REGIONS AND INDUSTRIES

REGIONS AND INDUSTRIES

A perspective on the industrial revolution in Britain

Edited by

PAT HUDSON

Senior Lecturer in Economic History,
University of Liverpool

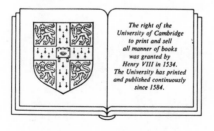

The right of the
University of Cambridge
to print and sell
all manner of books
was granted by
Henry VIII in 1534.
The University has printed
and published continuously
since 1584.

CAMBRIDGE UNIVERSITY PRESS

Cambridge
New York   Port Chester
Melbourne   Sydney

338.0941
R336

Published by the Press Syndicate of the University of Cambridge
The Pitt Building, Trumpington Street, Cambridge CB2 1RP
40 West 20th Street, New York, NY 10011, USA
10 Stamford Road, Oakleigh, Melbourne 3166, Australia

First published 1989

Printed in Great Britain by the University Press, Cambridge

British Library cataloguing in publication data
Regions and industries: a perspective on
the industrial revolution in Britain
1. Great Britain. Industrialisation,
1600–1850
I. Hudson, Pat, *1948–*
338.0941

Library of Congress cataloguing in publication data
Regions and industries: a perspective on the industrial revolution in
Britain/edited by Pat Hudson.
p.   cm.
Includes index.
ISBN 0 521 34106 X
1. Great Britain – Industries – History. I. Hudson, Pat, 1948–
HC253.R46   1989
338.0941 – dc 19   89 – 501   CIP

ISBN 0 521 34106 X

UP

CONTENTS

PART THREE THE DIVERSE NATURE OF THE OUTER REGIONS

FIGURES

MAPS

TABLES

CONTRIBUTORS

LESLIE A. CLARKSON is Professor of Social History at The Queen's University of Belfast. He has published extensively on the economic, social and demographic history of Ireland as well as on broader topics of central concern to historians of industrialisation. His publications include *Proto-Industrialization: The First Phase of Industrialization?* (London, 1985), *The Pre-Industrial Economy in England, 1500–1750* (London, 1971) and (as editor) *Irish Population, Economy and Society: Essays in Honour of K. H. Connell* (Oxford, 1981).

NEIL EVANS teaches history and Welsh studies at Coleg Harlech. His research interests centre on the social and economic development of Wales and he is currently preparing a book on Cardiff. He has published in a number of journals including *Past and Present, International Review of Social History* and *Welsh History Review.* He is secretary of Llafur.

PAT HUDSON is Senior Lecturer in Economic History at the University of Liverpool. She has written mainly on pre-factory industry and on the textile trades. Her other books include *The Genesis of Industrial Capital* (Cambridge, 1986) and, edited with Maxine Berg and Michael Sonenscher, *Manufacture in Town and Country before the Factory* (Cambridge, 1983, reprinted 1986).

JOHN D. MARSHALL is Emeritus Reader in Regional and Local History at the University of Lancaster. He is active in pursuing primary research, particularly on the economic and social history of the Lake Counties and he is interested in regions and regionalism in the development of Britain and Europe. He has published extensively and continues to produce a stream of stimulating articles as well as being a leading force behind CORAL. His major works include *Furness and the Industrial Revolution* (Barrow, 1958) and (with J. K. Walton) *A History of the Lake Counties from 1830* (Manchester, 1981).

ADRIAN J. RANDALL is a Lecturer in Economic and Social History at the University of Birmingham. His research has concentrated on the history of social protest in the eighteenth and early nineteenth centuries, with particular reference to the West of England. A major book *Before the Luddites* is in preparation and he has published several important journal articles notably in *Past and Present* and in *Midland History*.

MARIE B. ROWLANDS is Principal Lecturer in History at Newman College, Birmingham. She has expert knowledge of the industrial and social history of the West Midlands metalwares region, having pursued detailed research on the area for many years. She is also interested in religious and familial history. Her publications include *Masters and Men in the West Midlands Metalware Trades before the Industrial Revolution* (Manchester, 1975) and *The West Midlands from AD 1000* (London, 1987).

BRIAN SHORT is a Lecturer in Geography at the University of Sussex. His research has centred on the rural history of south-east England, especially the Weald and he is currently evaluating material arising from the Lloyd George Finance Act of 1910. His publications include 'The South-East: Kent, Surrey and Sussex', in J. Thirsk (ed.), *Agrarian History of England and Wales*, vol. 5, part 1: *1640–1750, Regional Farming Systems* (Cambridge, 1985) and (with P. F. Brandon) *The South-East from AD 1000* (London, 1989).

JOHN K. WALTON is Senior Lecturer in History at the University of Lancaster. His research and publications cover a broad spectrum of interests in social and economic history, mainly of Lancashire and the Lake Counties. He has written extensively on the economic development of these regions as well as on resort development and working-class leisure. His books include *Lancashire: A Social History, 1558–1939* (Manchester, 1986).

IAN D. WHYTE is Senior Lecturer in Geography at the University of Lancaster. He is an expert on Scottish agricultural history and migration patterns. His work includes *Agriculture and Society in Seventeenth-Century Scotland* (Edinburgh, 1979) and *A Historical Geography of Scotland* (London, 1983).

ACKNOWLEDGEMENTS

One cannot move from Barrow-in-Furness to London and successively live in the East Riding and the West Riding of Yorkshire then on Merseyside without being wholly convinced of the large extent to which regional character and identity pervade all aspects of social, cultural and economic life. My interest in this and its historical foundations stretches back many years and owes much to family, friends and colleagues who have sustained it. In particular I must thank my parents in Barrow, my sister in London and Tony whose knowledge of and enthusiasm about Liverpool have been a major source of inspiration. He has also been instrumental in allowing me to find the time to contemplate and to complete the editing of this volume.

The project started in 1985 at a Conference of Teachers of Regional and Local History (CORAL) held at Lancashire Polytechnic. Three of the papers presented there, by Neil Evans, Brian Short and Ian Whyte, provided a starting point for the volume and John Walton and John Marshall, who attended the conference, also agreed to participate in the book. The inspiration for the publication came from John Marshall whom I have much cause to thank for his continued encouragement and support. Other chapters were specially commissioned for this volume and I must thank all the contributors alike for their responsiveness and encouragement. Although I alone must remain responsible for its contents, Chapter 1 has benefited from the useful comments of an anonymous referee and from discussion with Maxine Berg, Gerry Kearns and Eric Taplin, who I thank for their time and patience. Finally, I must acknowledge the influence of a succession of friends and colleagues who have stimulated my continuing interest in industrial regions since my undergraduate days, most notably Arthur John, Sidney Pollard, Julia de L. Mann, Eric Sigsworth, Franklin Mendels, Jurgen Schulmbohm, David Jenkins, Jonathan Zeitlin and John Styles.

June 1988   PAT HUDSON

INTRODUCTION

There is growing dissatisfaction with studies at aggregate national level which attempt causal analysis, be they of demographic, social or economic phenomena. These sorts of studies have recently been prominent in reassessing the nature and importance of the industrial revolution in Britain emphasising gradualism and continuity and playing down the possibility of major discontinuity in either economic or social life.[1] Much valuable research of the last decade or so has rightly corrected an earlier tendency to exaggerate the discontinuities of the period *c.* 1750–1850.[2] But should the averaging out of changing experiences in different parts of Britain and the formation of an aggregate picture of components which happen to figure in the national income estimation persuade us that no discontinuity was present? Concern with change and progress may now be out of fashion: 'British historians today are mainly concerned to show that less happened, less dramatically, than was once thought.'[3] But there are problems in viewing history in terms of 'great arches'[4] of continuity or, as with much economic history, confining analysis to the 'economic' aspects of life as isolated by neo-classical economics. Both fail to capture that variety of experience and motivation which makes up the whole and neglect the significant transformations going on just under the surface of national economic indicators and national social groupings.

Thanks to the work of historians stretching back to J. H. Clapham and

[1] For discussion of this literature see Chapter 1.
[2] Some of this is discussed by D. Cannadine in 'The present and the past in the English industrial revolution 1880–1980', *Past and Present*, 103 (1984). The best of this literature has, however, always had an eye for the dialectics within continuity and for qualitative changes in levels of exploitation and in the competitive environment of seemingly 'traditional' forms of activity. See, for example, R. Samuel, 'The workshop of the world: steam power and hand technology in mid-Victorian Britain', *History Workshop Journal*, 3 (1977).
[3] D. Cannadine 'British history: past, present – and future?', *Past and Present*, 116 (1987), p. 183. See also B. Bailyn, 'The challenge of modern historiography', *American Historical Review*, 87 (1982), p. 3.
[4] The term is from P. Corrigan and D. Sayer, *The Great Arch: English State Formation as Cultural Revolution* (Oxford, Blackwell, 1985), although this book, as the title implies, by no means places exclusive stress on continuity. The term and the work is discussed in M. Barratt Brown, 'Away with all the great arches: Anderson's history of British capitalism', *New Left Review*, 167 (1988).

including Joan Thirsk, A. H. John, J. D. Chambers, J. de L. Mann, E. L. Jones and more recently F. F. Mendels, S. Pollard and J. Langton, we have been made aware that industrialisation in Britain and elsewhere occurred first and foremost within regions rather than within nations as a whole.[5] It is the contention of this volume that attempts to understand the industrial revolution as an economic, social and political process are best made with the regional perspective at centre stage. After all, both economic structure and human agency during this period, in important respects, operated at a regional level.[6] Furthermore, there was something unique about the industrial regions of the late eighteenth and nineteenth centuries. They were dominated by particular sectors (principally by various combinations of textiles, coal, engineering and shipbuilding) in a way never experienced before. Nor was this to be experienced subsequently, as the twentieth century has seen the growth of intra-sectoral spatial hierarchies with high-order, capital-intensive and research and development functions being located away from other processes. Furthermore, it can be argued that despite the continuing influence of London, the industrial regions of the industrial revolution period were freer of metropolitan economic, social and political influence than they had been in the seventeenth and early eighteenth centuries or were to become from the late nineteenth century. The canal-based economies of the period were regionally as well as nationally and internationally orientated and the region was a powerful focus of social and political identity across the social spectrum.[7] Sectoral specialisation and regional integrity largely explain the distinctive social and class relations found in the industrial areas of the period and suggest why these regions continued to have important elements of economic, social and political coherence long after the later nineteenth-century innovations in communications and in business and financial institutions. This alone makes their study essential in understanding the overall growth of the national economy at this time.

[5] J. H. Clapham, *An Economic History of Modern Britain*, vols. 2 and 3 (Cambridge, Cambridge University Press, 1932, 1938); A. H. John, *The Industrial Development of South Wales 1750–1850* (Cardiff, University of Wales Press, 1950); J. D. Chambers, 'The Vale of Trent, 1660–1800', *Economic History Review*, Supplement 3 (1957); J. de L. Mann, *The Cloth Industry in the West of England from 1640 to 1880* (Oxford, Clarendon Press, 1971). Other works by authors mentioned here are noted in Chapter 1.

[6] By 'human agency' I am here referring to the economic and social action and identity of the mass of the population. Its manifestation in terms of regional institutions of employers, pressure groups, trade unions and political movements, as well as the nature of regional economic structures is discussed by J. Langton, 'The industrial revolution and the regional geography of England', *Transactions of the Institute of British Geographers*, 9 (1984). For his own definition and account of human agency in this context see D. Gregory, *Regional Transformation and Industrial Revolution: A Geography of the Yorkshire Woollen Industry* (London, Macmillan, 1982). For further discussion see Chapter 1.   [7] See Langton, 'The industrial revolution'.

Some may be surprised that this volume nowhere attempts to define what is meant by a region. There is scope, of course, for another book on the heuristic and other qualities of the region as a dynamic concept. But this sort of discussion has largely been avoided here because the contributions themselves highlight the dangers of seeing the region as a static and pregiven category. Unlike nation states and other political units, regions emerge in the course of analysis and become finite in different ways depending on where and when we place the emphasis of our study. Regions are always historically relative and contingent although their spatial, economic, social and cultural integrity can endure for long periods despite considerable changes in communications, markets, technology and control. One such long period was experienced by British industrial regions from the early nineteenth century to at least the interwar years.

This book is about provincial concentrations of manufacturing activity. The role and importance of London as a centre of production as well as trade and finance form scope for another very different but parallel story of the industrial revolution which is not addressed here. The history of the metropolis and its concentration of wealth, political power and consumer markets must never be separated from the history of the provinces, however. The effect of London on regional specialisation, on finance and on culture remained and remains crucially important.

The volume started out with a set of integrating themes given as an agenda to the contributors. It was not envisaged that each chapter would address all or even most of the themes but that there would be common preoccupations sufficient for some general conclusions to be drawn and for one region to be compared with another. The themes cover four major aspects vital to understanding the emergence, the functioning and the long-term prospects of manufacturing regions during the period of industrialisation. They are discussed to some extent in Chapter 1. The first theme suggested to contributors was to consider factors in the environment of pre-factory industry including the agrarian and institutional settings, the role of urban centres and the nature of markets and competition. The second theme related to the nature of industrial activity itself: its evolution, its diversity, the organisation of production and trade, the sources of capital and credit and the role of transport and communications systems. The third theme concerned the relationship within a region between economy, population and labour supply including the question of a demographic dynamic associated with industry and including the working of the poor law and inter-regional migration. Finally, the question of the dynamism of early manufacturing regions was addressed. What role did the nature of pre-factory industry, its organisation, finance and workforce play in influencing the pace and nature of transition to more centralised and mechanised production? How important were political as well as economic forces acting at regional, national and international levels in explaining the history of manufacturing regions? What factors influenced the diversification of industry in a region and that region's ability to survive periods of economic depression?

The contributions to this book each deal with the varied experiences of different industrial regions during periods which include that associated with the British industrial revolution. The essays are clearly articulated, address overlapping themes and are thus largely left to speak for themselves. They are mentioned in the introductory chapter but no attempt is made fully to summarise their arguments as the concern of that chapter is to provide an analytical framework within which the various contributions can be placed and considered. The function of these essays is illustrative of various debates rather than an attempt to present an entire alternative and regionally oriented picture of the economic history of Britain in this important period. Given the shortcomings and limits of the mass of recent aggregative studies the idea here is to take a modest step in the direction of identifying and evaluating the industrial revolution as a political and social as well as an economic process which initially occurred in certain very limited and somewhat self-contained regions of Britain only and which had both spread and backwash effects on other manufacturing areas. It was a process which added up to more than the sum of its parts. And it was from these varied regional industrial bases that a gradual revolutionising of economy and society across a broad front began. There is much current research activity on British regions and there are a few excellent vintage texts but there has hitherto been no convenient format which provides both a taste of the varieties of regional experience subsumed under the heading of the first industrial revolution and which at the same time gives a guide to the existing theoretical and empirical literature about the importance of economic and social change at this level. It is thus hoped that the volume will appeal to research specialists and to students alike and will encourage a renewed search for discontinuities as well as for continuities in the economic and social history of Britain and her component regions.

🔊 *Chapter 1* 🔊

The regional perspective

PAT HUDSON

Disaggregated analyses of the industrial revolution in Britain are currently out of fashion. The influence of the 'New Economic History' on the growing macro-economics school has resulted in new calculations of the movement of aggregate variables: national income, industrial output, the rate of capital formation, the growth and composition of the labour force, living standards and demographic trends. Aggregate estimates, incorporating wide margins of error, have been accompanied by cross-national comparisons and by the formation of hypotheses about the causal relationships between different elements of change.[1] Valuable though this work has been in suggesting a macro-framework and in speculating about national characteristics of cause and effect its perspective on industrial change and economic development is limited. Thus, aspects of economy and society which were innovative or unique to the period have been neglected. And the industrial revolution remains as inscrutable as ever.

This chapter aims to highlight the importance of the regional perspective in understanding the extent of fundamental economic and social change

---

[1] See N. F. R. Crafts, *British Economic Growth during the Industrial Revolution* (Oxford, Clarendon Press, 1985), a book which consolidates the results first published in several journal articles; idem, 'Patterns of development in nineteenth-century Europe', *Oxford Economic Papers*, 36 (1984), pp. 438–58; C. K. Harley, 'British industrialisation before 1841: evidence of slower growth during the industrial revolution', *Journal of Economic History*, 42, 2 (1982), pp. 267–89; C. H. Feinstein, 'Capital formation in Great Britain', in P. Mathias and M. M. Postan (eds.), *Cambridge Economic History of Europe*, vol. 7, part 1 (Cambridge, Cambridge University Press, 1978), pp. 28–96; D. N. McCloskey, 'The industrial revolution: a survey', in R. C. Floud and D. N. McCloskey (eds.), *The Economic History of Britain since 1700*, vol. 1 (Cambridge, Cambridge University Press, 1981); P. H. Lindert and J. G. Williamson, 'Reinterpreting Britain's social tables, 1688–1913', *Explorations in Economic History*, 20, 1 (1983), pp. 94–109; idem, 'English workers' living standards during the industrial revolution: a new look', in J. Mokyr (ed.), *The Economics of the Industrial Revolution* (Totowa, N. J., Rowman & Allanheld, 1985), pp. 177–205; J. G. Williamson, *Did British Capitalism Breed Inequality?* (London, Allen & Unwin, 1985); E. A. Wrigley and R. S. Schofield, *The Population History of England, 1541–1871* (London, Edward Arnold, 1981). Debate still rages between the various authors regarding their methods of estimation, accuracy and about how to explain the slow rates of change which they find. The most recent contributions to this debate, which survey many of the problems and issues, are to be found in *Explorations in Economic History*, 24, 3 (1987), which contains articles by Crafts, Williamson and Mokyr.

occurring between the mid-eighteenth and mid-nineteenth centuries. First, the limitations of the current aggregative, national income estimation approach are discussed followed by an assessment of causal analysis of demographic change at the national level. The regional approach is then outlined and justified as uniquely important for comprehending the economic and social history of the industrial revolution period. An agenda of issues ripe for study at the regional level is established which centres around the identification of regional dynamics and includes discussion of external economies, proto-industrialisation and critical mass. The analysis closes with a stress on the need to place regional studies within the wider context of changing structures of national and international political and economic power.

AGGREGATION AND GRADUALISM

Deane and Cole's aggregative work long ago rightly laid the foundations for a more gradualist interpretation of the overall growth of the industrial revolution period but unlike the current wave of macro-economic estimates and theorising their concern was to present an integrated picture of parallel but often unequally distributed growth in trade, industry, capital, agriculture and population.[2] They still talked of an industrial transformation but stressed the need to look back to the early eighteenth century for its beginnings. By contrast the main thrust of the diverse findings of the last decade on the movement of aggregate indices has been to dethrone the industrial revolution altogether apart from the broad structural aspect of deployment of population. Productivity change continued in its slow early eighteenth-century fashion, fixed capital proportions, savings and investment changed only very gradually, workers' living standards and personal consumption remained largely unaffected before 1830 and were certainly not squeezed.[3] The macro-economic indicators of industrial and social transformation were not present and certainly Prometheus himself was absent.

Harley's estimates indicated that the size of the industrial sector of the early eighteenth century was nearly twice as large as previously thought but its subsequent growth and transformation were thus much less

---

[2] P. Deane and W. A. Cole, *British Economic Growth 1688–1959*, 2nd edn (Cambridge, Cambridge University Press, 1967).

[3] The exception to this picture of gradualism was provided by Feinstein in his estimates of capital formation and productivity growth but he has been criticised by Crafts for using Deane and Cole's inflated economic growth measures. Crafts regards the bulge in productivity growth 1800–30 found by Feinstein as an artifact of index number problems in Deane and Cole's work, Crafts *British Economic Growth*, Ch. 4.

dramatic.[4] Crafts has calculated that change in investment proportions was very gradual in the eighteenth century and that total factor productivity growth in manufacturing was only around 0·2 per cent from 1760 to 1801 and 0·4 per cent from 1801 to 1831. Even total factor productivity growth across the entire economy, inflated in Crafts' opinion by the performance of agriculture, grew very slowly: 0·2 per cent from 1760 to 1801, 0·7 per cent from 1801 to 1831, reaching 1·0 per cent only from 1831 to 1860.[5] Crafts argues that one small and atypical sector, cotton, possibly accounted for half of all productivity gains in manufacturing.[6] In his words 'not only was the triumph of ingenuity slow to come to full fruition, but it does not seem appropriate to regard innovativeness as pervasive'.[7] Crafts believes that his work should occasion the rewriting of textbooks on the period.[8] But this would be certainly premature.

The new gradualist view of economic change in the industrial revolution is based on the assessment of the growth of aggregates from the weighted averages of their components. Apart from the scope for mathematical error, this involves as Crafts himself admits a classic index-number problem.[9] The difficulties of assigning weights to industrial and other sectors of the economy, allowing for changes in weights over time and for the effects of differential price changes and value-added changes in the final product are insurmountable and will always involve a range of subjective decision.[10]

[4] Harley, 'British industrialisation before 1841'.

[5] Crafts, *British Economic Growth*, pp. 31, 81, 84. Crafts' computations have been severely criticised by Williamson, Mokyr and others. As Mokyr has pointed out in 'Has the industrial revolution been crowded out? Some reflections on Crafts and Williamson', *Explorations in Economic History*, 24, 3 (1987), 'Crafts' figures imply that Britain's industrial revolution was a grave mistake because it should really have become the First Agricultural Nation ... judging by the way Crafts refines (Deane and Cole's) figures, one might have thought that the numerator in these estimates was relatively reliable and that the highest marginal product of scholarly labour was in correcting and adjusting the price deflator ... estimates of nominal product (agricultural output) made by Deane and Cole cannot possibly have been intended for the use which Crafts makes of them. They repeatedly use words like "largely guesswork" and "highly arbitrary" in describing their assumptions' (p. 306). Crafts ignores these sorts of qualifications made by Deane and Cole and also by Feinstein (where he utilises the latter's estimates). Furthermore, his calculations of several measures such as agricultural total factor productivity and productivity of the 'unmodernised' sector depend on the estimation of residual figures which embody and often therefore magnify the errors endemic in all the additional major calculations of economic growth and, especially, of sectoral breakdowns.

[6] Crafts, *British Economic Growth*, p. 85.   [7] Ibid., p. 87.

[8] N. F. R. Crafts, 'British economic growth, 1700–1850: some difficulties of interpretation', *Explorations in Economic History*, 24, 3 (1987), p. 268.

[9] Crafts, *British Economic Growth*, p. 17. A gross error of either calculation or transcription occurs in Crafts' assessment of the growth rate per annum of national product 1780–1801 at 1·42 per cent. From his own calculations this should read 1·32 and the error seriously lowers his estimation of the per capita measure, ibid., Ch. 2.

[10] R. V. Jackson has recently highlighted the certain underestimation by Crafts of the size of the government component in national income at this time. 'Government expenditure and British economic growth in the eighteenth century: some problems of measurement', paper presented to the Annual Conference of the Economic History Society (University of East Anglia, 1988).

What is certain is that cotton and some of the other more dynamic sectors of the economy have been overemphasised in studies of the past. Though they grew at a phenomenal rate, revolutionising industries were initially small and their effect on aggregate statistics was very modest compared with agriculture and more 'traditional' manufacturing sectors. In fact dualistic growth models which distinguish between a vanguard and a traditional sector of the economy make abrupt changes in the economy as a whole a mathematical impossibility. Even if changes in the vanguard sector itself were discontinuous its share in the economy would grow very gradually while the traditional sector would lose ground slowly and only in the long run would the 'modern' sector become dominant in the overall economic indicators.

Drawing a dichotomy between a 'traditional' economy which, although not stagnant, developed gradually along conventional lines with slow productivity growth and slowly rising capital and labour ratios and the 'modern' sector consisting of cotton, iron, engineering, mining and some other consumer goods such as pottery and paper is certainly no simple matter. Mokyr is one of the few historians who whilst extolling some of the virtues of recent aggregative analysis is prepared to countenance their fundamental difficulties. He admits that at first only small segments of the advanced sectors underwent 'modernisation' so that dualism existed within as well as between industries making calculations about the performance of the 'modern' sector rather tricky.[11] But even Mokyr fails fully to examine the dynamism of the 'traditional' economy which could and did contain significant cumulative innovations. Although not discontinuous these probably accounted for a very large part of productivity gains in the economy in the period before 1830.[12] Relegation of this sector, in much current literature, to the role of backward survivor or even to the role of a contemporary subordinate of the revolutionised sector is inappropriate.

Embodied in the entire macro-economic approach to the history of the industrial revolution is a type of modernisation theory which assumes that the 'traditional' sector is just catching up with the vanguard march of the factory, certainly not that it might represent a more permanent feature of the dualism inherent in all advanced societies (and often increasingly

[11] J. Mokyr makes this point very clearly: 'The industrial revolution and the new economic history', in Mokyr (ed.), *The Economics of the Industrial Revolution*, p. 5.

[12] G. N. Von Tunzlemann, 'Technical progress during the industrial revolution', in Floud and McCloskey (eds.), *The Economic History of Britain*, p. 143; D. N. McCloskey, 'The industrial revolution 1780–1860: a survey', in Mokyr (ed.), *The Economics of the Industrial Revolution*, pp. 53–74. For the best descriptive account of the productivity changes in the traditional economy defined correctly in the broadest terms to include organisation and work practices, external economies of concentration, etc., see M. Berg, *The Age of Manufactures* (London, Fontana, 1985), *passim*.

apparent as economic growth continues). In reality the 'traditional' sectors are more justifiably seen as representing a different path or pattern of development within the complex of industrialisation which gets lost in the aggregate studies. They were sometimes complementary to, sometimes competitive with (and often as dynamic in their own way as), the factory and heavily capitalised sectors. The 'traditional' sectors were as much, if not more, a part of the dynamic of the industrial revolution as the factory although their qualitative changes are not well reflected in the quantitative indicators. The labour force in the 'traditional' sectors, for example, gets lost in the failure of statistics to record much part-time and female or juvenile work. Furthermore, organisational and commercial changes in these sectors did not entail massive injections of fixed capital which would show up in the aggregate figures.[13] It would be better if we abandoned the terms 'modern' and 'traditional' entirely in this context. The contrast arises more out of the functional differences between labour-saving and labour-using development than out of a chronological sequence of growth.

The labour-using sector partly arose, at a regional level, from the demands of the factory and the expansion of heavy-goods industries, urbanisation and improved transportation: a major reason why its size in overall national income and in manufacturing remained and remains so large. Developing more independently, artisan and workshop manufacture could also by the use of flexible technologies and constant adaptation to, and stimulation of, changing taste and fashion function in dynamic form throughout the nineteenth century as the examples of the Sheffield and Birmingham regions testify. This usually occurred within a well-defined industrial region where flexible specialisation and small production units were the dominant characteristics. These districts not only exhibited their own specific social values and institutions but they also created, often on the basis of collective effort, a range of external economies of technical, commercial and financial support which contributed vitally to their continuing success.[14]

It is becoming clear that the current spate of aggregative studies has an inbuilt problem of identification in posing questions about the existence of an industrial revolution. Is there any justification for identifying such a

---

[13] For fuller discussion of the shortcomings of dual-economy models, the neglect of technological and organisational change outside the factory and the role of female and child labour in the period see M. Berg, 'Technology and productivity change in manufacture in eighteenth-century England', in J. A. Davis and P. Mathias (eds.), *Technology and Innovation from the Eighteenth Century to the Present* (Oxford, Blackwells, forthcoming). I am grateful to Maxine for allowing me to see this unpublished paper. See also, M. Berg and P. Hudson, 'Is the industrial revolution dead?', unpublished seminar paper, 1988, which emerged from our discussions.

[14] C. Sabel and J. Zeitlin, 'Historical alternatives to mass production: politics, markets and technology in nineteenth century industrialisation', *Past and Present*, 108 (1985), pp. 133–76.

phenomenon with high investment ratios, factory mass production, high productivity manufacturing techniques and their influence on overall aggregate indicators? Clearly, technological progress was not growth and rapid growth did not everywhere imply the revolutionising of production functions: 'Some industries which grew slowly were mechanising and switching to factories (e.g. paper after 1801, wool and chemicals like soap and candles) while construction and coal mining, in which manual techniques ruled supreme with few exceptions until deep into the 19th century, grew at respectable rates.'[15] There is also a problem in relying too heavily on measures which happen to be included in national income estimation. Increased efficiency in the tertiary sector is one major omission. The growth of the service sector and its concentration in London and the south-east is a major part of the story of Britain's industrialisation, argues Lee.[16] Furthermore, changing social relations of production were not always and everywhere a function of changing forces of production spawned by new technologies. The changing relationship between capital and labour, the degree of subordination or even of subsumption of the latter by the former, and the increasingly competitive world in which employers (across the spectrum down to penny-capitalists) became enmeshed were marked features of the period. These were as much a part of the discontinuity of the industrial revolution (as a social and political as well as an economic process) as the physical measures of industrial output and productivity.

The social and cultural as well as the economic impact of the modernising sector, its reciprocal interrelationship with the 'traditional' sector and the innovative possibilities of the latter cannot be comprehended in aggregate statistical analyses. At the regional level of study the false dichotomy between 'modern' and 'traditional' and the shortcomings and assumptions embedded in this terminology become thoroughly exposed. Growth was an uneven process and it took very different qualitative forms both within and between sectors and regions. This complexity and its precise impact and importance eludes the national-level quantitative methods so fashionable in the current historiography.

---

[15] Mokyr, 'Has the industrial revolution been crowded out?', p. 314.

[16] C. Lee, 'Regional structure and change', in J. Langton and R. J. Morris (eds.), *Atlas of Industrialising Britain 1780–1914* (London, Methuen, 1986), pp. 30, 140–3, and *The British Economy since 1700* (Cambridge, Cambridge University Press, 1986).

DEMOGRAPHIC ANALYSIS AT NATIONAL LEVEL

The aggregate and pessimistic view of a period of economic achievements once regarded as revolutionary has a methodological counterpart in the demographic work of Wrigley and Schofield.[17] They have argued that, despite considerable growth in numbers, there was no significant discontinuity in demographic *behaviour* in England between the sixteenth and the mid-nineteenth centuries. Wrigley and Schofield's work highlights some of the more general problems of the aggregative studies. Although their new population estimates have been the subject of some debate they have been seen as a breakthrough in our knowledge of English population trends. Their causal analysis, however, has occasioned much more scepticism.[18] They have argued that nuptiality and hence fertility change in England occurred as a delayed response to changes in living standards as indicated by real wage trends. Leaving aside the considerable doubt as to the reliability of the Phelps Brown and Hopkins wage index as an indicator of general trends in economic well-being and ignoring the criticism they have received of back projection techniques and for introducing a seemingly arbitrary lag into their correlation analysis, there remains grave disquiet about their creation of various series of national demographic trends. There would be no problem so long as their work remained descriptive of the national scene but the danger lies in using these aggregate results to analyse patterns of individual motivation. There is the strongest likelihood that their national estimates conflate opposing tendencies in different regions, sectors of industry and among different social groups. 'If labourers acted in response to different stimuli from those that prompted craftsmen, miners or textile workers, this response is lost in the process of aggregation', argues Levine.[19] Real progress in understanding the mainsprings of aggregate demographic trends will only come with regional, sectoral and class breakdowns which are able to address the possibility that different sorts of workers or social groups within different regional cultures are likely to have encountered different sorts of stimuli or

[17] Wrigley and Schofield, *The Population History of England*.
[18] D. Gaunt, P. Levine and E. Moodie, 'The population history of England 1541–1871: a review symposium', *Social History*, 8, 2 (1983); M. Anderson, 'Historical demography after the population history of England', *Journal of Interdisciplinary History*, 15, 5 (1985); J. Mokyr, 'Three centuries of population change', *Economic Development and Cultural Change*, 32, 1 (1983); M. L. Olney, 'Fertility and the standard of living in early modern England: in consideration of Wrigley and Schofield', *Journal of Economic History*, 46, 1 (1983); P. H. Lindert, 'English workers' living standards, population growth and Wrigley and Schofield', *Explorations in Economic History*, 20, 2 (1983); R. D. Lee, 'Inverse projection and back projection: a critical appraisal and comparative results for England, 1539–1871', *Population Studies*, 39, 2 (1985).
[19] Levine, in Gaunt, Levine and Moodie, 'The population history of England', p. 155.

to have varied in their reaction to economic trends creating a range of demographic regimes.

The parish reconstitution studies emerging from the Cambridge database is yielding little evidence of the movement of vital variables that line up well with the temporal movement of the aggregate series. Levine and Wrightson in a study of nine parishes in the seventeenth century have shown that few places exhibit the aggregate trend of a rise in the age of marriage in the late seventeenth century let alone the inverse relationship between age of marriage and illegitimacy rates which is a major feature of the aggregative data:[20] 'evidence from the nine family reconstitution studies shows no clear pattern in the age of marriage but rather a variety of demographic adjustments which reflected changing local conditions'.[21] These conditions were clearly not just a matter of real income changes:

Deindustrialisation in Colyton and the shift away from labour intensive corn farming in Bottesford may have produced the rise in age of marriage whereas, on the other hand, the coming of domestic industry to Shepshed and the commercialisation of the agriculture of Terling in response to the London food market's growing demand may have led to a fall in age at marriage.[22]

For Levine and Wrightson then, and exemplified in their Terling study, the most important causal variable affecting population change was the local economic setting. For Terling this included in the seventeenth century the increasingly impoverished labouring population, inflation, crises, insecurity and the activities of an increasingly self-conscious parish elite especially regarding the administration of poor relief and the settlement laws from the mid-century on.[23]

Aggregate demographic indicators are thus difficult if not impossible to use in identifying the mainsprings of change across a range of varied regional and even local economies. Similar assumptions about a national norm toward which regions and localities tend pervades the demographic analysis just as it dogs the macro-economic work of Crafts and others. As Seccombe has eloquently observed of the work of both the Cambridge and Princeton groups of demographers:

The multi-class and mixed region totals which are compiled, statistically manipulated and interpreted, inevitably mask structural variation along these lines.

[20] D. Levine and K. Wrightson, 'The social context of illegitimacy in early modern England', in P. Laslett, K. Oosterveen and R. M. Smith (eds.), *Bastardy and its Comparative History* (London, Edward Arnold, 1980).   [21] Ibid., p. 161.   [22] Ibid., p. 160.

[23] K. Wrightson and D. Levine, *Poverty and Piety in an English Village: Terling, 1525–1700* (New York, Academic Press, 1979). For the importance of the local economic setting and particularly of the influence of domestic employment and proletarianisation on demographic trends in the eighteenth and early nineteenth centuries see D. Levine, *Family Formation in an Age of Nascent Capitalism* (New York, Academic Press, 1977).

The result is an excessive preoccupation with national comparisons ('the French versus the English pattern'). Class and regional variations are generally treated as an afterthought in a lead and lag framework ... premised on a conservative cultural-diffusionist assumption; lower classes and backward regions lag behind their superiors, but eventually follow them on the road to modernity and progress.[24]

Almost three decades ago Wrigley himself made similar observations about the study of the mechanics of industrialisation in Europe; observations which apply equally to demographic analysis:

it is always possible ... that it is misguided to seek 'national' features to explain Germany's industrial growth or France's relative stagnation, since these are observations about average conditions whose origins may lie in regional differences affecting comparatively small areas of each country.[25]

industrial growth was essentially a local rather than a national affair. In this regard it is perhaps unnecessarily inexact to talk of England and the continent rather than, say, of Lancashire and the valley of the Sambre-Meuse. Each country was made up of a number of regional economies.[26]

Schumpter shared these fears in 1939 when he warned that relations between aggregates are entirely inadequate in teaching us anything about the nature of the processes which shape their variations.[27]

THE REGIONAL APPROACH

It is not enough to criticise aggregate studies: we must also provide a justification for turning to the regional rather than say local or sectoral level of analysis in identifying the nature, causes and corollaries of industrialisation in Britain. Crafts cites three justifications for choosing aggregative analysis for this purpose[28] but conversely these actually highlight some of the advantages of a regional approach. The first is purely practical: that most data are available at national level. But in fact estimates no less accurate than the aggregate series could be made for many variables from data available at regional level.[29] Indeed aggregate figures of fixed capital

---

[24] W. Seccombe, 'Marxism and demography', *New Left Review*, 137 (1983), p. 35. For discussion of an alternative approach to the demographic history of the period employing the concept of proto-industrialisation see P. Hudson, 'Marx or Malthus: models of English demographic change in the eighteenth century', unpublished seminar paper, 1986. See also the chapters by Clarkson, Whyte and Walton in this volume.

[25] E. A. Wrigley, *Industrial Growth and Population Change, a Regional Study of the Coalfield Areas of North West Europe in the Later Nineteenth Century* (Cambridge, Cambridge University Press, 1961), p. 89.

[26] E. A. Wrigley, 'The supply of raw materials in the industrial revolution', *Economic History Review*, 15, 1 (1962), p. 16.

[27] Quoted by Mokyr, in 'The industrial revolution and the new economic history' p. 6.

[28] Crafts, *British Economic Growth*, p. 3.

[29] An example of this is found in D. T. Jenkins, *The West Riding Wool Textile Industry, 1770–1835: A*

formation and of manufacturing output are formed from regional and
sectoral building blocks. Secondly, Crafts argues that events such as the
financing of wars with France were burdens on the national economy and
that changes in external policy similarly had repercussions on the structure
of the whole economy. This is a more substantial point but can only justify
limited sorts of analysis for this period because central government policies
always had a regional, sectoral and/or class-specific origin and emphasis in
their impact. The Land Tax, for example, by its peculiar fixity in terms of
regional and local distribution, approximately in line with later seventeenth-
century values, favoured the advancing northern industrial districts by not
raising their share as their property values rose.[30] And, with respect to
Europe as a whole, Pollard has suggested: 'The levying of protective tariffs
in order to support home industry, and even more the direct subsidy paid
to manufacturers, tended to tax the backward regions in order to enhance
the lead of the advanced ones. State action, if indeed it had any positive
effect whatever, tended to confirm the regional structure of industry.'[31]
Furthermore, the effect of much central government policy at this time was
overlain at regional and local level by wide variations in administration and
implementation. A crucial question will always be: why was regional
economic development so diverse in relation to national economic policies?
Crafts' final point is that 'the national economy of Britain represented for
many products a well-integrated national goods market by the early
nineteenth century'.[32] This appears to be an act of faith rather than
informed judgement. Although the national spread of fashionable consumer
goods was increasing,[33] it simply cannot be substantiated, certainly before
the second quarter of the nineteenth century, that the British economy had
a 'fairly well integrated set of factor markets'.[34] The really important spatial
unit regarding the market for factors, especially capital and labour and for
information, commercial and credit networks in the pre-railway period was

Study of Fixed Capital Formation (Edington, Pasold, 1975). And econometric studies using regional-
level estimates have been attempted for the regional coalfields of the Ruhr and the Nord as well
as to the whole of the French Nord: C. L. Holt Frerich, Quantitative Wirtschaftsgeschichte des Ruhr
Kohlenbergbaus in 19 Jahrhundert (Dortmund, 1973); M. Gillet, Les Charbonnages du Nord de la France
au XIXe siècle (Paris and The Hague, 1973); M. Wolf, 'Eléments pour la construction d'un indice de
la production industrielle dans le Nord 1815–1914', Revue du Nord, 54 (1972), pp. 289–316.

[30] S. Pollard, Peaceful Conquest: The Industrialisation of Europe, 1760–1970 (Oxford, Oxford University
Press, 1981), p. 38.
[31] S. Pollard, 'Regional markets and national development', unpublished paper presented at a
conference on Custom and Commerce in Early Industrial Europe, Centre for Social History,
University of Warwick, April 1987, p. 7.
[32] Crafts, British Economic Growth, p. 3.
[33] See J. Brewer, N. McKendrick and J. H. Plumb, The Birth of a Consumer Society: The Commercialisation
of Eighteenth-Century England (London, Hutchinson, 1983); Colin Campbell, The Romantic Ethic and
the Spirit of Modern Consumerism (Oxford, Blackwell, 1987).
[34] Crafts, British Economic Growth, p. 3.

undoubtedly the often clearly delineated economic region. Construction of the improved navigation and canal systems on which the economic growth of this period depended did much to endorse the existence of regional economies even making them more insular for a time than before. Waterway networks were largely regionally constructed (at first almost entirely regionally financed and promoted) and largely inward-looking: 'The key function of canals lay in servicing a quantum leap in the scale and efficiency of regional economic systems ... canal traffic was fundamentally short-haul acting to bind discrete sub-regional resource fields, production sites and markets into a complex expanding system of symmetry and triangular reciprocity'.[35]

Langton has joined Freeman in stressing this result of English canal development:

Dense patches on the [canal] network ... developed highly integrated economies largely separate from one another ... As they developed on the basis of their comparative advantages and the external economies of scale available to particular industries within them the canal-based economies became more specialised, more differentiated from each other and more internally unified.[36]

Most recently, Turnbull has analysed the nature of canal networks in exactly these terms stressing in particular the distribution fields of coal supplies and the advantages to most industries of canal siting.[37] Knowledge of the nature and operations of the canal-based transport systems should give a salutary warning to those who believe in the existence of nationally integrated factor markets at this time easily amenable to general equilibrium analysis and to the other techniques of current neo-classical macro-economics.

Where canal systems did connect inter-regionally it was most often with the ports and with the international economy than with the patterns of trade and influence which had flowed via London in earlier centuries. And it is no accident that during the period when canal haulage articulated the economy that the large commercial cities of the provinces grew most rapidly in relative and absolute terms. Nor were the railways quick to destroy regionally oriented transport systems. Freeman, summarising the research in this field, argues that: 'Most companies found it in their best interests to structure freight rates so as to encourage the trade of the regions they served. The result was often to favour short-distance freight

---

[35] M. Freeman, 'Transport', in Langton and Morris (eds.), *Atlas*, p. 86.
[36] J. Langton, 'The industrial revolution and the regional geography of England', *Transactions of the Institute of British Geographers*, 9 (1984), p. 162.
[37] G. Turnbull, 'Canals, coal and regional growth during the industrial revolution', *Economic History Review*, 40, 4 (1987), pp. 537–60.

flows. And where companies exhibited discrete territorial identity this acted to cement existing resource grouping almost forming a policy of regional development.'[38]

The regional nature of factor markets is illustrated if we take the case of labour. Hunt's recent work on regional wages has gathered evidence of a major and widening shift in differentials in the period 1760–1790s in favour of the northern industrialising regions.[39] This is not consonant with the assumption of current macro-economic work: that markets will reduce spatial differentials with industrialisation. Hunt sees his findings as more consistent with a growth pole interpretation which is only compatible with a regional perspective and analysis. The growth pole approach predicts that in several respects market forces may operate to reinforce the initial advantages of industrialising areas. The development of external economies and economies of scale will encourage the clustering of new economic activities creating backwash effects in more peripheral regions which prove unable to compete and which lose their most vigorous population through out-migration. The slow-moving aggregate figures of Britain's economic performance between the mid-eighteenth and the mid-nineteenth centuries disguise a great deal of activity of this kind where rapidly expanding and intensively industrialising regions had their counterparts in areas of stagnation and decline.

The markets for both industrial capital and for commercial credit were regional before the 1830s and 1840s and the region remained an important financial unit well beyond these decades especially before the widespread adoption of the joint-stock form.[40] In the eighteenth and early nineteenth centuries capital rarely flowed outside of the industrial region where it was generated and the bulk of finance raised by industrialists came from their locality and its wider region from within a network of commercial, social and familial links where face to face knowledge and trust were important. Personal knowledge of the respectability and reliability of trading partners was also important in the raising of credit and short-term loans. There were regional networks of capital supply articulated in the eighteenth century through the role of attorneys active at the level of the county legal circuit. Land Tax collectors, with their important seasonal balances, were regionally based and had detailed knowledge of the landed security of their potential

[38] Freeman, 'Transport', p. 92. See also G. Hawke, *Railways and Economic Growth in England and Wales 1840–1914* (Oxford, Oxford University Press, 1970).

[39] E. H. Hunt, 'Industrialisation and regional inequality: wages in Britain, 1760–1914', *Journal of Economic History*, 46, 4 (1986); idem. 'Wages', in Langton and Morris (eds.), *Atlas*, pp. 60–8.

[40] All points in this paragraph are well substantiated for the West Riding textile region in P. Hudson, *The Genesis of Industrial Capital: A Study of the West Riding Wool Textile Industry c. 1750–1850* (Cambridge, Cambridge University Press, 1986). See also Pollard, *Peaceful Conquest*, p. 37.

short-term borrowers. The banking system throughout the period also had distinctive regional features. It was quite common for the private banks within each industrial region to bail each other out in time of crisis with declarations of support. And the basis of the banking system – the acceptance of each other's notes and cheques – occurred through a much denser network of agreements and recognition within the region than occurred inter-regionally. The banking system did also transfer funds from areas of capital surplus to areas of capital need but the differential interest rates which provided a motive force for this transfer were themselves an illustration of the existence of specifically regional capital markets. The regional nature of commercial crises and waves of bankruptcies provides further testimony of the regional level of the great bulk of financial links during the industrial revolution.

The recently published *Atlas of Industrialising Britain* contains further material which encourages a reassessment of the regional approach for the analysis of economic, social and cultural change in this vital period.[41] The various chapters especially those on population, wages, chemicals, textiles and iron show that changes in spatial organisation, with the establishment of more clearly defined industrial regions, both preceded and accompanied the major changes in output, technology and productivity which have attracted most attention from historians. These spatial shifts are a central identifying feature of the industrial revolution period. The editors identify three spatial processes at work in the nineteenth century each making a contribution to the regional patterns of economic activity and the cultural forms observed. First there was the continuing core-periphery relationship between metropolitan and provincial Britain. It could be argued that this relationship was significantly different during the era of the canal-based economies than it had been before and than it was to become with the greater integration of the national economy and the growing power of London from the late nineteenth century. Secondly, the pattern of resource-based industrial development of areas rich in water power, coal and other minerals was important, and finally there were processes operating 'on a smaller scale to link the way in which people think act and organise themselves through their work, daily routines and relationships to the resources of their immediate environment'.[42] These three spatial processes recur again and again, usually implicitly rather than explicitly, in the existing literature on the history of the English regions and one or more are obvious in each of the contributions to the present volume. The dialectical interplay between a region's social and economic history and its response

---

[41] Langton and Morris (eds.), *Atlas*.
[42] Ibid., 'Introduction', p. xxvii.

to changing commercial and industrial experiences remoulded rather than destroyed old assumptions, relationships and behaviour patterns. Thus as illustrated in the *Atlas* clear differences emerged between the economic bases and the cultural forms of well-defined regions especially within the north and Midlands: 'between the four northernmost counties and the rest of northern England, between south-east and south-west Lancashire, between the northern and southern parts of the West Riding of Yorkshire, between the East and West Midlands and between the champion and wood-pasture regions in the south'.[43]

Of course, these observations do not prove (nor seek to prove) that the differences produced distinct, integrated and coherent regions economically or culturally. But the argument that there was a growth of regionalism during the industrial revolution period and in the mid-nineteenth century is convincing.[44] There occurred a growing identity among all social groups with the economic, social and political interests of their region. Although this may have been no more important than the other identifications which people were creating based on class, religion, nation or community, it certainly grew with and reacted upon the rest. And its source can only be understood in the context of regional levels of economic and political influence and of economic and social relationships.

REGIONAL SOCIAL IDENTITY

Langton traces the origins of regionalism in the growth of county society in the seventeenth century. County towns acted as a focus for the fiscal, judicial and political concerns of the whole shire. Smaller towns, especially market centres, also played a part in cementing local and regional identities, especially where towns and their hinterlands came to specialise in the production of particular craft goods for distant markets. Finally, agrarian geography did much to create clearly identifiable and reciprocating regional agricultural economies. Everitt suggests that eight types of agrarian *pays* were identifiable in Britain from the seventeenth century each with different social and cultural corollaries: fielden or champion, forest, fell and moorland, marshland, heathland, fenland, downland and wold.[45] The more general division between fielden and wood-pasture regions has long been stressed. Fielden regions were characterised by arable farming, communal

---

[43] Ibid., p. xxx.

[44] Langton, 'The industrial revolution'. I have drawn strongly on this article in the following section on regional social identity.

[45] A. Everitt, 'Country, county and town: patterns of regional evolution in England', *Transactions of the Royal Historical Society*, 29 (1979), pp. 79–108, quoted by Langton, 'The industrial revolution', p. 149.

behaviour and increasingly polarised societies of yeomen and their labourers dominated by squirearchy and established church. Looser social structures based on kin, pastoral industrial by-employments, the importance of commons for resources and colonisation, and the anti-authoritarian attitudes, expressed most clearly in religious non-conformity characterised wood-pasture areas and created a favourable environment for expanding industry and commerce.[46]

With growing industrialism from the late eighteenth century clear regional characteristics of this type were overlain with the influence of increased commerce and manufacturing and regional identifications grew. Industrialisation accentuated the differences between regions by making them much more functionally distinct and specialised. Economic structures varied from one region to another in initial pattern, changing composition and in their changing pace and nature of development. Economic and commercial circumstances were thus experienced regionally and social protest movements with their regional fragmentation can only be understood at that level and in relation to regional economic and social structures.[47] Likewise, issues of national political reform came to be identified with particular regions, for example, factory reform with Yorkshire, the anti-poor-law campaign with Lancashire, currency reform with Birmingham: 'These regional differences of preoccupation generalised beyond particular issues, entered people's consciousness ... and became one of the major currencies of English literature when the regional novel emerged as an important genre in the 1840s.'[48] As sub-regional economic specialisms made the links between different places within the same region more obvious and more necessary, the tendencies towards region-wide integration and identity were further encouraged. Often the clearly identifiable industrial region was forged through the links created by provincial centres such as Manchester, Liverpool, Birmingham, Bradford, Leeds and Newcastle, and the force of regional integration was made complete by the intra-regional nature of migration, by the formation of regionally based clubs and societies and by the growth of the provincial press.

Of course it is easy to underplay both the economic and cultural role of

---

[46] Langton, 'The industrial revolution', p. 149. For more sophisticated divisions of farming types in England and Wales and for detailed discussion of regional systems see J. Thirsk (ed.), *Agrarian History of England and Wales*, vol. 5, part 1: *1640–1750 Regional Farming Systems* (Cambridge, Cambridge University Press, 1985).

[47] Langton provides a stimulating survey of the regional fragmentation of trade unions, of Chartism and other movements, and of regional differences in work practices and work customs, in 'The industrial revolution', pp. 150–5. See also D. Read, *The English Provinces 1760–1960: A Study in Influence* (London, Edward Arnold, 1964).

[48] Langton, 'The industrial revolution', p. 156.

London and the pervasiveness of popular nationalism, neither of which can
be ignored for the very period most affected by regional economic and
social identification.[49] Provincial newspapers depended on the dissemi-
nation of national information from London, which was the centre of
conspicuous consumption influencing fashion and tastes far and wide, and
a large proportion of the population continued to have regular and
immediate contact with the capital through trade, training, social life or
travel routes. Colley's recent study of the nationalistic vocabulary of
popular radicalism in the earlier nineteenth century must also be set against
the regional articulation of its activities.[50] It was the former which, she
argues, made class increasingly salient but the latter was of paramount
importance in keeping latent class activities within strict parameters.
Furthermore, the state after 1815 began to foster identification with local
customs and regional traditions as a means of combating the possibilities
of nation-wide opposition. This was obviously made possible only by
existing popular identification with locality and region which shows up in
so many aspects of economic and social life. To explain this regionalism in
the mid-nineteenth century, illustrated by the flowering of dialect literature,
requires 'an account of why economic development was so diverse
between regions, so markedly variable in relation to national commercial
policies from region to region and so cohesive within the different regions
themselves'.[51]

REGIONS AND ECONOMIC CHANGE

The geographical matrix of study should obviously be determined by what
the historian is trying to explain and many fundamentally important
questions about this key period concern regional activity. What forms did
industrialisation occurring within regions take? How did regions of
revolutionising industry differ from those changing more slowly or
stagnating? What factors determined the outcome of structural change at
regional level? What role did pre-existing agrarian structures play in
creating a regional environment conducive to particular sorts of trajectories?

---

[49] These are points stressed by Gregory in his critique of Langton: D. Gregory, 'The production of
regions in England's industrial revolution', *Journal of Historical Geography*, 14, 1 (1988), pp. 50–8.
See Langton's reply: J. Langton, 'The production of regions in England's industrial revolution: a
response', *Journal of Historical Geography*, 14, 2 (1988), pp. 170–6. Here Langton argues 'There may
be room for argument about how far regional differences were due to integration within a national
nexus of flows articulated through London, how far to links between groups of regions without the
interposition of London, and how far to the separate and independent integration of different
regions into different sectors of a ... world system' (p. 172).

[50] L. Colley, 'Whose nation? Class and national consciousness in Britain, 1750–1830', *Past and Present*,
113 (1986).   [51] Langton 'The industrial revolution', p. 162.

How important were political processes and power structures at regional, national and international levels in accounting for the success or failure of regions and what role did regionally specific forms of work organisation, work practice and technological adaptation play?

We must now turn to some of the literature which has employed a regional approach to the study of industrialisation in order to survey what such an approach may comprise and to see what sorts of issues have so far been raised. The region has too often been used merely as a convenient box into which masses of descriptive material is stuffed. Regional analysis to be worthy of its name must aim to do more than this but it must also avoid the trap of a determinism which finds an almost mechanical connection between soil and society or even between natural resources more generally and economic development. Pounds' massive project on the historical geography of Europe takes note of this but disappointingly tends to relegate non-locational factors to the realm of the random or the irrational.[52] On agricultural change Pounds gets closer to the constraints or otherwise imposed by the historical factors of cultural and political environment arguing that developments were not necessarily those which examination of the resources would lead one to expect. Rural change and adaptation were hindered by a complex web of social obligations and relationships especially those concerning rights over commons and wastelands.[53]

This point is reminiscent of the recent work done by Martin and by Neeson on Warwickshire and Northamptonshire respectively which show just how important common rights and enclosure were in the viability of rural manufacturing.[54] This is not a 'soil to society' argument but one which considers the interface between the 'traditional' economy, expanding sectors and the local social, institutional and cultural environment.

Clearly the relationship between investment and location depends on factors such as mutable systems of landownership, the power and influence of local elites, the nature of local government and a host of other variables not comprehended by straight locational analysis. As Pollard has stressed: 'modern location theory ... tends not only to be ahistorical and static, but also fails to make a clear distinction between the causes for concentration of industry in regions as such and for the growth of *particular* industrial regions' (my italics).[55]

---

[52] N. J. G. Pounds, *An Historical Geography of Europe, 1800–1914* (Cambridge, Cambridge University Press, 1985), p. xx.   [53] Ibid.

[54] J. M. Martin, 'Village traders and the emergence of a proletariat in South Warwickshire 1750–1851', *Agricultural History Review*, 32, 2 (1984); J. M. Neeson, 'The opponents of enclosure in eighteenth-century Northamptonshire', *Past and Present*, 105 (1984), p. 55.

[55] Pollard, *Peaceful Conquest*, p. 113.

There is a considerable body of recent literature which has provided useful insights into the nature and role of regions in industrialisation. And much of it has concentrated on examining those factors and circumstances (widely conceived) which prompted industry to grow and decay in some regions rather than others and in some regions earlier than others. Pollard is one of the most significant contributors to this recent debate. He has adopted a specifically regional approach to his study of the process of diffusion of innovation in Europe and of European industrialisation more generally. He points out that 'In... Inner Europe [1760 onwards]... the differences in income between regions were much greater than the average difference in income between countries and represented much the more significant economic reality of structural and trade inter-relations and complementarity.'[56] It was this complementarity created by the inter-regional immobility of factors of production which created regions which were increasingly functionally distinct. Thus, the economic development of the industrial revolution period created regions different in kind to those existing before. In the eighteenth century and earlier very similar pre-industrial regions could and did exist side by side largely cut off from one another because of poor communications and lack of the economic complementarity which might stimulate major transport improvements. These sorts of regions disappear from the mid-eighteenth century and especially in the nineteenth century to be replaced by distinct and internally integrated regions whose extra-regional export base became the single most important foundation of their success.

By 1750 the pattern of regional industrialisation in Britain was obvious but not fixed. On the contrary, patterns of regional specialisation and concentration were in a state of flux during the entire period of the industrial revolution and especially in the second half of the eighteenth century. Some areas succeeded where others failed and this mixed pattern of success contributed more significantly than anything else to the picture of relatively gradual growth of the macro-economic indicators. Qualitative changes in the economy were marked but their unevenness meant that they were only little transformed into changes in quantity before the nineteenth century. For example, an increase in the output of the wool textile sector by about 150 per cent during the entire eighteenth century seems very modest but this conceals the dramatic relocation taking place in favour of Yorkshire whose share in national production rose from around 20 per cent to around 60 per cent. From the aggregate perspective, an increase of 150

---

[56] Pollard, *Peaceful Conquest*, p. 123. It can, of course, be argued that national state policy was partly, if not largely, responsible for these regional inequalities and that the nation state must also, therefore, remain a unit of the highest analytical importance.

per cent over the course of a century could have been achieved simply by gradual extension of traditional commercial methods and production functions but Yorkshire's intensive growth necessarily embodies a veritable revolution in organisational patterns, commercial links, credit relationships the sorts of cloths produced and (selectively) in production techniques. The external economies to be achieved when one region took over more than half of the production of an entire sector were also of key importance.

The massive amount of spatial shifting of industrial concentration occurring in Britain in the eighteenth century contributed to changes in the nature of goods produced and production and marketing methods. Different regions tended to specialise in different ranges of goods suitable to specific sorts of markets. The organisation of work and work practice prevalent in successfully expanding regions often came to influence the methods of an entire sector. And the growth of specialised mercantile and financial services within the dominant regions served to increase the external economies and significantly to reduce both intra-regional and inter-regional transaction costs.

The dynamic forces at work in the economy in the second half of the eighteenth century went on to make a cumulative major impact on a broader front and eventually to influence the aggregate growth indicators of the entire economy. The reason Pollard stresses for this dispro-portionately small leaven being able eventually to activate the wider mass is that it was crucially concentrated in regions. Thus Pollard argues that the influence of Britain as the pioneer industrial nation: 'was grounded on the existence of ... relatively limited regions providing as it were a system of walls within which the new ideas could reverberate and gain reinforcing strength ... instead of being diffused ineffectively across the length and breadth of a mostly unreceptive island'.[57]

The industrial region of the late eighteenth and early nineteenth centuries had a dynamic and operative function and not just a descriptive meaning. Industrial regions generated an interaction which would have been absent if their component industries had not been juxtaposed in this way. And the dynamism of these industrial regions spread out to influence other manufacturing areas. The Sheffield region, for example, could tap capital, technological aids, commercial information, foreign markets and the protection of the British navy, all of which had been built up for the use of the earlier-advanced export regions of Britain.[58] The interactions and self-reinforcing drive created by the development of industry in its regional concentration must lie at the heart of analyses of the industrial revolution in Britain and elsewhere.

[57] Ibid., p. 19.   [58] Ibid., pp. 28–9.

PROTO-INDUSTRIALISATION

Pollard's work on the importance of the region in the process of industrialisation has run parallel to and has a significant interface with the hefty literature of the last two decades on the subject of proto-industrialisation.[59] The separate strands of the original proto-industrialisation thesis from Mendels and from the work of Kriedte, Medick and Schlumbohm have in common a major stress on the dynamic effects of regions of expanding domestic and handicraft manufacture of goods for distant markets. These regions are seen to have experienced a form of industrialisation before industrialisation based on a growing functional interrelationship between merchant capital (involved largely in the putting-out system) and the family economy (with effective ties to the land but not solely dependent on it). Within the region of proto-industry capital and skills were accumulated and demographic increase stimulated thus creating the entrepreneurial and proletarian conditions for more fully fledged industrial expansion using centralised forms of organisation and technology. Furthermore, Mendels in particular stressed the interplay between regions of proto-industry and those concentrating on commercial farming: an interplay initiated on the basis of comparative advantage but becoming self-reinforcing as two way trade endorsed the specialisation of regions in the production either of foodstuffs or manufactures.[60]

By establishing the possible links between the nature of industrial change, peasant ecosystems, family life, demography and culture and by viewing these as integrated rather than separate fields of study the concept of proto-industry has significantly changed the way in which the region is perceived in the analysis of industrialisation.[61] No longer are those wishing

[59] For a survey of this literature see L. A. Clarkson, *Proto-Industrialization: The First Phase of Industrialization* (London, Macmillan, 1985). Important statements of the initial hypotheses are contained in F. F. Mendels, 'Proto-industrialisation: the first phase of the industrialisation process', *Journal of Economic History*, 32, 1 (1972) pp. 241–61; P. Kriedte, H. Medick and J. Schlumbohm, *Industrialisation before Industrialisation: Rural Industry in the Genesis of Capitalism* (English transl., Cambridge, Cambridge University Press, 1982). Important discussions and critiques of the concept include M. Berg, P. Hudson and M. Sonenscher (eds.), *Manufacture in Town and Country before the Factory* (Cambridge, Cambridge University Press, 1983); *Proceedings of the Eighth International Conference of Economic History, Budapest 1982: Session A2, Proto-Industrialisation* (1982); R. Houston and K. D. M. Snell, 'Proto-industrialization? Cottage, industry, social change and industrial revolution', *Historical Journal*, 27 (1984), pp. 473–92; D. C. Coleman, 'Proto-industrialization: a concept too many', *Economic History Review*, 36, 3 (1983), pp. 435–48.

[60] F. F. Mendels, 'Seasons and regions in agriculture and industry during the process of industrialisation', in S. Pollard (ed.), *Region und Industrialisierung* (Göttingen, Vandenhoek und Ruprecht, 1980).

[61] Thirsk's work is an important precursor here, see J. Thirsk, 'Industries in the countryside', in F. J. Fisher (ed.), *Essays in the Economic and Social History of Tudor and Stuart England* (Cambridge, Cambridge University Press, 1961), pp. 70–88.

to analyse the mainsprings of industrial growth in a region satisfied merely to explore a shopping list of factors or preconditions. It is now necessary to consider how manufacturing meshed in with agriculture through the seasons, how systems of landholding, inheritance and wealth distribution conditioned the nature, organisation and finance of industrial activities in an area, how urban production functioned in relation to rural manufacturing, how the family, household and personal life adapted to changes in work regimes and market opportunities, how these were reflected in demographic behaviour and how all these variables related to one another.

In accounting for the growth of rural domestic manufacturing in certain regions of western Europe from the seventeenth century Mendels and others initially stressed the importance of areas of high ground and infertile soils where loose systems of inheritance and population increase created an increasingly proletarianised group within the population whose livelihood could only be supported by manufacturing sidelines. The part-time nature of much early proto-industry allowed farming and other activities of the rural calendar effectively to subsidise low manufacturing piece rates. Unlike urban manufacture which often involved guild regulation and restrictions rural labour was cheaper and more flexible.

Since these characteristics of proto-industrial regions were first stressed considerable empirical work has unearthed a more complex picture of the sorts of regional environments which favoured the extension of manufacturing at this time. By no means all dynamic proto-industry occurred in regions where agriculture was poor, neither were populations everywhere driven to manufacturing out of dire necessity. Commercial manufacturing successfully existed alongside commercial farming in several regions especially where the gender or social division of labour or the seasonality of agricultural work created a pool of available labour at low cost. Gullickson's work on the Pays de Caux has shown this where men worked in agriculture and women comprised the proto-industrial work-force.[62] Whyte's chapter in this volume also throws interesting light on this question indicating that the social institutions and the organisation of arable farming in north-east Scotland created a workforce for the textile industry alongside commercial agriculture.

At issue amongst the proto-industrial theorists and their critics is not just the environment of proto-industry but also, of course, the limits and possibilities of the transition of a proto-industrial area into a region of more fully developed industrialism. Mendels stressed that the transition from phase one (proto-industrialisation) to phase two (the development of

[62] G. L. Gullickson, *The Spinners and Weavers of Auffay* (Cambridge, Cambridge University Press, 1986).

industrial capitalism) in a region was never automatic. But he implied that this would usually occur, in the absence of severe institutional obstacles, because of increasing marginal costs and lack of control over the workforce.[63] Kriedte is much more explicit in recognising a disjunction between the proto-industrial/consumer-goods phase of industrialisation and a phase two most often based on producer goods and heavy industries necessarily involving different sectors, skills and often also different locations.[64] In the British case, as Coleman has pointed out, the success rate for proto-industrial regions during the late eighteenth and early nineteenth centuries was very poor. Only four out of the ten English proto-industrial regions which he identifies witnessed early industrial revolution.[65]

Coleman argues that coal supplies were a more important determining factor in successful industrialisation than was proto-industry. In this he follows Nef, Brinley Thomas and Wrigley.[66] And the latter has most recently stressed that the whole question of Britain's undeniable industrial revolution revolves around the shift from organic to inorganic sources of energy and raw materials with its obvious effects on industrial relocation.[67] Although, as we shall see, careful attention must be paid to the pull of coalfields in the mid-nineteenth-century spatial pattern of Britain's development, the eclipse or otherwise of earlier proto-industrial regions had mostly occurred long before coal became a vital locational influence as a source of either heat or power. Short's chapter on the Weald illustrates this rather well. This region had an advanced putting-out system, an export base, agricultural specialisation, a growing population and a developed iron-producing sector, yet it de-industrialised just when other regions were taking off. The reasons for its demise were not a simple matter of coal availability.

General comparative advantage models employed to explain the considerable spatial shifts between proto-industry and 'phase two' are similarly inadequate: too much of their causal analysis is inferred from the end result, as Berg has argued.[68] For example, the shift of capital from the textile industries back to the land in Norfolk and Essex in the later eighteenth century is not satisfactorily explained by examining the

---

[63] Mendels, 'Proto-industrialisation: the first phase'.

[64] Kriedte, Medick and Schlumbohm, *Industrialisation before Industrialisation*, Ch. 6.

[65] Coleman, 'Proto-industrialization: a concept', p. 443.

[66] J. U. Nef, *The Rise of the British Coal Industry* (2 vols., London, Routledge, 1934); Wrigley, 'The supply of raw materials'; Brinley Thomas, 'Towards an energy interpretation of the industrial revolution', *Atlantic Economic Journal*, 8, 1 (1980).

[67] E. A. Wrigley, *Continuity, Chance and Change: The Character of the Industrial Revolution in England* (Cambridge, Cambridge University Press, 1988). I am most grateful to Professor Wrigley for the opportunity to read the manuscript of this work before publication.

[68] Berg, *Manufactures*, p. 118.

agricultural potential of the area. It leaves untouched the question why these regions did not change to new types of cloths or even why they produced cloths at all in the first place. Finally, if the comparative advantage of agriculture was so great why did these areas see the growth of other sorts of domestic industries alongside agriculture at this time: silk, lace, straw plaiting? The answers would seem to lie in social and institutional factors concerned with the way in which established industry was organised in both town and country. The changing gender division of labour in agriculture in the south and east was also important in the drift to female-specific forms of domestic crafts alongside agriculture.[69] These sorts of factors elude the standard proto-industrial model of ideal types of proto-industrial region and are also passed over in much comparative advantage theorising which emphasises specialisation in agriculture *or* industry, rarely both.[70] We need to be able to ask how successful agriculture could contribute to industrial growth *within* a region.

Berg places major stress on the social and institutional factors influencing the locational shifts of manufacturing industry in the eighteenth century and particularly in explaining the decline of formerly buoyant manufacturing regions.[71] Certainly the way industry was organised, the regional institutions and practices of finance and commerce and the traditions of organised labour could radically influence the sources of capital, entrepreneurship and labour for expanding industry. Sometimes regional trades could become dominated by a clique of large employers whose interaction, power and control militated against injections of new initiative and new methods. Sometimes capital came largely from outside the region (as was the case with the Weald and later with south Wales) or the power over markets was held outside the region (as was the case with the power of the Blackwell Hall factors over the textile trades of East Anglia and the south-west). It is often argued that in the textile industry the master clothier and worker structure in the south compared unfavourably with the socially more uniform and technologically more flexible small weaver communities of the north. The organisation of trades affected innovation because resistance to mechanisation occurred mainly where innovation most upset the established structures of the trade and of labour hierarchies. Randall's chapter in this volume addresses this issue, stressing also the importance of

---

[69] See K. D. M. Snell, *Annals of the Labouring Poor: Social Change and Agrarian England 1600–1900* (Cambridge, Cambridge University Press, 1985), Ch. 1.

[70] See, for example, the otherwise stimulating articles by E. L. Jones: 'The agricultural origins of industry', *Past and Present*, 40 (1968), and 'The constraints on economic growth in southern England, 650–1850', in *Proceedings of the Third International Congress of Economic History* (Munich, 1965); also, Mendels, 'Seasons and regions'.

[71] Berg, *Manufactures*, pp. 118–22.

local traditions of community solidarity and consciousness in providing an environment for the resistance to innovation by the workforce.

CRITICAL MASS

In the first half of the nineteenth century industrialisation in Britain was even more than in the eighteenth century a regional phenomenon and, unlike on the Continent, the advent of railways did not materially affect the regional concentration of industry. Although the locational influence of coal supplies came into its own at this time it was by no means the sole locational variable and it explains neither the differential nature of coalfield development nor the longer term differences in the trajectories of different industrial coalfield areas. Furthermore, the industrial region in Britain in the nineteenth century differed from its proto-industrial predecessor. By the nineteenth century, as Pollard argues, there seemed to be a minimum critical mass (which generated significant external economies) necessary for a progressive industry to maintain its momentum in a region and to keep up technically with its competitors.[72] In contrast, the proto-industrial concentrations were of very mixed size and structure: sometimes small towns even cities, most often dispersed in hamlets and villages but over areas varying greatly in size from relatively isolated pockets to entire counties. Proto-industry clearly did not require the same sorts of external or scale economies as centralised more capital-intensive production.

It is necessary to enquire what the critical mass comprised and what factors determined the ability in the nineteenth century for these sizeable industrial concentrations to maintain their status as major industrial regions and to influence the wider economy. The critical interactive mass is well summarised by Pollard:

What was important was interdependent diversity, in terms of backward and forward integration, service trades, infrastructure including a good transport system and close linkage with markets and suppliers to enable the region to react quickly to changing costs and prices or fashions. Where these elements were present the tendency would be for the region to pull ahead of the rest and for regional inequality to increase cumulatively for very long periods.[73]

A vital factor in creating the interdependence of sectors and firms in a region was the regional nature of the labour market; the availability of a pool of experienced labour was one of the most important external economies. Trade unions and other workers' organisations met and organised regionally, as did industrialists. The latter depended on this

[72] Pollard, *Peaceful Conquest*, p. 106.   [73] Ibid., p. 39.

regional co-operation to control such matters as unreasonable credit practices and embezzlement, and to blacklist and otherwise curtail the role of trade union activists. The transfer of technology occurred between regions, following skill-specific migration, and was diffused within a region aided by complex and overlapping networks of regional commercial and social life. In addition, as we have seen, the banking system was regionally oriented at this time, as was the market for industrial capital and credit. The critical mass of the interactive region was also served by considerable external economies in the sphere of trade and commerce. Specialised merchants and brokers established firm links with major markets and the flow of knowledge concerning changing tastes and fashion was easier to lock into within the established industrial region than without. Supply side linkages were also important in the efficient supply of industrial raw materials, engineering and other skills.[74]

The vibrancy and indeed the viability of industrial regions could be and often was eventually tested. Sometimes the major mineral resource base failed, for example iron ore in Shropshire, lead in Derbyshire. Cumulative success could also give way to cumulative failure where complacency and conservatism created an inability to respond to structural change in the markets for products. This was particularly crucial in regions where a single sector dominated, as was the case with many of the European textile regions. This is why Pollard stresses the importance of diversity as well as interdependence in the critical mass. In England the major industrial regions surviving into the twentieth century were those which saw a succession of distinctive economic bases overlapping and also taking over from one another as earlier successful sectors were overtaken by competition from elsewhere. Both Lancashire and Yorkshire had coal and iron to take them through from the phase of textile domination to the broader bases of economic diversification into engineering, services and chemicals. Similar sequences of mixed industries evolving in succession characterised the growth of the Clyde region, and the north-east, whereas the vast array of different metal and hardware trades of South Yorkshire and the West Midlands served to create a balanced growth with a spread of potential quite apart from the existence of coal in both regions. These conditions eluded north Wales, the West Country and East Anglia; this was by no means mere accident nor solely dependent on the absence of coal as the north Wales example illustrates.

The presence of multiple industries was important but the nature and trajectory of an industrial region must also be examined in the context of

---

[74] Ibid., pp. 33–8, and Langton argues similarly about trade unions and employers' associations, and about intra-regional economic relations, in 'The industrial revolution', pp. 150–7.

the role of central and local state activity, and of the prevailing economic power structures at regional, national and international levels.

POLITICAL AND ECONOMIC POWER

As Evans argues in the present volume: 'We must avoid giving regions personalities and then blaming them for lack of growth or praising them for success ... people within *and without* the regions still make the decisions: analysis of class and power structures cannot be evaded'.[75] Class and power structures including the influence of politically powerful elite groups, the functioning interrelationship between 'core' areas of development and more 'peripheral' regions, the working out of international as well as national divisions of labour and the power of dominant ideologies concerning the limits and possibilities of different technological combinations all had a powerful impact on the development and nature of regional concentrations of industry and their long term survival prospects.

Pollard has argued that national state policies in nineteenth-century Europe tended to endorse existing regional inequalities despite the support and privilege given to certain state manufacturing establishments and the active role played by continental states in railway development.[76] In England the state played a much smaller role in promoting regional development in any direct sense. And where it did (not necessarily consciously), such as with the earlier Mines Royal or the Mineral and Battery works, the drain of profits out of the region and back to state coffers and the eventual withdrawal of support often had grave deleterious effects.[77] When one comes to analyse the role of the state directly and specifically in promoting British regional growth it is the role of *local* government at county and sub-county level which requires attention. This is a much-neglected field despite the fact that the county administration of the legal system, taxation and forms of economic regulation was the arm of state activity which most directly and immediately affected regional economic activity. And at parish level, often responding to the wider prevalence of regional practices, the forms of administration of poor relief, the implementation of the settlement laws and the billeting of pauper apprentices could significantly affect the supply of labour to industry and its cost.[78] Local and regional political structures, embedded in the long histories of particular regions, also determined the distribution of wealth

[75] See p. 224.
[76] Pollard, 'Regional markets and national development', pp. 6–7, and *Peaceful Conquest*, pp. 159–63.
[77] Marshall and Evans both give examples of this in their contributions to this volume; see pp. 133, 141, 209.
[78] For the importance of this in the later seventeenth century, see Wrightson and Levine, *Poverty and Piety in an English Village*. See also Snell, *Annals of the Labouring Poor*, Ch. 3.

(including wealth held in land) and the nature of the land market via inheritance practices, controls over the transfer of copyholds and influences on the marketing of freehold land. Thus, the availability of land as a vital factor of production (both in itself and as collateral for raising capital) alongside labour and capital was fundamentally influenced by forces acting at the level of specific localities. These forces were important in the siting of manufacturing and commercial activity outside of the major towns and cities and as important as the agrarian potential of a region when one searches for the agricultural origins of industry.[79]

There is a similar need to comprehend the political character of towns and cities of the industrial regions. Their corporate or non-corporate status could be important in restricting or prompting the growth of trade.[80] The nature of urban oligarchies could affect everything from the control and functioning of markets to the building of commercial and industrial premises. The origins and history of a town whether long established or newly developing was also crucial and this in turn was a major factor in explaining the nature of its dominant political groupings.[81] Rowlands' descriptions of the nature and growth of the West Midlands towns and Whyte's allusions to the restrictive Scottish burghs provide examples in this study of the importance of urban structures and urban politics for the dynamism of the wider manufacturing areas.

The emergence of distinct social classes and of class antagonisms also varied from region to region: a product of the interplay between historical factors and the nature of changing industrial structure. Important in this was the emergence of an increasingly proletarianised and often increasingly urban workforce. Equally a factor was the transformation of labour discipline and work culture. These occurred in an uneven spatial pattern. Gregory has recently argued that it is important to recognise that the structural transformation of labour and of the labour process was in many respects a regional affair: struggles around the control and character of work were undertaken largely at regional level.[82] Randall's chapter shows this rather well. Regions like the West Riding of Yorkshire and the West Country found it difficult to link their interests in a common cause (such as opposition to the deregulation of the woollen industry in the early

[79] P. Hudson 'Proto-industrialisation: the case of the West Riding wool textile industry in the eighteenth and early nineteenth centuries', *History Workshop Journal*, 12 (1981), pp. 34–61; E. L. Jones, 'The agricultural origins of industry'; Thirsk, 'Industries in the countryside'.

[80] A. P. Wadsworth and J. de L. Mann, *The Cotton Trade and Industrial Lancashire 1600–1780* (Manchester, Manchester University Press, 1931; reprinted 1965), Ch. 3.

[81] P. Clark and P. Slack, *English Towns in Transition 1500–1700* (Oxford, Oxford University Press, 1976); P. Corfield, *The Impact of English Towns, 1700–1800* (Oxford, Oxford University Press, 1982).

[82] D. Gregory, *Regional Transformation and Industrial Revolution: A Geography of the Yorkshire Woollen Industry* (London, Macmillan, 1982), p. 292.

nineteenth century) partly because of longstanding regional rivalries but mainly because of differences in expectations and experiences which arose from fundamental differences in the regional constitution of class relations. Kearns in discussing (and decoding) Gregory has recently stressed an important point worth pursuing in regional studies of cultural and social as well as economic change: 'While the separation of the worker from the means of production was a general feature under industrial capitalism, the links between production, circulation and distribution were established in ways which varied regionally.'[83]

My own work on the West Riding has shown the very specific way in which industrial, mercantile and finance capital interacted but also remained very separate. In other industrial regions, because of the varying commercial and investment requirements of their dominant sectors, the relationship between manufacturing and trading took other forms. The degree of vertical integration or disintegration and the implications which this had for investment sources and institutions was one major variable in this which had considerable implications for the regional constellation of class forces.[84] A further feature which influenced the nature of class relations across the social spectrum was the differing regional distributions of income which could sustain and reproduce a given social structure or contribute to its transformation. To understand this is to understand the nature of the dominant employment sectors of the region: the nature of labour hierarchies, skill divisions, the extent of women's employments, the degree of centralisation of production and of labour intensity. Such elements get lost in attempts to understand the wider politics of class at the national level particularly for the period before the Second World War.

The prevalence of ideologies at national and international levels concerning the nature of economic and technological development may also play a crucial role in determining the success or otherwise of industrial regions. This is particularly the case, argue Sabel and Zeitlin, where an industrial region has based its specialism on a form of production at odds with the general trend.[85] Sabel and Zeitlin present an interesting argument about the relationship between politics, markets and technological choice in their analysis of the relative decline of economically viable alternatives to mass production in the nineteenth century. These alternative forms of 'flexible specialisation' were so often associated with specific regional concentrations, or industrial districts as Alfred Marshall termed them, that the Sabel/Zeitlin analysis is of some importance in studying the origins and

---

[83] G. Kearns, 'The age of regions? The historical geography of the industrial revolution', unpublished paper, 1987, p. 10.
[84] Hudson, *The Genesis, passim.*   [85] Sabel and Zeitlin, 'Historical alternatives'.

futures of those regions which successfully industrialised without a dominating sector of mass production: 'Silks in Lyon; ribbons, hardware and speciality steels in Solingen, Remscheid and Sheffield; calicoes in Alsace; woollens in Roubaix; cottons in Pawtucket and Rhode Island; textiles of all kinds in Philadelphia – the history of all these industries challenges the classical view of economic progress'.[86] And all these depended, as Sabel and Zeitlin argue, on the creation of regional institutions that balanced co-operation and competition among firms so as to encourage permanent innovation.[87] But why did many of these innovative regions fail to survive in recognisable form down to the present? And why were they not more numerous to begin with? Sabel and Zeitlin's explanation is a political one: that the direction of technological development is crucially dependent on the distribution of power and wealth in society:

Those who control the disposition of resources and the returns from investments choose from among the available applications of technology the one most favourable to their interests as they define them...In time the logic of the dominant paradigm becomes so compellingly self-evident that competing lines of innovation become almost inconceivable.[88]

Thus, explanation of the way an industrialising region develops is as difficult to reduce to a list of purely economic causes as explanations of which regions industrialise. The non-economic, political influences on the organisation of industry and its use of technology have localised historical, cultural and institutional elements but the position of regions within the larger political and economic arenas of the national and international economies is a crucial variable in determining their viability.

CURRENT DEVELOPMENT THEORY

Theories of contemporary development and underdevelopment, particularly analysis in terms of formal and informal imperialism or structures of economic core and periphery, have thrown up another set of power relationships relevant for understanding both sub-national and international patterns of the concentration of economic activity and wealth.[89] This sort of analysis is important because too often regional problems get identified

---

[86] Ibid., p. 142.   [87] Ibid., p. 144.   [88] Ibid., pp. 161–2.

[89] Influential in these theories has been the work of A. G. Frank, e.g. *Latin America: Underdevelopment or Revolution* (New York, Monthly Review Press, 1970), and S. Amin, *Unequal Development* (Brighton, Harvester, 1976). One of the best known historical applications to uneven regional development is M. Hechter, *Internal Colonialism: The Celtic Fringe in British National Development, 1536–1966* (London, Routledge, 1975). For a review of some of the historical applications of core-periphery ideas to British history, see K. Robbins, 'Core and periphery in modern British history', *Proceedings of the British Academy*, 70 (1974).

solely with the region in which they occur. Factors such as lack of entrepreneurial talents, worker militancy, unfavourable resource endowments get pushed to the forefront of analyses of regional differences whilst wider national and international political and economic power structures are ignored. In this way the perception of political struggle and protest in regions gets split off from struggles elsewhere and any wider questioning or understanding of the relationships between disparate regional problems gets discouraged. Although most of the theorising of unequal development during the last decades has revolved around the analysis of international power structures,[90] much of it can throw light on regional imbalances also. Just as in the international sphere, factor flows between regions are not simply a matter of the working of free markets but relate closely to the siting and operation of political as well as economic power.

There are, however, a number of dangers in transposing models largely evolved to study uneven development between national economies to the study of regional inequalities. One problem arises because a region is much more open both economically and politically than a nation and it almost invariably has a narrower industrial base arising from its specialisation of function. Both of these affect the way in which national and international divisions of labour are experienced. Most importantly, as stressed by Massey, theories of the development of nations and underdevelopment tend to take nation states as objects given to analysis:

Whether or not this is correct at an international level...'regions' are *not* necessarily pre-given to the study of intra-national spatial differentiation...regions must be constituted *as an effect* of analysis; they are thus defined in relation to spatial uneven development in the process of accumulation and its effects on social (including political) relations.[91]

What is thus required is a transposition of some of the ideas evolved in the context of dependency models (for example, peripheralisation, colonisation) to a dynamic understanding of what makes and sustains a region's attractiveness as a site for intense economic activity and profitability. Short's chapter in this volume does just this in analysing the decline of the Weald.

Such a dynamic model of regional development must also include consideration of the effects of economic fluctuations (at both national and international levels) upon existing regional structures which are themselves a product of waves of historical evolution. In both the analysis of Sabel and

[90] For an important early exception, see G. Myrdal, *Economic Theory and Under-Developed Regions* (London, Duckworth, 1957). This discusses spread and backwash effects in particular.

[91] D. Massey, 'Regionalism: some current issues', *Capital and Class*, 6 (1978), p. 110.

Zeitlin and in those studies where industrialisation and de-industrialisation, development and underdevelopment are seen as two sides of the same coin, the role of cyclical fluctuations both long and short term assume an important place. According to Wallerstein, for example, periods of long-term economic expansion (the A-phase of logistic cycles lasting a century or more) create the circumstances for endorsing the established core/periphery structures at both sub-national and international levels.[92] According to Sabel and Zeitlin these conditions will also confirm the position of the dominant technological path.[93] It is periods of crisis and general involution which shake up both the established structures and hierarchies (radically affecting spatial patterns) and open up the possibility of divergent technological breakthroughs.

The critical issue is of course why, confronted by similar beneficial spread effects during the same cyclical upswing, some regions prosper in a sustained way, achieving the sort of critical mass required for longer term stability or expansion whereas in other regions the industrial development for an upswing proves incomplete or ephemeral making them easy prey to the acute backwash effects of the next cyclical downswing. In a recent overview of Ulster's industrial history, Othick writes that regional industrialisation

is best comprehended as a sequence of challenges and responses: the former emanated from a periodically widening set of production possibilities, which were determined by the rhythms of the world economy and Britain's changing international role; the latter were constrained by the local economic, social and institutional structures that had resulted from the previous interaction of regional, national and international influences.[94]

It is this sort of dynamic approach to understanding the interaction between the past and the present, between the political and the economic and between forces acting at regional, national and international levels that we need to be working towards as a first step in identifying just what the industrial revolution was as an economic and political process. This sort of regional approach also has the advantage of getting away from the complacent assumption about the self-sustaining character of economic

[92] I. Wallerstein, *The Modern World System*, vol. 2: *Mercantilism and the Consolidation of the European World Economy 1600–1750* (New York, Academic Press, 1980), pp. 2–35. Wallerstein has, of course, been heavily criticised from a number of perspectives, most notably (with respect to European industrialisation) by P. O'Brien, 'European economic development: the contribution of the periphery', *Economic History Review*, 35, 1 (1982). But few critiques have addressed his spread/backlash arguments regarding long cycles of development.

[93] Sabel and Zeitlin, 'Historical alternatives', pp. 162–3.

[94] J. Othick, 'The economic history of Ulster: a perspective', in L. Kennedy and P. Ollerenshaw (eds.), *An Economic History of Ulster, 1820–1940* (Manchester, Manchester University Press, 1985), p. 228. This sort of analysis is prominent in Evans' chapter in this volume.

growth. Because a region much more than a nation tends to specialise in certain economic functions and because it is more open to external competition it is inherently vulnerable to the changing context of wider political and economic forces. This context is felt by a region through its manifold linkages with other regions, with the national economy and with the world economy in which both region and nation are enmeshed. Whether these linkages are beneficial or harmful to a region depends, as Othick argues,

on the relative strength of spread effects which encourage the diffusion of industrialisation, as against backwash effects which produce the opposite result ... Spread effects encompass the transfer of technology capital and business enterprise from a more to a less developed industrial region ... Backwash effects occur when the less developed region experiences an outflow of capital, or skilled labour, to a more advanced region; or when its local industries succumb to ... competition.[95]

The task for the historian is to be able to identify in what circumstances the backwash effects may dominate the spread effects and where linkages may prove disadvantageous in the long term. Echoing Pollard, Othick argues that the linkages most likely to produce lasting benefits are those which encourage the economic diversification of a region. The linkages spawned by Ulster from its textile sector were not capable of supporting a more diversified economy. Before shipbuilding and engineering took off in the second half of the nineteenth century, the pattern of industrialisation that had occurred in Ulster endorsed rural population increase whilst discouraging large-scale urbanisation. Even in the late nineteenth century the industrial base of Ulster remained precariously narrow: it generated a disproportionately large amount of low-paid female labour and the level of urbanisation remained low by British standards. Thus although Ulster had become established as a major industrial region within the United Kingdom economy, its fundamental weaknesses were soon to be revealed as that economy's fortunes declined. And Ulster's possibilities were further circumscribed by national priorities and policies: an affliction common to other regions.[96]

Massey has a similar perspective in her conceptualisation of the dynamics of spatially uneven development, which centres on understanding the interplay between a region's history and its response to newly emerging spatial divisions of labour.[97] She stresses that a region's

---

[95] Ibid., p. 226.

[96] Ibid., pp. 234–5. See also Clarkson's chapter in this volume, pp. 261, 270.

[97] Massey, 'Regionalism' and D. Massey, 'In what sense a regional problem?', Regional Studies, 13 (1979), pp. 233–43. See also D. Massey, Spatial Divisions of Labour: Social Structures and the Geography of Production (London, Macmillan, 1984), and A. Lipietz, Le Capital et son espace (Maspero, Economie et Socialisme, 1977).

attractiveness or otherwise to economic activity will respond especially to changes in the organisation and control of its dominant sectors. She suggests a schematic way of approaching this as a historical process: to conceive of it as a series of 'rounds' of investment in each of which a new spatial division of labour is evolved. These rounds of investment are distributed, as Harvey has argued, out of fundamental tension between preserving the values of past commitments made at a particular place and time, or devaluing them to open up fresh room for accumulation.[98] The new distribution of economic activity will be overlaid on and combined with the pattern produced in previous periods.

The combination of successive spatial divisions of labour may not, of course, produce, in any sense, coherent regional economies. But with respect to nineteenth-century Britain, industrial regions proved both enduring and expansive during the period of general buoyancy of the Victorian economy. Furthermore, they had fairly distinctive social relations and continued to have important elements of economic, social and political coherence long after the mid-century innovations in finance transport and communications. This makes their study essential in understanding the overall growth of the national economy at this time. The endurance and spatial integrity of British industrial regions throughout the nineteenth century occurred largely because they were dominated by investment in particular sectors: principally in various combinations of textiles, coal, engineering and shipbuilding. When sectoral crisis came with the change in imperial relationships and with the decline of the United Kingdom as a dominant industrial economy, regional depression ensued.[99] Restructuring and geographical redistribution of economic activity since the Second World War has occurred along different lines. Intra-sectoral spatial divisions of labour have become much more important, spread on a pattern of locational hierarchies of production (research and development in the south-east, labour-intensive and low value added processes in more peripheral regions).[100] It is at this point that the pull of the metropolis and the importance of London as the centre of financial power came back into its own and when it became obvious that the British state was very well adapted to serving the needs of finance rather than industrial capital.[101] This

---

[98] D. Harvey, *The Limits to Capital* (Oxford, Blackwell, 1982), pp. 419–22.

[99] Uneven levels of regional unemployment predate the interwar period largely because of sectoral specialisation of the regional economic base, see H. R. Southwall, 'The origins of the depressed areas: unemployment, growth and regional economic structure in Britain before 1914', *Economic History Review*, 41, 2 (1988).

[100] See Massey, 'In what sense a regional problem?', *passim*.

[101] See G. Ingham, *Capitalism Divided? The City and Industry in British Social Development'* (London, Macmillan, 1984); C. Leys, 'The formation of British capital', *New Left Review*, 160 (1986); P. Anderson, 'The figures of descent', *New Left Review*, 161 (1987). For a critique of the dominant importance in British economic and political development of the Treasury–City–Bank nexus, see

explains the growing dominance of London and the Home Counties over the provinces in the twentieth century, a trend initiated in the nineteenth century by the concentration there of high-order service activities.[102] In this context as Dyos argued long ago: 'The shift of resources into the exploitation of the northern provinces...:in the eighteenth and nineteenth centuries might be represented as an interlude ... in a much longer historical trend (towards London)'.[103] Whether or not this was an interlude, it certainly implies the need to look closely at regional industrial concentration and development patterns for the crucial period of the industrial revolution and its aftermath. And with contemporary fears of the breakup of Britain[104] and the creation of the new north/south divide, understanding the interplay between region and nation in historical perspective assumes a renewed relevance and importance.

M. Barratt Brown, 'Away with all the great arches: Anderson's history of British capitalism', *New Left Review*, 167 (1988).

[102] C. Lee, 'The service sector, regional specialisation and economic growth in the Victorian economy', *Journal of Historical Geography*, 10 (1984).

[103] H. J. Dyos, 'Greater and greater London: notes on metropolis and provinces in the nineteenth and twentieth centuries', in J. S. Bromley and E. H. Kossman (eds.), *Britain and the Netherlands*, vol. 4: *Metropolis, Dominion and Province* (The Hague, Martinus Nijhoff, 1971), p. 91, reprinted in D. Cannadine and D. Reeder (eds.), *Exploring the Urban Past: Essays in Urban History by H. J. Dyos* (Cambridge, Cambridge University Press, 1982), quoted by Kearns, 'The age of regions?', p. 19.

[104] T. Nairn, *The Break-Up of Britain* (London, New Left Books, 1981).

PART ONE

THE TEXTILE HEARTLANDS OF THE INDUSTRIAL REVOLUTION

Proto-industrialisation and the first industrial revolution: the case of Lancashire

JOHN K. WALTON

In the last few years the literature on proto-industrialisation has almost achieved its own take-off into self-sustaining growth. The theories and agenda advanced by the pioneers of the concept have been applied to regions and economies far removed from its original settings in north-western and central Europe. Russia and Japan now feature in the proto-industrial canon, and the concept has also migrated from country to town, with studies of urban proto-industrialisation in settings as economically and geographically diverse as Lisburn (Northern Ireland) and Bologna.[1] But, surprisingly, nothing has yet been said about the applicability of the theories to the Lancashire textile industries. This is extraordinary because south-east Lancashire, especially, has a strong claim to having become the first full-fledged industrial society during roughly the last quarter of the eighteenth century and the first half of the nineteenth. At any rate, it combined factory industry, using steam power, continuous operation and a high level of mechanisation, with the rapid rise of distinctively industrial towns on an ever-growing scale, and the emergence of the first concentrated, purely industrial proletariat. Whatever qualifications one might want to make about the persistence of older ways of working alongside the factory, this was a remarkable set of developments. If a transition from pre-industrial through proto-industrial to industrial economy and society took place anywhere in its pure form, uncontaminated by the influence of prior innovations elsewhere, it should have been in the Manchester area of Lancashire. But the economic history of the Manchester region between the early seventeenth century and the late eighteenth century has hardly been touched since Wadsworth and Mann brought out their classic work on *The Cotton Trade and Industrial Lancashire* in 1931. Subsequent, and recent, syntheses reflect this lack of research: Peter Kriedte, for example, in a book which develops proto-industrial themes in the context of 'Europe and the World Economy 1500–1800', says next to

---

[1] See citations in R. Houston and K. D. M. Snell, 'Proto-industrialization? Cottage industry, social change and industrial revolution', *Historical Journal*, 27 (1984), pp. 473–92.

nothing about Lancashire in the text, while recognising in passing the excellence and importance of Wadsworth and Mann's contribution.[2]

I do not claim that this chapter will make up for this damaging and distorting neglect. Major research projects are needed, especially on the relationships between economic change, social formations and demography, on the division of labour within the household, and on the organisation of work more generally. More has been done on entrepreneurship and markets, but mainly for the late eighteenth and nineteenth centuries. I cannot fill these gaps; but I can hope to locate interesting problems and suggest intermediate hypotheses. This chapter does not rest on a heavy research base, but I hope that it will stimulate others to carry on where I leave off.[3]

Even without a substantial research project, the proto-industrial characteristics of what became 'cotton Lancashire' are clearly identifiable in outline in the seventeenth and eighteenth centuries. This applies not only to Manchester and its immediate surroundings, but also to a wider area extending to Burnley and Blackburn to the north and north-west, and to Preston, Wigan and (more debatably) Kirkham and Warrington in the west. We shall see that different kinds of manufacture prevailed in different places, and that the pattern shifted over time. Rural domestic industries did develop, especially but not entirely in upland and agriculturally inhospitable areas. We shall see that the more fertile plains and valleys were not immune to the contagion. These manufactures depended increasingly on distant markets, and came to be organised systematically by (mainly) urban capitalists. The rise of domestic manufacture was associated with accelerating population growth, and as textiles became economically dominant the area came to rely on food brought in from emergent areas of agricultural specialisation and investment, especially parts of west Lancashire and the Cheshire plain, later reinforced by canal-borne produce from Lincolnshire and the eastern counties, and by the widening influence of the port of Liverpool.[4] Ultimately a vicious spiral of falling piece rates,

---

[2] P. Kriedte, *Peasants, Landlords and Merchant Capitalists: Europe and the World Economy, 1500–1800* (Leamington Spa, 1983), p. 180. See also John T. Swain, *Industry before the Industrial Revolution* (Manchester, 1986), pp. 1–2.

[3] For the late eighteenth century in Lancashire, see especially M. M. Edwards, *The Growth of the British Cotton Trade, 1780–1815* (Manchester, 1967); K. Honeyman, *Origins of Enterprise* (Manchester, 1983); S. D. Chapman, 'Fixed capital formation in the British cotton manufacturing industry', in J. P. P. Higgins and S. Pollard (eds.), *Aspects of Capital Formation in Great Britain, 1750–1850* (London, 1971), pp. 57–107.

[4] J. Aikin, *A Description of the Country from Thirty to Forty Miles around Manchester* (London, 1795; reprinted Newton Abbot, 1968); J. Holt, *General View of the Agriculture of the County of Lancaster* (London, 1795; reprinted Newton Abbot, 1969); S. Marriner, *The Economic and Social Development of Merseyside* (London, 1982), p. 48; J. P. Dodd, 'South Lancashire in transition: a study of the crop returns for 1795–1801', *Historic Society of Lancashire and Cheshire*, 117 (1965), pp. 89–107; C. Hadfield

over-production and 'self-exploitation' can be identified, at least among the hand-loom weavers by the second quarter of the nineteenth century. At the level of introductory generalisation, the first industrial revolution had clearly proto-industrial roots. But the problems begin as soon as we start to probe below the surface.

One of the main difficulties with the concept of proto-industrialisation is that of showing when the phase begins or ends. How, in the beginning, does a proto-industrial economy differ from the many well-established 'dual economies' in which agriculture and domestic manufacture had long co-existed? How far, and in what ways, does development have to proceed before something justifies the label 'proto-industrial'? At the other end of the process, where the transition to 'industrialism' is 'satisfactorily' completed, at what point between the coming of the first factories and the demise of the last artisan outworker should the proto-industrial phase be held to have ended? If our terms are loosely defined, the concept of the 'proto-industrial' is spread thinly and amorphously across many centuries and loses its analytical bite; but if they are narrowly and specifically delimited, we may find it hard to identify any proto-industrial place and period with any conviction, as the concept is ground into nothingness between the millstones of what comes before and what comes after. These problems are particularly relevant to the Lancashire experience, and as I analyse the changing economy and society of this pioneer industrial region in the light of proto-industrial theory, I shall take care to keep them in mind.[5]

At the outset, we need to set our themes more precisely in their geographical context. The processes of proto-industrialisation are held to have operated at a regional level; but as Coleman in particular has pointed out, the proponents of the concept have tended to dodge the question of what a region might actually be. This is understandable, for the term is essential but embarrassingly elastic. It provokes argument because it becomes so Protean and elusive whenever a precise frame of reference is needed for empirical enquiry. The area which became the Lancashire cotton district is problematic because different parts of it evolved in different ways, so that what was recognisable as a distinctive economic region by 1840 had been a jigsaw of contrasting experiences less than a century earlier. Moreover, here as elsewhere economic and social change was no respecter of political boundaries, and when I speak of Lancashire's cotton industry I

and G. Biddle, *The Canals of North-West England*, vol. 1 (Newton Abbot, 1970), pp. 164, 176, 267, 279–80; C. S. Davies, *The Agricultural History of Cheshire, 1750–1850* (Manchester, 1960).
[5] For criticisms see especially Houston and Snell, 'Proto-industrialization?'; L. A. Clarkson, *Proto-Industrialization: The First Phase of Industrialization?* (London, 1985); D. C. Coleman, 'Proto-industrialization: a concept too many', *Economic History Review*, 36, 3 (1983), pp. 435–48.

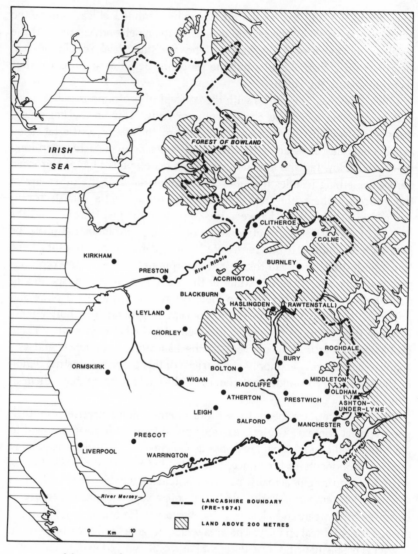

Map 2.1   The Lancashire textile area of the eighteenth century

include those areas of north-east Cheshire and north-west Derbyshire
which came under the same influences and experienced the same changes.
I propose to examine the nature of the changing economies of different
parts of the county, deciding which are worth considering as potential
components of a proto-industrial region on the criteria used by the

theorists, and stirring in some additional ingredients which may help to explain the distinctive nature of the Lancashire experience.[6]

The complexities of Lancashire's pre-industrial economy were brought out long ago by Wadsworth and Mann. Different areas specialised in different cloths using different raw materials; but there was considerable overlap between the textile industries, and the boundaries of their areas of predominance changed over time. There were also important mining and metalworking industries, especially in the south-west of the county; but I shall concentrate my attention on the textile industries. This narrowing of the field of analysis is a general feature of explorations of proto-industrialisation, and it has attracted adverse comment. In the Lancashire context, however, it seems a defensible approach, if only because it was in textiles, and specifically in cotton, that the first factory-centred industrial revolution occurred.[7]

At the beginning of the seventeenth century a well-developed woollen industry was operating in symbiosis with agriculture over much of north-east Lancashire, with strong connections with the West Riding of Yorkshire. Woollens predominated east of Clitheroe and the upper Ribble Valley, east of a line running from Blackburn southwards to Bolton, and north of a line from Bolton to Ashton-under-Lyne. Manchester and Salford also made rough woollens, and Manchester and Bolton were centres of woollen finishing. But linen was the prevailing textile manufacture over most of the rest of the county, apart from an outpost of the declining Westmorland woollen industry around Cartmel and Hawkshead, north of Morecambe Bay in what has (since 1974) become Cumbria. Linen was especially important in and around Manchester, and Manchester also manufactured smallwares and wove silk; but the linen manufacture was widespread throughout the county wherever woollens were unimportant. There were complications: apart from the diversities of the Manchester economy, which was already acquiring some regional metropolitan characteristics, Wadsworth and Mann point out that 'Linen overlapped with woollens in the Blackburn area, and there was some woollen manufacture at Preston and Wigan', some distance to the west. In the early seventeenth century, too, major changes were beginning.[8]

---

[6] Coleman, 'Proto-industrialization: a concept', p. 441.

[7] A. P. Wadsworth and J. de L. Mann, *The Cotton Trade and Industrial Lancashire 1600–1780* (Manchester, 1931; reprinted 1965). See also Stephen Kenny, 'The location and organisation of the early Lancashire cotton industry: a systems approach', *Manchester Geographer*, 3 (1982), pp. 9–11. For a general survey of the Lancashire economy in this period, see John K. Walton, *Lancashire: A Social History, 1558–1939* (Manchester, 1986), Chs. 2, 4 and 6. For coal and related industries in south-west Lancashire, J. Langton, *Geographical Change and Industrial Revolution* (Cambridge, 1980).

[8] Wadsworth and Mann, *Cotton Trade*, p. 24; see also N. Lowe, *The Lancashire Textile Industry in the Sixteenth Century* (Manchester, 1972); T. S. Willan, *Elizabethan Manchester* (Manchester, 1980);

The key change in Lancashire's product inventories involved the introduction of cotton through the medium of fustians, which in this context (though not in others) were relatively heavy cloths which combined a linen warp with a cotton weft.[9] Fustian manufacture was spreading rapidly in and from the Blackburn and Bolton areas from the early seventeenth century. It was 'firmly established' in and around what later became Oldham by 1630, and it was penetrating the economy of the Manchester district itself by the late seventeenth century. By this time cotton was also being introduced into the traditional Lancashire linen industry, in a variety of manufactures known generically as cotton-linens. The relative importance of cotton in all these processes increased steadily during the first half of the eighteenth century, and by mid-century most of south-east and central Lancashire was largely given over to the manufacture of cotton and cotton-using goods. The pure linen industry was becoming confined to the west of the county, although it retained outposts of late eighteenth-century strength, especially around Preston, Kirkham and Warrington. But the woollen manufacture, which had itself diversified to embrace lighter and more up-market cloths from the early seventeenth century, remained firmly established in its Lancashire heartlands around Rochdale and Colne, in the Bury area and in Rossendale. It was not until the great cotton boom of the late eighteenth century and the early factory age that the frontiers of the woollen industry began to be rolled back. In and around Rochdale, especially, the manufacture of various woollen fabrics remained important into the second quarter of the nineteenth century and beyond, and in 1824 Baines' Lancashire directory found that cotton firms were far outnumbered here by woolstaplers, wool carders, and flannel and baize manufacturers. Manchester itself still filled four columns with woollen and worsted firms in the same directory: no doubt these were mainly the warehouses of putting-out manufacturers, in keeping with the town's role as commercial capital of Lancashire textiles, which was already firmly established at the end of the Napoleonic Wars.[10]

Even if we confine our analysis to textiles, then, the area which became identified as the Lancashire 'cotton district' was far from homogeneous in its industrial make-up at any point between the early seventeenth and the

---

E. Kerridge, *Textile Manufactures in Early Modern England* (Manchester, 1985), pp. 20, 23–4; A. P. Wadsworth, 'The history of the Rochdale woollen trade', *Transactions of the Rochdale Literary and Scientific Society*, 15 (1923–5), p. 93.

[9] Wadsworth and Mann, *Cotton Trade*, p. 527; Kerridge, *Textile Manufactures*, pp. 49–50.

[10] Wadsworth and Mann, *Cotton Trade*, especially Chs. 1 and 9; G. H. Tupling, *The Economic History of Rossendale* (Manchester, 1927), Ch. 6; E. Baines, *History, Directory and Gazetteer of the County Palatine of Lancaster*, vol. 2 (1825; reprinted Newton Abbot, 1968), pp. 347–8; R. Lloyd-Jones and M. Lewis, 'The economic structure of "Cottonopolis": Manchester in 1815', *Textile History*, 17 (1986), pp. 71–89.

mid-nineteenth centuries. To complicate the picture further, silk weaving was making inroads, not only in Manchester but at Middleton to the north and in the Leigh and Ormskirk districts to the west, especially during the 1820s and 1830s.[11] If we are to speak of 'proto-industrialisation' in textiles in a Lancashire 'region', we shall have to lump together the experiences of the cotton, woollen, linen and silk industries, each of which had its own internal sub-divisions in terms of products, organisation and markets, and each of which followed its own distinctive trajectory of development in terms of technology, mode of production and relationship with agriculture. Any attempt to generalise about the area which eventually became the Lancashire cotton district, a process which was not completed until the second half of the nineteenth century, must take account of this diversity of backgrounds: a diversity which also extends to such important influences on economic development and proto-industrial theory as agriculture, land tenure, inheritance practices and the strength or weakness of large landowners and manorial overlords. Is there a case for applying the label 'proto-industrial' to any or all of this complicated pattern of sub-regions, which arguably only attained a real measure of coherent regional identity with the completion of the transition to factory-centred industrialisation? Even then, of course, the differences between the spinning and weaving areas, and between the industrial and employment structures of individual towns, remained considerable and pervasive.[12]

THE LINEN MANUFACTURE

The linen industry which persisted in the western part of Lancashire provides the least difficult case. It misses out on too many of the theoretical desiderata to stand much chance of aspiring to the 'proto-industrial' label. But the situation was not clear-cut. Much of the raw material for the linen manufacture was imported from Ireland and increasingly in the middle decades of the eighteenth century from the Baltic. Kirkham, about which we know most, developed a colonial export trade in twine and sailcloth at mid-century, and the Langtons and other leading merchant families were eagerly cultivating further overseas outlets by the 1770s. A putting-out system was in full swing by this time, employing hundreds of weavers in the surrounding countryside as well as in Kirkham itself. This seems to have been exceptional, although Warrington, like Kirkham, sold sailcloth to the royal navy, and its merchant manufacturers also competed in the overseas

---

[11] R. Sykes, 'Popular politics and trade unionism in south-east Lancashire, 1829–42', unpublished Ph.D. thesis (University of Manchester, 1982), pp. 200–9.
[12] See especially D. Farnie, *The English Cotton Industry and the World Market, 1815–96* (Oxford, 1979).

markets of the 1770s. Before 1750, indeed, a Warrington sailcloth manufacturer was said to be employing 5,000 people, and a sale notice of 1759 showed that some of the work was becoming concentrated into urban workshops. At Prescot, too, a putting-out system in sailcloth and linen was well established by 1765.[13] Much more important here, however, was the manufacture of watch parts and files, whose workers were 'numerously scattered over the country from Prescott to Liverpool, occupying small farms in conjunction with their manufacturing business', and supplying 'all Europe ... more or less' by 1795.[14] Elsewhere, indeed, the linen manufacture seems to have been low-key and locally orientated. This was true of Preston and Wigan before the importation of the cotton industry, and also of Ormskirk.

These latter judgements are particularly impressionistic, and linen and its related manufactures were locally important to a lot of families over a wide area. But we run into problems when we try to assess *how* important, and to *how many* or *what proportion* of families. The bailiff of Clitheroe suggested in 1695 that flax spinning mattered a great deal to the local poor, who

mostly employ the winter in spinning flaxen yarne, and formerly made advantage thereof; which forreigners seeing, have undermined us, buying the best of flax and imploying their owne poor to spin, about Hamborow, etc., where they live cheap and send us the yarne, which we must either take at their rates or bee content with the worst sort of flax, little else now comeing; by which meanes, our poore complaine they cannot get for their yarne what their flax cost, and must either turne beggars or worke to no purpose. And soe the poore are ruined.[15]

This was part of a plea for protection against foreign competition in the home market, and as such it may well exaggerate the importance of the industry to domestic economies in normal times. It seems likely that over most of western Lancashire, even in the eighteenth century, the linen industry was a supplement to primarily agricultural domestic economies, rather than the main prop of a rural industrial proletariat. We lack the detailed local analyses which might help us to take matters further. We know that for various short periods in the first quarter of the eighteenth century quite impressive proportions of the fathers of baptised children might be recorded as having textile-related occupations: almost half at Walton-le-dale, near Preston, in 1704–8, though rather less twenty years

[13] Aikin, *Manchester*, pp. 311–12; Wadsworth and Mann, *Cotton Trade*, pp. 211, 302–3; F. Singleton, 'The flax merchants of Kirkham', *Historic Society of Lancashire and Cheshire*, 126 (1977), pp. 73–108; T. S. Ashton, *An Eighteenth-Century Industrialist: Peter Stubs of Warrington, 1756–1806* (Manchester, 1939; reprinted 1961); and information from Joan Wilkinson.
[14] Aikin, *Manchester*, pp. 311–12.
[15] Quoted by Wadsworth and Mann, *Cotton Trade*, p. 90.

later, and nearly one in five at nearby Penwortham. At Upholland in the early 1720s a peak of more than one in four was reached.[16] Around Kirkham, of course, the proportions may well have been higher; and these figures will exclude those households in which agriculture clearly dominated a family economy in which textiles also featured. We know, too, that the linen and sailcloth industries were capable of employing whole families. Arthur Young found at Warrington in 1769 that spinning and warping were performed by men, winding by women, and starching and weaving by men, women and boys; and his evidence suggests that perhaps a thousand people or more were employed there in sailmaking alone. But many of these may have been urban Warringtonians, and the evidence for the linen manufacture in the nearby villages which became St Helens is pervasive but not specific. This is what one would expect in dealing with a subordinate activity which augmented the proceeds of farming rather than attaining parity of importance with it or rising to predominance over it.[17]

The evidence for rural textile manufacturing on a scale which might be called 'proto-industrial' is thus less than convincing for west Lancashire as a whole, although the pockets of intense activity around Kirkham and Warrington might lend credence to a localised version of the thesis, if closely examined. In the south of the area, of course, coal mining and metalworking were rapidly expanding as industrial employers; and at Prescot, Chowbent near Atherton and Ashton-in-Makerfield the latter might be organised in a similar way to domestic textiles.[18] These developments were probably more important than the linen manufactures as influences on the population growth of the seventeenth and eighteenth centuries. Between 1660 and 1760 the population of selected townships on the coalfield grew three times as fast as the 'national' rate calculated by Wrigley and Schofield, accelerating sharply in the early eighteenth century, while the predominantly agricultural townships seem merely to have kept pace with the nation at large. There was no direct evidence of the emergence of 'proto-industrial' demographic patterns on the coalfield, however. Although the mining-dominated township of Whiston showed a median age at first marriage three years below its agricultural neighbours Halsall and Downholland in the second quarter of the eighteenth century, birth intervals within marriage followed very similar patterns in all three places. It was not until the 1750s that the coalfield ceased to be a net

[16] Ibid., p. 314.
[17] Ibid., p. 303; T. C. Barker and J. R. Harris, *A Merseyside Town in the Industrial Revolution: St Helens, 1750–1900* (Liverpool, 1954), p. 120.
[18] Aikin, *Manchester*; Langton, *Geographical Change*.

exporter of population, principally to Liverpool, and agricultural parishes in south-west Lancashire lost population heavily by migration throughout the century after 1660. On parts of the central and south-west Lancashire coalfield, especially at Prescot, there was a marked tendency towards the fragmentation of holdings and to sub-letting in the first half of the seventeenth century, accompanied by manifestations of severe poverty. There were parts of a potentially proto-industrial jigsaw, then, but not enough resulted from them to justify the label.[19]

The agricultural systems of the area were in any case very different from those classically associated with proto-industrialisation, although these expectations have had to be modified in the light of recent case studies which show that apparently proto-industrial developments are not incompatible with fertile land and intensive arable agriculture. But these exceptions usually involve industries which use labour which is not in demand for agriculture, and this seems not to have been the case in west and south-west Lancashire. Although much maligned by outside commentators in the later eighteenth century, the various farming regimes of western and indeed central Lancashire were more identified with arable and genuinely mixed farming, and more open to innovation in crops and methods, than was the case on the county's eastern uplands, where soils and climate were decidedly inhospitable. Warrington, for example, was surrounded by 'rich meadows ... pasture and garden ground. It is noted for its gooseberries .... Potatoes are raised in large quantities, and thirty or forty thousand bushels have been shipped at Bank-quay in a year.'[20] This comment comes from the 1790s; but much of the area was already intensifying its specialisations in beef, dairying, potatoes and market gardening long before 1760. Compared with the rest of Lancashire, too, the west was relatively well-endowed with resident gentry who invested in agriculture and took an active interest in developing their estates. This reinforces the evidence that this was not a proto-industrial region or sub-region in the sense envisaged by the coiners of the concept. It was a balanced economy, agriculturally dominated and agriculturally self-supporting (except in crisis years in the first half of the seventeenth century), with no built-in tendency to specialisation in textiles or other manufactures for distant markets and no runaway land sub-division, population explosion or landless rural proletariat (apart from the growing number of miners). The evidence is circumstantial, and two or three small

---

[19] A. J. Rawlings, 'The rise of Liverpool and demographic change in part of south-west Lancashire', unpublished Ph.D. thesis (University of Liverpool, 1986); W. King, 'Illegal behavior in seventeenth-century Lancashire', unpublished Ph.D. thesis (University of Michigan, 1977), especially Ch. 2, for Prescot.

[20] Aikin, *Manchester*, p. 306.

areas would repay closer analysis, but on the whole this picture is convincing.[21] At most, one might invite the wrath of Professor Coleman by calling west Lancashire 'sub-proto-industrial' in the third quarter of the eighteenth century.[22] Parts of the area industrialised rapidly from the late eighteenth century onwards, but the driving forces were coal mining and heavy metallurgical industries, which do not really fit into the proto-industrial package, and a cotton industry which was brought in from further east. We must now look at developments in the eastern half of the county.

THE WOOLLEN MANUFACTURE

Developments in the woollen manufacturing district were much further advanced even in the early seventeenth century, when the introduction of bays, a woollen/worsted mix, was changing the area's output inventory at the same time as fustians were coming in further south.[23] But even the coarse kerseys which predominated at the end of the sixteenth century were already being exported overseas in large quantities. In Elizabethan times they were going to Spain, Portugal and France, and a very large number went from north-east Lancashire to the Baltic via Hull. Mercantile connections with London and the West Riding were well established in the furtherance of these export links; and Swain points out that the importance of Baltic exports to the economy of the Colne area was shown by the severity of trade depression in the 1620s and 1630s, when competition from Prussia and Silesia, 'monetary manipulation on the Continent' and the effects of the Thirty Years War brought prolonged impoverishment and helped to convert harvest failure into famine in 1623–4.[24] In Colne, Trawden and Pendle, by the early seventeenth century, 'the overwhelming majority of all households were involved in some part of the clothmaking process'; and among the wealthier stratum of those who left inventories at death, 'no less than 70 per cent owned cards, combs, spinning wheels and looms'. Moreover, much of the raw material was brought in from a considerable distance: not only from the West Riding, but also from the wool-producing counties of the Midlands and south-west. The sub-division of holdings was advancing: in Colne manor the number of copyholds doubled between 1527 and 1617, and by the latter year nearly half were of five Lancashire acres or less, not enough for a family's subsistence unless it had some extra source of income. But there was less sub-division, and less

[21] Rawlings, 'Rise of Liverpool', p. 191.
[22] Coleman, 'Proto-industrialization: a concept', p. 443.
[23] Wadsworth and Mann, *Cotton Trade*, p. 5.
[24] Swain, *Industry*, pp. 202–3.

reliance on cloth manufacture, in nearby Trawden, where 'cloth production was no more than useful supplementary income'.[25] Around Burnley, substantial stone houses were being built by the greater yeomanry and lesser gentry in this period, and Sarah Pearson suggests that their prosperity was founded on the increased rents which textile manufacture made possible, if not on direct involvement in the industry themselves.[26]

The evidence for the precocious advent of the proto-industrial in the Burnley and Colne areas in this period must be qualified in various ways. Swain makes clear that we are still dealing with a dual economy, in which cloth output increased in 'the less labour-intensive periods of the agricultural year, and contracted during the haymaking and harvesting seasons'. Despite the dependence on middlemen, too, which was vital to an industry with far-flung markets and sources of supply, there was no evidence of an extensive putting-out system, although weavers might employ nearby families to card and spin for them. 'Each household was independent in that it owned and was responsible for the disposal of the cloth which it made'.[27] Moreover, we still cannot be sure what the balance of effort and income between agriculture and manufacturing was in a notional 'average' household; and, relatedly, we remain unable to reconstruct the prevailing demographic regime, especially as the paucity of surnames vitiates attempts at family reconstitution. The evidence for population increase is compelling, but we are unable to say how it was generated, or to resolve the classic chicken-and-egg question of how far industrial opportunities promoted population growth, and how far population growth provided entrepreneurial opportunity. The evidence of increasing squatting on common land, of rising rents for the sub-tenants of copyholders (whose own manorial rents were pegged during the long inflation of this period) as well as the tenants of freeholders, and of the recruitment of economically vulnerable bastards and younger sons into textiles, combines to suggest that population growth was creating an attractively cheap labour force for domestic manufacture. But we lack the wherewithal to test the hypothesis that a recognisably proto-industrial demographic regime was emerging in response to these pressures and opportunities. In any case, the upward population trend was halted by the depression of the 1620s and 1630s, with compelling evidence of famine in 1623-4 and widespread defaulting on rents over the two decades, coupled with a spate of sales and mortgages, a sharp decline in the number of marriages (and an equally significant rise in illegitimacy), and a high level

---

[25] Ibid., pp. 199-204.
[26] Sarah Pearson, *Rural Houses of the Lancashire Pennines, 1560-1760* (London, 1985), pp. 34-6.
[27] Swain, *Industry*, pp. 199-204.

of out-migration. All this provides a reminder that the course of transition to an industrial economy was not necessarily smooth or linear, even in Lancashire; and subsequent events in Rossendale and the Rochdale area, further south in the Lancashire woollen district, reinforce this point still further.[28]

Swain's excellent analysis of north-east Lancashire unfortunately stops in the 1640s, and there has been no comparable follow-up study of that particular area. From the mid-seventeenth century, however, we can pick up the evidence from Tupling's classic study of Rossendale, a few miles to the south, and splice in King's recent amplification, supplemented by Wadsworth's work on the Rochdale area and Gray's more fragmentary material on Bury. Indeed, the Lancashire woollen district has attracted more research for the period between the mid-seventeenth and the mid-eighteenth centuries than the area which became the early heartland of the cotton industry itself.[29]

The Rossendale of Tupling and King had reached a similar stage of development to Swain's north-east Lancashire by the mid-seventeenth century. But there were interesting differences, too. Although the sub-division of holdings was a pronounced and sustained phenomenon in both districts, for example, it seems to have been associated with differing inheritance practices. In Rossendale, partible inheritance was at least as common as primogeniture, whereas primogeniture was the norm in north-east Lancashire, and was if anything increasing its predominance in the seventeenth century. But primogeniture did not prevent the sub-division of estates, for heirs had to provide for widows and younger children, and the calls on their resources were often such that the integrity of the inheritance had to be broken by sale or threatened by borrowing on mortgage. This is an interesting example, and perhaps a telling one, of economic trends being strong enough to overcome the obstacles presented by custom and legal practice. We shall return to this theme in a wider setting at the end of the chapter .[30]

King's findings on Rossendale after the mid-seventeenth century suggest stagnation and uncertainty, with 'no major or sustained increase in local cloth production'.[31] We should remember that commentators on neigh-

[28] Ibid.; C. D. Rogers, *The Lancashire Population Crisis of 1623* (Manchester, 1975).
[29] Tupling, *Rossendale*, Ch. 6; W. King, 'The economic and demographic development of Rossendale, c. 1650–c. 1795' unpublished Ph.D. thesis (University of Leicester, 1979); Wadsworth, 'Rochdale woollen trade'; A. P. Wadsworth, 'The early factory system in the Rochdale district', *Transactions of the Rochdale Literary and Scientific Society*, 19 (1935–7), pp. 136–56; M. Gray, *The History of Bury, Lancashire, 1660–1876* (Bury, 1970), Ch. 1.
[30] Tupling, *Rossendale*, pp. 76–7, 90–5; Swain, *Industry*, pp. 202–3.
[31] King, 'Rossendale', Ch. 9. The copy of this thesis in the Lancashire Record Office, Preston, which I used, is unpaginated.

bouring areas of woollen manufacture were more optimistic. Wadsworth believed that 'the scale of Rochdale industry grew considerably during the period of commercial expansion after the Restoration'.[32] Gray provides a similar impression for Bury, stressing 'the growing importance of the textile trade, the extent of financial enterprise and the persistent problem of poverty', although these assertions are not supported very convincingly with hard evidence.[33] Would work in similar depth to King's modify the picture for Rochdale and Bury in a pessimistic direction? Or did Rossendale's experience differ markedly from those of its southern and south-eastern neighbours, just as it probably followed a different trajectory from the Forests of Pendle and Bowland to the north-east and north-west, where textile development occurred more slowly and bit less deeply into local economies? We do not yet know the answers to these questions. But it would clearly be dangerous to generalise too glibly about the Lancashire woollen district as a whole from the experience of Rossendale. We know that it shared similarities with nearby wool manufacturing areas; but it also differed from them in economic performance, as far as present knowledge goes, and perhaps in other important respects. Parts of the Rossendale experience may form a basis for plausible generalisations about the wider Lancashire woollen district; but we do not know which aspects of Rossendale's circumstances applied elsewhere, and which were peculiar to the locality.

But King's work is suggestive. Despite a high level of involvement in textiles in the mid-seventeenth century, he finds no evidence of sustained growth in textile manufacture or population until well into the eighteenth century. Rossendale remained a poverty-stricken area in the later seventeenth and early eighteenth centuries, with the median farm occupying between 20 and 30 acres, many falling below 10 acres and 'a substantial proportion' of the inhabitants already landless in 1660. The vast majority of the population lived between the 600-foot and 1,100-foot contours, avoiding the unhealthy valley bottoms and preferring the windswept hillsides. In 1663 only 15 householders in the whole district paid the Hearth Tax on more than two hearths, out of a total of perhaps 670 families, nearly half of whom were exempted on the grounds of poverty. This compares interestingly with Bury, where as many as 28 of the 222 dwellings had three or more taxable hearths, although here again nearly half the total were exempt. Evidence of textile manufacturing activity was found in nearly 60 per cent of Rossendale probate inventories between 1660 and 1715, and by the early eighteenth

---

[32] Wadsworth, 'Rochdale woollen trade', p. 98.
[33] Gray, *Bury*, p. 25.

century the parish registers ascribed textile-related occupations to nearly 40 per cent of the adult male entries. Markets were distant, and a large proportion of the area's textiles was sent via London; but there is no evidence of a locally based putting-out system nor of any increase in the scale of manufacturing units, although some putting-out may have been organised from Rochdale. Much of the area's finishing was done there. It seems likely that textile manufacture was still a supplement to agriculture for most families, as most farms combined cattle-raising with a small amount of arable, perhaps as an insurance against high grain prices or supply difficulties in hard winters. The interesting variations in demographic patterns within Rossendale support this assessment. Growth, such as it was, was concentrated around Newchurch, where textiles were relatively strong. In the Haslingden area, on the other hand, pastoral agriculture was more important and population at best stagnated. But the difference is largely accounted for by Haslingden's higher death rates; and there were frequent mortality crises, the most clear-cut of which occurred in 1672–6, 1683, 1700 and 1712–13, although they were far less damaging than those of the first half of the seventeenth century. They seem to have been caused more by bad weather and bad harvests than by trade depression, although the earlier crises contained elements of both ingredients; and the trade depressions of 1696 and 1703, which were reasonable harvest years, were not accompanied by high mortality. This evidence suggests a vulnerable, semi-subsistence agricultural system, whose vulnerability was mitigated in those areas where textile manufacture was most fully developed; and in these areas wealth levels seem to have been higher. But there is still no evidence of the early marriages and high birth rates postulated by proto-industrial theory: indeed, birth rates in Newchurch were actually lower than in Haslingden, with its more agriculturally orientated economy. Rossendale between the 1650s and the 1710s was stagnating after earlier growth, and it showed no real advance on the position in north-east Lancashire at the beginning of the seventeenth century. Matters may have gone further in the Rochdale district, but on the evidence we have it would be rash to describe the Lancashire woollen manufacture as in any sense 'proto-industrial' in the early eighteenth century, so far as the vital demographic characteristics are concerned.[34]

The ensuing decades, however, saw rapid and accelerating developments. Between 1717 and 1778 the population of Rossendale probably trebled, and a growing proportion of the families were visibly dependent on textiles. In the Haslingden area and south Rossendale, textile-related occupations were allocated to more than half the parish register entries in

[34] King, 'Rossendale', Chs. 1–9; Gray, *Bury*, p. 11.

1722–6, and to about two-thirds in 1741–5. We have no figures for Newchurch, where the textile base was stronger in the early eighteenth century; but its experience may have approximated more closely to that of Saddleworth, two valleys to the east, where the corresponding proportion was 76 per cent as early as 1720 and 88 per cent by 1760. Elements of a dual economy persisted, of course; but what these figures show is that throughout Rossendale the 1720s and 1730s saw the crucial transition to an economy in which most families were perceived to owe their livelihood more to textile manufacture than to agriculture. There were other, obviously interrelated developments. Worsteds, with their elastic demand potential, took over from the traditional kerseys from the 1720s onwards, and the putting-out system, organised within Rossendale, spread rapidly during the second quarter of the eighteenth century. So did the local development of the finishing trades; and the direct marketing of cloth to the London merchants also began to be locally organised, although Rochdale remained important. All this both reflected and encouraged the concentration of resources in the hands of substantial clothiers, and it is no surprise to find associated changes in the social structure. The average value of surviving inventories (which account for 11·5 per cent of adult male burials over the whole period) was £91 in 1711–15, £127 in 1721–30 and £230 in 1741–50. Levels of domestic comfort improved among these higher social strata, as mirrors, maps, pictures and candlesticks became more frequent. The listing of rooms in inventories also suggests that a belated 'great rebuilding' was taking place, with larger houses and extensions to existing ones. The other side of this coin is the proliferation of the landless, wage-earning and impoverished. By the mid-eighteenth century over 500 small cottages had sprouted in Rossendale and the fragmentation of landownership recommenced. 'A substantial wage earning element' emerged in the local population, and from the 1750s a 'dramatic' rise in poor relief expenditure began, while at least four townships opened workhouses between 1730 and 1759. King concludes that local trading conditions were becoming more strongly determined by the state of the textile industry than by the harvest or the level of food prices.[35]

These far-reaching changes were accompanied by the advent of a recognisably proto-industrial demographic regime. The annual percentage population growth rate nearly doubled to 2·4 per cent in 1726–35, and although the higher level was not sustained through the mid-century, it reasserted itself in the later 1760s and 1770s. Birth rates rose sharply from less than thirty per thousand in 1716 to nearly forty-one per thousand in 1731, after which they stabilised at or near the higher level until the 1760s,

[35] King, 'Rossendale', Chs. 10–16.

when a further increase occurred. Marriage rates also went up between 1706 and 1721, stabilising at their higher level thereafter. It is impossible to calculate ages at marriage, but it seems almost certain that, as in Saddleworth at the same time, they fell significantly. Birth intervals certainly fell sharply between the early 1720s and the early 1780s, from an average of 27·8 months to one of 22·3. So Rossendale's population growth was being fuelled by its own natural increase, and there may even have been some out-migration to the Manchester area. Even in 1780, however, urbanisation was still small scale, and the population remained widely spread through an inhospitable countryside. All this suggests that the expectations of Medick and others about proto-industrial population growth were being faithfully worked out in eighteenth-century Rossendale; and the more general expectations of proto-industrial theorists were being met quite convincingly by the middle decades of the eighteenth century.[36]

We lack similar painstaking analyses for Bury and Rochdale; but the impressionistic evidence suggests that they may have continued to anticipate developments in Rossendale on a rather larger scale.[37] But here we come to a paradox. On all the established criteria, the Lancashire woollen district was fully 'proto-industrial' by the third quarter of the eighteenth century, and its leading merchants and clothiers were accumulating substantial capitals, which could have been used to fuel a transition to factory industry. But the woollen manufacture did not make this transition at this time, despite its extensive trade with distant markets which ranged as far as Russia and beyond. Water power was applied to the carding process in the late eighteenth century, but where the spinning jenny was adapted to the woollen industry it was almost always hand-operated, and weaving likewise remained on the hand-loom.[38] Even in the early 1830s only two woollen mills in Rochdale seem to have 'spun and wove by power',[39] and in Rossendale there were 'possibly ... not more than two' woollen spinning mills before 1830.[40] Wadsworth suggests that the merchant capitals of the woollen manufacture went into landed estate purchase or banking rather than into the next stage of industrial development in the late eighteenth century: in Rochdale,

Landowning carries its own social prestige; the merchant is always in the land market, and builds his mansion .... His sons and grandsons become more landlords

[36] Ibid., Chs. 10–11; H. Medick, 'The proto-industrial family economy: the structural function of household and family during the transition from peasant society to industrial capitalism', *Social History*, 1 (1976), pp. 291–316.

[37] Wadsworth, 'Rochdale woollen trade'; Gray, *Bury*, Chs. 2–3.

[38] Tupling, *Rossendale*, pp. 197–8.

[39] Wadsworth, 'Early factory system', p. 137.

[40] Tupling, *Rossendale*, p. 198.

than traders; the stimulus to acquisition has passed. They become country gentlemen, or they may take advantage of the great field for credit opened by the industrial revolution and become bankers. With them ends one stage of industry. The typical employing capitalist of the early nineteenth century, the small factory owner, is once again of a new social class. Like the founders of the earlier dynasties he begins in a humble way.[41]

It would be interesting to explore this suggestion further: it does not accord with recent findings about the social origins of early factory masters in the cotton industry, who follow the proto-industrial model much more closely.[42] But this evidence sits interestingly alongside a further crucial point: the industrial revolution, as conventionally understood, came to Rochdale, Bury and especially Rossendale through the advent of the cotton industry rather than the development of the woollen manufacture. It was imported, rather than indigenous. As Tupling says of Rossendale, 'The Valley had in 1770 a woollen organisation which was well established and on the high road to a development of some importance. That organisation was now in part usurped by the new textile trade, which adapted it to its special conditions and ultimately completely recast it.'[43] Not that the woollen industry disappeared, of course: indeed, it was probably not displaced from predominance in Rochdale until about 1840.[44] But it was cotton that brought extensive factory development and town growth to these areas, as its invasion gathered momentum from the late eighteenth century. So why did a proto-industrial woollen manufacture yield pride of place to an industrial economy whose origins lay elsewhere, and whose techniques and markets were significantly different?

Part of the answer may well lie in the unwillingness of the established capitalists to invest in the next stage of the woollen industry's development. Such attitudes were probably affected in turn by their perceptions of the growth potential in woollens, worsteds and flannel, especially in the light of the rapid rise of the cotton industry; and the new machinery, especially in spinning, was better suited to the characteristics of cotton than to those of wool. This may have been partly because the new machines were created with the needs of and opportunities in the cotton industry at the forefront of the inventors' minds. It might also be argued that the woollen industry in Lancashire was held back by one of the most obvious difficulties inherent in proto-industrial theory's analysis of the transition to industrialisation: its

---

[41] Wadsworth, 'Rochdale woollen trade', p. 101; and see J. Cole, 'Chartism in Rochdale', unpublished M.A. dissertation (Manchester Polytechnic, 1986), pp. 3–5, which qualifies this only slightly.

[42] See above, n. 3.

[43] Tupling, *Rossendale*, pp. 203–4.

[44] Cole, 'Chartism in Rochdale', p. 8.

demographic regime was expanding the labour force so effectively that for many years there was not sufficient inducement for capitalists to introduce labour-saving machinery. To substantiate this suggestion for the Lancashire woollen district we would need to know a great deal more about wage rates and attitudes to embezzlement and manufacturing delays than we do at present.[45] But the key point is the overwhelming potential for expansion in cotton as compared with wool; and the demographic block did not prevent the cotton industry from making its own transition, and generating enough additional dynamism to become the vehicle for the full-scale industrialisation of the old Lancashire woollen district. We must now attempt to explain this giant leap, which involves posing a familiar kind of question in a restricted geographical setting. Why was south-east Lancashire first?

THE COTTON INDUSTRY

The manufacture of cotton-using cloths was firmly established over a wide area of south-east Lancashire, with Manchester emerging as its hub, by the late seventeenth century. By mid-century, and perhaps a little earlier, pure cotton cloths were being exported in growing quantities, including hollands among the cotton-linens and velvets among the fustians. Cotton wool imports averaged just over £1 million during 1698–1710, topped £2 million in 1741–50 and passed £5 million in 1771–80. They were supplemented by yarn imports which reached a peak in 1731–40 and never fully recovered from a sharp decline in the next decade; but Wadsworth and Mann point out that the raw material import figures should be 'nearly doubled for comparison with later statistics'[46] if a valid rendering of the industry's growth is to be obtained. Up to the 1770s a considerable amount of linen was still being used for warps, but by 1787, when cotton wool imports had leapt to £22 million, the new machinery was enabling cotton to be used for warps as well as wefts. This puts the pace of growth in the 1780s in less spectacular perspective, compared with earlier decades. But a growing proportion of these expanding imports was being worked in the Manchester area, as cotton manufacture declined in other parts of England, continuing to develop only in the Glasgow district.[47]

The concentration of cotton-using manufactures into south-east Lancashire was accompanied by intensifying specialisation and the development of all the stigmata of the classic proto-industrial model. Already in the mid-1720s more than half the fathers of children baptised in

[45] Houston and Snell, 'Proto-industrialization', pp. 490–1.
[46] Wadsworth and Mann, *Cotton Trade*, p. 170.
[47] Ibid., pp. 170–7.

Oldham parish had textile-related occupations ascribed to them. The same applied at Radcliffe in the 1740s, and by 1776–82 the proportion had risen to more than two-thirds. At Middleton it was five-eighths in the early 1730s and more than 70 per cent by the late 1740s.[48] Further west, towards the edge of what was becoming the 'cotton district', a census of Roman Catholic households at Samlesbury, in the Ribble Valley, listed 68 per cent of the male household heads as cotton hand-loom weavers. Hodge tells us that 'many other entries begin with women on their own described as cotton spinners; perhaps these were households where the husband was Protestant and therefore not included in our lists'. Fewer than one in five of Catholic households had no member working in cotton manufacture. As Hodge comments, 'Unless the Catholics named in this list were far more likely to take up these occupations than the rest of the population ... this list suggests that domestic industry was already crucial to the local economy in 1767'.[49] This density of domestic manufacture must have been the norm closer to Manchester; and in the emergent regional capital itself a census in 1751 found 4,674 looms in the parish, approximately one to every household. Most of the master weavers owned two or more looms, admittedly, but the concentration remains impressive.[50]

Population growth and the sub-division of holdings accompanied the development of manufacturing. Comparison of the imperfect but wide-ranging episcopal visitation surveys of 1717 and 1778 suggests that the population of Manchester and Blackburn deaneries more than doubled during this period. The Oldham parish register entries tend to confirm this pattern. So do Aikin's extracts from the parish registers of Eccles, Radcliffe and Middleton, while Prestwich seems to have been growing faster still.[51] Wadsworth and Mann assembled a telling array of comments by contemporary observers which bring out the small size of the landholdings in the later eighteenth century. Their examination of surveys suggests that 'many of the cottages had small plots of land attached, and that a considerable proportion of the larger holdings were too small to be economic agricultural units'. Important though it was, agriculture had become 'secondary to industry' by this time.[52] As Aikin said of Mottram-in-Longdendale,

The smaller farms are let very high; nor could the tenant pay such prices but for the industry of himself and family, who are in general weavers, hatters or cotton

[48] Ibid., pp. 314–16.
[49] A. Hodge, *History of Samlesbury* (Preston, 1986), pp. 38–9.
[50] Wadsworth and Mann, *Cotton Trade*, pp. 326–7.
[51] Walton, *Lancashire*, p. 77; Aikin, *Manchester*, pp. 222, 234, 245, 259.
[52] Wadsworth and Mann, *Cotton Trade*, pp. 317–21.

spinners .... The chief article of the farm is a roomy house, and their two or three cows produce milk or butter for family use, with a little to spare for making up the rent. Some wheat and oats are grown and potatoes are cultivated.[53]

We cannot yet document the pace and extent of the sub-division of holdings with any precision, and nor can we unravel the mechanisms of population growth, although natural increase was clearly the basis of it, and birth rates in the area were to be remarkably high in the early nineteenth century. The circumstantial evidence overwhelmingly points to the development of a proto-industrial demographic system. Landless or almost landless cottagers, dependent entirely on manufacturing, were growing in numbers rapidly by mid-century, and most of the population increase was spread thickly through the countryside in the 1770s. Towns were beginning to grow, but only Manchester had attained a substantial size: it grew fivefold between the Restoration and 1773, when a house-to-house enumeration found 22,481 inhabitants.[54]

The other desiderata of proto-industrial theory were also in evidence. Much of the dynamism of the cotton-using textile manufactures came from the exploitation of distant markets, although home sales remained important throughout. Ireland was particularly prominent as an outlet for fustians in the first half of the eighteenth century, but the 1750s, especially, saw a great boom in cotton piece-goods exports to America, the West Indies and Africa. From the 1760s onwards, however, it was the expansion of the European market which provided a secure foundation for longer term growth. The increasing use of an exotic and problematic raw material of distant provenance, coupled with the need to find outlets for products in far-flung markets, necessitated the generation of substantial mercantile capitals and a sophisticated credit system. The first Manchester bank was not founded until 1771, but the bill of exchange system provided adequate access to short- and medium-term credit, often drawing on London merchants and finance houses. Long-term borrowings tapped the savings of local gentry, professionals, traders, farmers and widows. Family and friends were sources of first resort, but Lancashire attorneys played a particularly prominent role as loan brokers, finding investment outlets for capital in lumps of varying sizes, and providing a vital service for textile manufacturers.[55]

[53] Aikin, *Manchester*, p. 23.

[54] R. K. Fleischman, jr, 'Conditions of life among the cotton workers of southeastern Lancashire during the Industrial Revolution', unpublished Ph.D thesis (State University of New York, Buffalo, 1973); Walton, *Lancashire*, p. 65.

[55] Wadsworth and Mann, *Cotton Trade* pp. 91–6, 248–50, and Ch. 8. Edwards, *Cotton Trade*, Chs. 9–10; B. L. Anderson, 'The attorney and the early capital market in Lancashire', in J. R. Harris (ed.), *Liverpool and Merseyside* (London, 1969), pp. 50–77.

Contemporary Mancunians took pride in the humble origins of their great capitalists, many of whom, by the 1750s if not earlier, were buying their way into landed estates in the same manner as the Rochdale woollen merchants and manufacturers. Below the highest strata, who might dabble in government loans and financial services to the aristocracy as well as extending their activities into the slave trade, there were many intermediate levels: middling and lesser merchants and manufacturers in Manchester itself, and clothiers in the surrounding districts who might trade with London on their own account. It seems to have been mainly from these intermediate strata that much of the capital for the transition to the factory system was drawn in the late eighteenth century. In terms of property values, if not of employment structure, Manchester was probably always predominantly a mercantile rather than a manufacturing town, as the work of Lloyd-Jones and Lewis on the 1815 rate-books confirms.[56]

Innovations in organisation and technology were proliferating by the middle decades of the eighteenth century. The putting-out system did not begin with the introduction of cotton, but by the 1680s it was becoming increasingly prevalent, as Manchester and Bolton merchants operated through subordinate agents in outposts up to 20 miles distant as well as putting work out directly on their own account. Many of the smaller independent manufacturers, whether stringing together individual transactions or working on commission, were gradually drawn into dependence on putters-out and became, effectively, employees operating on a piece-rate wage: so there was downward as well as upward mobility out of the middle ranks in cotton.[57] It is impossible to chart the intermediate stages of the spread of putting-out with any conviction, but by the mid-eighteenth century it was certainly the norm. This transition to a form of wage-labour proceeded alongside the gradual and piecemeal introduction of new forms of machinery. In the Manchester smallwares manufacture, which produced tapes, garters and similar goods, the so-called Dutch loom was introduced soon after the Restoration, and by 1750 there were at least 1,500 in the town. The Dutch loom saved labour but involved relatively high capital investment, and its use was increasingly concentrated into substantial workshops which by 1751 might contain twelve or more machines apiece, whose operation was defined as a masculine preserve. By this time a new variant, the swivel loom, was being introduced for the manufacture of higher quality tapes, and in the 1760s a Manchester merchant attempted to apply water power to a collection of such looms in

---

[56] Ibid., Chs. 13–14; Lloyd-Jones and Lewis, 'Economic structure'.
[57] Wadsworth and Mann, *Cotton Trade*, pp. 78–87; Lloyd-Jones and Lewis, 'Economic structure', p. 82, for an extension of the field of influence to 30 miles.

a recognisable anticipation of the factory system. Weaving technology was improved more generally by the widespread adoption of Kay's fly shuttle, which increased productivity considerably: it spread rapidly in the cotton-using manufactures from the 1750s onwards, after earlier beginnings in woollens.[58] In the finishing processes, too, the pace and scale of change accelerated after mid-century, with the migration of calico printing as a large-scale operation from London and the introduction of new technologies and larger production units in bleaching and dyeing, which had long been centralised under the control of merchant capitalists.[59]

By the middle decades of the eighteenth century the cotton-using manufactures of south-east Lancashire exhibited all the characteristics required by proto-industrial theory, and to the fullest extent. There were intimations of an imminent transition from domestic manufacture to factory industry, too, as a ferment of invention and experiment bubbled.[60] But other places and industries, at other times, had shown similar symptoms, without going on to transform themselves into full-fledged industrial societies. The woollen and worsted industries of Lancashire and Yorkshire, indeed, were in a similar condition at this very time; but their transformation began later, took longer and was influenced by the pattern of events in the cotton industry. Why did this industry, at this time, crash through the barriers into the new world of the power-driven factory and the industrial town?

We must resist the temptation to exaggerate the suddenness of the transition. It was at first confined to the spinning and preparatory processes, and to calico printing. Weaving remained dominated by the hand-loom and the domestic system until well into the nineteenth century: a point to which we shall return. The famous successful cotton spinning inventions ascribed to Hargreaves, Arkwright and Crompton followed several decades of sustained experiment and trial in pursuit of similar goals. Early applications of the jenny, and of related developments in carding and other preparatory processes, were adaptable to domestic workshops and slightly larger collections of hand- or horse-operated machinery; and the water frame, which was more demanding in scale of operation and separated home and workplace from the start, was developed mainly on rural sites.

[58] Wadsworth and Mann, *Cotton Trade*, pp. 14, 103–4, 284–8, 301–2, 465–71; M. Berg, *The Age of Manufactures* (London, 1985), pp. 150–1.
[59] Wadsworth and Mann, *Cotton Trade*, pp. 303–8; S. D. Chapman and S. Chassagne, *European Textile Printers in the Eighteenth Century: A Study of Peel and Oberkampt* (London, 1981); Berg, *Manufactures*, p. 205. Berg summarises the importance of this industry thus, quoting from Chapman and Chassagne: 'Calico-printing workshops were effectively "proto-factories", a "transitional stage in evolution from dispersed domestic manufacture to the factory system"; and a number of leading calico printers were associated with the introduction of mechanized spinning and weaving.'
[60] Wadsworth and Mann, *Cotton Trade*, pp. 411–48, 472–88.

Technological change was not always large scale or capital-hungry, either; and its social impact had been anticipated for half a century by the water-powered silk-throwing mills which were extending their influence in the Macclesfield area, within easy reach of Manchester, by the 1750s. It was the coming of the mule, and the application of steam power to it, which really made the crucial difference, concentrating cotton spinning on urban sites; and the major transformations associated with these developments were only just beginning at the turn of the century. It was in the early decades of the nineteenth century that the really dramatic increases in raw cotton consumption and urbanisation took place.[61]

Even so, there is something cumulatively impressive to explain. Nothing like it had been seen before. To explain the chain of events which began in the 1770s and gathered such overwhelming momentum in the nineteenth century, we need to go beyond the proto-industrial mode of analysis. For south-east Lancashire to become the first industrial economy and society, it needed to start from a recognisably proto-industrial set of circumstances; but our explanations must analyse what it was that made it *different* from everywhere else. Explanations for the 'first industrial revolution' often start from arguments about poor land, high population densities, the availability of merchant and domestic manufacturing capital and a credit infrastructure, and the existence of foreign markets; but the literature on proto-industrialisation shows that these attributes were widespread in Europe. Taking these widely shared characteristics as our starting point, and accepting that they applied to south-east Lancashire, we must now explore some additional and distinctive themes in our search for explanations.

The key difference is that south-east Lancashire was already, in the 1770s, firmly identified with the cotton manufacture. Cotton was, after all, a uniquely versatile raw material. It could be made into, or incorporated into, an astonishing variety of fabrics, suitable for export to every corner of the world. Its supply was much more elastic than that of flax or wool, especially when American output began to rise rapidly during the 1790s. These characteristics enabled it to take the fullest advantage of the boom in world trade and in British exploitation of overseas markets. If any commodity was going to spearhead the breakthrough from proto-industrial to industrial society, cotton seems (admittedly with hindsight) to be ideal for the purpose. But contemporaries were well enough aware of its

[61] Walton, *Lancashire*, pp. 105–8; G. Malmgreen, *Silk Town: Industry and Culture in Macclesfield, 1750–1835* (Hull, 1986); Edwards, *Cotton Trade*, Ch. 9. Retained raw cotton imports stood at 4·2 million pounds in 1772, 24·7 million in 1789, 41·8 million in 1800, 65 million in 1811, 141 million in 1821 and 249 million in 1831. The increments tell a very different story from the percentage growth figures. These totals come from P. Mathias, *The First Industrial Nation* (London, 1969 edn), p. 486.

potential to invest in it and encourage its cultivation. Indeed, it is arguable that the sheer scale of growth in demand for cotton products may explain the breaching of the demographic block which made the transition from the proto-industrial so difficult. It generated such a high level of demand for labour that it outpaced population growth and set a premium on labour-saving investment and productivity maximisation. Despite the unprecedented rises in productivity on the spinning side of the industry, however, the expanding labour force was kept in sufficient employment by the need for hand-loom weavers, with only temporary difficulties as the transition to the factory in spinning took place during the 1770s. The mechanics of this process would repay much closer examination.[62]

But why was it south-east Lancashire that reaped the benefits from the peculiarities of cotton? At the most obvious level, its commitment to cotton-using cloths was certainly much more intense than anywhere else in Britain by mid-century; and it was probably unmatched elsewhere in Europe. It therefore had a wide spread of expertise in the purchasing, working and marketing of this complicated, difficult and rewarding material, having built successfully on the compatibility of cotton and linen and utilised the overseas trade outlets which had been developed in connection with the local linen and woollen industries. These established traditions and areas of expertise were probably more important than the institutional and geographical features of which so much has been heard; but we cannot ignore them altogether. Fustians and cotton manufactures were internally unregulated by central or local government, enabling a symbiotic rather than a competitive relationship to develop between town and country, and allowing growth to proceed with a minimum of artificial restraint. Manchester, like its satellite towns, remained immune from guild restrictions and from the regular strife and corruption of parliamentary elections. But Corfield has recently produced a convincing denial of the view that 'constitutional differences caused the differential economic performance of eighteenth-century towns';[63] and Manchester, at least, had plenty of bitter and sometimes violent internal political wranglings despite its unincorporated status.[64] Nor is Farnie's recent attempt to rehabilitate the damp Lancashire climate as an explanation for south-east Lancashire's specialisation in cotton completely convincing. The high humidity of Manchester, Bolton and surroundings may have made cotton easier to

---

[62] Edwards, *Cotton Trade*, Chs. 5 and 8. But for opposition to the scale and pace of innovation in the spinning and (importantly) the preparation processes, see *An Impartial Representation of the Case of the Poor Cotton Spinners in Lancashire* (1780: copy in British Library). This came in the aftermath of the riots of 1779, and shows, among other interesting things, that many of the rioters were women.

[63] P. Corfield, *The Impact of English Towns, 1700–1800* (Oxford, 1982), pp. 91–2.

[64] Walton, *Lancashire*, pp. 101, 135–6.

work, but it would be difficult to prove that it was enough to tip the scales between this and other potentially suitable areas.[65] Possibly the diffusion of basic mechanical skills through the area, and especially the proximity of skilled watchmakers around Prescot, assisted the rapid transition to mechanised spinning, although it would be hard to set a value on this contribution.[66]

Transport improvements were more important in enabling growth to continue than in sparking it off. Cotton suffered less from high transport costs than did other industries using and producing materials of lower value in relation to their bulk; and the spread of a Manchester-centred web of canals during the last quarter of the eighteenth century was more important in providing coal for steam-powered factories and domestic hearths, and in guaranteeing the food supply of coalescing industrial populations, than in servicing the early development of a water-power-based cotton factory system. Road improvements were also of vital importance, though their impact is even more difficult to assess comparatively and quantitatively. But transport innovation was only becoming essential to further growth at the turn of the eighteenth and nineteenth centuries, when accelerating urbanisation coincided with the transition to steam. At this stage, the existing pattern of canal provision may have helped to concentrate growth into south-east Lancashire for a time, at the expense of the northern outposts of the industry around Blackburn, Burnley and Colne: it took the completion of the Leeds and Liverpool Canal through this area in 1816 to redress this balance.[67] It was only in the 1790s, too, that the proximity of Liverpool became an important advantage to the Lancashire cotton industry, as the proportion of the cotton import and export trade channelled through the port began to grow rapidly, and its merchants came to exercise a strategic influence on the cotton district. By this time, too, Liverpool merchants and interested landowners had combined to create a road and canal transport system for their own purposes, which reached out to link up with the Manchester-centred network, bringing Liverpool and the rest of the world into easier reach. But Liverpool's development in the eighteenth century had been based on completely different trading patterns. It became available as a significant fortunate factor endowment in time to contribute to the second phase of cotton Lancashire's industrial revolution, in the early to mid-nineteenth century; but its importance in the formative transitional years was quite limited.[68]

[65] Farnie, *Cotton Industry*, pp. 49–51.

[66] A. E. Musson and E. Robinson, 'The origins of engineering in Lancashire', *Journal of Economic History*, 20 (1960), pp. 209–33, and especially pp. 219–22.

[67] Walton, *Lancashire*, pp. 72–4, 115–17, and references cited therein.

[68] Marriner, *Merseyside*, for a summary and references. See also Langton, *Geographical Change*, and his 'Liverpool and its hinterland in the late eighteenth century', in B. L. Anderson and P. J. M. Stoney

This is a reminder that the industrialisation of south-east Lancashire was a long process. The transition from domestic manufacture to factory production in cotton came much earlier in spinning, where it was largely accomplished during the 1770s, than in weaving, where the triumph of the power-loom was still far from complete in the early 1850s, when a 'dual economy' survived in parts of the Ribble Valley and, no doubt, elsewhere. It took the 'Cotton Famine' of the early 1860s to apply the *coup de grâce* to cotton hand-loom weaving; and in woollens and silk, of course, the transition took longer still.[69] Even within cotton itself, complicated fabrics for counterpanes kept highly skilled and specialised domestic weavers in business in Bolton into the 1890s.[70]

The upshot of this was that whole parishes, covering wide areas of the county, could still be dominated by the domestic cotton manufacture in the 1810s, 1820s and beyond: well into the 'factory age'; and many villages still specialised in cotton hand-loom weaving beyond mid-century. Timmins has calculated that in 1813–22 about 80 per cent of the bridegrooms in Newchurch-in-Pendle were hand-loom weavers, and the parishes of Blackburn, Oldham, Rochdale and Bolton all fluctuated around 50 per cent. The percentage in the rural areas of these extensive parishes probably approached the Newchurch-in-Pendle figure.[71] This was the last full generation of men to be recruited into hand-loom weaving; and as piece-rate wages fell sharply in the 1820s and 1830s their family incomes became more dependent on children's factory work. In many cases they became a reserve army of labour for factory masters who economised on fixed capital by installing enough power-looms to cope with normal demand, and made full use of the domestic workers only when the pace quickened. The lengthy decline of cotton hand-loom weaving could be seen as the last phase of spiralling exacerbation of misery anticipated by Hans Medick's model of the economic consequences of proto-industrial demography, although in this case matters are complicated, as Lyons points out, by the availability of factory work *alongside* domestic manufacture, enabling complex mixed domestic economies to emerge. All this took place in a setting which was neither proto-industrial nor yet fully industrial.[72] What

---

(eds.), *Commerce, Industry and Transport* (Liverpool, 1983), pp. 1–25. For further comment see Walton, *Lancashire*, pp. 111–12.

[69] J. G. Timmins kindly provided unpublished material from work in progress for his Lancaster Ph.D. thesis on the hand-loom weavers in Lancashire cotton and related manufactures. John Wardman also provided information on the Ribble Valley. See also Farnie, *Cotton Industry*, pp. 278–84, and G. Greathead, 'A study of hand-loom weaving in the mid-nineteenth century', unpublished M.A. dissertation (Manchester Polytechnic, 1986), for Bolton.

[70] Farnie, *Cotton Industry*, pp. 283–4. [71] Timmins, work in progress.

[72] J. S. Lyons, 'The Lancashire cotton industry and the introduction of the power loom, 1815–50', unpublished Ph.D. thesis (University of California, Berkeley, 1977), especially pp. 34–99; Medick, 'Proto-industrial family economy'.

should we call this transitional phase between the proto-industrial economy of the later eighteenth century and the recognisably industrial situation of the mid-nineteenth century? With tongue slightly in cheek, but with a genuine belief that the label may have its uses, I suggest that it is 'post-proto-industrial'.[73]

Several concluding points emerge from this exercise, heavily dependent on the synthesis of secondary sources though it is. In the first place, it is astonishing that a work written in 1987, on a topic of such central importance, should be so conspicuously indebted to a book first published in 1931. It is a tribute to the excellence and durability of Wadsworth and Mann's work, but it points up the need for further research on the formative years of the cotton industry in the pre-factory era. Secondly, the analysis of Lancashire textiles suggests that the concept of the proto-industrial does have useful descriptive value. It sets standards against which regional and sub-regional economies can be evaluated; and it is clear that by the second quarter of the eighteenth century the woollen- and cotton-using districts of Lancashire were meeting these standards. Thirdly, however, it should be noted that the Lancashire experience as a whole reinforces the point that the 'proto-industrial' phase was not only a dead end in many periods and places: it was also not the only possible transitional route to a recognisably 'industrial' economy, as the equally rapid but contrasting growth experience of the south-west Lancashire coalfield bears witness when set alongside developments in south-east Lancashire.[74] Fourthly, even on its own territory the model falls short at an explanatory level. The transition to an industrial economy and society in south-east Lancashire was complex and protracted, as we have seen; but cumulatively it involved major shifts in the location of industry, in the nature of entrepreneurship, the composition of capital and the age/sex structure and work experience of the labour force. To account for these changes, we need to go beyond the proto-industrial model and look for other factors. But at least the concept of the proto-industrial gives us certain basic criteria which can be held constant as a necessary background, enabling us to try to isolate what is different and how it works. As it stands, the concept has its limitations at a descriptive level, and it lacks explanatory power where it matters most: in explaining the transition to industrialisation. The next stage of research should be moving on beyond the proto-industrial model, exploring the difficult problems which surround the nature and causation of this transition. Further work on Lancashire in the eighteenth century should be an early item on this agenda.

---

[73] Jenny Smith originated this expression, although she would not wish to be held responsible for it.
[74] Langton, *Geographical Change*, and his 'The industrial revolution and the regional geography of England', *Transactions of the Institute of British Geographers*, 9 (1984), pp. 145–67.

Chapter 3

Capital and credit in the West Riding wool textile industry c. 1750–1850[1]

PAT HUDSON

As is well known, the West Riding of Yorkshire grew to dominate the British production of woollen and worsted cloths and yarns during the course of the eighteenth century eclipsing the older centres of East Anglia and the West Country. Spatial concentration of much of an entire sector of industry within a clearly defined industrial region was to become a major feature of British industrialisation, one which lasted into the twentieth century. Sectoral concentration must therefore play an important part in analysis of the dynamics of the industrial revolution but it has largely escaped much of the recent literature on this subject which has concentrated on national aggregates and their interaction.[2] The rapid growth of the Yorkshire textile industry proved to be the first example of major new concentrations of production occurring at this time and, as such, it is important to consider the foundations of its success. What influences conditioned the emergence of dynamic forms of pre-factory and early factory manufacture and why were these influences so bounded in space that it is possible to be quite specific about the geographical extent of activity for a century or more? Put another way: what made this industrial region? On what foundations did its continuing success rely? And how did the network of social and economic relationships at regional level get formed and reformed in the process of economic growth?

This chapter concentrates on networks of credit and capital supply which were important in cementing diverse and dispersed manufacturing localities into a more integrated region. As capital supply was vital both in the extension of production and in its intensification via innovations in organisation and technology, this subject is a central one in understanding the pace and nature of industrialisation.[3]

---

[1] This is a considerably altered version of my paper 'Industrial organisation and structure in the West Yorkshire wool textile industry, c. 1780–1850', presented at the Anglo-Japanese Conference on Textile History, Kyoto, Japan, September 1987. I am grateful for the helpful discussion of my paper at the conference and my thanks also go to an anonymous referee for useful comments.

[2] For a discussion of this literature see Chapter 1 in this volume, pp. 6–13.

[3] The chapter relies heavily on research undertaken for and discussed at length in my book, *The Genesis of Industrial Capital: A Study of the West Riding Wool Textile Industry c. 1750–1850* (Cambridge,

It has recently been argued that Britain's industrial regions arose because the national economy was based for more than a generation upon canal and waterway haulage. Canal-based systems of transport were regionally orientated, long-distance flows being interrupted by variations in widths and depths, by weather and by transfers between carriers. Thus the transport of raw materials and finished goods were regionally articulated with the vast majority of shipments being over short distances to and from the major ports. It was this, Langton claims, which underpinned the regional nature of both manufacturing specialisation and of social and cultural life before the mid-nineteenth century.[4] This study concentrates on capital supply because, unlike the flow of material goods, capital and credit networks fall outside of any pattern directly dictated by canals. They depended very much upon historical factors of land and wealth distribution in specific localities, on information flow and on the work of financial intermediaries. Their history thus provides an additional element in our understanding of the functioning of specialised manufacturing regions during the industrial revolution.

The chapter begins with a discussion of the agrarian and institutional environment in which woollen and worsted manufacturing flourished during the eighteenth century. Not only is this a very necessary part of the story of the rise of the West Yorkshire industry but it also, as we shall see, had much to do with the supply of both short- and long-term capital to industry. In discussing the influences of landownership and farming on the development of textile manufacturing this study recognises the importance of the context of locality as well as region in analysing the origins of proto-industrial structures and their transformation. Commercial impulses occurring at the national, international and regional levels worked themselves out in particular ways in different small localities as they reacted to them against the backcloth of their own history and social relations. The exogenous stimulus of the market was confronted first by the internal structure and dynamic of the manufacturing locality whose nature did much to determine the extent to which communities were able, or felt it necessary, to respond positively (or negatively) to the opportunities which presented themselves. Thus the process of industrialisation moved at different paces in different parts of the region (as it did in others) and the

Cambridge University Press, 1986). Aspects of that work are summarised in the last four sections of the chapter but they are here placed within a rather different and more developed analytical perspective: that of the region and its importance in forming *the* vital catchment area for capital and credit during crucial decades of technological and organisational innovation.

[4] J. Langton, 'The industrial revolution and the regional geography of England', *Transactions of the Institute of British Geographers*, 9 (1984), pp. 145–67. See also, G. Turnbull, 'Canals, coal and regional growth during the industrial revolution', *Economic History Review*, 40, 4 (1987), pp. 537–60.

outcome in terms of such things as the nature of centralised production, sources of capital and enterprise, the extent of sweating and outwork, could vary enormously between places a few miles from one another. Despite this, as we shall see, there was a very real sense in which the major links between land, labour and capital were intra-regional rather than local by the first half of the nineteenth century.

In considering the agrarian and institutional environment of manufacturing activity in the West Riding in the eighteenth century one necessarily focuses on developments outside of the established large towns of the region: Leeds, Bradford, Wakefield and Huddersfield. Because of their size and nature, and particularly because of the presence of untypically large and early centralised manufacturing concerns and of immigrant groups, these towns had a different constellation of influences acting upon them than the industrial villages, hamlets and small towns so characteristic as sites of wool textile manufacturing throughout the period. One cannot, however, comprehend the functioning of the regional economy without addressing the pivotal role played by the larger urban concentrations. It was the towns which were instrumental in forging extra-local ties and those national and international commercial relationships which created the specialised industrial region out of its diverse parts. Towns were traditionally the marketing, finishing and merchanting centres for virtually all woollen cloths before the end of the eighteenth century and for an increasing proportion of worsted yarns and fabrics. Attorneys and private banks often operated from towns as did the joint-stock banks which mushroomed in number after the 1826 joint-stock enabling legislation. The urban location of financial institutions together with the growth after the Napoleonic Wars of foreign mercantile communities (who had their own lines of financial supply) increased the pull of the towns over the textile region as a whole especially by the second quarter of the nineteenth century. The wholesale food markets of the region, increasingly supplied from the East Riding and elsewhere during the eighteenth century, also pivoted on the larger towns and there was a constant flow of traffic, both people and goods, between the towns and their overlapping circles of influence in the region. Thus the town-country dynamic and the extra-regional relationships of the towns as centres of national and international commerce, functioned alongside the influence of locality and region endorsing the functioning of the textile area as an internally integrated yet outward-looking whole. Towns tended to undermine, whilst by no means destroying, the importance to rural manufacturing of the relationships forged in village and parish. Our understanding of the balance of forces involved in the emergence of factory-based industry from its more scattered and more rurally located predecessors is best advanced against this interface of region and locality, town and world market.

TIME AND SPACE, AGRICULTURE AND INDUSTRY

There has been a long debate about the causes of Yorkshire's success in the eighteenth century compared with the older centres of commercial textile pre-eminence.[5] In addition to Yorkshire's specialisation at the rapidly expanding 'cheap and nasty'[6] end of the market, most recent analysis has stressed the importance of cheap rural labour, the resident and responsive mercantile group and, in the case of the woollen branch, the structure of small masters.[7] There was, it is argued, greater identity of interests between masters and journeymen than between large clothiers and their domestic employees in other regions. This conditioned the reception of innovations and attitudes to the flexibility of production.[8] In the worsted sector the putting-out capitalists themselves often undertook their own merchanting even in the growing export trades. Thus control over access to markets remained in the region and was not, by the later eighteenth century, mediated through Blackwell Hall factors or any other external group to any significant extent.

In so far as Yorkshire's success was founded on the organisational structure of the two branches of the industry it is important to understand how they emerged and how they related to the agrarian history of the region. As indicated in Map 3.1, the production of different types of cloth came to take place in overlapping but quite distinct sub-regions. The most important division was that between woollen manufacture in the south and east of the textile belt and worsted production which concentrated on the higher Pennine regions to the north and west. Although the distinction between the mode of organisation of the two industries was not always clear-cut, the spatial division was endorsed by the dominance of systems of putting-out in the worsted area and small master artisans with only limited putting-out in the woollen branch. Heaton's classic study stressed this distinction as did Sigsworth but neither examined its foundations.[9]

---

[5] See, for example, J. H. Clapham 'The transference of the worsted industry from Norfolk to the West Riding', *Economic Journal*, 16 (1910). R. G. Wilson, 'The supremacy of the Yorkshire cloth industry in the eighteenth century', in N. B. Harte and K. G. Ponting (eds.), *Textile History and Economic History: Essays in Honour of Miss Julia de Lacy Mann* (Manchester, Manchester University Press, 1973), pp. 225–46.

[6] Wilson, 'The supremacy of Yorkshire', quoting contemporary opinion in Norwich and the West Country, p. 245.

[7] Ibid., *passim*.

[8] M. Berg, *The Age of Manufactures* (London, Fontana, 1985), pp. 118–22.

[9] H. Heaton, *The Yorkshire Woollen and Worsted Industries from Earliest Times to the Industrial Revolution*

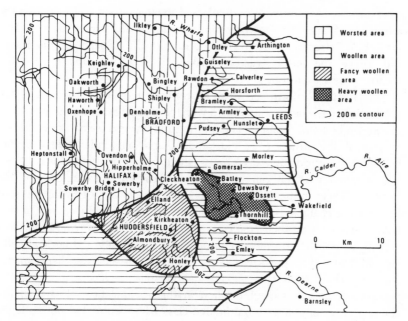

Map 3.1   The location of Sowerby and Calverley within the worsted and woollen areas
respectively of West Yorkshire, *c.* 1780–1830
Source: Based on Hudson, *The Genesis*, p. 28

There were no overriding technological or commercial reasons why
Yorkshire's woollen cloths should have been manufactured by small
masters. And although there were some advantages of scale in worsted
manufacture in order to finance direct mercantile contact and to explore
new markets in competition with East Anglia, there is still much to explain
about the contrasting structures of the two industries. As I have argued in
more detail elsewhere, a major clue to understanding the different structures
and the dynamics of their operation lies in the peculiar spatial pattern which
they occupied within the textile region as a whole.[10]

Yorkshire's long-established manufacture of woollens was conducted by
artisan households who typically bought their raw materials on credit and
sold their finished or semi-finished products at weekly markets in the urban
Cloth Halls. Usually, clothmaking was undertaken as a by-employment
alongside farming or smallholding. In the woollen belt, soils and climate

(Oxford, Oxford University Press, 1920; 2nd edn 1965). E. M. Sigsworth, *Black Dyke Mills: A
History with Introductory Chapters on the Development of the Worsted Industry in the Nineteenth Century*
(Liverpool, Liverpool University Press, 1958).
[10] Hudson, *The Genesis*, Ch. 3.

were suitable for a mixture of arable and grazing which had increased the attraction of large estate ownership, a legacy of the earlier manors. This institutional structure affected the land market, the influence of inheritance and, hence, the social structure, making it peculiarly amenable to the durability of artisan forms.

The area to the north and west, by contrast, moved over from woollen production to the newly established worsted manufacture during the course of the eighteenth century. The putting-out system came to dominate instead of the structure of independent and semi-independent artisan households. Considerable division of labour between households occurred and spinning was put out over a wide area which extended into the Yorkshire Dales in the north and into Lancashire in the west. The worsted belt became characterised by increasingly proletarianised weavers' households dependent on their employer (and the parish). This region, much of it lying above the 200 metre contour, was climatically and agriculturally less attractive than the lower-lying woollen belt and was hence never strongly manorialised. Here subinfeudation, an active land market, and the process of enfranchisement resulted in the accumulation of land in the hands of a socially diverse but limited class who then rented out cottages to the larger army of the landless group. I have argued that this type of social structure and institutional history was a favourable environment for putting-out to flourish. Potential commercially minded employers with landed assets existed side by side with a proletarianised group whose landlessness made it difficult to function independently as household manufacturers.[11]

In order to test these notions vigorously and to enquire exactly how the institutional and agrarian environment functioned to influence the social structure via landholding, inheritance, poor relief systems and in other ways, two townships, Sowerby and Calverley (see Map 3.1), one from each of the major sub-regions, are the subject of current micro-level research.[12]

---

[11] For more detail of these arguments see ibid., and P. Hudson 'Proto-industrialisation: the case of the West Riding wool textile industry in the eighteenth and early nineteenth centuries', *History Workshop Journal*, 12 (1981), pp. 34–61, and P. Hudson, 'From manor to mill: the West Riding in transition', in M. Berg, P. Hudson and M. Sonenscher (eds.), *Manufacture in Town and Country before the Factory* (Cambridge, Cambridge University Press, 1983), pp. 124–44.

[12] Various separate parts of this major project at the University of Liverpool have been financed by grants from the Pasold Fund, the Twenty-Seven Foundation, the Leverhulme Foundation, the Nuffield Foundation, the British Academy and the Economic and Social Research Council. For more detailed discussion of this project and some of the findings on Sowerby and Calverley see P. Hudson and M. Davies, 'Two eighteenth-century locality studies and the use of the SQL data-base', *Computing History Today*, February 1988. P. Hudson, 'Landholding and the organisation of textile manufacture in two Yorkshire townships c. 1660–1800', unpublished paper presented at a Conference on Custom and Commerce in Early Industrial Europe, Centre for Social History, University of Warwick, April 1987.

Table 3.1. *Percentage distribution of Land Tax payers in Sowerby (S) and Calverley (C), 1782, 1788 and 1794*

Land Tax assessment category	Percentages paying					
	1782		1788		1794	
	S	C	S	C	S	C
1 < 4s	14	33	15	41	14	41
2 4s–< £1	36	48	35	39	35	36
3 £1–< £2 10s	29	15	30	16	30	19
4 £2 10s–< £5	12	2	13	2	11	2
5 £5–< £10	7	—	4	—	6	—
6 £10–< £20	—	—	1	—	1	—
7 £20 and over	2	2	2	2	2	2
Total percentage	100	100	100	100	100	100
Total cases	122	46	111	44	107	42
Percentage of owners with direct involvement with their own land	41	35	45	38	50	45

Source: Land Tax returns for Sowerby and Calverley, West Yorkshire Archive Service, Wakefield.

Although Sowerby and Calverley both have distinctive histories and social features peculiar to themselves, they are also representative in many respects of the sub-regions of which they form a part. Tables 3.1 and 3.2 give some illustrations of their very different patterns of landholding and hence social structure as revealed by just one source: the Land Tax returns. Similar contrasts also show up using earlier Land Tax data and even from Hearth Tax returns of the 1660s.[13]

Table 3.1 illustrates the percentage distribution of Land Tax payers in the two townships, which reflects their differences in social structure nicely.[14] In Calverley, Thomas Thornhill paid more than £70 in 1782 rising to £95 in 1794. By the latter year, he paid more than nineteen times that of the next person on the tax scale. In Sowerby, on the other hand, George Stansfield and Sir Watts Horton shared the top tax bracket but both paid only £25 to £35 throughout the period and several others paid more than

[13] See Hudson, 'Landholding and the organisation of textile manufacture', Tables 4a, 4b and 5. There has been long debate about the Land Tax and the difficulties in using it as an historical source representing land values. Most of these problems are avoided in the approach used here which is focused on comparative sizes of holdings for two townships under the same assessment area. See M. Turner and D. Mills (eds.), *Land and Property: The English Land Tax 1692–1832* (Gloucester, Alan Sutton, 1986), especially the chapter by M. Turner: 'The Land Tax, land and property: old debates and new horizons', pp. 1–38.

[14] The following three paragraphs are based on evidence from the Land Tax Returns for Sowerby and Calverley, West Yorkshire Archive Service, Wakefield.

Table 3.2. *Percentage distribution of occupiers of land in Sowerby (S) and Calverley (C), 1782, 1788 and 1794*

| | Percentages paying | | | | | |
| | 1782 | | 1788 | | 1794 | |
Land Tax assessment category	S	C	S	C	S	C
1 < 4s	10	15	9·5	28	10	25
2 4s–< £1	48	65	46	57	47·5	59
3 £1–< £2 10s	36	16	38	11	34	9
4 £2 10s–< £5	6	3	6	2	8	4
5 £5–< £10	—	—	0·5	—	0·5	—
6 £10–< £20	—	1	—	2	—	3
Total percentage	100	100	100	100	100	100
Total cases	221	106	211	119	208	118

Source: Land Tax returns for Sowerby and Calverley, West Yorkshire Archive Service, Wakefield.

£2 10s. Many of those in the under 4s tax bracket in Calverley paid less than 1s, but the lowest Sowerby payment was 3s, indicating either the existence of a stratum of poor taxpayers in Calverley or the fact that many smallholders owned and were liable for only part of the land which they held. Supplementary copyhold land was probably also held or small plots rented from Thornhill.

A difference is also indicated in the proportions of owner-occupiers and owner-part-occupiers. Sowerby had a greater proportion of people directly involved in working their own land which, along with the greater dispersal of ownership, implies that there was a much greater freedom in the land market. Most of the owner-occupiers of Sowerby were in the 4s–< £1 tax category. In Calverley, owner-occupiers were predominantly found in the under 4s group, those with bigger farms were mainly tenants, many of whom rented land from Thornhill who could exert considerable control over the land market.

Turning to the size of tenanted farm plots most common in the two townships, as detailed in Table 3.2, it becomes obvious that the typical farm in Calverley was one on which 4s–< £1 was paid in Land Tax. There also existed a sizeable number of cottages with small patches of taxable land attached. It is my contention that these farms were the province of the dual-occupation clothier. Large units were occupied mainly by specialist yeomen farmers and graziers working to supply the Leeds market in particular. In Sowerby, the most common farm-size group was also the 4s–< £1 taxed but the next category of £1–< £2 10s was also very substantial and several persons occupied farms taxed at £2 10s–< £5. But unlike in Calverley almost no one classed themselves as farmers in the parish register entries of the period.[15] and many Sowerby yeomen, as evidenced by probate inventories, were involved in textile putting-out and trade.[16] The sizeable farms of Sowerby were thus intimately related to textile manufacture and trade, acting as a source of collateral and spreading risks for putting-out concerns just as the small farms and holdings of Calverley enabled balancing of occupations amongst the clothier group.

The structure and practice of inheritance tended, in both townships, to perpetuate the traditional structure of landholding and the importance of leasing and short-term transfers so important to the financing of the industry.[17] The proliferation of copyholders in Calverley ensured some continuation of traditional use-rights particularly until the (partial) Enclosure Act of 1758. At this point the continuation of the same inheritance practices (primogeniture with portions) in new circumstances accelerated the process of proletarianisation of a section of the population whilst maintaining the more substantial copyholder clothier dynasties on a stable footing.

In Sowerby enclosure by act came late – in the 1840s. Primogeniture with portions here did not result in the decline of the 'yeomanry' but meant that those who survived, flourished and bought up the land which others were forced to sell were those involved in the lucrative spheres of trade and putting-out. This was the new yeomanry class of Sowerby. They never called themselves clothiers (though that is what, in many respects, they were) but instead termed themselves yeomen[18] and rose during the eighteenth century to positions of power and authority in the township elite. Here they administered the poor law, relief, pauper apprenticeship and settlement in a very different manner to that found in Calverley. In the latter the old substantial landholding and farming families functioned alongside a group of stable landholding clothiers. They exhibited aspects of communal organisation, affiliations and loyalties in the sphere of familial affairs and in local government and religion. The small clothiers of Calverley were also active in founding communal scribbling and fulling

---

[15] See Hudson 'Landholding and the organisation of textile manufacture', pp. 6–8 and Tables 2 and 3 derived from parish registers of Sowerby St Peters and from Calverley parish, West Yorkshire Archive Service, Halifax and Leeds (microfilm) respectively.

[16] Based on a study of 111 probate documents for Sowerby, 1690s–1790s, Borthwick Institute, University of York. These can be interestingly compared with over 100 similar documents surviving for Calverley during this period: see Hudson, 'Landholding, and the organisation of textile manufacture', Table 1.

[17] Based on study of tax returns and probate records of the two townships; see ibid., pp. 17–23.

[18] Parish register occupational data, West Yorkshire Archive Service, and probate descriptions, Borthwick Institute, University of York.

mills on a joint-stock basis whose success depended on mutuality and trust. Sowerby, by contrast, seems to have manifested a more 'individualistic' culture in both local government and in trading activities.[19]

Thus inheritance practices, together with the initial structure of landownership and holding from the sixteenth century and earlier, served in Sowerby to aid the rise of a 'new yeomanry' of commercial manufacturing employers. In Calverley it seems to have ensured the relative stability of a huge group of small landholding clothiers in the population throughout the eighteenth century. The example of these two townships serves to illustrate developments which took place more generally, despite some localised variations and exceptions, in the two basic textile sub-regions of West Yorkshire. It further indicates that differences in agrarian environment and manufacturing forms could be accompanied by significantly different cultural and political structures and hence by different expectations about the legitimacy (as well as possibility) or otherwise of certain sorts of social and economic behaviour.

Although, by the second quarter of the nineteenth century, historical influences of landholding and social structure were being overlain in many localities by the growth of the major towns of the region, by the influence of migration and settlement of labouring and mercantile groups, and by the effects of the extension of national communications, it is certainly the case that the manufacturing villages and hamlets of the West Riding looked inwards and upon themselves for most of their vital social and economic relationships throughout the period under discussion. And these vital relationships continued to owe much to the nature of the elite group and of local government, to old-established notions of respectability and legitimate behaviour, and also to the traditional locations of financial and mercantile wealth and influence within the parish or township.

Capital supply, for example, was immediately dependent on the social as well as economic relationships existing between lenders and those in need within the locality. Most loans throughout the textile region, both short and long term, took place within a radius of 10–15 miles and occurred between persons known to one another. For example, of £89,625 raised in eighty-four separate loans by Benjamin Gott and Co. during the period 1780–1871, 67 per cent was raised within Leeds itself and the two biggest single sources of funds, accounting for almost half of the total, were relatives of the partners and other individuals involved in the local textile trades.[20] Although the Gott concern was atypically large, it is likely that its

---

[19] Hudson, 'Landholding and the organisation of textile manufacture', p. 22.
[20] Promissory notes and loan details 1758–1812, B. Gott & Co., John Goodchild MSS, Wakefield Central Library, Archives Department.

pattern of borrowing underestimates the general degree of reliance on family and local trade contacts: the partners were well established in trade and could command the attention of banks and attorneys. Furthermore, the flexibility of the localised credit network in response to more general trends depended a great deal on personal contact and trust. The possibilities of obtaining external, particularly bank, credit were influenced by the origins and ownership of banks and the social and business relationships between local bank owners or directors and shareholders, and their clients.[21] Similarly, the reception of new techniques and methods of organisation owed much to the strength of traditional practices. Worker resistance to machinery and the speed and extent of innovation varied in different parts of the Riding.[22] This can only be comprehended by attention to local detail of the ways in which new methods complemented or destroyed established notions of legitimate business practice.[23] At the same time local ideas about social justice and the nature and policy of local government regarding the vexed question of poor rates, relief and settlement vitally influenced the supply of local labour and its cost. Labour supply in relation to demand together with local assumptions about fair rates of pay and conditions of work influenced the extent to which credit could be extracted from labour through use and abuse of truck and token payments and also conditioned the potential of an area to move into sweatshop production.[24] Local labour supply and labour costs influenced the economic rationale of labour-saving innovation which in turn conditioned the possibility of accelerating the turnover time of capital in production.

   Although local social structure and custom thus conditioned a broad spectrum of environmental factors for wool textile manufacturers in the first half of the nineteenth century only one will be discussed in detail here as an illustration of the importance of study at the level of both locality and region. We here concentrate upon local and regional influences affecting access to credit and to capital finance.

---

[21] Hudson, *The Genesis*, Chs. 3, 4 and 9.
[22] See, for example, F. Peel, *The Risings of the Luddites, Chartists and Plug-Drawers* (Brighouse, 1895); J. Mayhall, *The Annals of Yorkshire from the Earliest Period to the Present Time* (Leeds and London, 1860), vol. 1, p. 236; E. P. Thompson, *The Making of the English Working Class* (London, Penguin, 1963), Chs. 6, 8, 9 and 12.
[23] Thompson, *The Making*. See also the chapter by Randall in this volume and Hudson, *The Genesis*, p. 43.
[24] The use of truck and delayed wage payments varied within the West Riding: Hudson, *The Genesis*, pp. 149–53.

THE CAPITAL OF COMMUNITIES

Most studies of industrial finance during the industrial revolution period have drawn a somewhat false dichotomy between fixed and circulating capital: their sources and their importance in understanding the transformation of industry. Fixed and circulating capital were rarely distinguished in contemporary accounting and the two were often interchangeable. For example, a short-term bank loan could become longer term by default and could be used *de facto* to finance fixed capital construction. Similarly lump-sum loans of mortgage finance could be used to pay off pressing book debts. Thus the impact of changes in credit practice on the viability of different types of concerns were mediated by their possibilities of access to other forms of finance. Here the basic spatial division between woollen and worsted production, outlined above, appears fairly crucial although the conditions to which it gave rise could, of course, vary somewhat from one manufacturing locality to another.

In townships like Calverley where as many as 50 per cent of the male population were clothiers in the second half of the eighteenth century, the parish registers testify that there was a tendency for trades to run in families and occupational endogamy was a feature.[25] Thus many of the clothier families were closely related to one another through descent, marriage, work co-operation and often all three. Links created in this way facilitated the flow of funds from one concern to another. Families and friends were known to bolster each other through hard times.[26] The close ties between farming and landholding and woollen manufacture also had an important influence. Not only could careful balancing of activities between textile manufacture and farming help to ride out the storms of commercial life, but contacts made through farming and the paternal structure established between landowners and their tenants could provide an economic safety net.[27] Thornhill, the largest landowner in Calverley, and his predecessor, saw the letting of plots suitable for clothiers and the dual economy as an important part of estate management and it was in their own interest to bolster the fortunes of textile production generally where possible and for individual tenants where necessary.[28] Furthermore, the holding of both copyhold and freehold land on the part of clothiers was an important asset

[25] Calverley parish registers (microfilm), West Yorkshire Archive Service, Leeds.

[26] One can see this in the probate inventories showing both debts and credits, Borthwick Institute, University of York. And in the charging and credit policies of fulling and scribbling mills, see Hudson, *The Genesis*, pp. 141–6.

[27] For discussion of these and following points regarding the woollen area as a whole see Hudson, *The Genesis*, Ch. 4.

[28] Ibid., p. 86.

in raising loans on mortgage. The social structure of woollen townships comprising a large stratum of lower bourgeois small tenant clothiers was also conducive to communitarian attitudes and behaviour on their part in both economic and social life. It is no accident that Calverley was a major locality for the building and operation of 'Company Mills' (the joint-stock co-operative ventures between the clothiers).[29] Neither is it fortuitous that Calverley parish proved receptive to the ideals of the Moravian Church with its notion of the community of goods and the commonwealth of many.[30] Even the early Co-operative movement proved stronger in the woollen area of the Riding.[31]

Rural mass production of worsteds in places like Sowerby, dependent on the absorption of unapprenticed and cheap labour scattered over a wide area of poor soils and cottages built on waste land, represents a contrasting picture of rural social relations and of the possibilities of credit and fixed capital financial flows within the localities. Impersonal lending appears to have been more fully developed in these regions by the late eighteenth century with both attorneys and private banks active in this.[32] Private bankers were also more likely to be involved in textile manufacture and/or trade in the worsted area although the directors and shareholders of joint-stock banks which emerged from the late 1830s appear to have been closely connected with textiles throughout the entire textile region.[33] There appears to have been a more developed market for money in the rural worsted localities of the eighteenth century and although patronage, clientage, family and religious ties remained influential, a market it was nevertheless. And it appears to have been readier to look outwards in search of funds from the localities to the landed wealth in particular of the wider region and beyond.

The money market of the worsted areas needed more objective criteria of assessment of credit worthiness than the less-formal channels more common in the woollen townships. Here 'respectability' was all-important.

---

[29] Ibid., p. 79.

[30] The Moravian Church was established in 1777 at Fulneck in Calverley parish.

[31] Mid-nineteenth-century trade directories, Leeds City Reference Library. G. J. Holyoake, *The History of Co-operation* (London, 1908).

[32] Commercial directories of the wool textile area indicate the prevalence of attorneys resident in the worsted regions, and Sowerby yields more evidence of the activities of attorneys than Calverley which is almost certainly not merely a result of selective survival of data. See P. Barfoot and J. Wilkes, *The Universal British Directory*, vol. 3 (London, 1793), and the records of J. Howarth, attorney of Ripponden, who did a great deal of business for various textile traders in Sowerby, West Yorkshire Archive Service, Halifax. A sample of more than 100 probate inventories for Sowerby also indicate attorneys very active as creditors as well as debtors, Borthwick Institute, University of York. For further substantiation of these points see Hudson, *The Genesis* Ch. 9.

[33] See M. Collins and P. Hudson, 'Provincial bank lending: Yorkshire and Merseyside, 1826–1860', *Bulletin of Economic Research*, 31, 2 (1979); P. Hudson, 'The role of banks in the finance of the West Riding textile industry', *Business History Review*, 55, 3 (1981).

It was a notion found also in places like Calverley but there it was tied up with social morality and with corporate norms of behaviour. In the worsted areas respectability had little to do with social morality as such. Here the respectable were the propertied (especially those with land or tangible assets outside of those sunk in business), the well-known, long-resident in the locality (local church or local government office was important here) and those with a reputation for avoiding speculation or similar unsound commercial dealings. If a manufacture gained respectable status he could be assured of continuing support from institutions of the capital market and was in a good position to extend the use of bank credit.[34] Each worsted manufacturing township had its stratum of respected merchants and manufacturers who united to tackle problems of embezzlement, trade unionism or threats to social order.[35] However, individual worsted manufacturers were not generally in a position to lend within the locality as their own circulating requirements were heavy[36] and, assuming Sowerby and Calverley to be reasonably representative of their wider areas, there appear to be fewer examples of close family connections or endogamy between putting-out employers compared with the extended families in woollen manufacturing.[37]

REGIONAL ORIENTATIONS IN THE CAPITAL MARKET

We have indicated that there is a clear sense in which the market for medium and longer term capital was dominated by influences acting at the sub-regional or even parish level; this market being clearly influenced by historical factors of social and agrarian environments. However, the credit market increasingly operated at a different spatial level: that of the textile region as a whole. And even in the flow of longer term funds there were clear regional orientations which overlay the localised influences throughout the period. One can see this in the geographical spread of the attorney's varied activities. Attorneys linked borrowers to lenders across a geographical area determined by their legal activities in the County Court and as estate stewards and trustees of wills. These placed the attorney in a pivotal position for gaining knowledge of the location of idle funds

---

[34] Hudson, *The Genesis*, Ch. 9 and pp. 265–6.
[35] For these aspects, especially the attempts made by the Worsted Committee to tackle embezzlement, see J. Styles, 'Embezzlement, industry and the law in England, 1500–1800', in Berg, Hudson and Sonenscher, *Manufacture*.
[36] See Hudson, *The Genesis*, Ch. 8.
[37] Parish register of Sowerby with Calverley, preliminary analysis of surnames and occupations covering more than 24,000 vital events for Calverley parish 1681–1750 and for Sowerby township 1688–1750.

seeking a return and of respectable and secure borrowers. The estates which attorneys administered were frequently dispersed in different parts of the county and activities at court in Wakefield made the textile region as a whole the major orbit of the attorneys' financial dealings. Thus attorneys found their lenders and borrowers throughout the region although the latter tended to concentrate in the immediate locality of the attorneys' residence or main centre of operations. It was more important for an attorney to know the status and reliability of borrowers than of lenders hence the formers' generally narrower location amongst that series of face to face commercial and social relationships which underpinned the attorney's immediate locality.[38]

When the role of the attorney as the major intermediary in local and intra-regional medium and longer term lending declined from the early nineteenth century onwards, it was taken over by the activities of private and (from the 1830s) joint-stock banks. But again, banks had both localised and regional orbits of influence. Private banks in the West Riding usually gathered their partners from a narrow locality and often emerged from textile business partnerships of traders and to a lesser extent of manufacturers.[39] The bulk of their deposits were gained from their locality from clients who were in a position to know the bankers well enough for trust to develop. But medium and longer term lending occurred on both a local and a regional level: largely to the immediate and close business and family contacts of partners and directors.[40] The lines of connection through business followed those of the trade in material goods with the regional waterway networks and the towns as marketing centres delineating the geographical limits of much of the banks' lending business.

As surviving private banks grew bigger, some developing branches within the region, they were joined by a mushrooming of joint-stock banks in the textile area during the 1830s. This endorsed the regional nature of potential capital supplies just at the time when the factory and mechanised production was starting to gain considerable ground. Thus the industrial revolution in Yorkshire textiles (the development of mechanised factories and parallel spread of a web of smaller more traditionally organised, specialised or sub-contracting firms) was underpinned by an essentially regional supply of capital funds. Joint-stock banks operated largely from the towns of the region taking their shareholders and directors from the business interests of the town and its immediate locality.[41] Both

---

[38] Hudson, *The Genesis*, pp. 211–17.
[39] Hudson, 'The role of banks', p. 381; idem *The Genesis*, pp. 217–18.
[40] Hudson, 'The role of banks', pp. 384–7.
[41] Collins and Hudson, 'Provincial bank lending', p. 70. See also idem, 'Provincial bank lending', School of Economic Studies Discussion Paper, University of Leeds, 1977, Tables 1 and 2.

directors and shareholders were given some priority in securing loans and credit so it was vital for the success of business not to be excluded from active involvement in one or more of these institutions. Together they covered the entire region in a series of overlapping circles of activity and influence. Few spread their activities beyond the textile area apart from their necessary links with the London money market through discount houses. The banking system of the region was further held together by inter-bank business (especially in discounting) and by the role of the Leeds branch of the Bank of England (from the late 1820s) which gave greater regional access to metropolitan capital and aided the ability of country banks to supply advances to their clients.

REGIONAL INNOVATION AND REGIONAL CREDIT PRACTICE[42]

When one comes to consider the supply of short-term capital and credit to the Yorkshire textile sector the importance of credit practices peculiar to the structure and system of trade in the sector and region becomes even clearer. To understand how this functioned and to examine its influence on innovation in organisation and production, we must first describe in outline the changes going on in manufacturing and in trading in the two branches of the industry.

By the 1780s and 1790s, although the artisan structure still dominated the woollen branch of the industry, and putting-out the worsted branch, these organisational forms by no means represented a static picture. In the woollen sector two developments were of considerable importance in changing the pattern. First, innovation of mechanised carding and scribbling occurred which required water power and thus tended to be established, alongside fulling, in water-powered mills. These had been traditionally owned and financed by landowners (a legacy of manorial monopolies) but now in several areas including Calverley such mills were established by groups of artisan clothiers on a joint-stock basis. This system avoided the delays and monopolistic charges of traditional establishments and was of considerable advantage to subscribers who were often treated preferentially with charges and credit terms. These mills did not arouse opposition and were consciously not even termed factories as they fitted in with the needs and structure of the domestic artisan system, strengthening it rather than challenging it.[43]

Unlike the scribbling mills a second development, the growth of

---

[42] Unless otherwise noted, the material in this and the following section derives from Hudson, *The Genesis*, Ch. 8.

[43] Ibid., pp. 33–7.

merchant manufacturers, did arouse great hostility and opposition amongst the generality of artisan concerns. Not only did these merchant manufacturers by-pass the Cloth Halls and often also the staplers, but they began to build centralised units which gathered workers under one roof for spinning and weaving as well as for the preparatory and finishing processes. Although the number of integrated woollen manufactories increased during the 1790s and (at a slower pace) during the 1800s and 1810s, the average size of factory concern remained small and most employed domestic as well as centralised workers.[44] The most notable feature of the woollen sector remained the domestic clothier whose position was in fact endorsed, as we shall see, not only by the proliferation of commission scribbling and fulling mills, but also by the financial and credit matrix which prevailed in the industry within West Yorkshire until the 1820s.

The worsted sector lagged behind the woollen in moves to centralisation before the widespread mechanisation of worsted spinning in the 1820s. Putting-out concerns grew in size but very few included sizeable units under one roof and most employers continued via sub-contractors to employ large numbers of men and women, weavers and spinners, scattered over a wide geographical area. The slow pace of centralisation before the 1820s, indicated in estimates of fixed capital formation,[45] was not a function of technological drag: after all the spinning technology of cotton was close to hand, requiring relatively minor adjustments and worsted fibre was proving suitable for the Arkwright technique of roller spinning. But the domestic system remained dominant for three major reasons.

First, it remained viable because of a large supply of cheap female labour which had few alternative sources of income and which used the hand mule or throstle with great efficiency. Secondly, the volatile trade conditions during the Napoleonic Wars and their aftermath increased the relative attractiveness of high- rather than low-liquidity ventures. Most importantly, and related to trade conditions, was the influence of the credit matrix within which worsted manufacturers were forced to operate. This was unfavourable for capital intensive expansion before the late 1820s, when shorter credits became the practice in sales and when specialist mercantile and finance houses stepped in to take an increasing share of the trading risks especially in the growing transatlantic and Far Eastern trades.

In the woollen and worsted sectors, although varying a great deal between firms of different sorts, the fixed/circulating capital proportion may well have been generally lower than a third before the 1820s and

---

[44] Ibid., pp. 40–1.
[45] D. T. Jenkins, *The West Riding Wool Textile Industry, 1770–1835: A Study of Fixed Capital Formation* (Edington, Pasold, 1975), p. 176.

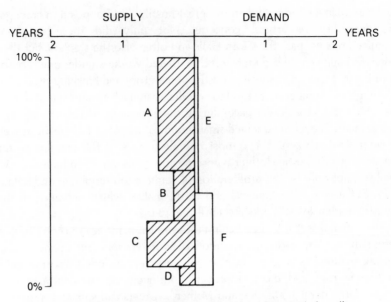

A   Purchase of wool from staplers at average of 6 months' credit
B   Labour payment (largely weaving and spinning) at 3–4 months' credit
C   Fulling, scribbling and carding at 6–8 months' credit
D   Other inputs, tools and rents at 2–3 months' credit
E   Sales at cloth halls at under 14 days' credit
F   Direct sales to merchants or middlemen for short bills at 3 months

Figure 3.1   The credit matrix of the domestic artisan woollen manufacturer, pre-1815
Source: Hudson, The Genesis, p. 191.

rarely exceeded one half before the 1850s.[46] Thus the credit matrix was bound to be a major determinant of the financial flexibility and viability of manufacturers and of their capacity to extend and advance production. Ashton's work first stressed the importance of regional factors in eighteenth-century credit particularly the level of immediate knowledge and trust required for the extensive system of bills of exchange which developed in the Lancashire cotton area. Anderson's research on the same region further emphasised the regional activities of attorneys in short- as well as long-term capital provision during the crucial decades of the late eighteenth century expansion of cotton manufacture and trade.[47]

[46] Hudson, The Genesis, pp. 50–2.
[47] T. S. Ashton, 'The bill of exchange and private banks in Lancashire, 1790–1830', In T. S. Ashton and R. S. Sayers (eds.), Papers in English Monetary History (Oxford, 1954); B. L. Anderson, 'The attorney and the early capital market in Lancashire', in J. R. Harris (ed.), Liverpool and Merseyside (London, 1969); and idem, 'Provincial aspects of the financial revolution of the eighteenth century', Business History, 12 (1969).

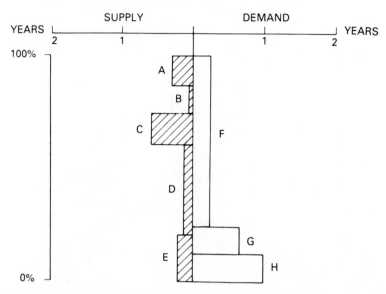

A   Purchase of wool from growers and dealers at 3–4 months' credit
B   Purchase of wool from growers and fairs at 14 days' credit or less
C   Purchase of wool from staplers at 6–8 months' credit
D   Labour payment at average of 1–2 months' credit
E   Tools, carriage, oil, soap, etc., at 2–3 months' credit
F   Cloths sold to Leeds merchants at 3 months' credit
G   Cloths sold direct to Europe at average of 8 months' credit
H   Cloths sold direct to American market and to the home trade at average of 12 months' credit

Figure 3.2   The credit matrix of the worsted putting-out manufacturer, *c.* 1780s–1810
Source: Hudson, *The Genesis*, p. 192.

As a first step in understanding the credit matrix for wool textile manufacturing and its regional character, its importance to different sorts of concerns and hence to the possibilities of development from less-centralised to more centralised forms of production, it is useful to establish a typology of wool textile manufacturing business. The diversity of organisational and technological structures of production within the industry, together with the different raw materials used and the varying products and markets served, ensured that credit practices would impinge differentially on different types of manufacturers. In the real world, of course, firms would also feel the effect of face to face commercial and personal relationships and the build-up of mutual trust between trading partners which seems to have been so important in the formation of the credit matrix. Nevertheless, there were certain broad conditions of normal credit practice which firms of a particular sort faced. Figures 3.1–3.7 attempt to illustrate some of the

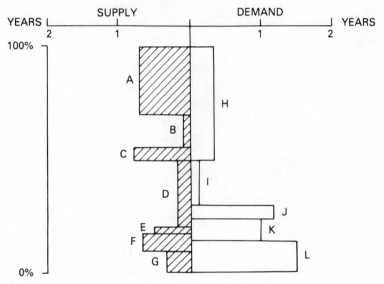

A   Purchase of wool from staplers at 6–10 months' credit
B   Direct purchase of wool from growers and middlemen at an average of 1
    month's credit
C   Purchase of wool from importers at 6–11 months' credit
D   Labour, part centralised, part domestic, at an average of 2 months' credit
E   Rental of premises at 6 months' credit
F   Dyeing and dressing services at 6–12 months' credit
G   Other inputs: oil, soap, tools, carriage at an average of 4 months' credit
H   Sales to local merchants at 4 months' credit
I   Sales to shippers for advances at 6 weeks' credit
J   Direct sales to Europe at credit averaging 14 months
K   Sales to the home trade at credit averaging 12 months
L   Sales to North and South America at 18 months' credit

Figure 3.3   The credit matrix of the large-scale manufacturer in the woollen branch,
c. 1800–20s
Source: Hudson, The Genesis, p. 193.

variations between different types of manufacturers in the composition of
both their input costs and their sales outlets and associated credit
relationships. They are based on estimates of inputs and sales structures
derived from a variety of primary and secondary sources, particularly
business records. These figures simplify a very complex picture at the
aggregate level for different broad types of manufacturing concern. They
are intended as no more than an aid to conceptualising the liquidity
position of different sorts of manufacturers acknowledging the impossibility
of properly representing flows of finance in such a static form.

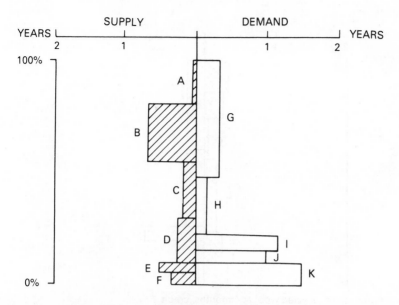

A   Purchase of wool from growers at 2 weeks' credit
B   Purchase of wool from staplers at 8 months' credit
C   Labour at credit averaging 2 months
D   Machinery, tools, equipment, oil at around 3 months' credit
E   Rental of premises/fixed capital charges at 6 months' credit
F   Dyeing and carriage at an average of 4 months' credit
G   Cloths sold to merchants at 4 months' credit
H   Sales to shippers for 'immediate' advances – 2 months' credit
I   Cloths consigned direct to Europe to agents on commission at 14 months' credit
J   Direct sales to the home trade at 12 months' credit or more
K   Direct sales to North and South America at 18 months' credit

Figure 3.4   The credit matrix of the worsted manufacturer with centralised, mechanised
spinning, pre-1830s
Source: Hudson, *The Genesis*, p. 194.

Credit practices on both the supply and the demand sides of the industry
changed noticeably during the period 1750–1850.[48] On the supply side,
despite the irregularities introduced by the disruptions of the Napoleonic
War period, the long-term change in credit practice was in favour of shorter
and more uniform allowances. By the 1830s and 1840s the late eighteenth-
century wool (and other input) credits of six to twelve months or more had
given way to two or four months or, as in the case of auctioned wool, cash

---

[48] A more detailed discussion of the changes described in the following three paragraphs is to be found
in ibid., Ch. 8, where the primary source material from business records, upon which the analysis
rests, is cited in full.

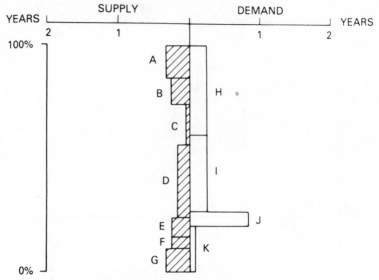

A   Purchase of recycled wool at 4 months' credit
B   Purchase of wool from staplers at 3 months' credit
C   Purchase of wool at auction at 2 weeks' credit
D   Labour at credit averaging 2 months
E   Dyeing and carriage at 3 months' credit
F   Rental of premises/fixed capital charges at an average of 3 months' credit
G   Machinery, tools, utensils, residual inputs at 4 months' credit
H   Direct sales or through intermediaries to the home trade at 3 months' credit
I   Direct sales abroad at 3 months' credit
J   Direct sales abroad on long credits
K   Direct sales to foreign houses in England for immediately discountable bills: 1 month's credit

Figure 3.5   The credit matrix of the factory woollen manufacturer, 1820s–40s
Source: Hudson, The Genesis, p. 195.

terms. Scribbling and carding mills appear to have moved from half-yearly to quarterly pay days and had begun to charge for any additional credit. By the 1830s even commercial rentals seem to have been increasingly confined to quarterly rather than half-yearly payments. Labour became the most flexible of input costs regarding credit by the 1830s and 1840s, hence the extended use and abuse of truck and token particularly by the smaller firms of the worsted sector. Overall, internal credit on the supply side of the industry had curtailed by the late 1820s and 1830s making the credit matrix less favourable for setting up and for the viability of small concerns with little access to the now much-needed external sources of accommodation via banks in particular.

On the demand side of the industry the cash and short-credit sales

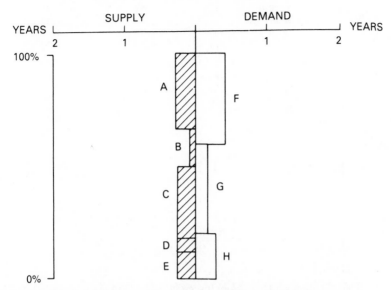

A Purchase of wool from staplers at 3–4 months' credit
B Purchase of wool from growers and at auction at 2–4 weeks' credit
C Labour payment (mainly factory female spinners) at 3 months' credit
D Rental of premises/fixed capital charges at 3 months' credit
E Machinery, tools, equipment at 3 months' credit
F Yarn sold to the home trade at 4–6 months' credit
G Yarn sold to merchants, including foreign merchants in England, at 6–8 weeks' credit
H Yarn sold direct abroad at 3–4 months' credit

Figure 3.6   The credit matrix of the factory worsted manufacturer, *c.* late 1820s–40s
(spinning branch)
Source: Hudson, *The Genesis*, p. 196.

commonly found with the Cloth Hall system were replaced, in the case of many larger concerns from the 1790s, by very long credit terms, commonly twelve to twenty-four months. This was associated with the evolution of merchant manufacturers in the woollen branch and with the struggle to gain a competitive position in the volatile and especially the long-distance trades made essential by the disruption of European markets in the 1790s to 1810s. It was also associated with the 'Bradford Principle', so called in Yorkshire, which came to prominence at this time: the idea of expanding sales aggressively at low unit prices and profit relying on bulk sales and a rapid and large turnover to ensure high overall profits. At first this principle was adopted and financed by the larger merchant manufacturers themselves, particularly in the worsted yarn and cloth branches. They used the

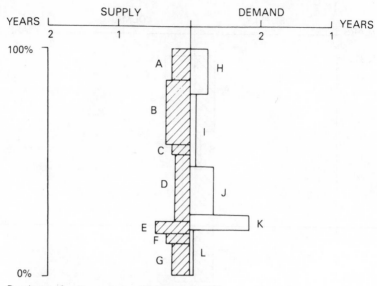

A   Purchase of cotton warps at 3 months' credit
B   Purchase of worsted yarn at 4 months' credit
C   Purchase of other fibres at 3 months' credit
D   Factory labour at 2–3 months' credit
E   Rental of premises/fixed capital charges at an average of 6 months' credit
F   Dyeing and carriage at 4 months' credit
G   Machinery, engine, tools, etc., at 3 months' credit
H   Direct sales to the home trade at 3 months' credit
I   Direct sales to domestic merchants in home and foreign trades at 1 month's credit
J   Direct sales abroad at 4 months' credit from invoice date
K   Direct sales abroad, e.g. to South America, on long credits
L   Direct sales to foreign houses in England for immediately discountable bills: 2 weeks' credit

Figure 3.7   The credit matrix of the factory worsted manufacturer, c. late 1820s–40s
(weaving branch)
Source: Hudson, The Genesis, p. 197.

consignment system and auction, particularly in the transatlantic trade, as the principle depended on full exploitation of the elasticity of the export markets. But many manufacturers got their fingers burnt or worse in the periodic overstocking crises of the American market and, following the mass bankruptcies of 1825, a definite change occurred in the length of credit manufacturers offered to merchants. From the mid-1820s credit extended in the sale of yarn and cloth in domestic as well as foreign markets was curtailing once more from the extremes reached in the first quarter of the nineteenth century and from this time manufacturers themselves were rarely involved in long credit extension. This coincided with the decades when cost-competition increased in the trade and the accent was placed on cheapness of both production *and* circulation costs. Credit figured prominently in the latter. Credit-competition of the sort experienced particularly during the Napoleonic Wars became restricted to periods of speculative activity. At the same time mechanisation and vertical disintegration quickened the turnover time of capital in production, facilitating the use of shorter credits, and improvements in communications reduced the period of realisation. The stabilisation and reduction of credit terms, on the demand side of the industry in the climacteric of the mid-1820s, seems to have remained a characteristic feature of the trade through much of the rest of the nineteenth century.

In the 1830s and 1840s curtailment of open or internal credit on both the supply and the demand sides of the industry was eased by the expansion of external credit associated with the growth of banking facilities. Bank discounts were crucial in enabling manufacturers to contract the amount of finance they formerly were forced to devote to the sale of their commodities. Bank overdrafts enabled firms to buy raw materials for cash at auctions or on very short credit thus taking advantage of periods of low prices. The West Yorkshire textile region was one of the main areas experiencing rapid expansion of banks following the legislation of 1826. This may well have placed the larger and more influential concerns with links to the local banking fraternity at an advantage *vis-à-vis* the smaller manufacturer or the new entrant to the industry. The directors' lists of Yorkshire banks of the 1830s and 1840s show the dominance of medium- and large-scale industrialists on the boards and in positions of directorial influence and only the largest and most substantial concerns were allowed discount facilities with the Bank of England.[49]

THE IMPACT OF CREDIT[50]

This brings us to consideration of the ways in which these regional sectoral trends in credit practice affected the relative position of proto-industrial as opposed to more centralised forms of manufacturing business within the textile area. It is easiest to identify the changed position of the woollen artisan. It was a matter of note of contemporaries that the credit available

[49] Collins and Hudson, 'Provincial bank lending' (Discussion Paper), Tables 1 and 2. Only firms which were estimated to have upwards of £25,000 invested in business and which had a local reputation for reliability were allowed discount accounts with the Bank: Leeds Branch Letters 1830s, Bank of England Archives.

[50] For full references to the primary sources upon which this analysis rests, see Hudson, *The Genesis*, pp. 190–207.

on raw material supply in the late eighteenth and early nineteenth centuries made it very easy to set up in business in the woollen branch of the Yorkshire industry: 'It is one recommendation of the domestic system of manufacture that a young man of good character can always obtain credit for as much wool as will enable him to set up as a little master manufacturer.'[51] One witness before the 1806 Parliamentary Inquiry spoke of the ease with which a journeyman could become a sizeable master and attributed this to 'the facility of credit, as soon as they have accumulated a sum of money that they can procure material, they send it to the mill and we scribble it for them; or if they have not money, we give credit; and they have credit upon every operation it undergoes'.[52]

Figure 3.1 shows the relatively favourable credit matrix of the woollen artisan compared with that of the larger-scale manufacturer with some centralised production and more direct and distant sales (indicated in Figure 3.3). The credit position of the proto-industrial structure of woollen manufacture also compares favourably with that in the worsted branch (shown in Figure 3.2) which made greater use of domestic wools directly bought on short credits and had no real equivalent of the Cloth Hall system of sales for ready cash.

Through the oscillations of trade and credit following the deflation of the 1810s, entry eased by generous credit terms began to disappear and by the 1830s staplers' credit had stabilised at two to four months. At the same time, for those who could afford to do without credit, directly purchased and auctioned wool gave big price advantages. From 1815 to the 1820s, the longer credits needed on the demand side to expedite sales made it more difficult to set up in business except in very specialised branches of the trade, sheltered from the brunt of competition. However, this also made life difficult for the bigger firms with centralised labour who had much cloth to shift whilst the survival of a portion of sales for cash through the Cloth Halls, or even direct for merchants' orders, helped to maintain the viability of existing artisan units.

In the 1830s and 1840s a very different climate of credit prevailed. The shorter credits common on cloth sales were now predicated more than ever before on shifting the burden by having access to bank discount facilities. The cost advantage of buying wool for cash at auction increased as Australian imports flooded the auction rooms with staples suited to the woollen branch of the industry. Thus not only did the potential newcomer of the 1830s and 1840s need higher initial fixed capital outlays than his or her predecessors but also needed the status to command extensive credit

[51] *British Parliamentary Papers*, 1806 (268), III, Report, p. 10.
[52] Ibid., evidence of James Walker, Wortley, p. 182.

from the local financial sector. The position of existing artisan concerns began to be seriously undermined for the first time by their larger rivals using cheaper wools and extensive short-term bank accommodation. Some representation of these larger concerns and their credit matrix is given in Figure 3.5. The traditional small concerns, by contrast, were living from hand to mouth, their existence predicated on the long open credits endemic in the earlier phase of manufacture. During proto-industrialisation the net credit gained by a small manufacturer in the woollen trade could almost cover the time of production and circulation (or realisation). The system of ready cash for sale at the Cloth Halls and long credit extended by staplers and fullers had provided an environment for capital accumulation enabling the gradual evolution of larger concerns from the ranks of the manufacturers and the building of carding and scribbling mills on a joint-stock basis. This world was fast disappearing in the textile region of the 1830s.

The worsted putting-out capitalist of the eighteenth century Yorkshire trade generally purchased English wool from growers and dealers on short, often no, credit and sold yarn and/or cloth at three to four months minimum, often more. This unfavourable credit position was one factor ensuring the domination of the industry in the late eighteenth century by concerns of larger capital than in the woollen branch (see Figure 3.2). The credit matrix, furthermore, may well have contributed, along with the disarray of markets in the early nineteenth century, to the relatively slow move to the centralisation of production. Putting-out capitalists certainly seem to have been slow to move to factory production. As well as a prior build-up of capital it required an obvious shift in mentality to move from high- to lower-liquidity, longer-gestation ventures. As indicated in Figures 3.2 and 3.4, worsted firms had all their capital, and more, tied up in the circulating needs which the regional industry required. Thus it may have been the credit matrix which slowed down the shift to more centralised production of Yorkshire worsteds. The turnover time of capital was also very long in eighteenth-century worsted production, two years or more was not uncommon. It involved a larger number of processes than woollen work; more time was spent in collecting and distributing materials, only limited use was made of the jenny in Yorkshire and wools were commonly oiled and stored for up to twelve months prior to combing. Thus credit could never, as in the woollen branch, be stretched to cover production time. When centralisation did get off the ground it is no surprise that it was accompanied by vertical disintegration into spinning, weaving and combing concerns which cut the turnover time immeasurably for individual businesses (compare Figure 3.4 representing a vertically integrated firm with Figures 3.6 and 3.7). When sales credit practices changed in the 1820s and competition in the industry concentrated on costs, the benefits of mechanised spinning became vital. Furthermore, this mechanisation halved the turnover time of capital in the space of a decade. Staplers and banks came to regard specialist spinners as less risky credit clients than integrated manufacturers whose turnover time was slower, so spinners often had the option of any staplers' credit available. This goes a long way to explain why the mechanised worsted spinning sector (whose favourable credit matrix is represented in Figure 3.6) was the fastest growing part of the Yorkshire textile trade in the 1820s to 1850s, trading much of its product far outside the confines of the local industry, particularly in central and eastern Europe. Once spinning was mechanised, weaving soon followed, as it became essential to speed up turnover. Comparing Figure 3.4 with Figure 3.7, it looks likely that the credit matrix did not favour continuation of weaving as solely a hand or putting-out industry even within integrated firms. Worsted weaving concerns from the late 1820s were able to gain three to four months' credit on yarn or warps. Although they commonly sold at shorter credit than that, only specialisation and mechanisation could turn the credit matrix in their favour by speeding up production.

Despite the foregoing argument it is only at the level of the region as a whole and by generalising that one can speak of the overwhelming advantages of large centralised units over smaller decentralised ones. From the mid-1820s the balance of commercial forces in the regional industry may well have been in favour of the growth of factory production but proto-industrial structures proved remarkably tenacious especially in the woollen branch through the rest of the nineteenth century. This was largely because of the strength of supporting financial, social and cultural institutions, and influences acting at the level of certain localities and parishes. Credit changes do not explain everything as each concern met the challenges of the commercial and financial world with a mixture of responses derived in part from the possibilities formed in the localised context. The nature of agrarian links, interpersonal socio-economic and familial relationships, local labour supply conditions, the nature and origin of the local financial sector: all of these contributed to the specific environment in which businesses functioned. Their flexibility and latitude of action in circumstances of changing commercial and credit conditions at regional and national level was formed within the local and face to face context of their very different townships and parishes.

THE REGION AND THE FINANCE OF INDUSTRY

In the foregoing survey of changes in regional credit practice, set against the backcloth of the initial rural environment of textile manufacture, several points have emerged which prompt us to look closely at the specificities of the region and its economy in locating the sources of innovation and in gaining an understanding of the pace and nature of industrial change. Of course many of the changes in credit practices associated with the wool textile trade (especially those concerning international sales and national retailing) mirrored wider changes occurring simultaneously in other sectors. The integrating links provided by London discount houses and, later, by the Bank of England together with the increasingly efficient flow of commercial information by the second quarter of the nineteenth century worked to ensure that the capital and credit markets of the industrial regions were firmly linked to national trends and tendencies. However, each industrial region was also characterised by the practices peculiar to its own sectoral composition. Each industrial sector had, like wool textiles, a set of different and changing organisational and trading structures and its own (again changing) customs regarding capital and credit supply. These regional customs have been the focus of this chapter.

We are drawn to conclude that the region is not a static or pregiven category but becomes finite in different ways depending on where and when we place the emphasis of our analysis. In the eighteenth century the emerging Yorkshire textile region took in two separate and distinct areas geographically, agriculturally and socially in addition to possessing a wide penumbra of the putting-out of worsted wools to female labour in North Yorkshire and north-east Lancashire. The two main areas were separately supplied with wools from different locations. The worsted industry used mainly English long staples bought direct from the wool counties by the larger manufacturers or their specialised agents. The woollen industry mainly used short stapled imported wools bought through the important intermediary of the credit-granting woolstapler. The woollen and worsted branches also served different markets with the worsted industry being rather more dependent on exports especially to Europe.[53] Halifax and Bradford became the main centres for worsted marketing whilst Leeds and Wakefield merchants dominated the woollen trade. The woollen/worsted contrast was not always so clear-cut as the ideal types described here indicate. Mixed fabrics were made and staplers and merchants did connect firms in the two branches. Furthermore, the whole region had a centuries-long tradition of indigenous woollen manufacture which had spawned its

[53] Hudson, *The Genesis*, pp. 66–8.

own regional contacts. Intra-regional links were certainly present: the role of attorneys in finance and of banks in discounting regional bills were important alongside the flows of goods (raw materials and finished products) which occurred largely within the clearly defined region and to the main outport at Hull and, later, Liverpool. The evidence of settlement certificates also shows that migratory labour came largely from within the textile region and specifically moved within the two specialised areas. But all these elements of regional integration were to increase in the first half of the nineteenth century particularly from the 1820s which coincided with the quickening pace of both commercial and manufacturing innovation. It was at this time also that the importance of localised economic and social life in village, hamlet and parish felt a major impact from the rapidly growing centres of commerce and production in the towns. And the textile region began to contract somewhat, with the loss of rural spinning, to an area which serviced the principal towns and the more specialised outposts.

The story of the textile region during this period is illustrated rather well by considering the impact of the changing supply of finance to industry, especially of credit. As banks became more important financial inter-mediaries than attorneys (a trend accelerating from the 1820s), the regional nature of the capital market was endorsed because, until the 1860s or so, banks were very regional institutions linked together in a functioning system of regional credit and intelligence networks. The importance of family and locality in financial and business dealings did not disappear but it became very much overlaid by the more powerful institutions of regional finance in the second quarter of the nineteenth century. And as internal credit contracted markedly in favour of external finance after the crisis of 1825, those firms which remained most successful were those able to lock into the regional network of bank and mercantile credit. Thus we could say that in the Yorkshire textile area before the late 1820s the capital and credit markets were local as well as regional, personal yet reasonably open to large and smaller firms alike depending as they did on localised assessments of respectability and credit worthiness. Relatives were perhaps the major source of long- and medium-term loans for manufacturers whilst direct business contacts who extended credit on materials supply were the major source of circulating capital. Even the family and local community of the workforce played its part by enduring long delays and truck in wage payments. And attorneys directly assessed the trustworthiness of their clients showing a strong tendency to lend within their immediate locality. From the late 1820s the capital and credit markets, affected by the growth of urban mercantile communities and urban banks, became more regionally oriented which had implications for their accessibility. Large and more well-established firms now had better opportunities to raise finance, as they carried more influence and generally had more collateral than small localised businesses. At the same time the vertical disintegration in worsted production prompted by changes in the regional credit matrix made the region and its external economies all the more vital as a site for the expansion of single process concerns. We are thus alerted to the second quarter of the nineteenth century as a time when the separation of merchanting from manufacture, the growing importance of external credit, product specialisation and a quickening pace of innovation and of turnover of capital were all occurring as a function of the increasingly regionally integrated system of finance, manufacture and trade.

After the mid-century the improvement of national communications networks particularly of information flow, started in train a process which was to see the gradual decline of some of the financial aspects of the region's integration. Faltering of profit margins in textile mass production combined with increased awareness of potentially lucrative investments elsewhere (both at home and abroad especially in government stock and railways) to attract funds away from the region.[54] The process of bank amalgamation in the third quarter of the nineteenth century also changed the complexion of regional finance as lending decisions became increasingly a function of extra-regional head-office policy. And that policy tended to follow the trend of British banking and of city finance in this period: to look outward to government stock or international financial and commercial dealings rather than to domestic industry for a major source of its reward. The balance of political power in the national state supported this role of the British economy: city-based and internationally oriented.[55] And this continued in the twentieth century to affect the fortunes of indigenous manufacturing industry with results which are readily apparent today. Thus, in the third quarter of the nineteenth century some of the most important foundations of the regional manufacturing economy were permanently undermined.

[54] For examples of this from the 1840s through the second half of the nineteenth-century, see P. Hudson, *The West Riding Wool Textile Industry: A Catalogue of Business Records* (Edington, Pasold, 1975), pp. 155–6, 158–71, 300–6, 332, 344, 349, 376, 392, 433, 468, 471.

[55] See G. Ingham, *Capitalism Divided? The City and Industry in British Social Development* (London, Macmillan, 1984), especially pp. 108ff. C. Leys 'The formation of British capital', *New Left Review*, 160 (1986); P. Anderson, 'The figures of descent', *New Left Review* 161 (1987). For a critique of these analyses of the importance of the City–Treasury–Bank nexus in British economic and political development of the last 200 years, see M. Barratt Brown, 'Away with all the great arches: Anderson's history of British capitalism', *New Left Review*, 167 (1988). Barratt Brown rightly argues that the British capital investment that was encouraged overseas was not just in merchanting but in production and that it was never wholly undermining of investment at home.

PART TWO

OTHER PATHS, OTHER PATTERNS

~~ Chapter 4 ~~

Continuity and change in an industrialising society: the case of the West Midlands industries

MARIE B. ROWLANDS

In the West Midlands industrialisation was a long process rather than a series of discrete economic stages. It was the outcome of a continuous interplay of innovation and of continuity, and of diverse responses to pressure and to opportunity. The experience of this region supports recent work on industrialisation at national and international level, which stresses the importance of economic growth and structural change in society before 1760, and which suggests that between 1760 and 1850 economic growth was slower, and innovation more piecemeal, than was formerly believed.[1]

The West Midlands displayed many of the features which have been recognised as encouraging industrialisation, including a pastoral economy, early agrarian capitalism, weak manorial controls and strong market incentives. Nevertheless, the region had its own special features, and adds another alternative to the many differing modes of industrialisation in the English regions. Its characteristics included marked continuity in the relations of production, the multiplication of units of production and the persisting importance of high-level skills of hand, brain and eye in the context of mass production. The most notable characteristic of the Midlands was diversity: of soils, of sizes of community, of products, of tenurial relations, of modes of organisation, of units of production and capitalisation, and of levels of wealth and poverty. This diversity was to prove an important influence in generating industrialisation in a form which was a significant alternative to factory mass production.[2]

The process will be considered in three chronological periods, the first from about the mid-sixteenth to the mid-seventeenth centuries when the

[1] N. F. R. Crafts, *British Economic Growth during the Industrial Revolution* (Oxford, 1985), p. 69.
[2] F. F. Mendels, 'Proto-industrialisation: the first phase of the industrialisation process', *Journal of Economic History*, 32, 1 (1972), pp. 241–61; P. Kriedte, H. Medick and J. Schlumbohm, *Industrialisation before Industrialisation: Rural Industry in the Genesis of Capitalism*, with contributions from H. Kisch and F. F. Mendels (English transl., Cambridge, 1982); J. Thirsk 'Industries in the countryside', in F. J. Fisher (ed.), *Essays in the Economic and Social History of Tudor and Stuart England* (Cambridge, 1961); C. Sabel and J. Zeitlin, 'Historical alternatives to mass production: politics, markets and technology in nineteenth century industrialisation', *Past and Present*, 108 (1985), pp. 133–76.

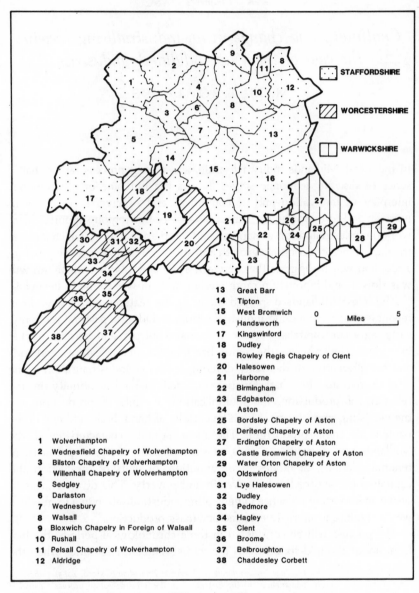

Map 4.1   The parishes of the West Midlands manufacturing area

West Midlands was establishing a national market for metalware and glassware; the second between the mid-seventeenth and the mid-eighteenth centuries when the West Midlands developed under the influence of an expanding home and international market; and the third during the period known as the 'industrial revolution'. Comparative examination of these three chronological periods makes it evident' that the transition from one phase to another was not marked by great discontinuities or sudden restructuring of economy or society.

The area to be discussed in this chapter covered roughly 100 square miles and comprised thirty-two parishes which lay in what was then south Staffordshire, north Worcestershire and north-west Warwickshire (see Map 4.1). These parishes were pastoral woodland communities with settlements dispersed through groups of hamlets. They were all either on the south Staffordshire coalfield or sufficiently near to it to draw supplies of fuel from it. The open arable fields were extremely irregular, and comprised only a small proportion of the available land. By the sixteenth century there was a multiplicity of small closes, some open-field arable and much open heath and waste, pasture and woodland. There were five seigneurial boroughs within the area: Wolverhampton, Walsall, Dudley, Halesowen and Birmingham. In addition, Stourbridge, the main hamlet of Oldswinford parish, was increasingly urban.

1560–1660

By the mid-sixteenth century the area was already more populous than the predominantly agricultural areas of the rest of Staffordshire, Worcestershire and Warwickshire. The population of the whole area had more than doubled 100 years later. The population of the rural industrial villages within the area had increased even more, in some cases as much as fourfold. This took place at a time when the national population increased by only about 75 per cent. Rising population was combined with inflation, and parish registers reveal the immiserising effects on the poorer families in rural parishes of Warwickshire. In contrast, there are fewer such indications in the industrial parishes of the West Midlands and it seems probable that the industrial villages gained rather than suffered from rising prices and numbers of people.[3]

[3] E. A. Wrigley and R. S. Schofield, *The Population History of England, 1541–1871* (London, 1981); J. M. Martin, 'Population and industrialisation in Tudor and Stuart Warwickshire 1973', typescript, Warwick Record Office; D. Palliser, 'Dearth and disease in Staffordshire 1540–1670', in C. W. Chalkin and M. A. Havinden (eds.), *Rural Change and Urban Growth* (London, 1974), pp. 54–75; P. Frost, 'The growth and localisation of rural industry in South Staffordshire 1560–1720', unpublished Ph.D. thesis (University of Birmingham, 1973), pp. 280–344; V. H. Skipp, *Crisis and*

The principal landowners were the Earls of Dudley, the Lyttletons of Hagley and the Holts of Aston, who between them held about one third of all the manors in the area. These larger landowners were all gradually replacing traditional tenures by leaseholds. The greater part of the other manors were in the hands of resident gentry, men of modest estates who held two or three small manors at most but who were nevertheless influential in their locality. There were also gentlemen without manors and superior yeomen occupying moated houses or large farmhouses, who held freehold, leasehold and copyhold land, and formed a very stable core in many parishes. In Sedgley, for example, almost all the freeholds, copyholds and leaseholds were in the hands of five such families. The remaining families of the parish must have held their land as sub-tenants, or as cottagers on the waste. Both gentry and richer yeomen often held land in several different manors and although they went through the formalities of reporting to the manor courts as appropriate, the social status of at least some of the 'copyholders' makes it unlikely that they recognised any limitations upon their organisation of cultivation and sub-letting. The land was usually acquired over many generations by inheritance, marriage, purchase and lease. Parts of such assorted holdings were demised and sold for commercial reasons and could be used as a basis for raising small mortgages. These developments in land tenure within manors promoted agricultural capitalism, and facilitated small-scale industrial activities.[4]

Peers, gentry and yeomen developed the industrial potential of their lands very much as one element of the general management of the whole property, whether large or small. From 1568 mineral rights belonged to the lords of the manors, but mining was permitted to the tenants on freehold and leasehold land. Copyholders had long claimed the right to mine and in Sedgley, Darlaston and some other manors, 'free' copyholds carried the right to mine but even 'base copyholders' could do so on payment of a small fee.[5] Even where lords sought to check mining by copyholders they were unable to enter the tenancy or recover coal once mined, and in those places on the 'ten yard seam' where coal could be dug from open pits, control must have been difficult. In the sixteenth century the manor court of Amblecote frequently dealt with coal mining, making orders for the

    Development (Cambridge, 1978); idem, 'Economic and social change in the forest of Arden, 1530–1649', in J. Thirsk (ed.), *Land, Church and People: Essays Presented to Professor H. P. H. Finberg, Agricultural History Review Supplement* (1970).

[4] Dudley Record Office, Dudley MSS 7/10, a survey of the manor of Sedgley; manor court rolls of Kingswinford, Sedgley, Rowley Regis. M. B. Rowlands, *The West Midlands from AD 1000* (London, 1987), pp. 115–23, 150–8.

[5] J. F. Ede, *A History of Wednesbury* (Wednesbury, 1962), pp. 114–16; F. W. Hackwood, *Sedgley Researches* (Dudley, 1898), p. 39; S. Shaw, *The History and Antiquities of Staffordshire*, vol. 2 (London, 1801), p. 226.

filling of pits and the amount of coal to be worked, supervising the removal of coal, controlling competition and limiting sales. The court exercised less day-to-day control in the seventeenth century but the lord of the manor was paid over 20s a week per pit, by tenants holding leases of pits. Coal worked in this parish was at a depth of 25 yards which must have meant that costs of exploitation were high, but this was presumably counter-balanced by the lively demand from nearby finery, chafery and fulling mills, from the smiths' hearths, the brickworks, and, in the seventeenth century, the new glassworks.[6] In other parts of the region particularly good seams of ironstone were exploited by small-scale undertakings in Rushall, Wednesbury and Netherton, and limestone works in Sedgley and Wren's Nest were exploited either directly by the lord or leased out to yeomen and others.

The lessees of the larger coal mines put in gins and gear, provided horses, and employed pikemen and grubbers to work below ground and banksmen to sort and sell the coal above. Horse gins were erected for drainage and for hauling up the coal or ironstone. Sometimes leases were taken jointly by three or four men, and partnerships between members of associated families begin to be indentifiable. These connections might extend over several parishes and be maintained for two or three generations. However, all mineral products were difficult to transport and were profitable only if they could be sold locally to serve the needs of manufacture, building and agriculture. Work in mineral mining and carrying was widespread but intermittent, and undertaken by men whose main livelihood was farming.[7]

Other important assets of a landed estate were the streams and small rivers capable of providing water power. In the upper reaches of the local streams the waters ran swiftly and the construction of pools was easy. In the lower reaches of the Rea and Cole the gradients were not steep but long mill leats were constructed to provide a sufficient head of water. By the end of the fourteenth century there were twelve fulling mills serving the textile industry in addition to numerous corn mills. Water power was being employed to hammer iron by the end of the fifteenth century, and by the end of the sixteenth century many landowning families were establishing water-powered iron furnaces, chaferies and fineries. Slitting mills were introduced from the early seventeenth century. The Earl of Dudley, the Whorewood, the Wyrley and the Persehouse families were particularly

---

[6] *Victoria County History of Staffordshire*, vol. 20 (Oxford, 1984), pp. 54–6.

[7] Dudley Record Office, Dudley MSS leases; J. Roper, *Probate Inventories of Sedgley* (Dudley, n.d.); *Victoria County History of Staffordshire*, vol. 2 (Oxford, 1967), pp. 68–9; Rowlands, *The West Midlands*, pp. 147–8.

active and by 1660 there were, within the area, some fifteen furnaces, forges and slitting mills producing iron, and others in the neighbouring parishes of Kinver, Womborne, Wolverley and Bushbury.[8]

The landowners who erected iron mills in the late sixteenth century engaged in competition sometimes amounting to violence, and direct exploitation often ended in disaster for the owner.[9] From the 1630s iron mills were usually leased to specialist ironmaster families such as the Foleys who proved to be outstandingly successful. Most of the lessees were townsmen with some experience in selling ironware. They built up widespread networks of mills, which were planned, managed and developed in the light of commercial judgements relating to power, fuel, markets and communications'. They employed professional clerks and specialist skilled workmen, and actively sought out new customers and markets. The iron mills were of great economic importance in the sequence of production, but like the mines and quarries their presence did not significantly alter the social composition of the communities in which they were located. They were often sited some distance from the main settlements, and the specialist skilled craftsmen were few in number and formed networks of their own, moving from mill to mill. Local people were employed for casual labour and carrying services in the iron mills, as in the mines and quarries, but this work was not sharply differentiated from general agricultural labour and services. Water was also increasingly used to drive blade mills for sharpening edge tools. These required little power and were relatively cheap to erect and maintain. The adaptation and management of blade mills were usually undertaken by lessees, most of whom were individual craftsmen, or more usually partnerships of two craftsmen. They did not normally undertake more than one mill, and were for the most part members of local families.[10]

Whereas the exploitation of minerals and water power were both aspects of land management, the development of handicraft manufacture for the retail and wholesale trades owed little directly to landownership or tenurial relations, and Midland landlords provided neither leadership nor

---

[8] J. R. Gould, 'Excavation of the fifteenth century ironworks of Simon Montford at Bourne Pool, Aldridge Staffs.', *Transactions of the South Staffordshire Archaeological and Historical Society*, 11 (1969–70), pp. 58–64; R. Pelham, 'The migration of the iron industry towards Birmingham in the sixteenth century', *Transactions of the Birmingham Archaeological Society*, 66 (1945–6); *Victoria County History of Staffordshire*, vol. 17 (Oxford, 1976), pp. 30, 185, vol. 20, pp. 34, 54–5, 72–3, 85, 142–5, 168–9, 178–9, 192, 213; *Victoria County History of Warwickshire*, vol. 7 (Oxford, 1964), pp. 253–70.

[9] 'Calendar of Staffordshire quarter sessions rolls. Part iv', *Staffordshire Historical Collections* (1936); G. R. Morton and M. Wanklyn, 'Dud Dudley – a new appraisal', *Journal of West Midland Studies*, 1, 1 (1967), pp. 48–65.

[10] R. Dilworth, *The Tame Mills of Staffordshire* (Newton Abbot, 1975); *Victoria County History of Staffordshire*, vol. 2, pp. 108–118; L. H. R. Schubert, *The History of the British Iron and Steel Industry* (London, 1957).

investment. The organisation of production grew out of the medieval experience of the manufacture and distribution of textiles. It involved a major shift of products and diversification of skills, but it did not involve any new modes of organisation. The manufacture of hardware used local supplies of raw materials, and depended critically upon readily available supplies of cheap fuel. However, the existence of local raw materials was not by itself a sufficient reason for the success of the region's specialisms. Already in the sixteenth century many raw materials were being imported from further afield. The scythemakers used steel, the braziers, brass, and the pewterers, silver and tin, none of which were available in the locality. While local resources might account for the early appearance of a regional craft specialism, its development into a manufacture for wider markets depended far more on the concentration and interchange of specialist skills and commercial expertise.

During the period 1560 to 1640 nails, locks, edge tools, agricultural implements and saddlers' ironmongery were all needed in greater quantities as population expanded. The 'great rebuilding' created a demand for nails for flooring and roofing laths. The improvements in domestic furnishing created a demand for locks and hinges, more pewter, more brassware and more glassware and window glass. The growth of internal travel and trade created demand for more metal parts for harness (known as lorrimy). Agricultural improvements stimulated trade in farming implements – the scythe, for example, replacing the sickle for some tasks, to the advantage of the scythemakers of Belbroughton and Chaddesley Corbett. Even when national population growth slowed down in the mid-seventeenth century, internal trade and travel, coastal shipping, the rebuilding of the navy, agricultural improvement and rising standards of domestic comfort continued to provide expanding consumer markets for Midland products. Plague interrupted trade only temporarily and while the civil wars made the roads hazardous for the packhorse trains, the ironmasters prospered, producing iron for both sides, lockmakers made locks for muskets and nailers made bullets. By the Restoration the Midlanders were regularly supplying London, most areas of England and Wales, Ireland and the early American settlements with a widening range of hardware.

The Midlands had long been crossed by important roads which by contemporary standards provided sufficient access to river and coastal ports and to London. The medieval textile trade in the Midlands had been dominated by Coventry but men of Wolverhampton, Birmingham and Kings Norton had also been active commercial capitalists. There were already men of commercial experience in the region, to collect, market and deliver the goods made in the Midlands. By the mid-sixteenth century a number of Midlanders had made fortunes in London while retaining their links with their home town. Some were Merchants of the Staple, or members of other London companies. They were able and willing to extend and diversify their activities to meet the demand for consumer goods. Several Wolverhampton and Birmingham townsmen were importing iron from Spain, and others were buying iron from the new water-powered iron mills, though they continued to be called 'fuller', 'draper' or 'goldsmith'.[11] Their capital was circulating capital, financing the purchase of raw materials and payments for work. The enterprise, the capital and the links and connections which made the growth of trade possible were generated almost entirely from within the trading community itself.

The commercial leaders lived mainly, though not exclusively, in the towns in substantial houses with large shops on the ground floor, opening on to the market place. Some were already concentrating on wholesale trade in metalware by 1600, and successfully invaded the London market. Their ranks were joined by a number of men who, having built up their capital as craftsmen, bought iron and other materials, employed others and marketed goods. Gradually they came to be designated 'ironmongers', grew in wealth and social status, and some of them achieved temporary political prominence during the Interregnum.[12]

The towns were the main centres of retail trade, distance marketing and commerce but the distinctive roles of town and country in industrialisation can easily be overstressed. The towns of the Midlands in the early seventeenth century were only imperfectly distinguished from their manorial and parochial context. All were originally seigneurial boroughs, and each had an associated area of 'Foreign' or continued to be part of a large parish. Only Walsall had a formal urban government and a craft guild and was described as wholly built up.[13] Craftsmen were numerous in both the towns and the villages. Those requiring imported or expensive raw materials or those producing luxury goods were to be found mainly,

[11] Rowlands, The West Midlands, pp. 142–50; R. Pelham, 'The trade relations of Birmingham in the middle ages', Transactions of the Birmingham Archaeological Society, 62 (1939), pp. 33–40; idem, 'The cloth merchants of Warwickshire in the middle ages', Transactions of the Birmingham Archaeological Society, 66 (1945–6), pp. 130–41; G. Mander and N. Tildesley, History of Wolverhampton (Wolverhampton, 1960), pp. 25–60; Royal Commission on Historical Manuscripts, 'Papers of John Smythe of Bristol, merchant, 1538–1550' (London, 1974), pp. 17–18.

[12] M. Flinn, Men of Iron (Edinburgh, 1962); W. Harrison and C. Willis, The Great Jennens Case (Sheffield, 1879), p. 43; D. H. Pennington and I. A. Rootes, 'The Committee at Stafford 1643–5', Staffordshire Historical Collections, fourth series, vol. 1 (1957).

[13] Victoria County History of Staffordshire, vol. 17, pp. 180–200; E. J. Homeshaw, The Corporation of the Borough and Foreign of Walsall (Walsall, Walsall Corporation, 1960), pp. 29–82; Mander and Tildesley, Wolverhampton, pp. 41–100; C. Gill, A History of the Corporation of Birmingham (2 vols., Birmingham, Birmingham Corporation, 1952), vol. 1, pp. 32–62; J. Roper, Dudley: The Town in the Sixteenth Century (Dudley, Dudley Libraries, 1963).

though not exclusively, in the towns. Walsall was undoubtedly the most industrial of the towns with a concentration of pewterers, braziers and makers of saddlers' ironmongery. However, Birmingham, Wolverhampton, Dudley and Stourbridge, although they had numerous braziers, pewterers, locksmiths and edgetool makers, were nevertheless essentially market towns, with a mixed economy. In addition to the metalworkers, there were numerous textile workers and woodworkers and service trades and the craftsmen were usually of lower social and economic status than the mercers, drapers and innkeepers who were the elite of the towns.[14] Conversely, in the industrial villages of Aston, Sedgley and Rowley Regis there were tanners, locksmiths and edgetool makers of wealth and status. The prestigious glassmakers from Lorraine located their glass works in the rural parts of the manor of Oldswinford not in the town of Stourbridge, and in the more rural parts of Sedgley, Halesowen and Chaddesley Corbett the scythesmiths combined their industrial work with substantial agricultural enterprises. The towns and the villages both contained some craftsmen producing goods for distant markets but this did not mean that they ceased to make for local sale. The same individual might be both an independent artisan selling directly to his customers and also making goods for the ironmongers, working on other men's materials and sending off his products to warehouses to fulfil orders obtained by men he never knew and for customers with whom he had no contact. The same man might be a putter-out of work on his own behalf and a taker-in of work for other men. He might work on the whole or part of the product. The evidence is too scanty to establish which form of organisation predominated.[15]

Substantial numbers of craftsmen were recorded in probate documents, parish registers and Quarter Sessions papers. In the parish of Sedgley, for example, of 550 adult men whose occupations were recorded in the parish registers between 1581 and 1616, 165 were metalworkers, 36 were ironworkers, and 33 were colliers. In the villages, the majority of craftsmen were also husbandmen, dependent like most people of the period on a variety of sources of income and support. There is no evidence to show

---

[14] J. Roper, *Dudley Probate Inventories, first series, 1544–1603* (Dudley, 1959); idem, *Dudley Probate Inventories, second series* (Sedgley, 1966); idem, *Stourbridge Probate Inventories* (Sedgley, 1966); D. Hilton, *Birmingham Probate Inventories* (Birmingham University Extra Mural Department, 1986); R. F. Homer and D. W. Hall, *Provincial Pewterers* (London, 1985).

[15] K. McPh. Buchanan, 'Studies in the localisation of Worcestershire industries', *Transactions of the Worcestershire Archaeological Society*, 17 (1940), pp. 40–50; ibid., vol. 18 (1942), pp. 31–41; ibid., vol. 19 (1943), pp. 45–55; E. A. Fry, *Index of Wills and Administrations in the Consistory Court at Worcester* (2 vols., Worcester, 1904, 1910); Frost, 'Rural industry in South Staffordshire', pp. 425–526; *Victoria County History of Staffordshire*, vol. 2, pp. 224–30, vol. 17, pp. 143–275; J. Roper, 'North Worcestershire scythesmiths', *West Midlands Studies*, 3 (1969); *Victoria County History of Staffordshire*, vol. 2, pp. 224–30.

whether rural rates of payment and production costs were lower than in the towns, so there is no means of knowing whether the villages supplied a cheap workforce. It is evident that they provided a very flexible labour supply, for since most of them had other sources of income from farming, casual carrying and labour, industrial activity could be intensified or reduced as the market demanded. By 1660 the duality of occupations had enabled many families to respond gradually and with limited risk to new opportunities.[16]

It does not seem that traditional manorial controls inhibited families from increasing industrial activity. Cottages on the waste were pulled down in West Bromwich but the population of nailers and other metalworkers continued to grow.[17] In Walsall there were complaints that the metalworkers refused to help with the harvest, and in West Bromwich that they worked on holy days.[18] Neither the Statute of Apprentices nor the Elizabethan poor law seem to have had much effect in inhibiting the mobility of labour or diversification of occupations. There was an attempt on the part of agents of the Earls of Dudley to enforce the Statute of Apprentices, and various initiatives were taken to regulate the metalware trades, but they came to nothing.[19] The pewterers of Walsall had their ware seized for illegal sale by the London company but continued to prosper.[20] An attempt to prosecute certain wholesalers of nails and other hardware as engrossers resulted in minimal sentences and a petition of support from the handicraftsmen.[21] Those whose industrial or commercial enterprise brought them into conflict with the law often had family connections with those whose duty it was to enforce it. There was no particular group among the wealthy or dominant classes whose interests were threatened by economic change; on the contrary, all owners and lessees of mineral-bearing land gained from the growth of manufacture. There was no tradition of strong manorial, parochial or guild control. Manorial boundaries were sometimes so confused and intermingled that jurors could not identify them, and parish boundaries were not much better with many extra-parochial places. The only recognisable urban trade guild, that of Walsall, comprised a wide variety of tradesmen, and was in severe financial straits.

[16] H. R. Thomas, *Sedgley Parish Register 1558–1684* (Newcastle, Staffordshire Parish Register Society, 1940–1); Frost, 'Rural industry in South Staffordshire', pp. 200–12, 524–7; R. A. Davies, 'Community, parish and poverty Oldswinford 1660–1730' unpublished Ph.D. thesis (University of Leicester, 1987), pp. 77–88.

[17] West Bromwich Library, Lissiemore transcripts of West Bromwich manor court rolls.

[18] Staffordshire Record Office, QS'b Trinity 1600, Q/SR M.1658.

[19] W. H. B. Court, *The Rise of the Midlands Industries* (Oxford, 1938), pp. 55–61.

[20] Homer and Hall, *Provincial Pewterers*; pewterers' searches, Guildhall Library, London, Guildhall MSS 71–56.

[21] J. Thirsk and J. P. Cooper, *Seventeenth Century Economic Documents* (Oxford, 1973), pp. 188–9.

There was no very evident connection between inheritance and economic processes; a recent study of Oldswinford concludes that 'the devolution of property across the generations played a very incidental role' and that 'it is difficult to conclude that industry ... developed ... as a result of the process of excessive land division'.[22] It is equally difficult to discover any connection between inheritance and industrialisation in other west Midland parishes. Primogeniture was the norm, but by this date the actual disposition of the property depended on the particular circumstances of the family rather than upon manorial custom. In some cases the testator clearly intended to enable several sons to set up workshops, or to encourage family connections useful in trade, but in this, as in so much else, Midlands practices were characterised by flexibility and adaptation to specific circumstances.

In the Midlands the gradual transition from an agricultural to an industrialising society was made possible by the concentration of commercial wealth, and the growth of a large, adaptable workforce, both skilled and unskilled. This took place in an area where there was much marginal and under-used land, and within a society which could readily accommodate change. The resident gentry played a role alongside the urban merchants in the gradual creation of a mining and a manufacturing region. Landowners and tenants were both encouraged by the pull of growing markets and pushed by their exigencies into more commercial exploitation of their assets. The development of leasehold and the opportunities to sub-let land facilitated commercial exploitation, and capital could be raised by small mortgages by men of very modest means. Small loans were frequently raised from neighbours and kindred, and money was invested on behalf of third parties. The commercial leaders were finding national markets for a great diversity of Midland metalwares; there were more producers and greater continuity of production. At the same time agriculture and other occupations cushioned the producers from the worst effects of overproduction, seasonal demand and trade interruptions. Gradually the experience, skills and contacts were being built up which were to sustain an even more remarkable development in the next hundred years.

1660–1765

The next hundred years brought a great quickening of economic growth and social change in the Midlands. In the late seventeenth century, many Midland manors changed hands and some were bought by men who had made wealth in industry, commerce or the law. Landowners old and new

---

[22] Davies, 'Community, parish and poverty', pp. 180–5.

continued in varying degrees to participate in the exploitation of mineral wealth and water power. The Foley family acquired six manors, and dominated the supply of iron until the 1720s when they much reduced their Midland interests both in land and in ironworks. The Lyttleton family of Hagley lent money to the Foley enterprise and later invested over £3,000 for a period in the Knight ironmaster partnership which took over the Stour Valley works from the Foleys.[23] Sandwell was bought by the Earl of Dartmouth and an attempt was made to find coal, but without success.[24] The Leveson Gowers, although making important profits from coal on their estates in Shropshire and north Staffordshire, were not exploiting the coal on their properties in Wolverhampton, Bilston and Willenhall.[25] The Holts at Aston collected rents from iron mills but disliked the environmental pollution.[26] On the other hand, the Dudley and Ward family continued to be actively involved in industry, extracting clay, ironstone, coal and limestone from the land, leasing out many of the works but exploiting some directly.[27] On all the large estates, the trend to leasehold continued, and old long leases were called in and converted to shorter leases or tenancies at will. The manorial courts continued to function and provided a means of registering landholding, recovering petty debts and maintaining ways, fences and water channels. There was a widening distinction between the tenant farmer who leased the land and cultivated it and the landlord who drew rents, invested in government stocks, and made strict family settlements.

Leases of mineral-bearing land were usually for shorter terms than agricultural leases. They were taken by gentlemen yeomen, individual craftsmen and colliers, or by partnerships of two or three neighbours. The lessees were sometimes described in successive leases first as 'yeoman' then as 'coal master' then as 'gentleman'. There were enterprising men of little capital looking for quick profits in a high-risk industry, who specialised in taking short coal leases. They competed ruthlessly with each other, and disregarded both local manorial law and the convenience of the rest of the community. Pits were dug in the open fields and in roadways, water courses were disturbed, there were fires and accidents both above and below ground. In 1686 there were said to be twelve or fourteen pits 'in work' and

---

[23] R. L. Downes, 'The Stour partnership 1726–36', Economic History Review, second series, 3, 1 (1950), p. 90.

[24] Staffordshire Record Office, D(W)1778 v.1325, 1327.

[25] J. R. Wordie, Estate Management in Eighteenth Century England (Oxford, Royal Historical Society, 1982), p. 95.

[26] O. Fairclough, The Grand Old Mansion: The Holtes and their Successors at Aston Hall (Birmingham, Birmingham Museums and Art Gallery, 1984).

[27] C. H. Bailey, Two Rent Rolls of Lord Dudley (Dudley, privately printed, 1882).

as many again 'out of work', some producing as much as 5,000 tons a year others as little as 200 tons. All coal was sold 'at the bank' to consumers who fetched it away themselves or to waggoners who took it to the towns.[28] The production of coal was an essential service for the development of industry, as was the availability of water power, and both these assets were controlled by landowners, but their responses were reactive rather than pro-active. The driving force of change in the Midlands came not from landowners but from the rapid response of craftsmen and commercial capitalists to new markets for Midland products which were opening up both at home and abroad.

Between 1660 and 1760 the overseas market for Midlands goods extended to become world wide. The West Indies began importing nails and agricultural metalware from the Midlands from the 1650s and as sugar became almost their only crop, they required huge quantities of cask nails, plantation hoes, cane cutters, oxchains and slave collars. Maryland, Carolina and, later, Georgia also depended on exports of a single product to England. The planters built up surplus credits in London and these were used to purchase and import into the colonies manufactured goods. Even in colonies of mixed economy, metalware imported from England was cheaper than goods manufactured at home. Other markets opened up. Midlanders supplied merchants with hardware both for direct trade with Africa and for the triangular trade of the slavers.[29] Merchants sailing north-east balanced the import of Baltic and Siberian iron and timber by exporting Midland hardware to Sweden and Russia,[30] and by 1770, fourteen Birmingham merchants were members of the Russia company.[31] The export of ironware and brassware to Europe increased both absolutely and relatively to England's whole export. Until the middle of the seventeenth century manufactured goods exported from England and Wales consisted almost entirely of cloth, but in 1699–1701 metalware accounted for 3 per cent of exported manufactures. In the period 1722–4 this proportion had increased to 7 per cent and by 1752–4 to 9 per cent.[32] The Midland share

[28] R. Plot, *The Natural History of Staffordshire* (Oxford, 1686), pp. 127–8; Dudley Record Office, Dudley MSS 2/16, 5/5, 5/6, 5/9, 7/10.
[29] R. Davis, *The Rise of the Atlantic Economies* (London, 1973); R. Davis, *English Overseas Trade* (London, 1973); Birmingham Reference Library, Archives, Galton MSS 403, 404.
[30] Somerset Record Office, Dickenson MSS DD/DN/420–4.
[31] Information from J. Newman based on the archives of Russia company.
[32] R. Davis, 'English foreign trade 1660–1670', *Economic History Review*, second series, 7, 2 (1954), pp. 150–66; idem, 'English foreign trade 1700–1774', *Economic History Review*, second series, 15, 2 (1962); E. Schumpeter, *English Overseas Trade Statistics 1697–1808* (London, 1960), Table VIII; W. A. Cole, 'Factors in demand 1700–1780' in R. C. Floud and D. N. McCloskey (eds.), *The Economic History of Britain since 1700* (2 vols., Cambridge, 1981), vol. 1, p. 64; D. Richardson, 'The slave trade, sugar and economic growth', *Journal of Interdisciplinary History*, 17, 4 (1987), pp. 739–69.

of these developments cannot be quantified, but upswings in national overseas trade, especially marked 1700–15 and 1745–60, were also periods of marked diversification and intensification of industrial activity in the Midlands.[33] Conversely, interruptions to overseas trade were quickly reflected in overstocked warehouses, laying off the workers, and high poor rates in the industrial villages.[34]

At the same time there was an increased consumption of manufactured goods in England and Ireland, including items which, though cheap and mass-produced, were for comfort and adornment rather than mere utility. These 'decencies' included snuff boxes, buckles for clothing, metal buttons, glass drinking vessels and bottles, brass candlesticks, pots and pans, coffee pots and tea kettles.[35] The causes of this increased demand and of the movement of real incomes are debatable,[36] but it is clear that more people purchased more manufactured goods, both necessities and 'decencies', than their grandparents. There was no great difference in the nature of Midlands goods produced for the home and for the overseas market. As Samuel Garbett of Birmingham emphasised in 1759, 'the home trade supports the foreign'.[37] Guns, for example, were needed abroad, both for war and for trade, and at home, both for sport and for personal protection.

The increased manufacture of goods was sustained by the multiplication of small units of production, and by more extended networks of commercial credit and circulating capital. New specialisms such as gun making and button making, appeared in both towns and industrial villages between 1690 and 1720.[38] There was no discernible progression from town to village or village to town, but there was a marked degree of localisation to facilitate the circulation of specialist materials and the carriage of work from one shop to another in the different stages of production. There was increasing specialisation in particular products, and much sub-division of the processes of production into separate specialisms.

[33] M. B. Rowlands, *Masters and Men* (Manchester, 1975), pp. 124–45.

[34] William Salt Library, Stafford, Wilkes MSS vol. 1, p. 86.

[35] J. Brewer, N. Mckendrick and J. H. Plumb, *The Birth of a Consumer Society: The Commercialisation of Eighteenth-Century England* (London, 1983), pp. 1–33; Rowlands *Masters and Men*, pp. 124–7; D. E. C. Eversley, 'The home market and home demand 1570–1780', in E. L. Jones and G. E. Mingay (eds.), *Land, Labour and Population in the Industrial Revolution* (London, 1967), pp. 237–9; J. S. Moore (ed.), *The Goods and Chattels of our Forefathers* (London and Chichester, 1976); B. Trinder and J. Cox, *Colliers and Yeomen* (London and Chichester, 1980).

[36] P. O'Brien, 'Agriculture and the home market for English industry 1660–1820', *English Historical Review*, 34 (1985), pp. 773–86.   [37] *Journal of the House of Commons*, XXVIII, p. 854.

[38] Lichfield Record Office, probate records; Staffordshire inventories 1660–1720; Birmingham and Aston parish inventories 1520–1720; Worcester Record Office, north Worcestershire probate inventories, 1666–1720; P.R.O., inventories from the appropriate parishes 1660–1720; M. B. Rowlands, 'Industry and social change in Staffordshire', *Transactions of the Lichfield and South Staffordshire Archaeological and Historical Society*, 9 (1967–8), pp. 37–58; idem, *Masters and Men*, pp. 125–56; idem, 'Society and industry 1700', *Midland History*, 4, 1 (1977).

Diversification of products and increased production were both facilitated by the increased availability of partly processed metals in an easily workable form. From the 1680s the state monopoly of brass and copper production was abandoned and several English companies began manufacture in London and Bristol. Birmingham soon became their most important market.[39] In addition, there were brass houses in Birmingham and Wednesbury by mid-century.[40] Meanwhile, water power was applied to rolling plate-iron and later to tinning plate, and Midland ironmongers imported much tinned and black plate from Wales and Shropshire.[41] Small steel furnaces in Stourbridge, Kingswinford and Birmingham supplemented steel imported from Europe and Scandinavia,[42] and English smelted zinc was being used in quantity as well as that imported from the East Indies.[43]

The changing market conditions and the shift to the use of more malleable metals encouraged the use of the stamp, the turning lathe and the drawbench in the domestic workshops.[44] The new equipment required neither an intellectual breakthrough nor any great capital investment. The tools were all familiar from earliest times and very simple to make and use; much simpler, for example, than the tools used by the instrument makers of Lancashire at the same period. These simple innovations enabled large quantities of toys and fashion goods to be produced cheaply and quickly. They sold by their novelty and an increasing variety of 'new' ideas were patented. Many more were kept secret as the property of the particular workman. As the new branches developed some tradesmen specialised in supplying colours, oxides, files, planes and dyes.[45]

Water power was in ever greater demand and was soon being used in the newer trades. Richard Heeley, the gun maker, was using water power for grinding gun barrels from at latest 1720, and toy manufacturers used water power for rolling iron, brass and silver. Other mills turned out wire, buttons, thimbles and paper. Altogether there were some hundred mills in the area.[46] The charcoal iron mills continued to supply the Midlands with

[39] H. Hamilton, *English Brass and Copper Industries* (London, 1967), pp. 101–40; *Victoria County History of Warwickshire*, vol. 7, p. 88.
[40] Liverpool University Library, Raistrick MSS 71/22, Angerstein's narrative, pp. 22–5.
[41] Kidderminster Public Library, Knight MSS 243, 244; East Suffolk Record Office, Ipswich, Ashburnam MSS HAI/GD/4/13; Newport Record Office, Caerleon, tin works MSS 1758–9.
[42] Flinn, *Men of Iron*, pp. 12–29, 141; Plot, *Staffordshire*, pp. 373–4; Taunton Record Office, Dickenson Papers DD/Dn/404.
[43] Walsall Public Library, Parry MSS 33/2; E. J. Cocks and B. Walters, *Zinc Smelting Industry of Great Britain* (London, 1968).
[44] Probate records as at n. 38; Rowlands, *Masters and Men*, pp. 124–46.
[45] *Aris' Birmingham Gazette*, 1743–60. Work on this periodical was much facilitated by the index to metalware entries held at the Social and Economic History Department, University of Birmingham. I am indebted to Professor Harris for the use of this index.
[46] *Victoria County History of Warwickshire*, vol. 7, pp. 253–70; R. Pelham, 'The water power crisis in

cast iron, bar iron, rod iron, plate iron and cast anvils, but by the mid-eighteenth century supplies were drawn from all over England and Wales, from Sweden, the American colonies and from Siberia.[47] There was no lack of active interest in new techniques. Crowley sent his son on a carefully prepared journey through Sweden to discover their advances in technology.[48] Experiments to smelt iron with mineral coal continued. Frederick de Blewstone, a German living in Aston, was credited with some success and in 1735 George Sparrow was attempting the same feat at Rushall furnace.[49] The Knights mixed coke-fired and charcoal-fired pig iron and John Knight experimented with metal bellows.[50] Experiments were also being made to find new methods of refining the pig to wrought iron.[51] However, until the second half of the eighteenth century the balance of advantage for Midland ironmasters continued to be in the production of charcoal iron, the more so as local coal was of poor coking quality.[52]

The most momentous innovation was the application of steam power to mines drainage, for which local conditions were particularly suitable. A Savery engine was reputed to have been erected at Darlaston in about 1706. A few years later in 1712 the first Newcomen engine was erected at the Coneygre for the trustees of Lord Ward. By 1733 when the patent expired there were already nine Newcomen engines at work on the south Staffordshire coalfield out of a total for England and Wales of 104, and many more were erected subsequently.[53] In other industries too there was much experiment and when market conditions made it profitable there was no reluctance to invest in innovation. Samuel Garbett produced acid on an unprecedented scale and more cheaply than by traditional methods, and came to be regarded as one of the founding fathers of the chemical

Birmingham in the eighteenth century', *University of Birmingham Historical Journal*, 9 (1963); idem, 'The water mills of Edgbaston and Birmingham', *Transactions of the Birmingham Archaeological Society*, 77 (1962).

47 B. C. L. Johnson, 'The Foley partnerships in the iron industry at the end of the charcoal era', *Economic History Review*, second series, 4, 3 (1952), pp. 322–40; G. Hammersley, 'The charcoal iron industry and its fuel', *Economic History Review*, second series, 26 (1973), pp. 593–613; P. Riden, 'The output of the British iron industry before 1870' *Economic History Review*, second series, 30, 3 (1977), pp. 442–59; B. G. Awty, 'The charcoal ironmasters of Cheshire and Lancashire, 1600–1785', *Transactions of the Historical Society of Lancashire and Cheshire*, 109 (1957).

48 Friends' House, Euston, Lloyd MSS F18a, 3 Nov. 1701.

49 Birmingham Reference Library, Galton MSS 84; Plot, *Staffordshire*, p. 128.

50 Downes, 'The Stour Valley partnership'.

51 C. K. Hyde, 'The iron industry of the West Midlands in 1754', *West Midlands Studies*, 6 (1973), p. 39.

52 C. K. Hyde, 'The adoption of coke smelting by the British iron industry 1709–1790', *Explorations in Economic History*, 10 (1973), p. 410.

53 J. Allen and L. Rolt, *The Steam Engine of Thomas Newcomen* (Hartington, 1977); J. R. Harris, 'The Newcomen engine and historical studies', *Transactions of the Newcomen Society*, 50 (1978/9), pp. 175–80; J. Kanefski and J. Robey, 'Steam engines in eighteenth century Britain: a quantitive assessment', *Technology and Culture*, 21, 2 (1980), pp. 161–86.

industry.[54] It is perhaps worth stressing that those most interested in these innovations were the men of industry not the landed or the intellectual elites.

The carriage of coal, iron, manufactured goods and foodstuffs was already putting great pressure on the roads and rivers, and considerable efforts were made to maintain and extend the existing transport network. The Trent was made navigable to Burton, many new cartbridges were built and footbridges widened. Turnpike trusts were set up from 1727 and short stretches of artificial waterway were built at coalworks.[55]

At a time when the national population was stagnating the population of Midland towns and industrial villages was growing vigorously. The parish registers recorded more baptisms than burials in almost every year and a marked increase in the aggregate number of events. There was a setback in the 1720s but recovery was rapid and the upward movement continued. There was much building of houses and workshops on heathland and wastes, and in the towns much infilling and sub-division of town centre properties. The population of Birmingham doubled between 1680 and 1720 to about 9,000 and again increased to 23,000 by 1750. Wolverhampton's population was about 7,500 by 1751.[56] Meanwhile the populations of the industrial villages also continued to grow more rapidly than the national average. Clergymen's estimates made in 1767 gave the population of Bilston as about 5,000 (a fivefold increase on a listing made in 1700) and Wednesbury as 3,000.[57]

As the towns increased in size so also they became more distinctive in their economic functions and offered a wider range of social services to their region. Birmingham developed a new exclusive residential zone inhabited by the great ironmongers who in wealth and lifestyle overtook

[54] A. and N. Clow, *The Chemical Revolution* (London, 1952); *Victoria County History of Warwickshire*, vol. 7, pp. 84–93.

[55] William Salt Library, Stafford, Hand Morgan MSS uncatalogued. A. L. Thompson, 'Transport in North Staffs in the eighteenth century', *Collections for a History of Staffordshire*, part 1 (1934); C. C. Owen, *The Development of Industry in Burton on Trent*, Phillimore (1978); G. L. Turnbull, 'Provincial road carrying in England in the eighteenth century', *Journal of Transport History*, 4, 1 (1977); Rowlands, *The West Midlands*.

[56] St Martin's, Birmingham, parish register 1660–1740, St Phillip's register Birmingham 1718–40, St John's Chapel register Deritend 1699–1740, St Peter and Paul's register Aston 1660–1740, transcripts in Birmingham Reference Library; J. M. Martin, 'The growth of population in eighteenth century Warwickshire', *Dugdale Society Occasional Papers*, no. 23 (Warwickshire, 1976).

[57] Sedgley parish register transcribed and analysed by Mr F. Barnet, private communication; H. R. Thomas, *Bilston Parish Registers* (Newcastle, Staffordshire Parish Register Society, 1920); transcript of Wednesbury parish register 1562–1812, Birmingham Reference Library; P. Adams, *Rowley Regis Parish Register, 1539–1812* (Newcastle, Staffordshire Parish Register Society, 1912–15; idem, *Transcript of Tipton Parish Register, 1513–1736* (Newcastle, Staffordshire Parish Register Society, 1923); House of Lords Record Office, Main Papers, Return of Papists, 1767; Lichfield Diocese, Lichfield Record Office, B.A./1/12; Rowlands, 'Society and industry', p. 56; Frost, 'Rural industry in South Staffordshire', pp. 269–71.

the mercers and grocers, while the workshops became concentrated in Deritend and Digbeth. Stourbridge, Dudley, Wolverhampton and, above all, Birmingham were increasingly the location of the largest warehouses, and of the new show rooms for luxury goods. The inns in the towns were the nodal points of the network of waggoners and carriers. In the largest of the urban inns the commercial leaders met to exercise real if informal control over prices, wages and policies.[58]

There was much mobility into and out of towns. The upwardly mobile hardwaremen and ironmongers of the industrial villages and smaller towns tended to move to Birmingham in the early eighteenth century where they could take advantage of the central facilities for credit and exchange, of the postal service, and where they could readily be sought out by visiting merchants and gentry. Between 1697 and 1756, 1,300 pauper immigrants were registered, coming mainly from neighbouring industrial parishes and including some skilled men. Some immigrants came into the area from a distance, even from London, and the first Jews had settled in the town by 1751.[59] Birmingham masters registered 800 apprentices between 1720 and 1760, one third of all Warwickshire apprentices. Of the few who recorded their place of origin about half were living in Birmingham, and the remainder came mainly from the small towns and larger villages of Staffordshire, Warwickshire, Worcestershire and Northamptonshire.[60]

The towns enabled Midlanders to follow the fashions of London and of the nobility. Coffee houses and Cold Baths opened in Birmingham, and in Wolverhampton 'elegant' concerts and theatrical entertainments were held. *Aris' Birmingham Gazette* began publication from 1741. Some shops sold confectionery, fine glass and china ware, booksellers sold and loaned books, and doctors of medicine, apothecaries, hairdressers, travelling salesmen and entertainers appealed to the wealthy and fashionable. At the same time the growth in population ensured an increase in the basic food, clothing and service trades.[61] The twenty girls recorded as apprenticed in Birmingham between 1710 and 1760 were almost all bound to mantuamakers and sempstresses.[62]

There was little development of town government. The wealthy ironmongers and shopkeepers took their turn as bailiffs, vestry men and

[58] Based on a study of the Hearth Tax returns, probate records, poor rate books, vestry books and leases of Birmingham, Stourbridge, Wolverhampton and Dudley.

[59] Birmingham Reference Library, 244501, 286011, 298237, 334441, 661020, 68653; R. Pelham, 'The immigrant population of Birmingham 1686–1726', *Transactions of the Birmingham Archaeological Society*, 61 (1937).

[60] R. Smith, *Warwickshire Apprentices and their Masters*, 24 (Warwickshire, Dugdale Society, 1975); J. Lane, 'Apprenticeship in Warwickshire', unpublished Ph.D. thesis (Birmingham, 1977).

[61] *Aris' Birmingham Gazette*, 1743–60.

[62] See n. 60 above.

trustees of charities and schools, but they rarely served more than once in each office and no dominant oligarchy was established. The only corporate town, Walsall, was becoming a byword for disorder and rioting at this period. The lack of sustained interest in local political leadership was probably due in part to the nature of the work of the commercial capitalists which required them to be absent from home a great deal. Their activities and preoccupations were orientated to the world outside the region itself, especially to Europe, the Baltic nations and North America.[63]

Birmingham was beginning to operate as a provincial centre of exchange, and the leading ironmongers and manufacturers dealt directly with overseas merchants. All six towns in the Midlands were, in varying degrees, centres of contact, negotiation and credit for a wider region, responding to the opportunities for profit presented by the growth of the region's population, its increasing concentration of wealth and its improving local and long-distance networks of communication.

In the industrial villages open fields persisted in an attenuated form, although for years they had been subject to encroachment and piecemeal enclosure. There was a growing division between agriculture and industry. In parishes just off the coalfield such as Chaddesley Corbett the dual economy of the earlier period was almost replaced by specialisation in agriculture. It has been shown that in south Staffordshire parishes and in Oldswinford in the Stour Valley the farmers were maintaining crop production by more intensive cultivation but the metalworkers were keeping fewer animals. By the 1750s some farms were specialising in raising horses for carriage of goods.[64]

In the coalfield parishes the numbers of craftsmen far exceeded the numbers of land workers, and many must have been cottagers and landless craftsmen. The trades recorded in Bilston chapel register between 1716 and 1730 included 240 bucklemakers, 160 other toymakers but only 34 labourers and 13 yeomen and husbandmen. Four-fifths of the trades recorded in Sedgley parish register 1680–1740 were industrial and included over 5,000 references to nailers, over 1,200 to colliers and 750 to locksmiths.[65] In the village of Willenhall Dr Wilkes, an experienced and accurate observer, noted that about 1760, there were some 250 houses and

[63] Cambridge University Library, Plumstead MSS Add. 2798/31, 59, 138, 159, 221; Friends House Library, Euston, Lloyd MSS 1/53–75, 2/31–61.
[64] P. Large, 'Urban growth and agricultural change in the West Midlands', in P. Clarke (ed.), *The Transformation of English Provincial Towns* (Leicester, 1982), pp. 184–5; Frost, 'Rural industry in South Staffordshire', pp. 278–350; P. Frost, 'Yeomen, metalsmiths and livestock in the dual economy of South Staffordshire 1560–1720', *Agricultural History Review*, 24 (1981), pp. 32–4; Davies, 'Community, parish and poverty', pp. 64–78.
[65] Registers of Bilston, Sedgley, see n. 57 above.

150 were inhabited by families wholly dependent on lockmaking. When orders for goods fell off, such families were much at risk, and the poor rate was twice as high as in agricultural parishes only a mile or two away.[66]

Parish offices were undertaken in the industrial villages by successful toymakers, hardwaremen and glass manufacturers, but like their fellow officials in the towns they were busy men whose trade took them far afield. Much work was done: new churches were built at Willenhall, Wednesfield and Smethwick, and others were substantially rebuilt, parish schools and workhouses were established, staffed and supervised, but no stable village oligarchy emerged. There was a marked tendency for the local gentry to move away, and the industrial villages retained few leisured or educated families. There were some large houses belonging to doctors of medicine, land stewards and the wealthier tradesmen, and a few important inns and carriers' warehouses, but there were no mercers, drapers or apothecaries, no genteel entertainments and no intellectual opportunities.[67] These were increasingly the specialisms of the towns.

In most of the Midland trades the workmen took on work according to traditional price lists. In brisk times the skilled workman could exercise much bargaining power but when demand fell he and his family might be 'put off' without notice. In coal mining some were employed as individuals, others in teams, some were paid by the day, others according to the quantity of coal raised. In clay mining near the river Stour the 'getter' was paid by the ton, but the 'drawer', who dragged the clay through the wet tunnel to the surface, was paid day wages, a situation which created not only a conflict of interests within the works and of status in the community, but also inhibited the growth of bargaining power.[68] There were traditional ways of retaliating against an oppressive employer: nails were sent off without heads or points, locks without keys, and the gun barrel forgers in 1749 gave notice in the press that unless the price of work was raised the guns would be 'so much the worse'.[69] From time to time the nailers rioted against unemployment or reduced prices. The more skilled masters of family workshops could demonstrate their power by working for rival employers, by not completing orders to time and by combining to assert their terms. By 1759 advertisements were appearing in the press in which groups of workmen of a particular place, the fireshovel makers of Dudley, for example, gave public notice that they would raise the price of their

---

[66] William Salt Library, Stafford, Wilkes MSS vol. 1, p. 6.
[67] William Salt Library, Hand Morgan MSS, Wilkes MSS, Fernyhough newspaper transcripts; Bilston Library, Lawley collection of transcripts; West Bromwich Library, Lissiemore transcripts of vestry books; T. Underhill, *The Ancient Manor of Sedgley* (Sedgley, privately published, 1941).
[68] Dudley Record Office, Bundle 2/15.
[69] *Aris' Birmingham Gazette*, 19 May 1746.

goods 2s or 3s in the pound. The Walsall bucklemakers 'unanimously agreed' that they would allow no discount, and agree the price for metal perquisites, and keep the same credit limits in cash or bills.[70] Although the family workshop and sub-contracting were still the norm, there are occasional indications of skilled metalworkers becoming waged workers, employed in other men's premises, with workspace, power and even tools provided.[71] Like the small masters the journeymen of particular trades also advertised their grievances and demands in the press.[72]

By 1765 the region was already familiar with technological innovation, there was already a large skilled workforce dependent on industry for a living, and a wide diffusion of the experience of manufacture, marketing and management. Relationships of production in both agriculture and industry had long been based on commerce and cash. Potent agents of change, such as the coke-fired blast furnace, the rotative steam engine, and the long-distance canals, were introduced in the next generation not into an agricultural society but into a region which had already served a long apprenticeship to industrialisation.

1765–1830

Knowledge of the earlier phase of industrialisation in the Midlands considerably alters our perception of the developments which followed, revealing how greatly economic growth and social change depended upon a complex and long-drawn-out interaction between innovation and established practices.

The role of the aristocracy and larger landowners after 1765 changed in degree rather than in kind. They became much more active in developing the mineral assets of their estates, but took no direct part in manufacturing industry. On the Dudley estate mining and quarrying were greatly extended, Enclosure Acts facilitated the access to minerals and canals were built which gave access to wider markets for coal. The number of iron furnaces leased out on the Dudley estates increased from three to nine during the period but none were directly worked by the Earl.[73] Lord Dartmouth at West Bromwich ordered boring into the deeper seams and by the 1820s there were 128 coal mines in West Bromwich, including

---

[70] Ibid., 22 Nov. 1759, 27 Oct. 1759.
[71] Rowlands, *Masters and Men*, pp. 159–65.
[72] *Aris' Birmingham Gazette*, 28 June 1759, 26 Nov. 1759, 3 Dec. 1759.
[73] T. J. Raybould, *The Economic Emergence of the Black Country* (Newton Abbot, 1973), pp. 55–68 and 172–96; T. J. Raybould, 'Aristocratic landowners and the industrial revolution: the Black Country experience', *Midland History*, 9 (1984), pp. 59–87.

Heath colliery where coal was 900 feet down.[74] From 1808 the Leveson Gowers became active in developing mining in south Staffordshire.[75] The large aristocratic estates began to employ specialist mining agents, but systems of estate management and accounting remained essentially based on manorial stewardship and profitability and efficiency continued to be adversely affected by inefficient management. Nevertheless, landowners played a major role in enabling others to set up ironworks and coalworks, and in improving transport networks. They continued to promote self-interest directly and regional development indirectly, and in so doing maintained their dominance and continued to enjoy the deference of the community.[76]

There can be no question of the revolutionary impact of the introduction of the coal-fired blast furnace into the area from 1766. Within a single generation, the coke-fired blast furnaces with their accompanying puddling furnaces and rolling mills revolutionised not only the south Staffordshire economy but also its settlement pattern and its landscape. The output of pig iron in Staffordshire rose from 6,900 tons in 1788 to 125,000 tons in 1815 and the Black Country's share of national output rose from 9·8 per cent to 31·6 per cent.[77] The population of the south Staffordshire coalfield parishes more than doubled between 1801 and 1831, some individual parishes increased three and fourfold, and new settlements sprang up near the furnaces.[78] Agriculture became progressively more difficult, the night sky was illumined with flames and the day darkened with smoke, and the district began to be called the Black Country. By 1806 there were twenty-five firms with forty-two coke-fired furnaces in south Staffordshire. A minority of the masters of the new coke furnaces were immigrants from Shropshire, including Wilkinson, Bagnall and Adams, but most of the remainder, Grazebrook, Sparrow, Turton, Gibbons, Bradley, Hallen, Hunt, were men of families with a long tradition in West Midlands industry.[79] There was even some continuation of the interests of the charcoal ironmasters. The Knights and the Spooners converted some mills to the new techniques and the old partnerships were not wound up until the

[74] R. Sturgess, 'Landownership and mining in nineteenth century Staffordshire', in J. T. Ward and R. G. Wilson (eds.), *Land and Industry* (Newton Abbot, 1971), pp. 173–6.
[75] Wordie, *Estate Management*, p. 95.
[76] R. Trainor, 'Peers on an industrial frontier', in D. Cannadine (ed.), *Patricians, Power and Politics* (Leicester, 1982), pp. 69–133.
[77] C. K. Hyde *Technological Change in the British Iron Industry 1700–1870* (London, 1977), p. 114.
[78] G. Barnsby, *Social Conditions in the Black Country 1800–1900* (Wolverhampton, 1980), p. 2.
[79] The lists of ironmasters are derived from trades directories and correlated with the occupations lists built up for the mid-eighteenth century from probate, estate papers, Foley MSS (Hereford Record Office), Knight MSS (Kidderminster Library), Dickinson MSS (Taunton Record Office), Plumstead MSS (Cambridge University Library), Darby MSS (Shrewsbury Record Office); compare F. Crouzet, *The First Industrialists* (Cambridge, 1985).

1820s.[80] Some of the new blast furnaces and puddling works were established by members of the old ironmonger families. The Gibbons family of Sedgley had been lockmakers, ironmongers and coalmasters and now became both ironmasters and bankers.[81] Similarly, Charles and John Wood, and Richard Jesson, who pioneered the development of malleable iron from coke-fired pig, belonged to families long active in the local iron industry.[82] Iron casting and holloware were also developed by men trained in the traditional workshops. Izon and Whitehouse moved from Aston to Greet water mill to make hinges, lathe-turned and cast holloware, and Kenricks moved from bucklemaking in Birmingham to holloware production at Spon Lane.[83] Many established workshops moved to new sites alongside turnpike roads and the new canals, and greatly extended their investment and the size of their undertakings. A few enterprises, like Keir's chemical works, were set up from scratch by men with no previous experience in industry, but these were remarked upon precisely because they were exceptional.[84]

The local demand for coal was dramatically increased by these developments and in 1798 it was calculated that 16,200 tons were being raised weekly. This was achieved by a great extension of the numbers, depth and size of mines and a great increase in the numbers of miners. There were few changes in techniques and little evidence of any intensification of the hours of work. Employment continued to be based on sub-contracting, but the butty or charter system became dominant at this period. In contrast to the team leader of earlier days, the butty did not work in the pit but negotiated the price, collected his team and paid them according to traditional prices and allowances. He took about a quarter of the team's earnings but provided tools, skips and horses.[85]

Steam power continued to be readily adopted wherever water power, human or horse power was insufficient. On Lord Dudley's estates there were sixteen steam engines used for mines drainage by 1802 and thirty-eight by 1839. Boulton and Watt engines were used from 1776 but Newcomen engines continued to be used for both reciprocating and

---

[80] G. Hammersley, 'Did it fall or was it pushed? The charcoal iron industry in the eighteenth century', in T. C. Smout and M. W. Flinn (eds.), *The Search for Wealth and Stability* (London, 1977), pp. 67–87; Kidderminster Library, Knight MSS K 242.

[81] W. A. Smith, 'The contribution of the Gibbons family to technical development in the iron and coal industry', *West Midlands Studies*, 4 (1970), p. 71.

[82] G. R. Morton and N. Mutton, 'The transition to Cort's puddling process', *Journal of the Iron and Steel Institute*, 205 (1967), p. 722.

[83] Dilworth, *Tame Mills*, p. 170; R. A. Church, *Kenricks in Hardware* (Newton Abbot, 1969).

[84] N. G. Coley, 'James Keir, soldier chemist and gentleman', *West Midlands Studies*, 4 (1971), pp. 1–13.

[85] J. Keir, 'The mineralogy of the southwest part of Staffordshire', in Shaw, *History*, vol. 2, pp. 116–23; Barnsby, *Social Conditions*, p. 24.

rotative motion and so did engines built by Pickard, Hornblower, Smeaton and others. Steam power was essential at the furnaces and rolling mills, and was important in enabling large castings to be handled by steam cranes.[86] For many manufacturing processes, however, only small inputs of power were required. In Birmingham by 1835 there were 169 engines at work but they only provided a total of 2,700 horsepower, two-thirds of which was applied in metalworking. Steam power and machinery were not extensively used in the Midland hardware trades until the middle of the nineteenth century,[87] and water power continued to make a significant contribution, in the Midlands as elsewhere. Webster's wire works, for example, were major producers of steel wire turning out several hundredweight a day by water power.[88]

The oliver in various forms was very widely introduced at this time in most of the small metal industries using iron, especially nail, chain, lock, bolt and nut making. This was a treddle hammer which enabled a single workman or woman to operate at a forge alone whereas formerly two persons had been required at each anvil. It had been known and used in other regions for centuries, was made of the simplest materials and could be constructed by the operator himself. The oliver facilitated the manufacture of many items and extended the range and speed of work of the hand workman. The introduction of the fly press in 1790 for cutting out pieces of iron for locks, and a number of improved lathes and casting processes, were also introduced, which did not displace hand labour but enabled a wider range of goods to be produced more quickly. There were some innovations which did threaten to displace the hand worker, as, for example, the casting and machine cutting of nails. However, even these innovations affected only the least-skilled hand workers. The largest nails continued to be made by hand for many years and the skilled processes in brass casting, brass stamping, and plating were still done by hand in most workshops in the 1830s.[89]

[86] Raybould, *Emergence of the Black Country*, p. 224; J. Tann, *Papers of Boulton and Watt*, vol. 1: *The Steam Engine Partnership, 1775–1825* (London, 1981); J. Tann, 'Mr Hornblower and his crew', *Transactions of the Newcomen Society*, 59 (1981); Harris, 'Newcomen engine'; Kanefsky and Robey, 'Steam engines', pp. 161–86.   [87] Court, *Midlands Industries*, p. 257.
[88] J. Horsfall, *The Ironmasters of Penns* (Kineton, 1971); Kanefsky and Robey, 'Steam engines', p. 175; R. Gordon, 'Cost and use of waterpower during industrialisation in New England and Great Britain: a geological interpretation', *Economic History Review*, second series, 36, 2 (1983) pp. 240–59, which suggests that although very heavily used the water power of Midland rivers was by no means fully exploited by the late eighteenth century.
[89] R. Jenkins, 'The Oliver', *Transactions of the Newcomen Society*, 12 (1931); G. Price, *A Treatise on Fire and Thief Proof Repositories and Locks and Keys* (Wolverhampton, 1856); I. E. Davis, 'The home made nail trade of Birmingham and district', unpublished M.Comm. thesis (University of Birmingham, 1933); Church, *Kenricks*, pp. 30–5; R. Prosser, *Birmingham Inventors and Inventions* (Birmingham, 1881); S. Timmins, *Birmingham and the Midland Hardware District* (Birmingham, British Association, 1866), pp. 110–17.

Such simple hand-operated machines could be housed in the existing workshops or in uninhabited houses in the towns. New courts of workshops and houses were built in the towns, and new industrial hamlets of houses and workshops sprang up on the heaths and wastes, and in agricultural parishes neighbouring the coalfield such as Womborne and Northfield. In some workshops each workman operated independently at his own workbench or hearth, and workspace could be hired. Such workshops proliferated in town and industrial village alike. For example, fifty brass workshops were separately listed in the Birmingham directories in 1800 and 250 in 1830, and there were 107 separate buttonmakers in 1812.[90] By the 1830s workshop and home were often separated, especially in the towns, but in the villages the combination of home and workplace persisted until well into the twentieth century.

For the larger operators, there were powerful incentives towards the concentration of production. It was difficult to maintain output in brisk times, employers were frustrated by delinquent carriers, by workmen who failed to meet deadlines, went away at the wrong moment, embezzled materials, or were seduced by rivals offering higher prices for their work, and by customers who wanted to change their orders at short notice.[91] Some manufacturers were using water power and later steam power for part of the sequence of production. In the toy and engineering and glass trades particularly manufacturers needed to establish greater supervision and control of production. A number of much-publicised large firms were established which employed 400 to 700 workers in one place, and made use of machinery, specialisation of process and waged labour. There were also numbers of medium sized firms by 1820, and in both Birmingham and in the Black Country this was probably a significant group.[92]

Capital continued to be raised by industrialists from traditional sources: inheritance, marriage settlements, private loans from family and fellow religionists. From 1766 there were in addition local banks, many of them set up by former ironmongers Lloyd, Galton, Spooner, Molineux, Hordern and many others. By 1800, the West Midlands had a lower ratio of population to bank houses than any other region in the country.[93] It is, however, not clear how far banks assisted industrial development. Larger

[90] *Victoria County History of Warwickshire*, vol. 7, pp. 98–100; E. P. Duggan, *The Impact of Industrialisation on an Urban Economy* (New York, 1985), pp. 25–32; E. Hopkins, 'The trading and service sectors of the Birmingham economy 1750–1800', *Business History*, 28, 3 (1986), pp. 77–96.

[91] Birmingham Reference Library, Galton MSS. 405; B. Smith, 'The Galtons of Birmingham', *Business History*, 9 (1967).

[92] *Victoria County History of Warwickshire*, vol. 7, pp. 94–8; M. Berg, *The Age of Manufactures* (London, 1985), pp. 94–8.

[93] Duggan, *The Impact of Industrialisation*, p. 48.

enterprises were usually set up by means of partnerships. Stewards of trust funds and private investors were willing to invest large amounts with strangers through the intermediary of an attorney. On this basis firms like Chance and Homer could mobilise capital of tens of thousands of pounds and attract corresponding credit.[94] Trade credit and retained earnings continued to be the principal way of financing the operating costs of firms large and small.

The leading manufacturers established institutions which served their own needs such as the Chamber of Commerce, the Proof House and the Assay Office, they lobbied for canal acts and better postal services, and set up the Birmingham Brass Company. However, these were public facilities available to small masters as well as large manufacturers and thus promoted dispersed as well as concentrated production. This was also true of the extension of market opportunities; the larger manufacturers established foreign markets, developed advertising techniques and attracted wholesale customers to the Midlands, but in so doing benefited others besides themselves. Workmen with their own tools constantly imitated the products of the famous houses at cut prices, and the larger concerns had a very real fear of such competition.[95]

Much work continued to be charged according to traditional price lists. These were extended and adapted to include new products and processes and became subject to negotiated discounts or percentage reductions, which fluctuated with the availability of work.[96] Even in large undertakings many of the workers were sub-contractors hiring and paying their own assistants until far into the nineteenth century. In the furnaces the bridgestockers continued to be paid for the work of their assistants as well as their own, and so did founders. Casters were paid according to the price lists for customary quantities and employed as many assistants as they needed at a weekly rate, whilst glassworkers were paid for the production of articles as a 'chair' of four workers. Masters' associations met annually to fix prices and discounts.[97]

Women were widely employed both in larger works and in domestic workshops. At George Symcox' works cheap buckles, curtain rings and finger rings were cast in brass mainly by 'women, children and some men' in 1812. Women were employed in less-skilled, repetitive tasks and in packing. Children were frequently employed, though rarely in great

[94] Ibid., pp. 58–65; D. J. Moss, 'The private banks of Birmingham', Business History, 24, 1 (1982), pp. 79–95.
[95] British Parliamentary Papers, 1812, III, Minutes of Evidence on the Petition against the Orders in Council.
[96] Price, Treatise, p. 88.
[97] Timmins, Midland Hardware District, p. 110; Church, Kenricks, pp. 56–8; W. K. V. Gale, A History of the Black Country Iron Industry (Newton Abbot 1966), p. 24.

numbers in any one place, mainly to serve the adults and prepare the work for them. It was in the domestic workshop that women and children most frequently worked alone, a change facilitated by the introduction of the treddle hammer. Men worked away from the home in puddling mills and rolling mills or making large chain, whilst women and children continued to work in domestic workshops making small chain or nails. Flexible and irregular working hours persisted both in domestic workshops and in large works, a practice derived both from the antecedent domestic economy and from the nature of the work itself. It has recently been shown that there was no great increase in the hours or regularity of work in either Birmingham or the Black Country before 1830.[98]

Both old and new methods of employment had advantages to the employer. Some men worked full time for a single employer with tools and workspace provided. Such an arrangement might be formalised by employer and servant entering into binding indentures to work fixed hours at an agreed rate. Although Boulton at Soho made use of indentured employees and also of workers on time wages, his manager in 1772 urged a return to piece-work rates, with workmen providing their tools and paying rent for their bench space, and a combined system gradually emerged.[99] At Kenricks some employees were on piece work and some at day work rates, although some control was exercised by signed agreements with the pieceworkers binding them to Kenricks for a specified period.[100] Apprenticeship too was changing. Whereas formerly apprentices had been members of the master's 'family', educated, maintained and supervised by him, now many 'apprentices' lived in their own homes, and were paid to work in the master's shop at rates consonant with their youth and inexperience. The transition from semi-independent artisan to waged 'hand' was proceeding, but in a very gradual and erratic manner under a variety of social and economic pressures.[101]

The numbers of non-producing intermediaries and factors were increasing significantly in many Midland industries at this period, and the distance between employer and employed was widening. The multiplication of specialisms and sub-division of both the production and marketing processes led to the employment of agents, factors, warehousemen, riders,

[98] Berg, *Manufactures*, pp. 306–10; British Parliamentary Papers, 1833 (519) XXI, *Report of the Royal Commission on the Employment of Children*; British Parliamentary Papers, 1843 (430) XIII, *Second Report of the Royal Commission on Children's employment*; E. Hopkins, 'Working hours and conditions during the industrial revolution', *Economic History Review*, second series, 35, 1 (1982), pp. 52–67; D. Reid, 'The decline of St Monday', *Past and Present*, 21 (1976), pp. 76–102.

[99] N. Goodison, *Ormoulu* (London, 1974), pp. 13–15, 240–1.

[100] Church, *Kenricks*, pp. 38, 55–8.

[101] J. Lane, 'Apprenticeship in Warwickshire', unpublished Ph.D. thesis (University of Birmingham, 1977); *Aris' Birmingham Gazette*, 1760–90.

butties and intermediaries at every level. At the same time it was still open for many producers to make direct sales of their products to the consumers.[102]

The persistence of the traditional patterns of production, industrial organisation, techniques and processes was not merely an example of inertia in the face of inevitable change. The older modes of production had a continued economic value, and it is worth noting in this connection that three different detailed studies of Boulton and Fothergill's toy manufactory agree that the enterprise was overcapitalised, and never really financially successful.[103] The West Midlands was one of the most successful industrial regions of the late eighteenth century, yet its social and economic structures remained very different from those classically associated with the forefront of Britain's industrialisation in the cotton sector of south Lancashire. Work practices, commercial organisation and the structure of society in both town and village showed a remarkable continuity in their nature from the sixteenth to the nineteenth centuries. This continuity was in part the product of long-established agrarian regimes associated with scattered open settlements, where the continued availability of poor quality heath and open land facilitated the growth of rural handicrafts and accommodated population increase. The resident gentry also continued to play an important role alongside industrial leaders and urban merchants in the rise of mining and manufacturing and instead of becoming polarised into 'capitalist' and 'proletarian' elements, Midland society comprised an ever-greater range of social status.

A study of the West Midlands hardware district provides an alternative model of industrialisation, one of diversified responses and multi-faceted change. Adaptation and extension of existing methods could be as important as radical change, and tradition and innovation could be effectively and successfully combined. The particular regional outcome depended upon the particular products and production processes, the social and agrarian context and even upon individual responses to change and opportunity. It is probably a false simplification to create an academic dichotomy between the 'traditional' and the 'innovative'. Recent studies have shown that the differences in the process of economic transformation

---

[102] S. R. Jones, 'The country trade and the marketing of Birmingham hardware, 1750–1810', *Business History*, 26, 1 (1984), pp. 24–43; Hopkins, 'Birmingham Economy', pp. 87–8; Barnsby, *Social Conditions*, p. 50.

[103] E. Hopkins, 'Boulton before Watt: the early career reconsidered', *Midland History*, 9 (1984), pp. 43–59; J. C. Cule, 'A financial history of Boulton and Fothergill', unpublished M.Comm. thesis (University of Birmingham, 1932); Goodison, *Ormoulu*.

between Birmingham and Manchester have been exaggerated.[104] More and more regional studies of industrialisation in Britain and mainland Europe have been published in the last thirty years, and as a result, the Midlands experience no longer appears to be an exception to a 'normal' process of revolutionary and sudden change. Instead it appears to be a good example of one process of industrialisation by gradual transformation, a process which was holistic and not merely economic, and within which there was a necessary interaction of continuity and innovation.

[104] Duggan, *The Impact of Industrialisation*, pp. 200–8; Hopkins, 'Birmingham economy', pp. 80–4.

Chapter 5

Stages of industrialisation in Cumbria

JOHN D. MARSHALL

Cumbria[1] was undoubtedly one of Britain's recognised textile regions during the late medieval and early modern periods. It had a class of manorial tenants or small yeoman whose activities embraced the main stages of woollen production, and whose work took them into a variety of crafts and small industries. The region also employed water power in such a way as to cause economic historians of a past generation to take it seriously as one of the main seats of an 'industrial revolution' in the thirteenth century.[2] However, water power continued to play a significant part in the economic activities of the Cumbrian region until the twentieth century. If we are to write of an industrial transition in Cumbria, it was certainly a long time in the making and, furthermore, the seeds of later de-industrialisation were to some extent sown alongside it. Rural industries became varied and widespread, notably so between the Tudor period and the end of the eighteenth century, but none was powerful enough in its effects to act monocausally on population movements (save, briefly, the copper mining of the late sixteenth century), and none can be easily identified as having stimulated major social transformations. The north and west of the region certainly experienced some major industrial developments in the nineteenth century, but their leading sectors (cotton, coal and steel) bore little direct or organic relationship to the earlier, more widely diffused industries of the Cumbrian land-mass as a whole. Accordingly, the proto-industrialisation concept is hard to apply to the region. Nevertheless, distinct chronological stages may usefully be identified in analysing the economic and social development of Cumbria

The following abbreviations are used

CWAAS (NS)   *Transactions of the Cumberland and Westmorland Antiquarian and Archaeological Society* (New Series).

BJ   C. M. L. Bouch and G. P. Jones, *A Short Economic and Social History of the Lake Counties* (Manchester, 1961).

[1] The area discussed in this chapter is that of the modern administrative county of Cumbria, consisting of the former Cumberland, Westmorland and Lonsdale North of the Sands (i.e. Furness).

[2] See E. M. Carus-Wilson, 'An industrial revolution of the thirteenth century', *Economic History Review*, 11 (1941), pp. 39ff. This fashion for detecting 'industrial revolutions' has now died.

after the late middle ages, each stage shading gradually – but not too imperceptibly! – into the next. Each exhibited a rich and contradictory mix of pre-industrial, proto-industrial and industrialised characteristics, and each had elements of dynamism as well as elements of stability within it.

This chapter aims to discuss the nature and the dynamism of three stages in the development of Cumbrian industries and society between the thirteenth and the nineteenth centuries, starting with a summary of their main characteristics.

Stage One: feudalism, textiles and mining (c. 1300–1660)

This stage was notable for the prevalence of an internationally recognised manufacture of coarse woollen textiles, mainly in Westmorland. Of the centres of control and population, only Kendal was of real significance, and the main source of economic support for the region was agrarian, with a primarily subsistence economy which was held back by military insecurity at the border, feudal tenures, poor soils and small holdings. Although water power was used successively in fulling, iron smelting and copper smelting, feudal dues were claimed from such installations: a form of exaction which, with heriots and labour services, lasted into the following stage. The region was a poor one and, where parish registers make analysis possible for the sixteenth and seventeenth centuries, the population showed sensitivity to food shortage and disease.[3] From 1564, large-scale state-induced copper mining was brought into the central Lake District by the Company of Mines Royal. Some small-scale iron manufacture, coal mining and salt boiling operated on and near the western seaboard, as did a number of woodland industries, but their economic and social effects were clearly localised. The latter can also be said about the finishing stages of the Westmorland woollen industry, whereas the operations and effects of the Mines Royal were more diffused.

Stage Two: the consolidation of rural industry and the growth of towns (1660–1790)

Although the major event of this period was the development, under the Lowthers, of the coal industry of the Cumberland coast, there were also quantitative and qualitative changes throughout Cumbrian rural industry and throughout its farming economy. The latter did not experience an agrarian 'revolution', but instead there was an accumulation of peasant

---

[3] Andrew B. Appleby, *Famine in Tudor and Stuart England* (Liverpool, 1978), pp. 95–154; see also P. Laslett, *The World We Have Lost*, 2nd edn (London, 1971), pp. 121–3.

savings within it, one which was evidently related to the effects of a growing cattle trade as well as to the textile and a mass of smaller industries. Agrarian feudal tenures were weakened, partly because the peasantry resisted them and partly because manorial courts themselves declined in the eighteenth century, a process gradually assisted by the enfranchisement of many manorial tenants. Rural trades and industries developed and diversified, including those crafts like tanning and malting which were associated with woodland and farm. The country iron industry developed a more advanced technology, and the paper, gunpowder and cotton industries became firmly established in suitable localities, mainly in the south of the region. The woollen textile industry, increasingly supported by hand-knitting in the eastern dales, continued to use Kendal as a trading, productive and finishing centre, and during this stage linsey-woolseys and Kendal 'cottons' (rough woollens) found markets in the colonies. Other towns, like Carlisle, Cockermouth and Penrith, acquired secondary textile industries as linen manufacture developed in west Cumberland and as, ultimately, a calico industry appeared in the Carlisle area post-1760. Economic activity was vibrant enough to provide sustenance for a considerable regional increase of population following 1740, and market towns expanded accordingly. Since the numbers of Cumbrian farmholdings did not (judging by sample data) increase verifiably in the same period, there was a greater landless population, part of which migrated to the local towns or left the region altogether. Many local families were supported by rural or urban industry, but in some parts of the region, rural spinning and weaving declined during this stage. As before, water power was extensively applied to all the more advanced manufactures, and the factory system (in cotton) appeared at the northern and southern edges of the region by the 1780s.

Stage Three: the concentration of the iron, steel, coal and textile industries, and the quickening of rural and other de-industrialisation (1790–1914)

A phase of marked regional town growth (1790–1831) was accompanied by lower rates of population growth in the countryside. Rural and semi-rural industries, which now included spade manufacture, widespread bobbin turning, cotton spinning, flax and tow spinning and the weaving of cotton checks, developed rapidly, and the regional use of water power was at its peak by 1850. But the rural iron industry, which had been at its most productive in 1750, was already in a state of relative stagnation and ultimate decline - and other rural crafts followed this pattern in the second half of the nineteenth century. The rural economy was supported by considerable small-unit and traditional style mixed farming, which adjusted itself to the demand of town markets for beef, butter and milk. The small farmer with a dual occupation, although not the smallholder with under five acres, had all but disappeared by 1850, and after that date there was an increased movement of population from the Cumbrian countryside, some of it into the towns and industrial villages of the west Cumberland coastal plain. Farmers turned their land increasingly to grass, thereby helping the out-migration, relying themselves on family labour. Industry, and population, became more obviously concentrated in the coastal districts of west Cumberland and Furness after 1860. This rapid process, based on the existing coal industry and also on a national market for the rich haematite ore of those districts, was accelerated by the regional building of railways, 1836–60. After the latter date, advanced smelting technology was utilised to make iron in the west of the region, and the phosphorus-free nature of the local ores aided the rapid introduction of the Bessemer process. Great regional landlords, like the Lowthers, Cavendishes and Curwens, played a major part in this industrialising phase, and the towns of Barrow and Workington grew at great speed as a consequence of the steel and transport revolutions. But during these boom years of the 1860s and the early 1870s the important Carlisle cotton industry, isolated from its competitors, began to contract, and by 1870 the nationally important Lake District bobbin industry was facing destructive competition from Scandinavia. The gunpowder industry continued to cater for national markets, as did the copper, lead and silver mines of the Cumbrian massif, but de-industrialisation was progressively occurring. It worked selectively and slowly, at once cause and effect as rural population thinned. Water power continued to find new applications in a variety of small industries like silk manufacture, electro-plating and brushmaking, but these ventures did not call for much labour, and the outward drift of population proceeded to such effect that more than 100,000 people left Cumbria during the middle and late nineteenth century. By 1900, the seeds of west Cumberland industrial decline were making themselves manifest, as the great haematite deposits became more costly to work, and as the basic process of steelmaking destroyed the former near-monopoly of non-phosphoric ore and 'Bessemer iron'. During these late Victorian years, only one important and enduring 'industry' burgeoned: that of Lake District holiday provision and tourism.

Before proceeding to a more general discussion of these three stages, we should notice that several industrial strands are common to each, namely activity in iron manufacture, copper and coal mining, and textiles. But one must not on this account fall into the trap of analysing the region's development as a straightforward evolutionary process from one stage to the next. Significant discontinuities occurred, and developments in the second and third stages were not always closely linked to those within earlier centuries or within the previous stage.

STAGE ONE: FEUDALISM, TEXTILES AND MINING (c. 1300–1660)

The Kendal-based woollen textile industry was, without doubt, the most important textile manufacture in Cumbria between the thirteenth and the nineteenth centuries. Its influence was mainly felt in the southern and eastern dales of the region, however, and other woollen and linen industries of the north and west were undeveloped and local in their impact. Carlisle, in the mid-sixteenth century had guilds of merchants and weavers, but had no such bodies of shearmen and dyers:[4] craftsmen essential to a fully developed system of production. The border territories, which had contained scattered fulling mills before that period,[5] were subject to Scots raids and general insecurity up to the Union of the Crowns, and this area of the region does not seem to have produced a cloth with a distinctive or local title – unlike the famous Kendal Green which was produced and sold by 'Kendalmen', nor even the low-value coarse 'Cartmels' which, according to the terms of a statute of 1609, resembled other southern Cumbrian cloth in being sufficiently low-grade to be exempt from searching and sealing.[6]

The Kendal-based industry had deep historical roots. Carus-Wilson identified nineteen fulling mill sites, some of them undoubtedly connected with this industry, in remote parts of the Lake District for dates in the thirteenth century.[7] But it is hard to accept her claim for an 'industrial revolution' in a region which was fundamentally pre-industrial in its rigidity of social order and occupational structure. An insight into this structure is given by the lay subsidy rolls of 1332, which show that 'small-scale rural industry' was very much additional to and subordinate to animal husbandry.[8] The latter was indeed important for its production of raw wool, exploited by the regional monastic houses led by Furness and Holm Cultram, and supplies from Cumbria had found their way to Italian buyers by c. 1315.

---

[4] The eight Carlisle guilds of 1561 were the merchants, butchers, smiths, tailors, tanners, weavers, skinners and shoemakers, these bodies having agreed to the Dormant Book's rules for the good government of the town; information by courtesy of Mr B. C. Jones. There were, however, scattered dyers and shearmen in the Carlisle area in 1332; see C. M. Fraser, 'Cumberland and Westmorland lay subsidies for 1332', CWAAS (NS), 66 (1966), p. 152.

[5] Fraser, 'Lay subsidies for 1332', p. 152; Carus-Wilson, 'An industrial revolution', p. 48.

[6] This theme of the exemption of Cumbrian and northern cloth from sealing was an old one, and a statute of 1390, and others in 1407 and 1410, refer to it; BJ, p. 135.

[7] Carus-Wilson, 'An industrial revolution', p. 48.

[8] Fraser, 'Lay subsidies for 1332', pp. 152–3.

The drive towards local manufacture may well have come initially from the towns rather than from the abbeys or priories; hence, fulling mills appeared in Cockermouth *c.* 1200, and in both Carlisle and Kendal two or three decades later. Charters of the mid-thirteenth century for Kendal, Ulverston and Warton refer to fulling and dyeing as being monopolised by the lord of the borough in each case, and there is little doubt that fullers were driven into remote places by seigneurial exactions. There was certainly a movement of such mills into the country in the Cockermouth area,[9] and Kentmere tenants apparently preferred to full their cloth in Staveley rather than to perform suit at the lord's fulling mill in Kendal (in 1274). The establishment of the country mills, following those in the towns, meant that several of the preparatory textile processes (washing, combing, spinning and weaving) as well as fulling received additional stimulus and became more widely diffused in the countryside.[10]

The fourteenth century brought interruptions to trade from war, famine and pestilence, but a renewed development of the south Cumbrian cloth industry may have occurred in the fifteenth, with a lesser but parallel rise of the textile industries in central Cumberland.[11] There were, during this century, European customers for the region's cloth as well as for its wool, and packs of Kendal friezes went 'occasionally' to Spain via Bristol.[12] Such a widespread market was associated with a Kendal-centred collecting area for yarn and wool which had spread as far as St Bees by 1517, and the size of that area is measured by the presence of 'Kendilmen' in Low Furness and in Skipton in 1509–10.[13] This territorial measurement is important, for it underlines the fact that the cloth industry was not spread throughout Cumbria with equal effect or intensity. There is little doubt about the primacy of the controlling town of Kendal, for out of twenty-four 'Kendalmen' or chapmen exporting cloth through Southampton in 1552–3, twenty-two were entered in the Cloth Hall accounts of the port as coming from Kendal itself – the two remaining men came from Ambleside and Crook respectively. The Kendal and Westmorland merchants were responsible for transporting 1,999 cloths through the port in the years

---

[9] Data by courtesy of Dr A. J. L. Winchester, in advance of his book *Landscape and Society in Mediaeval Cumbria* (Edinburgh, 1987); for the charters, J. Munby, 'Mediaeval Kendal; the first borough charter', *CWAAS* (NS), 85, (1985), p. 103.

[10] M. L. Armitt, *Rydal* (Kendal, 1906), pp. 199–210; for confirmatory data based on original sources, indicating that the local fulling mills remained in use between the thirteenth and the sixteenth centuries, W. Farrer and J. F. Curwen, *Records Relating to the Barony of Kendale* (3 vols., Kendal, 1923, 1924, 1926), vol. 1, pp. 244, 323–5, 332, 333, 357, 370; vol. 2, pp. 1–4, 24, 47.

[11] Data on the Cumbrian woollen industry by courtesy of Dr Winchester.

[12] E. M. Carus-Wilson, 'The overseas trade of Bristol', in M. M. Postan and E. Power (eds.), *Studies in English Trade in the Fifteenth Century* (London, 1934), pp. 188, 216.

[13] *BJ*, p. 28; Winchester, *Landscape and Society*, Ch. 7, p. 3.

mentioned, of which just over 1,000 were 'cottons' (woollens with a particular kind of raised nap). The cloths or webs themselves were 13 yards long,[14] and must have taken up to a fortnight to weave. Up to eighty looms, then, would have been required to produce the *c.* 2,000 cloths export figure that is mentioned here. It is known that other regional cloth went to Ireland, and there was a real but unspecified home market, so that an annual regional manufacture of some 6,000 webs would seem reasonable for this particular period.

How much employment did this widespread industry bring in its train? And what was its economic and social impact? Westmorland's households, according to an ecclesiastical survey of 1563,[15] came to a total of 6,417, and, if we allow that some of these households were in inaccessible places or were not in a position to provide labour, then this figure will do as an approximation for the wider Kendal textile area (including Furness and the border dales of Yorkshire). Of these households, between 200 and 300 could have provided the full-time weavers or websters that were necessary for the late sixteenth-century cloth production (if we accept the rough calculations already given). Spinning was largely part time and seasonal, employing women and children especially in the winter months. If we allow up to ten spinning households per loom, it can be estimated that between one third and one half of all households in the Kendal-dominated textile area were involved in the industry. This level of involvement is partly supported in calculations based on later material in probate inventories.[16] Full-time employments, however, were relatively few. They included many of the weavers themselves (some of whom were yeoman occupiers with a farming background), about a hundred workers at between thirty and forty fulling mill sites, and the mainly town-operating finishers or shearman-dyers, forty or fifty in all.[17] These figures will show that the Kendal-based

[14] B. C. Jones, 'Westmorland packhorse-men in Southampton', *CWAAS* (NS), 59 (1959), pp. 65–84, and especially pp. 70-1, where the length of the webs is mentioned.

[15] Appleby, *Famine*, p. 25; the survey quoted here is from Harleian MS 594, fos. 85–7, 105–6.

[16] Principally from the Archdeaconry of Richmond collection of wills and inventories at the Lancashire Record Office, WRW. Rates of production in spinning and weaving depended to some extent on the type of work undertaken. It has been assumed in this calculation that the weavers were virtually full time, which many of them probably were not. Likewise much of the spinning and preparatory work was probably occasional only, and was performed in the winter. A full-time weaver in the Lancashire conditions of the eighteenth century might employ three to six spinners; see A. P. Wadsworth and J. de. L. Mann, *The Cotton Trade and Industrial Lancashire 1600–1780* (Manchester, 1931), pp. 90, 275. The inventories show very tiny quantities of yarn, and full-time Cumbrian spinners were few.

[17] MS of census held at the Record Office, Kendal (WD/Ry), and taken in August 1695, under the terms of the Acts of *6 and 7 William and Mary* Cap. 6 (1694) and *7 and 8 William and Mary* Cap. 35 (1695). This census gives the shearman dyers, weavers and others then resident in Kendal, which had not increased in population in the seventeenth century, and it is therefore a useful basis for calculating earlier occupational numbers. For late sixteenth-century Kendal occupations, see *A Boke Off Recorde*, ed. R. S. Ferguson (Kendal, 1892), pp. 137–44.

industry cannot have supported much more than about 500 full-time occupations. Outside that town, the main boroughs of the region, Cockermouth, Carlisle, Egremont and Appleby, clearly had much more modest involvements in cloth manufacture and sale, with Cockermouth in the lead. Nevertheless, textile activity brought very small incomes, usually part time, to at least one third of the region's 18,000 households,[18] although it should be noted that probate inventory entries relating to wool and yarn (1560–1640) rarely exceed the value of a few shillings. Yet it is almost certain that textile involvements helped to build up the considerable savings which are a feature of the inventories of the period.[19] Moreover, spinning, carding and weaving fitted into the farming calendar, and could be performed without detriment to the work in field or byre.

The spread and distribution of these employments was not even throughout the regional countryside. There is a useful illustration of this in data from the probate inventories for the Kendal area of influence, which become available from 1578. Some 60 per cent of households from a sample of 100 such inventories for Furness Deanery, 1578–1640, show no clear indicator of involvement in textile production, and this non-involvement related noticeably to the Low Furness area, where only seventeen out of fifty show signs of an interest in the spinning or the preparation of yarn – and the yarn was as likely to be hemp or flax as it was to be wool. But another sub-group within the same sample, made up of households from the Hawkshead district, demonstrates a striking degree of involvement, with seventeen out of twenty-five possessing three out of four desiderata, wool, yarn, wheels and 'studdles' or loom frames, in addition to the common household or farming gear.[20] It is known that Hawkshead stood in a close relationship with Kendal and its industries, and that it was a supplier of both woollen yarn and leather to the Westmorland town. This example raises the question of how far proto-industry could take the form of this kind of rural–urban productive continuum, perhaps commencing in 'patches' or specific localities. Even here, however, there were complexities, for Hawkshead, as will be shown, developed a mass of crafts and by-industries, not all of which had direct connections with local towns. Individual farm households could show signs of having several members of families engaged in different crafts.

[18] Appleby, *Famine*, p. 25, for supporting calculations; it has been necessary to make some allowance for Furness households, by adding 2,000 to the general Cumbrian total.

[19] This generalisation applies to the later seventeenth century, for which detailed figures are available from calculations relating to the Archdeaconry of Richmond collection. For the sixteenth century, samples show between a quarter and a third of the gross values of probate inventories held in bonds and specialities. It is unlikely that much of this was derived from the sale of cereals or animal products, and textile and other by-occupations suggest the original sources of the modest wealth. It should be borne in mind that the poorer members of society did not file inventories, however.

[20] Archdeaconry of Richmond collection, sample specimens from Furness Deanery files,WRW.

It is important to consider briefly the type of tenure and farming that was prevalent in Kendal area and the rest of Cumbria, and to outline the inheritance customs that were followed on the manors of the region, because these had some bearing on the occupations to which farming families turned. Farming was small scale, and occupiers of between 10 and 15 statute acres were common in the sixteenth century, pursuing a mixture of subsistence cultivation of oats and barley with animal husbandry, mainly of small sheep flocks that produced the wool for the cloth industry. The farmer himself was typically a manorial tenant, but his geographical position near the border with Scotland, and his consequent liability to perform military service in its defence, had given him a special fixity of tenure known as *tenant right*, and had caused many thousands of the tenants to call themselves *yeomen*. The existence of tenant right meant in practice that the lord of a manor could not prevent a nominated heir from succeeding to the tenement or holding, and the implicit succession was through primogeniture or through a nominee.[21] The aim of the inheritance custom was that of keeping the tenement intact for military purposes (in order that it could maintain its armed man), but there was nothing in the custom to prevent an occupier or tenant from setting a family of adult children, on or near the tenement, to a variety of occupations. It may be that a wholly unofficial system of splitting tenements appeared in Cumbria in the late sixteenth century, for there were complaints of such partition at that period.[22] But the system certainly did not last, and primogeniture undoubtedly contributed to the pressures making for an increase of by-occupations.

What other occupations and by-occupations were typical of the region by the sixteenth century? The most common ones occurring in yeoman inventories are tanner, carpenter, roughmason or waller and blacksmith, but there is evidence of others, like charcoal burner (collier), quarryman, salt boiler, cooper, turner and basketmaker (the last three being woodland occupations, perhaps of a seasonal or part-time nature). Many followers of

[21] It should be noticed that the concept of tenant right is subject to refinement, even though its military significance is not usually challenged; see R. W Hoyle, '"An Ancient and Laudable Custom"; the definition and development of tenant right in North Western England', *Past and Present*, 116 (1987), especially, p. 25, where the author does not accept border service as the sole distinguishing feature of the tenure. See also, for variations in partibility, R. T. Spence, 'The pacification of the Cumberland borders, 1593–1628', *Northern History*, 13 (1977), p. 63. Otherwise the present writer's assertion is based upon examination of numerous wills in the Archdeaconry of Richmond collection.

[22] See the well-known case of the provisions in the Customs of High Furness, 1576, complaining of the 'dividing and portioning of tenements' (P.R.O., Duchy of Lancaster; Special Commissions; No. 398), quoted *in extenso* in A. E. Bland, P. A. Brown and R. H. Tawney, *English Economic History: Select Documents* (London, 1914), pp. 232–4. The crown ordered that undue sub-division should cease; but this, as a crown manor, was probably not typical of others.

these crafts had farm gear, and were scarcely full time in the more recent sense. In addition, the region exhibited a number of key industries outside textiles, the most important of these being copper mining and iron smelting. These were accompanied by activity (on a much lesser scale) in coal mining and the extraction of lead, silver and iron ore. The coal mining was localised near the west Cumberland coast, and was on a small scale, whereas the copper enterprises were large and state-induced, having the greatest local impact of any single industry. The main copper mines were at Keswick and Coniston from 1564 to *c.* 1603, and were operated by the Company of Mines Royal. These enterprises were set going with the help of several scores of skilled miners from the Harz and the Austrian Tyrol, but they also made considerable use of local labour. A list of 1574 for wage and other payments contains over 360 names of persons in an area extending for 12 to 15 miles across the Lake District, with Keswick as a centre.[23] There was an appreciable population increase in the parish of Crosthwaite, of which Keswick is a part, between 1571 and about 1620, but this is the only known case in which one industry had an identifiable effect upon population, either by stimulating natural increase or by encouraging in-migration – or both. No other industry, local or regional, had such a traceable demographic effect in the period before the eighteenth century.

The early regional iron industry manifested a more or less continuous development in scale and techniques from one stage to the next. It was essentially small scale before about 1660, and until 1600 it could have been seen as an adjunct to peasant or yeoman farming, with a few men working with bellows at a small hearth and producing a 'make' of roughly 1 ton a year. By that time, however, the bloomsmithy, which made use of water-powered bellows, had effected its appearance, and in the early seventeenth century this type of production was established in the region with at least seven known examples.[24] The industry as a whole created a heavy demand for charcoal, one which clearly clashed with the needs of the Mines Royal,[25] and the requirements or exactions of the latter seem to have resulted in the closing of bloomsmithies in the Furness Fells from 1564.[26] Bloomery and other operators either turned to small-scale copper smelting or simply continued to work for domestic purposes.[27] The scale of operations at the

[23] *BJ*, p. 127; see also W. G. Collingwood, *Elizabethan Keswick*, Cumberland and Westmorland Antiquarian and Archaeological Society Tract Series, 8 (Kendal, 1912), especially pp.120ff.
[24] C. B. Phillips, 'William Wright, Cumbrian ironmaster', *Transactions of the Lancashire and Cheshire Antiquarian Society*, 79 (1977), pp. 34–45.
[25] See *BJ*, p. 128.
[26] Ibid., p. 128.
[27] The evidence here is archaeological; copper slag has been found in bloomery sites, identified and enumerated by Mr M. Davies-Shiel and others.

point of production gives no measure of the number of persons involved in the supply and carting of fuel or the carriage of ore and iron; one bloomery forge, with two or three men working in it, and producing about 20 tons a year, had as many as thirty men burning charcoal or otherwise engaged in the activities mentioned.[28] The bloomeries which have left their traces in some 300 identified sites in the southern, central and west Cumbrian dales were used for a few weeks at a time, which suggests that the iron industry directly employed as many as 100 men on a seasonal basis. Coal mining, often performed by yeomen, employed very few at this period, but the small pits of west Cumberland were sending modest tonnages to Ireland after 1605, thus helping to establish a trade which became of great importance regionally in the next stage.[29]

The survey of employment so far given, necessarily a very tentative one, can be seen to produce the equivalent of between 1,000 and 2,000 full-time industrial occupations. But, as we have seen, there were many part-time ones, so that anything up to one third of a regional population of 18,000 households could have been touched by industrial or craft activity. However, other indications suggest that the numbers of part-time occupations did not markedly increase until after 1660 and, especially, until the eighteenth century. Before 1660, industrialisation in Cumbria was significant for what it had to portend rather than for what it could actually achieve in altering the ways of life of the region's people or in transforming assumptions and traditional attitudes. One may detect a rise of individualism in the customaryhold disputes of the seventeenth century, when small yeomen and husbandmen combined forces in numerous manors to resist the exactions of landlords, or when George Fox and the Quakers found a ready response to their missionary work in the Kendal cloth area and its regional environs.[30] But there was little profound economic or social change to influence any demographic changes permanently or directly, despite some apparent population growth in Tudor and Stuart Cumberland.[31] The population of Kendal seems hardly to have grown at all in

[28] Brian G. Awty, 'Force forge in the seventeenth century', CWAAS (NS), 77 (1977), pp. 97–112.

[29] J. V. Beckett, Coal and Tobacco: The Lowthers and the Economic Development of West Cumberland, 1660–1760 (Cambridge, 1981), pp. 14, 39, for early Lowther enterprise and exports to Ireland from 1605.

[30] For outlines of the copyhold or tenant-right struggle, BJ, pp. 74–6, and also Mildred Campbell, The English Yeoman under Elizabeth and the Early Stuarts (London. 1942), pp. 149ff; for the Quakers, BJ, pp. 179–83.

[31] W. G. Howson, 'Plague, poverty and population in parts of North-West England', Transactions of the Historic Society of Lancashire and Cheshire, 112 (1960), pp. 29–55, but especially 43–4. The late Giles Howson, a pioneer of historical demography who aggregated numbers of Cumbrian parish registers, concluded that the regional economy was 'rigid' at this Stage One period. See the independent calculations in BJ, p. 82, and in Appleby, Famine, p. 29 and passim. It is most unlikely that any regional population growth was stimulated by the direct effects of industry at this time; Malthusian factors seem to offer more likely explanations.

the seventeenth century,[32] and this apparent stagnation contrasts curiously with a greater sensitivity of Kendal textile producers and traders towards the needs of markets in Ireland, the West Indies, the Baltic and France, as the town's cloth manufacture became more quality directed, using longer staples in the age of the New Draperies.[33] The regional ironmakers, for their part, were largely serving a Cumbrian market.[34]

It is striking, indeed, that a supposedly backward and poverty-stricken area[35] should have contained so many industrial and marketing connections and growth points within it, and the explanation may be that there were two forms of economic activity, one type with (in most cases) very limited effects on the region as a whole, like coal mining and metalliferous mining, and another, like textiles or iron smelting, which affected more people over wide areas but usually only on a part-time or subsidiary basis. The backwardness of the very large agrarian sector, with its profound traditionalism reflected in the standard possessions and farming gear within probate inventories, must at the same time be given full weight. A multiplication of non-textile handicrafts was occurring alongside a form of 'industrialisation' which was also partially non-textile, all of which had some impact on this agrarian economy. This general fact questions the role of the seasonality of labour as stressed in Mendels' work,[36] although it is true that some industrial tasks were more easily and conveniently carried on in winter than in summer, especially in a largely pastoral agrarian economy. Woodland industries, however, were more easily pursued in the summer or autumn, as were those involving much transport.

There were most certainly proto-industrial elements in the regional economy at this early stage, and it is possible to detect them in certain areas and localities. A region, however, is a complex organism, with layers and patches of activity within it. Some of these, like large-scale copper mining, died away temporarily, whereas comparison with the next stage shows that others, like iron smelting, were still in a rudimentary but developing state. This slowness of development is reflected in the low number of full-time industrial occupations. The region was also, not for the last time, colonised or exploited by external capitalists.

[32] C. B. Phillips, 'The population of the borough of Kendal in 1576', *CWAAS* (NS), 81 (1981), pp. 59–61.

[33] C. B. Phillips, 'Town and country: economic change in Kendal c. 1550–1700', in P. Clark (ed.), *The Transformation of English Country Towns* (revised edn, London, 1985), pp. 107–9.

[34] Phillips, 'William Wright', p. 43. Dr Phillips' actual phrase is 'operating in an area of low demand'. However, this situation was transformed in the course of the seventeenth century; see B. G. Awty, 'The charcoal ironmasters of Cheshire and Lancashire, 1600–1785' *Transactions of the Historical Society of Lancashire and Cheshire*, 109 (1957), especially pp. 98–9.

[35] G. P. Jones, 'The poverty of Cumberland and Westmorland', *CWAAS* (NS), 55 (1956), pp. 198–208.

[36] F. F. Mendels, 'Seasons and regions in agriculture and industry during the process of industrialisation', in S. Pollard (ed.), *Region und Industrialisierung* (Göttingen, 1980), pp. 177–9.

STAGE TWO: THE CONSOLIDATION OF RURAL INDUSTRY AND THE GROWTH OF TOWNS (1660–1790)

The period 1660–1750 was unquestionably one of widespread rural economic development within Cumbria, whether reflected in the growth of savings on the part of landholders or in the evident rebuilding of farmhouses as measured in the dating of buildings.[37] Nor is it merely arbitrary to extend this second stage beyond 1750, for a surge of town and population growth, and a marked development in road improvement, carried this phase to the onset of factory industry, c. 1790. This stage had at its heart a major upthrust of the west Cumberland coal industry, a peak of development of the rural iron manufacture, and a consolidation of widespread water-power use which also coincided with a greater spread of craft and by-occupations, not least those connected with farming and textiles. Quantitative growth in trade was leading to qualitative change within regional society and industrial organisation. The larger landlords, hitherto minor influences in trade and industry,[38] were developing coal mining, and the Lowthers, Senhouses and Curwens were notable in this respect. A small-scale coasting trade, based partly on the west Cumbrian ports, and dealing in a variety of consumer and other goods,[39] was now overtaken by the Whitehaven coal trade with Ireland, and an ensuing transatlantic connection helped to transform the Cumberland port into the major tobacco port of England during the 1730s. The controlling magnates, the Lowthers, branched out into a variety of local industries and encouraged an extensive trade with Europe and the Baltic.[40] The impact of this western trade and coalfield upon the interior should not, however, be exaggerated. There are clear signs of the development of two partially separated sub-regional economies at this time – so separated that Walter Lutwidge, the leading Whitehaven merchant, had to assemble general cargoes of assorted goods from distant western ports like Bristol and Liverpool, and only one out of eight widely spread Lutwidge factors or agents was in the Cumbrian interior, in Kendal.[41]

[37] See the comments of a recent authority on dating of farmhouses by regions: R. Machin, 'The Great Rebuilding – an assessment', *Past and Present*, 77 (1977), p. 39; for savings, J. D. Marshall, 'Agrarian wealth and social structure in pre-industrial Cumbria' *Economic History Review*, 33, 4 (1980), pp. 503–21, and especially pp. 510–11.

[38] See C. B. Phillips, 'The gentry in Cumberland and Westmorland', unpublished Ph.D. thesis (University of Lancaster, 1973), pp. 345–6; the Cumbrian gentry of the seventeenth century were relatively poor, and no more than 11 per cent of them drew incomes from sources other than rent or farming. The Lowthers, Penningtons and Curwens were notable for showing enterprise.

[39] T. S. Willan, *The English Coasting Trade, 1600–1750* (Manchester, 1938), pp. 182–8.

[40] Beckett, *Coal and Tobacco*, pp. 102–46; see also E. Hughes, *North Country Life in the Eighteenth Century*, vol. 2: *Cumberland and Westmorland, 1700–1830* (London, 1965), pp. 28–63.

[41] Beckett, *Coal and Tobacco*, pp. 142–3.

The existence of the two sub-regional economies is indicated in the development of packhorse movements and turnpike routes after 1739. There was more or less continuous pressure to improve the north–south routes linking Scotland, Newcastle, Carlisle and Kendal, but the improvement of roads on the western side of the region depended upon Whitehaven's prosperity, and produced only two east–west links.[42] By the 1770s, some 230 packhorses were regularly entering and leaving Kendal each week, but only thirty-five of these came directly from Whitehaven and Cockermouth, the remainder being engaged in north–south, eastern or local traffic.[43] Much of the Kendal cloth export went through Liverpool,[44] and twenty packhorses left Kendal weekly for London. Kendal became even more firmly established as the regional textile centre during this stage, a position it was to lose to Carlisle in Stage Three, and it was increasingly supported by an old-established hand-knitting industry which had in turn spread from North Yorkshire and the dales bordering on that county.[45] The outlets for the knitted goods lay often in military contracts or in London,[46] and by 1770, when Arthur Young wrote about the knitters, between 3,000 and 4,000 persons, mostly part-time workers, were engaged in it in the Kendal trade alone. Knitting, it should be noted, was non-seasonal, and could be carried on in road or field alongside other employment.[47] Nor did it directly stimulate the local wool trade, for it used long-stapled wools brought in from outside by Kendal and other merchants. However, the production of the local 'cottons', using the poorer wools of Cumbrian sheep, continued as before, and by 1771 their production was estimated as employing 300 to 400 persons, mainly women.[48] But, as will be seen, there are signs that some branches of domestic textile spinning and even weaving were declining by 1750, and the prevalence of hand-knitting would go far towards explaining this.

---

[42] There were in fact two linkroads into northern and central Cumbria respectively, the Cockermouth and Brough (turnpiked in 1762), and the Cockermouth and Carlisle (turnpiked in 1753). The Kendal link was improved in 1762. As regards northern Cumbria and the Solway, coastal shipping often provided the best means of carriage. For the turnpikes, L. A. Williams, *Road Transport in Cumbria in the Nineteenth Century* (London, 1975), pp. 29–35, 214.

[43] J. Nicolson and R. Burn, *History of Cumberland and Westmorland*, vol. 1 (London, 1777), p. 266.

[44] C. Nicholson, *The Annals of Kendal* (2nd edn, London and Kendal, 1861), p. 241; Thomas Pennant, *Tour in Scotland* (Chester, 1771), p. 219.

[45] M. Hartley and J. Ingilby, *The Old Hand-Knitters of the Dales* (Clapham, 1951), pp. 14–59. There is little real evidence that this industry was deeply rooted in Cumbria proper before 1600, perhaps because knitting caused little gear to be entered in inventories.

[46] T. S. Willan, *An Eighteenth Century Shopkeeper: Abraham Dent of Kirkby Stephen* (Manchester, 1970), pp. 109ff.

[47] See the revealing examples given in Hartley and Ingilby, *Hand-Knitters*, pp. 60–1, and also the somewhat romanticised ones, pp. 74–9. It is clear that the work was best done sitting and in social groups.

[48] Arthur Young, *A Six Months' Tour Through the North of England*, vol. 3 (London, 1771), pp. 133–4.

Certainly, increased economic activity in the countryside as well as in the towns was accompanied by general and steady population increase from about 1740. It is not clear whether one was the cause or the effect of the other, and we are left with the truism that the larger population of 1750–1800 could not have been supported without underlying economic development in town and country. Between 1688 and 1801, the combined populations of Cumberland and Westmorland increased from roughly 90,000 to just over 158,000, or by about 75 per cent, with most of the upturn in numbers occurring after 1740.[49] Strikingly, no more than an estimated 18 per cent of the total increase in numbers was recorded in the coal-bearing district and trading ports of west Cumberland,[50] constituting yet another reminder that we should not exaggerate the effects of the rapidly developing coastal sub-economy.

Much of the population growth, indeed, took place in the main market towns of the region, which acted as control and collecting points for partially local textile and other economies: in Carlisle, with its smaller satellites Brampton and Wigtown, in Penrith and Kirkby Stephen (centres for the Eden Valley), in and around Kendal, with its smaller market villages of the textile area, and in the Furness towns of Dalton, Ulverston and Broughton. Each of these was in some way affected by the woollen textile, linen or calico manufactures (the calico belonging to the mid-eighteenth century and later), as were Cockermouth and the Whitehaven–Egremont district, although the three latter places were influenced by economic cross-currents from the coal and ironfields. If we take the nine towns previously listed, and apply to them some reasonably realistic estimates of population size for the late seventeenth century,[51] then it appears that their combined population growth rate exceeded 100 per cent for the period 1688–1801. Not only does this addition to the regional population of some 34,000 people account for a large segment of the total growth outside the coalfield,

[49] See *BJ*, pp. 215–18. This generalisation is based also upon parish register aggregations performed at different times by the late G. P. Jones, the Cambridge Group for the Study of Population and Social Structure, the late W. G. Howson, and the present writer (dealing mainly with Furness but also with Cumbrian market towns); see also G. P. Jones, 'Some population problems relating to Cumberland and Westmorland in the eighteenth century', *CWAAS* (NS), 58 (1958), pp. 123–39.

[50] The initial estimates for seventeenth-century populations are based partly on the Denton Survey figures; the independent figure for Whitehaven of 2,222, (1693) has been used, the other 'coal' chapelries or townships employed being Maryport, Workington, Allhallows, Aspatria, Bolton, Brigham, Crosscanonby, Flimby, Dearham, Moresby, St Bees, Camerton. For population estimates for most of these, see Appleby, *Famine*, Appendix A, utilising both Denton's figures and those based on the Hearth Tax. The low contribution to the total population growth of the region is not after all surprising; most of these townships were in an undeveloped state in 1801.

[51] For the demographic development of market towns in the region, see J. D. Marshall, 'The rise and transformation of the Cumbrian market town, 1660–1900', *Northern History*, 19 (1983), especially pp. 162–3, where unrealistic figures have been checked and adjusted.

it tells us roughly how that segment was supported or employed and directs attention to the possible incidence and importance of the multiplying occupations in rural areas. Fortunately, occupational enumerations for Kendal (relating to Stricklandgate, an important part of the town) for the years 1695 and 1787[52] tell us that textile employment in this locality increased fourfold between those dates, the building employments may have increased more than three times and that service and retailing occupations increased between two and three times. The metal-using trades increased fivefold, reflecting developments in the regional countryside. Roughly comparable data for the period 1721–44 are available for the market village of Hawkshead and its country district, and these show that professional services, with a variety of retail occupations in food, drink and clothing or personal items like watches accounted for about 40 per cent of all jobs given in the parish registers, followed by building (21 per cent) and textiles (20 per cent).[53] In this instance, the purchasing power of an agrarian community was clearly creating an effect. In both surveys, the importance of the service sector is emphasised, as is that of building and textiles, Kendal's predominance in that last respect being hardly surprising.

It remains true that the countryside and its smaller population centres, like Hawkshead, succeeded in absorbing roughly 10,000 additional people for the period 1688–1801 by providing families (to the number of between 2,000 and 3,000) with employments. It is also clear that having regard to rural natural increase in Cumbrian parishes, there was considerable movement of migrants from country to town. There were several reasons for this movement; not only did inheritance customs remain unchanged, obliging non-inheriting members of families to seek work in country or town, but the numbers of holdings may well have declined, and can hardly have increased across large parts of the region.[54] There are also indications that some branches of rural textiles fell away in importance. This deduction is strongly supported by the relative numbers of textile-involved households emerging in a large sample of Cumbrian probate inventories, in

---

[52] For the 1695 census of Kendal, see n. 17 above; the 1787 survey is part of a census of Westmorland for that year, Kendal R.O., WQSP/C. This second enumeration is for Stricklandgate, a substantial part of the town.
[53] Occupations entered in the Hawkshead parish registers, in turn transcribed in K. and G. O. G. Leonard, *The Second Parish Register Book of Hawkshead, 1705–87* (Hawkshead, 1968).
[54] Searle has concluded, from detailed examination, that the numbers of small customary estates in Cumbria declined between 1650 and 1803: C. E. Searle, 'The odd corner of England: a study of a social formation in transition; Cumbria, c. 1700–c. 1914', unpublished Ph.D. thesis (University of Essex, 1983), p. 193. Seer also J. D. Marshall, *Furness and the Industrial Revolution* (Barrow, 1958), p. 57, Table 4, using Land Tax lists (1746, 1790) for Lonsdale N. of the Sands; the trends shown here are supported by similar data in Searle, *passim*, the point being that estates valued at 1s–10s tended to decline.

two batches of 775 each for the periods 1661–90 and 1721–50. In the first batch, 24 per cent of decedents' inventories for Furness, Copeland and the Diocese of Carlisle showed some sign of involvement in textile work through the listing of spinning wheels, cards, yarn or loom-frames, but in Kendal Deanery (outside the town) only 16 per cent did so. This could be attributable to eccentricity in the inventories themselves, but is conceivably the result of a movement towards knitting, which left no equipment worth recording in these sources. But those for a later period show much lower percentages in most districts, although 24 per cent of upland occupiers in the Kendal area still had such gear in 1721–50, and 14 per cent in High Furness – these decedents were mostly from yeoman households, and many of the local population were within reach of Kendal merchants, who could have supplied them with finer non-regional yarns for hand-knitting, which was replacing some spinning and weaving of the local wool.[55] Such by-employments were certainly sought by the families of the yeomanry, and by the population in general. Hence, out of 95 such Hawkshead decedents for 1661–90, 9 per cent had a by-employment in addition to farming, but, out of 108 sampled for the following 30 years, 15 per cent had an additional employment, and, for 1721–50, 23 per cent out of 120 had branched out in that manner.[56] The most popular by-employments were, in descending order, textiles, building and quarrying, metalmaking and metal using, leathermaking and leather using, woodland crafts and, last of all, commerce and retail (which drew full-time workers). It will be noticed that, first, most of these activities were related to agrarian life and its products, and that, secondly, the group of by-occupations represents no common type of seasonality. They were, on the whole, pursued by members of the lower and middle yeomanry, persons without great wealth, and by local cottagers with little or no claim to any land at all. The numbers of such poor persons increased during the eighteenth century, as local poor law documents testify.

The eighteenth century also saw a considerable augmentation of the wealth of the rural middle class, the upper yeomanry and the substantial farmers, just as an urban social equivalent, made up of merchants, manufacturers and clothiers, was enabled to accumulate capital rapidly.[57] There was a marked growth of both credit and savings in the Cumbrian countryside, the propensity to save having been strengthened by the traditionally austere lifestyle shown in the inventories. It should be stressed

[55] Knitting was certainly practised in the southern Lake District; see Pennant, *Tour in Scotland*, p. 36, where the inhabitants of Ambleside were 'knitting stockings for Kendal market' in 1771.

[56] These occupations are recorded in Hawkshead wills and inventories combined for the periods indicated; see Marshall, 'Agrarian wealth', p. 517, Table 5.

[57] Marshall, 'Agrarian wealth', and idem, 'Kendal in the late seventeenth and eighteenth centuries', *CWAAS* (NS), 75 (1975), p. 206, Table 4.

that this accumulation was achieved without an easily distinguishable agrarian 'revolution'. Yeomen dealt in Scottish or Irish cattle which were wintered or fattened en route for southern markets, and the minor gentry, too, gained from this trade.[58] Members of the minor squirearchy or the upper yeomanry were enabled to finance, e.g. the regional iron industry, but it was typical that in this instance capitalisation also came from Cheshire or the Severn Valley, just as lead and copper mining attracted the London Lead Company or Charles Roe, the Macclesfield entrepreneur.[59] Other water-powered industries, like gunpowder manufacture (from 1764) and papermaking, were developed by regional capitalists from the rural middle class, as were the spade and sickle forges that appeared as west Cumbrian offshoots of the iron industry after about 1770. A growth of food processing was accompanied by a proliferation of corn mills during this century, and these provided the technology and skills for the development of water power generally. In the field of the extractive industries, there was a widespread growth of small-scale metalliferous mining, and, with an increase in slate quarrying for export and local use, a marked and further increase in building activity occurred from about 1760.[60]

Each of these industries had some close connection with regional agriculture or markets for labour, but also with markets outside the region. Local farming families might provide transport workers for slate, iron ore or iron, or produce seasonal workers in fellside mines, or take an interest in charcoal production or woodland industries. The extent to which the iron industry could involve such workers has already been noted; by 1746 there were seven cold-blast furnaces, with related forges, in Furness alone, and a few years later, coke-fired furnaces appeared in west Cumberland. The Furness iron industry cannot have employed fewer than 200 full-time and 300 part-time workers in the mid-eighteenth century, and many of the latter were engaged in related occupations, like the woodland industries which have been mentioned. Several hundred yeomen had interests in coppice woodland for charcoal production.[61] After about 1770, when charcoal

---

[58] Searle, 'The odd corner of England', p. 146, points out that this trade (discussed in Marshall, 'Agrarian wealth', pp. 512–13) would tend to benefit the wealthier peasantry, who would overstock the common pastures.

[59] Alfred Fell, *The Early Iron Industry of Furness* (Ulverston, 1908), pp. 265–6, for the ironmasters; for the London Lead Company, A. Raistrick, *Two Centuries of Industrial Welfare* (London, 1938), *passim*; for Charles Roe, W. H. Chaloner, 'Charles Roe of Macclesfield', *Transactions of the Lancashire and Cheshire Antiquarian Society* 62 (1950–1), pp. 141–2.

[60] The continued development of building (after 1760) is stressed by R. W. Brunskill, *Vernacular Achitecture of the Lake Counties* (London, 1974), especially in table, p. 135. For details of the slate industry, B. Tyson, 'The Troutbeck Park slate quarries', *CWAAS* (NS), 84 (1984), pp. 167–90.

[61] A striking illustration of yeoman involvement in charcoal woods is embodied in the Penny Bridge Wood Articles (1748), Cumbria County Archives, Barrow R.O., Z15/1–3, an agreement to supply charcoal to one firm was signed by some 182 local wood owners. See also Fell, *Early Iron Industry*, pp. 145–51, and Appendix E, pp. 435–9.

prices were climbing and the leading ironmasters had already been obliged to find charcoal in western Scotland, the Furness iron industry began a gradual decline, and the rich haematite iron ore of the Furness and Cumberland mines was instead exported,[62] beginning to be profitable to great landlords like the Montagus (later Dukes of Buccleuch), Stanleys and Wyndhams. It was this trade that was to interest investors in the economic possibilities of the coastal territory some seventy years later, and which led to railway promotion in the west of the region. However, the discontinuities of local and regional history should not be glossed over. The coke-smelting iron enterprises which grew in west Cumberland from 1752 had very little impact. Likewise the charcoal-smelting furnaces of Furness carried on in the nineteenth century only as specialised curiosities, catering for narrow markets.

During Stage Two, the iron industry and trade straddled the two sub-regional economies, east and west, having outlets in both Whitehaven and Kendal,[63] and, like the two former, it had distant markets – in this instance in the south-west of England. It was a characteristic of this stage that the intra-regional and extra-regional transport networks became much more elaborate, the textile industries of the Cockermouth area tending to look westward,[64] and those of Kendal (as we have seen) to the south and east. The rapid and decisive emergence of the coal and tobacco trades transformed the west Cumberland economy, and these developments manifest a marked discontinuity from Stage One. They owed a great deal to the Lowther family, and their origins cannot be traced in the nature of an earlier economy or society, but rather in the opportunities offered by Irish or transatlantic markets. The growth of a national or inter-regional economy made the development of slate quarrying profitable[65] (this was essentially a Stage Two development), whilst the growth of northern and other quarrying stimulated gunpowder manufacturing at Sedgwick (1764) by John Wakefield, of a Westmorland woollen manufacturing family.[66] This, too, was a newly planted industry with no precedent in Stage One.

[62] J. D. Kendall, 'Notes on the history of mining in Cumberland and north Lancashire', *Transactions of the North of England Institute of Mining Engineers*, 24 (1884–5), pp. 89–91; Fell, *Early Iron Industry*, pp. 92–7; statistics in paper by Lord E. Cavendish relating mainly to Montagu mines, in *Barrow Times*, 27 July 1878.

[63] In 1713, the Backbarrow Company had 'warehouses' in Whitehaven, Penrith and Keswick as well as in Kendal, Ulverston and Hawkshead; Fell, *Early Iron Industry*, p. 300.

[64] In 1749, a Cockermouth merchant was sending goods to Jamaica, Barbados and the Baltic, an interesting illustration of the outlets afforded by the sub-region's international connections; Beckett, *Coal and Tobacco*, p. 143.

[65] Although the slate trade is generally thought to have developed markedly after *c.* 1770 (see Marshall, *Furness*, pp. 42–6), determined entrepreneurdom was causing it to be sent from the Westmorland Troutbeck to London in 1753–60; Tyson, 'Troutbeck Park slate quarries', pp. 169–71.

[66] John Somervell, *Some Westmorland Wills* (Kendal, 1927), pp. 91–3.

A principal distinction between Stage One and Stage Two resides in the extent of activity, within the latter, in the field of water-powered enterprises small enough to be capitalised by regional yeoman or middle-class families who had prospered in trade. This generalisation applied to paper manufacture, which appeared in seventeen Cumbrian locations between 1670 and 1770, utilising linen rags from local textile manufacturers,[67] and to spade and sickle manufacture in the coastal areas, just as it had applied to a number of iron and woollen (e.g. machine carding) enterprises. These sources of capital were important in the absence of a substantial layer of country gentry with a business-oriented attitude of mind.[68] A movement towards a more open middle-class society coincided with a weakening of the feudal ties and constraints embodied in the manorial system, as lords of manors and their stewards lost control over customs advantageous to the tenants, like the regulation of common grazing.[69] At the same time, increasing numbers of customary tenants became enfranchised, and the second half of the century saw the effective decline of manorial administration in Cumbria.[70]

STAGE THREE: THE CONCENTRATION OF THE IRON, STEEL, COAL AND TEXTILE INDUSTRIES, AND THE QUICKENING OF RURAL AND OTHER DE-INDUSTRIALISATION (1790–1914)

We must now return to Carlisle and northern Cumbria, which were influenced by the west coast industrial development of the eighteenth century, to the extent that Walter Lutwidge, the Whitehaven merchant, had an interest in a 'factory' in the border city in 1740.[71] The latter had remained a garrison and ecclesiastical centre, with some considerable trade in cattle by virtue of its key position on a main route from Scotland, and the Diocese of Carlisle, stretching across the northern half of Cumbria, had experienced some expansion in domestic textiles before 1720.[72] Carlisle grew rapidly in population after 1750, aided in this growth by a development of calico printing. This was a wholly new departure, perhaps

---

[67] Information by courtesy of Mr J. H. A. Gavin, based on graduate research.

[68] J. V. Beckett, 'Landownership in Cumbria, 1680–1750', unpublished Ph.D. thesis (University of Lancaster, 1975), pp. 375–7.

[69] R. S. Dilley, 'The Cumbrian court leet and the use of the common lands', *CWAAS* (NS), 67 (1967), pp. 167–90.

[70] Searle, 'The odd corner of England', p. 146. Signs of manorial decay were also noted in Marshall, *Furness*, p. 130.

[71] B. C. Jones, 'Carlisle's first factory', *CWAAS* (NS), 85 (1985), pp. 189–90.

[72] Probate inventories for the Diocese of Carlisle, 1660–1750, at the Cumbria County Record Office, the Castle, Carlisle. These show as much involvement in spinning and weaving as do the inventories for Cumbrian deaneries to the south.

stimulated by the Atlantic trade and the importation of cotton through west Cumberland and Solway ports. This northern part of the region had few competing industries, and once the weaving of calicoes and fustians had gained momentum around Carlisle from 1785,[73] then factory cotton spinning rapidly followed on. There was an attempt at the latter in Cockermouth in 1781,[74] and spinning mills did in fact become established in Cockermouth, Keswick and even Caldbeck. But the real centre was Carlisle, with its suitable river sites on the Eden and the Caldew, and it was there, far removed from Kendal, that Cumbria's main factory revolution in textiles had its seat between 1790 and the middle of the nineteenth century. The factory owners employed weavers in the Solway parishes and the border, in such numbers that the eleven cotton mills of the Carlisle district (1829) were said to be employing members of some 5,000 families in weaving of different kinds, although another figure for the late 1830s (1,963 weavers for the same district) seems more realistic.[75] By 1851, cloth manufacture of all kinds was by far the largest employment sector in Cumberland, representing 15 per cent of all census occupations, and it employed four times as many workers as did the coal industry of the coast.[76] The industrial balance of the region, in textiles at least, had tipped decisively northward, for Kendal's woollen manufacture no longer employed many domestic workers outside the town. Calico printing remained in the Carlisle locality, and showed the same ultimate tenacity as papermaking in Westmorland; both have survived through the twentieth century.

Cotton mills had also appeared in the southern and eastern extremities of the region (at Backbarrow, Cark, Milnthorpe, Ulverston and also near Brough), and from the late eighteenth century, another and remarkable industry established itself in Westmorland – bobbin manufacture. The growth trajectory of this water-powered industry followed that of cotton, and declined with it in the 1870s[77] – despite the fact that the bobbins went largely to distant extra-regional markets. Regional bobbin manufacture was effectively killed by Scandinavian competition and by alternative ways of making bobbins and cops. The gunpowder mills, rising to a total of seven in all, continued to flourish in Westmorland and Furness because they had

[73] BJ, pp. 266–7.

[74] Hughes, Cumberland and Westmorland, pp. 357–8.

[75] See D. Bythell, The Handloom Weavers (Cambridge, 1969), pp. 10, 57, 61, 266, quoting mainly parliamentary papers on handloom weavers.

[76] Census of Great Britain, 1851, Population Tables, part I, vol. 2, Occupations of the People, British Parliamentary Papers, pp. 768ff and 775. In Cumberland, 15,239 people were engaged in cloth manufacture, as against 3,804 in coal mining.

[77] J. Somervell, address to Newcomen Society visitors, Transactions of the Newcomen Society, 18 (1937–8), p. 242.

few competitors nationally, but Cumbrian cotton spinning never really recovered from the cost disadvantages created by the concentration of machine weaving in east Lancashire. Like the regional linen industry, which was found in water-powered factories in Cleator, Cockermouth and Holme in Westmorland after 1800, it very tardily applied steam power. In faltering, it provoked the decline of northern Cumbrian domestic weaving, which was accompanied by sharp social and political tensions as the weavers of Carlisle, Wigton and Cockermouth became politicised.[78] The age of the Chartists also heralded mass out-migration from the Cumbrian countryside, which had complex motivations, nevertheless. It has been estimated that well over 100,000 people left Cumbria for other counties and countries during the nineteenth century.[79]

Yet the first half of the same century had seen a considerable and continued development of water-power use and of agriculturally related industries and crafts in the region, concerned with woollens (Kendal specialised in making horse-blankets and duffle), linens and checks, mining installations, wood turning and sawmilling, and a score of minor trades. In parallel, some agrarian transformations occurred which did not fall far short of an agricultural revolution on the larger farms and estates, causing tile and lime burning to become widespread. But such changes were simply not enough to prevent country people from seeking new lives elsewhere. The appearance of railways in the region from 1836 certainly gave the latter an economic unity, but it also stimulated migration-proneness, aided by the turning of much land to pasture after 1870. Railway building helped to bring about the region's real and spectacular industrial revolution in the coastal areas, when the non-phosphoric haematite, increasingly sold out of the region hitherto, gave west Cumberland and Furness an immense technical advantage in Bessemer steelmaking when used locally between 1863 and 1880. This led to the establishment of a major iron-producing area between Carnforth and Maryport, with fifty furnaces in blast in 1871, producing the valuable acid pig iron for use in steelmaking in both Barrow and Sheffield, and making railway rails for the world. Such activity stimulated town building, and had the effect, by 1881, of concentrating 60 per cent of the region's population into its coastal strip and main towns

---

[78] June C. F. Barnes, 'Popular protest and radical politics: Carlisle, 1790–1850', unpublished Ph.D. thesis (University of Lancaster, 1981), *passim.*

[79] For the actual estimate, see 'Distribution of the Enumerated Natives of Counties', *Census of 1891*, vol. 3, *British Parliamentary Papers*, 1893–4, CVI, p. 482. Table 9.

Much of the subsequent detail in this paper is covered in J. D. Marshall and J. K. Walton, *A History of the Lake Counties from 1830* (Manchester, 1981). The writer would like to record his thanks to Dr C. B. Phillips for helpful suggestions on the same topic, made at the CORAL annual conference in Preston in September, 1985 and further thanks to Dr Hudson for many useful ideas.

combined. By contrast, in 1851 only 24 per cent of the region's occupied population was employed in agriculture, and by 1891, 14 per cent. (On the eve of extensive industrialisation, in the mid-eighteenth century, the figure would have been about 50 per cent.)

Massive de-industrialisation began to take effect from about 1880, with the decline of bobbinmaking and of some branches of cotton spinning affecting the northern and rural areas of the region (especially in the Carlisle district), followed by the slow but inexorable contraction of the iron and steel industries, and, even more markedly, iron mining in the same coastal areas. Local shipbuilding in timber and iron also declined from the mid-century, although this industry was successfully concentrated in Barrow, and copper mining, which had revived in Coniston through much of the nineteenth century, also failed by 1905. The general loss of textile industries and employments in the countryside was not counterbalanced by the small water-powered industries that remained. The rural iron industry left a single outpost to survive at Backbarrow into the twentieth century.

This account of Stage Three is necessarily much abbreviated, and throughout the discussion, attention has been directed towards likely continuities and discontinuities. The great iron and steel industry of Furness and Cumberland (1863–80) had seemingly little to connect it to the rural ironmaking of Georgian times, although there were a few tenuous links, like the entrepreneurial influence of the Lowthers round Whitehaven, or the continued operations of a Furness partnership, the Newland Company, between the eighteenth and nineteenth centuries. The great iron deposits of the region had otherwise remained unexploited until nineteenth-century technology could cause them to be unlocked and could, in doing so, create new industrial sub-regions and societies in Furness and west Cumberland. Yet there were continuities even through this vast upheaval; iron mining on a small scale had taken place since the middle ages, and if we are to treat monastic institutions as great landlords (which indeed they were) then great landlord influence was nearly continuous from that time. Massive changes in technology, however, had accompanied no less comprehensive transformations in society itself, and the successes of the Lowthers as coal owners did not belong to the eighteenth century merely by accident; they belonged to an age of growing international commerce.

Few industrial regions are self-contained or uninfluenced by others, and consequently a region like Cumbria, which depended heavily on external markets, did not move autonomously from one discrete stage to the next. It was also dependent, especially in the sphere of metalliferous mining, upon a measure of investment from outside the region – upon that of the

Mines Royal in the sixteenth century, the London Lead Company in the eighteenth and upon powerful capitalists like Schneider, the Barratts and John Stirling in the nineteenth century. These investors not only developed iron and other mining on a large scale, but also caused communities to spring up, and their opportunities were provided by the absence of a strongly established and wealthy stratum of gentry under the great landlords themselves. Similarly, one area within a region could develop at the expense of another by exploiting cheap labour in backward localities, and southern and western Cumbria may well have taken advantage of the more undeveloped dales and fell territory in seeking sources of yarn, charcoal, stockings and, later, labour.

It is a useful exercise to consider industrial evolution in terms of stages like those set out here, but it becomes clear that when a region gives rise to a mass of localised or varied industries, so it becomes more difficult to employ a concept like proto-industrialisation, or any other model which attempts to characterise the whole of one phase. The Stage One given here was undoubtedly proto-industrial as far as the cloth industry of Cumbria was concerned, but was probably pre-industrial in so far as the concept relates to regional society as a whole; that is, feudal attitudes remained dominant, and the social or psychological reach of the industrial sector is hard to determine. Certainly, the majority of people were not directly touched by the latter. Stage Two was marked by development in several regional and rural industries, by distinct capital accumulation in town and country and by the sloughing off of residual feudal attitudes and even of institutions. This stage was largely proto-industrial as far as the Cumberland coal industry was concerned, but was second-phase (whether 'proto' or not) in iron, textiles and other mining. No major common movements of population can be associated with these industries, and seasonalities of labour were disparate and even clashing. As regards that 'maturity' of industrialisation associated with the so-called revolutions in factory production, coal, iron and steel, here a real problem is once more revealed; substantial de-industrialisation was the twentieth-century fate even of the west of the region. Hence, just as proto-industrialisation theory fails adequately to encompass the nature of industrialisation where the latter develops, in the end, with capital goods as the leading sectors, so also the notion of a self-sustaining industrial revolution fails to recognise the possibility of decline which may shortly follow.

᷐ᷩ᷒ Chapter 6 ᷐ᷩ᷒

The de-industrialisation process: a case study of the Weald, 1600–1850

BRIAN SHORT

The fact of de-industrialisation in the Weald of Kent, Surrey and Sussex between 1600 and 1850 is well attested. In 1600 the Weald had been the major English producer of glass and iron, especially ordnance. It was also extremely important for its production of timber and timber products and textiles, especially dyed broadcloth. As many as forty-nine out of the total eighty-five English blast furnaces were in the Weald in 1600. Both cloth production and glass reached their peak of output around 1600 and clearly the Weald was one of England's leading industrial areas at this time. This contribution will examine a region which provides a clear example of the failed transition from proto-industrialisation to full industrialisation, and also one in which the place of industry was not taken up by commercial agriculture.[1] What were the processes behind this industrial decline? And why did such a vibrant proto-industrial region of the sixteenth century fail to sustain its early achievements?

PROTO-INDUSTRIALISATION OR UNDERDEVELOPMENT?

Although only industries producing goods which are sold outside the region can truly be said to be proto-industrial, and the manufacture of iron and glass does not fit comfortably into a Mendels-style framework of analysis, the Weald was certainly a proto-industrial region. And the decline of all the region's industries must be examined in order to appreciate the significance of the transformation that occurred.

Unified to some degree by the availability of industrial raw materials, the products and problems of a wood-pasture economy, and relatively abundant water power, the Weald not only expanded industrial output in the sixteenth century but drew on a long tradition of industrial exploitation traceable back to medieval and into Roman and prehistoric periods. By

---

[1] See F. F. Mendels, 'Proto-industrialisation: the first phase of the industrialisation process', *Journal of Economic History*, 32, (1972), pp. 241–61; and D. C. Coleman, 'Proto-industrialization: a concept too many', *Economic History Review*, 36 (1983), pp. 435–48.

1600 iron production was focused on the eastern and central High Weald, largely within Sussex, around the headwaters of the Eastern Rother, Cuckmere, Ouse and Medway (see Map 6.1). Window and vessel glass production was concentrated at the opposite, western end of the Weald, on the Lower Greensand and Weald Clay. The parishes of Chiddingfold, Alfold, Ewhurst, Kirdford and Wisborough Green represented the nucleus. Clothworking was differently located again – with its centre in the eastern, and almost exclusively Kentish, Weald in the parishes of Cranbrook, Benenden, Hawkhurst, and Biddenden.

The three main industries *c.* 1600 thus had different concentrations which overlapped spatially at their respective peaks of production: glass in the west, iron in the centre and cloth in the east. The ubiquitous timber and its products were scattered more evenly across the region. The overall concentration was in the High Weald, at the very centre of the south-east, where there was a complex geology of Tunbridge Wells Sands, Wadhurst Clay, and Ashdown Beds, with a limestone inlier of Purbeck Beds, and with a mixture of less significant sands and clays. Around this mixture was the low-lying Weald Clay which provided fewer industrial raw materials but did have significant timber, brick and tile production.

The locational criteria for such industrial activity have been well documented. Raw material was provided by clay ironstone, with 35–40 per cent iron content, found as a deposit of nodules and thin beds near the base of the Wadhurst Clay. There were also areas of more shelly, calcareous ironstone and ferruginous sandstone in the major Wealden formations, as well as subsidiary ferruginous ragstone in the Weald Clay in Surrey and west Sussex. Timber, charcoal and ashes came from the plentiful woodlands, although enormous amounts of timber had been cut in the half-century before 1600. Oak, beech and birch were converted into charcoal fuel, either from the lands belonging to the ironmasters or from elsewhere if necessary. The Kentish textile industry used wool from the North and South Downs or Romney Marsh; fullers earth from the Maidstone–Boxley Lower Greensand area of Kent, and teazles, flax and hemp which were grown locally. Suitable sand for glassmaking came from the different strata of the western Weald Lower Greensand or from sandy seams in the Weald Clay. For all the industries, energy could be harnessed from the small but swift and abundant (if seasonal) Wealden headwater streams, and from wood fuel. The south-eastern location was peninsular and its several estuaries and ports facilitated the export trades.[2]

[2] For accounts of the separate industries, see C. H. Chalklin, *Seventeenth-Century Kent* (London, Longman, 1965), part 3; G. H. Kenyon, *The Glass Industry of the Weald* (Leicester, Leicester University Press, 1967); C. S. Cattell, 'The historical geography of the Wealden iron industry',

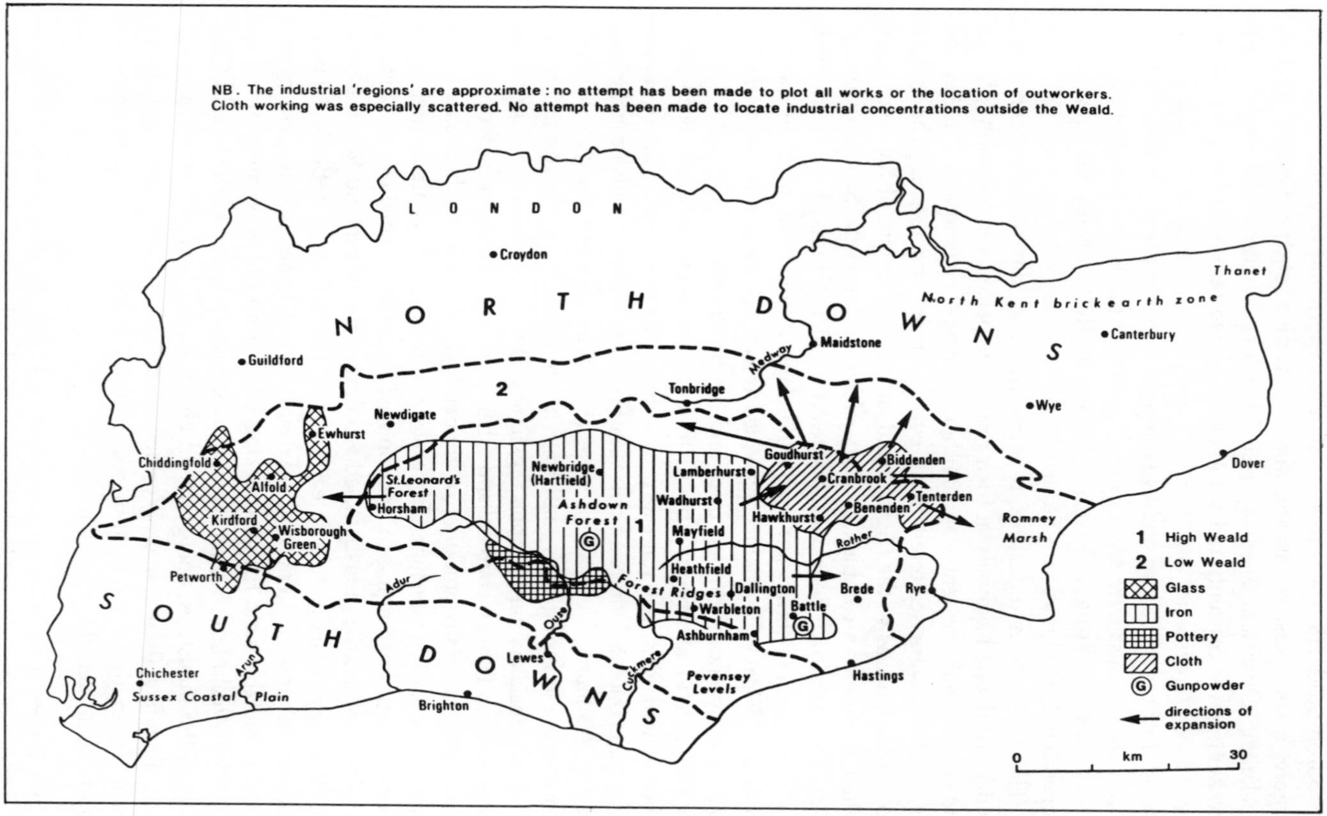

NB. The industrial 'regions' are approximate: no attempt has been made to plot all works or the location of outworkers. Cloth working was especially scattered. No attempt has been made to locate industrial concentrations outside the Weald.

Map 6.1 The industrial Weald, 1600–1850

However, the Weald was an underdeveloped region by the seventeenth century. This seeming contradiction arises because although the region was nationally important as an industrial complex, it had been continuously subordinated to political, economic and social decisions made outside its boundaries. London was, of course, a supplier of initiative and of both fixed and circulating capital, and the region had been dominated for centuries by peripheral manorial centres and older seats of settlement around its edges. It had for long been seen as a reserve of grazing land, timber, or as a source of raw materials. Agricultural investment had been minimal and this had resulted in a profusion of marginalised smallholdings, and a wood-pasture economy concentrating on the rearing and fattening of both imported and local cattle. As such, the Weald contrasted with its neighbours. In no sense was it a commercial corn-producing region like the neighbouring Downlands, and Brickearth regions of north Kent and the Sussex coastal plain, with their greater flexibility of operations and agricultural innovations. In the High Weald there was also still a great deal of common land in the chain of 'waste' stretching from St Leonard's Forest through Ashdown and eastwards along the Forest Ridges, areas of thin soils and scanty timber but guarded by commoners against the ever-increasing assault by cottagers. Such vigilance was necessary because the seventeenth-century Weald was one of the many English wood-pasture regions undergoing demographic change. Gavelkind tenure, partible inheritance and sub-divided holdings kept family labour within the region. There existed, therefore, the retention of stakes in family holdings, the possibility of obtaining part-time industrial work and the possibility of building a cottage on the waste. At the same time many smaller copyholders were being bought out and their holdings were being engrossed on the South Downs and the consequent depopulation also resulted in more demographic pressure on the Weald. The tell-tale signs of illegal cottage building, encroachment onto manorial wastes and the erection of poor houses all testify to this surge of population by the early seventeenth century. By this time by-employment was also allowing a lower age of marriage, which was important in producing high fertility rates which merged with the high rates of in-migration to produce an increasingly populous region.[3]

unpublished M.A. thesis (University of London, 1973). The standard text on Wealden iron, E. Straker, *Wealden Iron* (London, Bell, 1931; reprinted Bath, Chivers, 1967), is now greatly amplified in H. Cleere and D. Crossley, *The Iron Industry of the Weald* (Leicester, Leicester University Press, 1985). Wealden clothworking *inter alia* is dealt with in E. Kerridge, *Textile Manufactures in Early Modern England* (Manchester, Manchester University Press, 1985).

[3] C. E. Brent, 'Employment, land tenure and population in Eastern Sussex 1540–1640', unpublished D.Phil. thesis (University of Sussex, 1973); and J. Kirk, 'Colonists of the waste: the structure and evolution of nineteenth century economy and society in the central Forest Ridges of the Sussex Weald', unpublished M.A. thesis (University of Sussex, 1986).

In terms of Mendel's proto-industrialisation concept, the Weald presents a region offering some full-time and much part-time employment in both highly capitalised industry and handicrafts. It was both possible and necessary to supplement low agricultural incomes. The duality of employment could be seen, for example, in the mid-sixteenth century when the Wealden clothiers were referred to as men who 'dwel in great fermes abrode in the countrey, havying howses with commodities lyke unto gentylmen, where aswel they make cloth and kepe husbandry, and also grasse and fede shepe and catell'.[4] Much of the cloth industry rested on domestic carding, spinning and weaving put out amongst a dense scattering of cottagers. Although the industry was focused on the Kentish High Weald, the outworkers were also to be found in Sussex, from Wadhurst and Mayfield across to the fringes of the Ashdown Forest. Specialist craftsmen not found elsewhere in the Sussex Weald included kemmers, warp kemmers and warp spinners as well as some clothiers. The justices for the Upper Division of Pevensey Rape reported in 1630: 'As for worke for the poore, our parte of the contrey affordeth great plenty of its owne nature, by reason of our vicinity to the clothiers of Kent, who sett one worcke the weemen and children and by reason of our iron workes, which yeelde imployment for the stronger bodies.'[5] 'Eyling', the production of ash in a kiln or pit, was also common in this area with the demand from the Kentish dyeworks. In the clothing industry in this region the residents used their own equipment but materials were supplied by the clothier, who also controlled the dyeing and finishing processes. Only rarely were there weaving and clothing shops in the clothiers' own houses, but they frequently contained all the finishing equipment which was referred to in their probate inventories. Occasionally they possessed a fulling mill or a shearman's shop but most of the work was put out to weavers, fullers and spinners. Merchant capital was thus very significant here, and the clothiers also provided the necessary capital for the purchase of wool, dyes, vats and timber, and, of course, for wages. Enmeshed with pastoral farming, this putting-out system with its wage-labour employment largely supplied markets outside the region.

The situation with glassmaking was similar to that for cloth. The finance was supplied by a combination of merchant capital, the capital of the glassmakers themselves, which therefore may have come originally from the Continent, and from the local gentry. The latter offered credit for oak

---

[4] Cited in M. L. Zell, 'A wood-pasture agrarian regime: the Kentish Weald in the sixteenth century', *Southern History*, 7 (1985), p. 88.
[5] W. D. Cooper, 'Social conditions in Sussex 1631–1632', *Sussex Archaeological Collections*, 16 (1864), pp. 20–6 and 30–1.

and beechwood fuel which was usually the largest element in the overall costs. The number of people employed directly in the industry was small. A nucleus of skilled workers was needed, together with middlemen and labourers who could integrate their industrial work with agriculture. In 1614 Henry Strudwick alias Deane of Kirdford was buried. His inventory shows him to have been a glass carrier, with six small nags or packhorses, a cart, and with debts owing to 'William Strudwick his master', another member of this locally significant yeoman family, and who was both a glassmaker and ironmaster in Kirdford. Henry also died possessed of kine and young cattle, hogs, husbandry tackle and some crops.[6]

The iron industry was again similarly organised. At its peak in the late sixteenth century, the industry might have employed about 2,000 men and boys on a full- or part-time basis. A 1661 petition noted the many 'thousand poore people, farmers and others' being employed at the ironworks, although this was undoubtedly an exaggeration. The Petworth works were supplied with mine (ore) by two labourers who averaged 295 loads per annum in the early seventeenth century.[7] But a nucleus of skilled fillers, finers, hammermen and founders often passed their secrets down through generations, and they were in turn backed up by assistants, clerks and twice as many miners, colliers, woodcutters and carters. Mining was considered a low-status occupation, but the inventory of Thomas Reeve of Dallington indicates the alliance with husbandry. In October 1731, Reeve possessed his own cheap mining tools worth 12s 6d out of a total inventory worth £33 14s. His largest item was 'cash, apparel and debts' worth £27 13s 6d but there were also 'two small swines' worth £1 10s.[8] The consequences of such seasonal and part-time employment possibilities were far-reaching in the Weald.

An increasing population in the sixteenth and early seventeenth centuries was both a consequence and a cause of the proto-industrial activity. A comparison of taxpayers in 1524–5 with 1665 or 1670 shows that over most of the Weald their number had risen by between 12 and 38 per cent.[9] Fragmented Wealden pastoral farms were set within ample commons suitable for cottage construction and in a weakly manorialised countryside. The family, the hamlet or the isolated farm were the social and spatial units of production, and there were no communal farming institutions except for those connected with the use of common wastes.

[6] Kenyon, *Glass Industry*, pp. 112, 120; C. E. Brent, 'Rural employment and population in Sussex between 1560 and 1640, pt. 2', *Sussex Archaeological Collections*, 116 (1978), p. 47.
[7] J. L. M. Gulley, 'The Wealden landscape in the seventeenth century and its antecedents', unpublished Ph.D. thesis (University of London, 1960), p. 192.
[8] East Sussex Record Office, Inventories, Dallington 2361.
[9] Brent, 'Rural employment', pp. 241–4.

Kriedte has remarked that 'the social destabilization of the village was a pre-condition as well as a consequence of the spatial expansion of industrial commodity production'.[10] However, the Weald was never a countryside of socially cohesive villages at the level of manor, hamlet or parish as with common-field farming regions. Many smallholders and peasants dug and carted iron ore as supplementary occupations. Coopers, carpenters, millwrights and colliers rented woodland and farmland. Tanners sold iron ore, cordwood, cattle and corn. Smallholders included weavers, clothiers, spinners, hammermen, finers and gunfounders as well as mercers, tailors, millers and bricklayers. Therefore, it may be seen that proto-industry was spatially co-existent in the south-east not with agrarian capitalism but with the surviving peasantry of the Weald.

In terms of the underdevelopment of this Wealden peasantry, the caveat by Cardoso about dependency should be noted, namely that there exists, or existed, a variety of 'dependent capitalist development' in such regions, which was integrated into the emerging forms of broader monopolistic expansion.[11] A class of Wealden entrepreneurs (clothiers, ironmasters, timber merchants and glassmakers) thus emerged within the under-developed region, with their form of 'dependent capitalism' being linked more strongly to the external world than to their immediate locale. Living amongst dual-employed or agricultural peasants, this clique was never-theless guided by national or international market forces, and the social structures, processes and landscapes which they did so much to create were in tune with national and international, rather than regional, movements. Glass, cloth, ordnance and timber products were dispatched to metropolitan or foreign destinations and were controlled largely by monopolistic mercantile or landed wealth. Exports from the Wealden iron industry took the form of bar iron and ordnance and these went mostly to London. These were the most important of the Wealden iron goods, and only fire backs, nails and miscellaneous items were retained locally. London was also the chief market for cloth and glass as well as being the key reception centre for its export abroad. Also international was the movement of the expertise which had been crucial to the establishment of these Wealden industries. In the sixteenth century both technological and entrepreneurial expertise had come from Lorraine and Normandy to the glass industry, from northern France to the ironworks, and from the Low Countries to textile manufacture. Indigenous expertise developed from these migrant skills, but only timber seemed to be an English native preoccupation. One set of international links

---

[10] P. Kriedte, H. Medick and J. Schlumbohm, *Industrialisation before Industrialisation: Rural Industry in the Genesis of Capitalism* (English transl., Cambridge, Cambridge University Press, 1982), p. 16.
[11] F. Cardoso, 'Dependency and development in Latin America', *New Left Review*, 74 (1972), 89.

which Mendels did not take into account was therefore the international transfer of technical expertise (and the establishment of kinship links in due course) as well as finance and marketing skills. Without these, it would be difficult to envisage any of the main industries under discussion gaining the pre-eminence they achieved by 1600.

The linkages between the varieties of external and internal control engendered sometimes very complex arrangements for the running of the Wealden industries. The ironworks were run in many different ways. At its simplest, a Wealden landowner leased both land and ironworks to an ironmaster who then took the profit, less rent. In eastern Sussex, the Ashburnhams, Abergavennys, Gorings, Pelhams and Websters all took this line. Alternatively, the freehold might be sold, especially if the landowning family were in financial or political difficulties, as in the case of the Ashburnham family in the late sixteenth century. Here Giles Garton, a London ironmonger, was owed money, and there were sales to William Relf, the ironmaster. In this case, the land was subsequently re-purchased. But on top of these leasing and purchasing arrangements there were sub-letting agreements, partnerships involving half-tenancies, and time-sharing complexes. The operators in this capital-intensive manufacturing section were very much alive to the advantages of switching capital and technology between sites and between regions if necessary. Cardoso's concept of an 'integrated clientele class' with 'advanced consumption patterns'[12] might perhaps be pushing his Third-World analogy too far, but the whole context of Wealden industrial development and decline must be seen as the result of external stimulus and internal response.

Therefore, the internal dynamics of the Wealden iron industry were but the manifestation in a particular setting of national or international changes. Capital came into Wealden iron from London in particular. The monopolist Thomas Browne borrowed heavily in London to finance his furnaces. London wholesale ironmongers purchased diverse ironware from the region, while ordnance went either to the London-based Office of Ordnance or to the Tower of London for sale to merchant fleets. Ironworks might be established by Londoners, such as James Hooper and Francis Diggs at Pippingford in the armaments boom of the 1690s, or by Thomas Western at Brede and Ashburnham. Other Londoners, such as Samuel Gott, became ironmasters by purchasing into an existing works. The Ewood ironworks in Newdigate were owned by Christopher Darrell, 'citizen and merchant tailor of London',[13] while the goldsmith, Henry Fyner, had

---

[12] P. Cooke, 'Dependent development in United Kingdom regions with particular reference to Wales', *Progress in Planning*, 15, 1 (1980), p. 13.

[13] P. Brandon, *A History of Surrey* (Chichester, Phillimore, 1977), p. 53.

financed the erection of the first English blast furnace at the Newbridge complex on the northern edge of the Ashdown Forest in the 1490s. Midland interests were also represented in the shape of the Foley ironmasters or the Crowley–Hanbury consortium from the Forest of Dean in the seventeenth century; or the Staffordshire ironmaster John Churchill in the eighteenth.[14] One key result of such a diversity of external control and investment was, of course, to increase the vulnerability of the Weald to national and international structural and locational shifts in industry.

This vulnerable industrial base was not located among farmers noted for their productivity. There had been no concerted investment in food production in the Weald during this time. The Weald was perceived in agrarian terms as being difficult and residual by the early seventeenth century, and the survival of a flourishing peasantry with a self-sufficiency ethos derived in part from centuries of underdevelopment. By 1600 rural industry was thus the prominent Wealden feature, but in a situation which was externally controlled and increasingly dependent on national, metropolitan and international forces.

A FAILED TRANSITION

Why did these early-modern developments never precipitate the Weald into full industrial development? While timber and timber products continue to provide work in the twentieth century, the other industrial concerns had faltered by 1650, declined throughout the late seventeenth and eighteenth centuries and were quite dead by about 1820. The failure of the transition is explicable in terms which encompass all the Wealden industries, but past explanations for the decline have tended to look at each sector in isolation. These must be considered first.

The decline of Wealden iron can be correlated with fluctuating but generally decreasing demands for Wealden ordnance. By 1717 just 23 per cent of English furnaces were within the Weald, producing about 10 per cent of the total English pig-iron output. Swedish competition hit both the home market and the Dutch market. South Wales, the Midlands, and eventually Scotland also became rivals in traditional Wealden markets. One reason for the decline which has frequently been advanced is the high price and scarcity of timber. Ironmasters had to compete with demands from hop-growers, and with urban fuel and timber demands from such places as Rye and Hastings for the remaining resources. But much timber had for long been carefully coppiced. The decline in wood fuel as an explanation for Wealden iron decline simply does not square with the enormous

[14] Cleere and Crossley, *Iron Industry, passim.*

amounts of woodland still left in Sussex by 1850, when it was England's most wooded county. However, it must be allowed that the timber on the Ashdown and St Leonard's Forests had been virtually destroyed through neglectful management by the late seventeenth century. In *Sylva* John Evelyn, no advocate of ironworks, wrote that 'he that should deeply consider the prodigious waste which these voracious iron and glass-works have formerly made ... would be touch'd with no mean indignation'.[15] It had been noted, for example, that in 1649 the Bewbush furnace in St Leonard's Forest had been derelict for seven years through shortage of wood. In depositions on the management of woodland in the 8,000 acres of St Leonard's Forest, taken in the early 1680s, it was alleged that there had been 'great waste and destruction' since 1672, resulting in a significant loss of value. Agistment cattle and sheep had been taken into the Forest without the provision of adequate fencing, and heathland had been burned to improve rabbit grazings. Significantly, however, contemporary explanations of the decay of the ironworks in the Forest highlighted not the local timber shortages but the importation of cheap 'forreyn iron'. It does seem possible that the lack of demand for timber at the ironworks had been manifested in a wasting of the woodland in attempts to seek new uses for the local resources.[16] Indeed, Evelyn also wrote that 'I have heard my own father ... affirm, that a forge and some other mills, to which he furnished much fuel, were a means of maintaining and improving his woods ... by increasing planting and care'.[17] The decay of ironworking led to a decay in the woodlands, not vice versa.

Timber shortage can be seen as a localised, though severe, problem within the Weald. Perhaps as important was the fact that the entrepreneurs with water-powered sites experienced frustrating seasonal delays in production and more delay in the transport of the product, especially in the winter months. Despite the relatively high levels of capital investment in the construction of hammer ponds and bays it was noted, for example in 1653, that works were everywhere short of water. Rivers were used for transport in the eastern Weald wherever possible, since costs were thereby reduced and since roads were destroyed by the heavy loads. This latter was to the chagrin of local ratepayers who had to remedy the evils resulting from the activities of the industrialists. Roads were 'utterly decayed and spoyled'[18] by the carriage of charcoal, men and iron. The damage

---

[15] J. Evelyn, *Sylva or a Discourse on Forest Trees* (London, printed in 1776 edn as *Silva...*), p. 577.
[16] Public Record Office, E134 36 Chas II, East 22; Cleere and Crossley, *Iron Industry*, p. 315; Gulley, 'Wealden landscape', pp. 53, 193.
[17] Evelyn, *Sylva*, p. 568. The case against wholesale woodland depletion in the Weald is also made in M. W. Flinn, 'The growth of the English iron industry 1660–1760', *Economic History Review*, 11 (1958–9), pp. 144–53.
[18] J. S. Cockburn, *Calendar of Assize Records: Sussex Indictments, James I* (HMSO, 1975), p. 16.

incurred, external to the costs of the ironmasters themselves, had been the subject of increasingly severe Elizabethan legislation, but even by the 1620s it was still permissible to carry ordnance in four-wheeled carts. In 1666 problems associated with the carriage of heavy guns from John Browne's Chiddingfold furnace through Guildford were related in a letter from his agent.[19]

A mixture of political and technical explanations can be forwarded for the decline of the Wealden iron industry. The local political arguments relating to damage to the environment (e.g. damage to woodland and streams) and to infrastructure could probably have been resisted, certainly by landowners and ironmasters at the height of production. But more problematic were the political and economic processes external to the Weald. The revivals of the seventeenth-century Dutch War period and the eighteenth-century Seven Years War masked the underlying problems. After 1763 there was no way of competing. Carron guns undercut Wealden prices and the faithful Ordnance Office finally had to look elsewhere. In 1574 a reliable list of Wealden ironworks gives fifty-two furnaces and fifty-eight forges. By 1653 this had become thirty-six furnaces and forty-five forges, and in 1667 there were fourteen furnaces and twenty-one forges. By 1717 there were still fourteen furnaces but only thirteen forges, but by 1787 just three active furnaces were left. New works came on stream, but still more disappeared. In 1695 the Lamberhurst furnace was rebuilt as one of the largest in England, and there were abandonments and revivals, seasonal or infrequent workings, as well as changes in the pattern of output. Output did not, of course, reduce proportionally with the decline in works, but the overall pattern is apparent. Internal factions developed with the early seventeenth-century decline in demand for ordnance after the Spanish wars, and as holders of patents wrangled for assurances of income to tide them over their lean years. Such were the prime concerns of the King's gunstone maker, John Browne, who struggled through the early seventeenth century to secure for himself the supply of armaments to merchant fleets after the end of wartime demands. Similarly, the Fullers of Heathfield needed to use every ounce of political muscle to secure ordnance contracts by the mid-eighteenth century.[20]

Similar explanations are forthcoming for the decline of the eastern Wealden clothing industry, and for the western Wealden glass industry. The cloth industry was probably at its height between 1600 and 1630. Thereafter, its quality and skills remained but there was grave uncertainty

---

[19] Gulley, 'Wealden landscape', p. 193; Cleere and Crossley, *Iron Industry*, p. 339.
[20] Cleere and Crossley, *Iron Industry*, p. 166; H. C. Tomlinson, 'Wealden gunfounding: an analysis of its demise in the eighteenth century', *Economic History Review*, 29 (1976), pp. 383–99.

over export legislation in the early seventeenth century, and the trade never recovered from the slump of 1630–1. The wartime dislocations of the mid-seventeenth century were also significant, and the advent of the 'New Draperies' to Essex and elsewhere was decisive. By 1640 only Tenterden was classed among England's main cloth towns, although both Canterbury and Sandwich, outside the Weald, were included. Both were centres of settlement for refugee clothworkers from the 'Low Countries. Maidstone too had acquired a reputation as a cloth town for its manufacture of thread, a trade which certainly continued well into the eighteenth century. By the 1650s Wealden towns such as Tonbridge could still boast two or three clothiers on its outskirts. Tonbridge remained a convenient location for the organisation and collection of the produce from rural carders, spinners and weavers. The workshops for finishing the cloth were maintained as peri-urban sites, where dyeing and stretching were carried out. Thus in 1655 Thomas How, clothier, leased a house on the north side of Tonbridge with a warehouse and copper, hurdles, 'tainter', planks and joists. In many respects Tonbridge exercised the control over rural outworking districts that was noted by Mendels as a feature of proto-industrialisation. But the cloth towns in the Weald were parasitic on the cloth industry, and when the latter began to die, so too did the range of functions wither in those towns. Hasted noted in 1778 that both Cranbrook and Goudhurst still had woolstaplers, but that there were no clothiers left.[21] By 1650 suppliers of wool were selling to London, rather than to their traditional Kentish clothiers. Prosperity had deserted Goudhurst to the extent that its market place was taken down, and many people had migrated westwards into Sussex or left for the Palatinate or for the Low Countries again. In 1673 the inhabitants of Benenden complained of 'the great and general poverty in respect of the decay of the trade of cloth makeing with in the said parish, being the greatest support for most of the inhabitants there'.[22] The last product of the Cranbrook clothiers was rough linen hop-bagging. While flax continued as a popular crop in the Weald during the early eighteenth century, and there were still fulling mills operating, Defoe noted the great decline that had occurred by the 1720s:

There is not much manufacturing in this county: what is left is chiefly at Canterbury, and in this town of Maidstone, and the neighbourhood. At Cranbrook and Tenterden, Goudhurst and other villages thereabout, on the other side the Medway, there was once a very considerable clothing trade carried on ... but that trade is now quite decayed, and scarce ten clothiers left in all the county.[23]

[21] Chalklin, *Seventeenth-Century Kent*, Ch. 7; Gulley, 'Wealden landscape', pp. 209–11; C. H. Chalklin, 'A seventeenth-century market town: Tonbridge', *Archaeologia Cantiana*, 76 (1961), pp. 152–62.
[22] Chalklin, *Seventeenth-Century Kent*, p. 121.
[23] D. Defoe, *A Tour through the Whole Island of Great Britain*, 1724–6 (1974 edn), p. 115.

The Compton census of 1676 showed a density of population in the Kentish Wealden clothmaking area higher than the average for the Diocese of Canterbury, but in the 1660s half the inhabitants of Cranbrook had been too poor to be included in the Hearth Tax.[24] The interplay between clothworking, population growth and poverty was set out by one contemporary who viewed the decline of the industry with mixed feelings:

Tho' it sets the poor on work where it finds them, yet it draws still more to the place; and their masters allow wages so mean that they are only preserved from starving whilst they can work; when age, sickness or death comes, themselves, their wives or their children are most commonly left upon the parish; which is the reason why these towns [as in the Weald of Kent] where the clothing is departed, have fewer poor than they had before.[25]

Glass production declined far swifter than textiles. Peaking by 1600, the glassmaking industry had gone by about 1630. Only nine sites are thought to have been operating between these two dates, although a 1629 map of the southern part of Lodsworth parish still referred to the digging and selling of sand from the common to the glassmakers.[26] The 'Glasse houses' were small, with the furnaces being little larger than bread ovens. The limited capital involvement probably constituted something of a push factor, since there was no locational inertia produced by previous heavy investment. The Lorraine and Norman glassmakers had settled in Wisborough Green and Kirdford, and had developed well-established contacts with London glass dealers such as Lionel Bennet, a member of the Glaziers' Company. By 1605 Isaac Bungar, a Norman 'gentilhomme verrier' had established links with Bennet to such good effect that they had a virtual monopoly of Sussex glass for ten years. Temporary fuel shortages hindered the industry but it was the rise of coal-fired furnaces, monopolised by Mansell in Newcastle, that finished Bungar and the Frenchmen in the Weald. Their last furnace closed in 1618. Despite the prohibition on the importation of Venetian glass in 1615, the industry was now doomed; and in the same year the use of wood fuel in glassmaking was forbidden, with Mansell vigorously prosecuting any Wealden wood-burning transgressors. Bungar became increasingly interested in the mercantile aspects of the industry, and by 1620 he was a 'Freeman and Glazier of the City of London'. He was buried at Pulborough in Sussex in 1643, the only member

[24] C. H. Chalklin, 'The Compton census of 1676: the dioceses of Canterbury and Rochester', in *A Seventeenth Century Miscellany: Kent Records XVII* (Maidstone, 1960), pp. 172–4; B. M. Short, 'The south-east: Kent, Surrey and Sussex', in J. Thirsk (ed.), *Agrarian History of England and Wales*, vol. 5, part 1: *1640–1750 Regional Farming Systems* (Cambridge, Cambridge University Press, 1985), p. 308.
[25] Anon., *Reasons for a Limited Exportation of Wooll* (1677), quoted by A. Clark, *Working Life of Women in the Seventeenth Century* (London, Routledge, 1919), p. 149.
[26] Gulley, 'Wealden landscape', p. 201.

of the French glassmaking families brought over in the mid-sixteenth century to have stayed on. Other immigrant French masters had moved on to the coal-fired industries at Stourbridge or Newcastle upon Tyne, leaving the part-time Wealden producers to revert to their farming activities.[27]

DE-INDUSTRIALISATION: A WITHERED ENCLAVE?

It is a fairly general observation that industrialisation proceeds in enclaves within nation states. Different levels of growth and prosperity arise between regions, as well as between industrial sectors and between social classes. Ashworth observed that 'Some enclaves remain enclaves, though often somewhat enlarged: a few withered; some fused to become the dominant regions of great industrial nations.'[28] The Weald became a 'withered enclave'. By 1700 the de-industrialisation process in the Weald was almost complete, well before the generally acknowledged establishment of coal-fired manufactures elsewhere. Iron production was a relict industry, set for one last burst during the wars of the mid-eighteenth century; cloth and glass production had moved elsewhere, and the Weald was now left with more localised industries. These included tanning, leatherworking and gloving which were highly dispersed, bricks, tiles and pottery on the southern slopes of the High Weald and on St John's and other Low Wealden commons, and wood products such as baskets and tools, ashes and charcoal, hoops, barrels and sawn timber. Gunpowder production at such places as Battle and Maresfield had been a lesser Wealden concern, exploiting local charcoal together with imported sulphur and saltpetre. It was much reduced by the mid-seventeenth century, and of the five original sites, only that at Battle survived through into the late nineteenth century. However, some autumnal work was provided in the Ashdown Forest area in the gathering of alderwood which was used in coarse types of powder, and dogwood which was used in higher quality sporting powder. There were unauthorised as well as authorised powder mills. A Battle water mill was suppressed in 1627 as one of the former category, while the manufacture of gunpowder was officially licensed at Battle only in 1676.[29] Revealingly, Defoe noted that around Horsham it

---

[27] Ibid., 203; Kenyon, *Glass Industry*, pp. 20, 35, 114–35.

[28] Cited in C. H. Lee, 'Regional structural change in the long run: Great Britain 1841–1971', in S. Pollard (ed.), *Region und Industrialisierung* (Göttingen, Vandenhoek und Ruprecht, 1980), pp. 254–5.

[29] J. Lowerson, 'Sussex and "industrialization": economic depression and restrictive elements, 1700–1840', in M. Palmer (ed.), *The Onset of Industrialization* (Department of Adult Education, Nottingham, 1977), p. 19; Brent, 'Employment', p. 42; and J. Irons, 'Aspects of the impact of man on the historical ecology of Ashdown Forest, Sussex, before 1885', unpublished D.Phil. thesis (University of Sussex, 1982), p. 98.

was poultry production which was 'like a manufacture to the country people'.[30] In the Ashdown Forest many speculator landlords in the late seventeenth and eighteenth centuries sold timber and underwood recklessly to recoup their investments, thereby completing the deforestation of the area. Although they had existed for centuries, woodbrokers now became the most important middlemen for Wealden industry.[31]

At the height of production in the Weald, the 'inner contradictions' of proto-industry manifestly did not lead to a concentration of production in supervised workshops which then become mechanised. Instead, political and technical changes left the Weald as a spent industrial force. Some of the covering clauses used by theorists in dealing with de-industrialisation should therefore now be examined for their relevance to this particular English situation.

Both Mendels and Landes, in his discussion of Mendels' work, note that the absence of raw materials and power required for the transition to full industrialisation might lead to the decay of the older industries.[32] One can concur with this view without difficulty. Such was the fate of Brittany, Languedoc and parts of Normandy. Any attempt to modernise south-eastern English technology to maintain an industrial presence would have incurred a high importation cost for fuels. The possibility of using coal for Wealden manufacturing was considered more than once. Indeed, as early as 1637 John Browne, the ordnance monopolist, was urging Kentish clothiers to switch to coal to stave off their complaints against his over-use of local wood resources.[33] When William Ashburnham, that 'model of industry and efficiency'[34] had difficulty in finding a tenant for his ironworks in 1706, he took on the management himself, importing South Welsh coal from his own mines. But such ventures were generally quite uneconomic, and the use of coal at this juncture would only have served to prolong a decay which had already begun well before the advent of more sophisticated coal-fired technology.

Factors of comparative advantage might also work to stimulate agricultural development for the supplying of food to nearby urban areas. Mendels notes this particularly where railways act to shrink transportation costs. He conjoins this with the further point that a region may well exhibit soils and climate which are favourable for labour-intensive agricultural production. In either circumstance the region may switch its emphasis

[30] Defoe, *A Tour through the Whole Island*, p. 153.
[31] Irons, 'Impact of man', p. 88.
[32] Mendels, 'Proto-industrialisation: the first phase'; and D. Landes, 'Comments on papers by Hohenberg, Mendels and Mazzaoui', *Journal of Economic History*, 32 (1972), pp. 287–91.
[33] Brent, 'Rural employment', p. 170.
[34] G. E. Mingay, *English Landed Society in the Eighteenth Century* (London, Routledge, 1963), pp. 63–71.

from dual employment to agricultural specialisation. Thus the peasantry of Calvados in the Pays D'Auge in Lower Normandy became de-industrialised as butter and meat sales increased to supply urban areas as railway contacts grew.[35] But it is unlikely that such an explanation will suffice for the Weald. It is true, of course, that London represented the greatest potential market in England and that railways proliferated around and through the Weald. But Wealden farming did not oust manufactures. There were improvements in grassland management, in cattle breeding, in dairying and in poultry production, but these manifestly came later than the decline in cloth, iron and glass. Wealden cattle farmers were well within the orbit of the London food markets, of course, but perhaps real competition from agriculture could only have been offered with the advent of hop farming. Hops were both capital and labour intensive, were exhausting and high-risk products, but they were also capable of yielding great profit. Certainly the competition for woodland to be used for hop poles (needed by hop farmers at the rate of about 3,000 per acre) pushed up the production costs for late seventeenth- and eighteenth-century ironmasters. But again, maximum acreages in the Weald were not reached until the second quarter of the nineteenth century, and the risky nature of the crop did not make it realistic as a source of income for small farmers and peasants.

The relations between Wealden agriculture and industry had been extremely complex. Some of the relations were positive and truly complementary, such as the processing of hides, working of wool or milling. Some activities were associated positively and directly with agriculture, such as the manufacturing of implements. Some were associated indirectly and incidentally. Thus some Wealden land was treated with marl which might be derived from iron-ore bell pits, or with ashes from the ironworks. In these ways an industrial presence might actually stimulate agricultural change. However, a strongly competitive relationship may also be traced in claims for labour, land and capital, raw materials, fuel and power. Furnacemen could command wages double or triple those paid to farmworkers. In 1740 Fuller the ironmaster wrote of the negative effect on farmland in Warbleton where a succession of tenants had been 'done ill or almost broke upon it' since it was 'torn about so by drawing of mine'. But on the other hand, many of the tenants on the same Fuller Wealden estate could get by only through providing horses and carts for ironworking.[36]

Perhaps the very importance of Wealden industry by 1600 helped dampen the processes of agricultural change so noticeable in surrounding

---

[35] F. F. Mendels, 'Seasons and regions in agriculture and industry during the process of industrialisation', in Pollard (ed.), *Region und Industrialisierung*, p. 183.
[36] Cattell, 'Historical geography', p. 157; ESRO, SAS RF/15/25.

regions in the seventeenth and eighteenth centuries. Certainly the instances of internal transfers of capital between Wealden industry and agriculture were rare. However, many landowning families were forced to turn from ironworking back to agriculture and woodland in the late seventeenth and eighteenth centuries. In the case of the Fullers considerable income might still have been derived from sales of ordnance and bar iron in the first half of the eighteenth century, but stability in finances was sought by closer links with London society and national politics, and through income from Jamaican sugar plantations. Nevertheless, with the ending of ordnance contracts after 1763 the Fullers began to improve their estate management. Diversification now became essential. The inextricable mixture of land, trade, industry and the professions noted by Mingay for many eighteenth-century landowning families was in fact nothing less than a survival strategy in the Weald.[37]

Mendels' emphasis on comparative advantage as an explanation for de-industrialisation does not match the evidence from the Weald. Competition for resources between industry and agriculture was manifest, and the former activity clearly triumphed. Wealden farming could not compete with the returns to be gained from industry. Consequently, little investment by the larger landowners was successfully made, and when the key industries declined it was because of their internal and external problems – political, economic and technical – not because of the comparative advantages offered by agricultural prices.

One further point relating to the de-industrialisation of the Weald should be emphasised. Kriedte has noted that unequal terms of trade provoked an involuntary flow of capital from agriculture into commerce in the seventeenth century, and although generalisation across the seventeenth century is difficult in view of fluctuating prices in agriculture, he has seen this period as 'the High Noon of merchant capitalism...in England'. Thereafter industrial capital came to prevail nationally alongside merchant capital in the eighteenth century.[38] But he does not pursue the regional implications of his statement. With little identity of interest between merchant and industrial capital, those regions, such as the Weald, formerly receiving metropolitan mercantile investment were henceforth less favoured as government stocks and foreign investment became more attractive. And industrial capital in the eighteenth century was, to simplify the issue, a three-way flow between London, the Empire and the new manufacturing

---

[37] R. V. Saville, 'Gentry wealth on the Weald in the eighteenth century: the Fullers of Brightling Park', *Sussex Archaeological Collections*, 121 (1983), pp. 129–47; Mingay, *Landed Society*, p. 105.

[38] P. Kriedte, *Peasants, Landlords and Merchant Capitalists: Europe and the World Economy, 1500–1800* (English transl., Leamington Spa, Berg, 1983), p. 148.

regions. But in the Weald the old bonds between London financiers, ironmasters and landowners were weakened. Only where government or landed capital could continue to supply finance, as with the Fullers or Ashburnhams, could Wealden manufacturing be prolonged past 1750. The Fullers' Heathfield furnace closed in 1787 and the Ashburnham furnace in 1813.

When industrial capital did finally flow into the Weald it was as a cultural response to Victorian nativism, and it came in the form of gothic splendour and a retreat from unmannerly northern industrialism.[39] Here was a 'primitive' landscape, thrilling yet accessible. The image of the Weald as a retreat from industrial capitalism was fostered by the early nineteenth century and both those who benefited financially, and those who sought escape from its worst excesses in London, came to live in the region. Once this had happened, the death knell was sounded for any industrial investment. Indeed, it could be argued that even by the later eighteenth century, ironmasters could have invested more heavily in updating and modernising their charcoal iron techniques. Instead they turned to their estates as cultural and political investments, or increased their overseas commitments. It could even be argued that if a comparative advantage is to be sought, then it is to be found in the recreational and residential qualities, and sheer 'Englishness' of the Weald as perceived in the eighteenth and nineteenth centuries. It is the quality of landscape seen within the aura of Romanticism which has latterly been its most durable quality. An analysis of cultural attitudes is therefore needed to give more weight to the explanation of de-industrialisation in south-east England. Certainly changes in cultural and aesthetic notions affected the investment decisions of Wealden landowners, and the Victorian perception of the region as a reservoir of cultural refreshment is well documented.[40] Perhaps the preconditions for this change were laid down by the eighteenth-century withdrawal of gentry from industry, leaving scarcely a landscape trace, save for mannered Jacobean ironmasters' houses, serpentine hammer ponds, and fascinating ruins, half-hidden within the reclaiming woodland.

In the case of the Weald it seems more profitable to look to the changing patterns of national and international finance, politics and culture to understand de-industrialisation, rather than to seek explanations within the region itself or even, as Mendels has argued, within technological change.

---

[39] See M. Wiener, *English Culture and the Decline of the Industrial Spirit, 1850–1980* (Cambridge, Cambridge University Press, 1981).
[40] For a review of these ideas see P. F. Brandon and B. M. Short, *The South-East from AD 1000* (London, Longman, 1989).

Admittedly the intricacies of the relationship between technological change and political and economic decision-making are difficult to unravel. But several generations separate the peak of Wealden ironworking from the use of coal-fired bellows at Coalbrookdale in the 1770s, and a similarly embarrassing gap yawns between the demise of the Wealden putting-out cloth industry and the establishment elsewhere of the full factory system. Neither was the gap adequately filled by any agricultural developments sufficient to sustain viable regional employment.

The conflation of the theories of underdevelopment and proto-industrialisation allows us to see that the Wealden industries were oriented to the external world. They showed a marked spatial and sectoral specialisation within the region. Spatial overlaps occurred at times of boom, but retreats to three separate heartlands occurred at times of recession. Little evidence has so far been found for internal transfers of capital between the sectors or of any external scale economies which might have benefited all the industries. So, when economic retreat was in force, each industry could be 'picked off' separately, for it could not rely on security within an industrial complex.

Instead the Weald was left with an underdeveloped agricultural base, localised naked heathlands where timber had been stripped and a marginalised population whose size created a reputation for poor law stress and social crime that was only abated with rural depopulation, and the Victorian middle-class colonisation and gentrification after 1850. There was thus a 200-year gap between the end of proto-industrialisation in the Weald and the discovery of a new role as detached London suburb, a role that it still retains.

Chapter 7

Work, culture and resistance to machinery in the West of England woollen industry

ADRIAN J. RANDALL

The regional history of the British industrial revolution is one of marked contrasts of fortune; rapid growth and advance in one area, slow or sudden decline in another. Few industries, however, can match the remarkable contrast between the fortunes of the woollen cloth industry in the West of England counties of Gloucestershire, Somerset and Wiltshire and that of the West Riding of Yorkshire. As Wilson in a perceptive essay has shown, the West Riding woollen industry embarked on its road to supremacy early in the eighteenth century, but its progress was rapidly accelerated by the advent of early textile machinery.[1] The West of England, on the other hand, though dominant at the start of that century, was by its close already in rapid relative decline. Not long after the Napoleonic Wars this became an absolute decline. The West of England's failure to adapt to changed circumstances, its slower take up of new technologies, reduced it from the forefront of the cloth trade to little more than a backwater by 1850.[2] The work of Wilson and of Mann have done much to explain this eclipse, both stressing the importance of differences of product and especially in marketing practices as major reasons. While accepting that these were indeed important factors, this chapter is addressed to another aspect of this pattern, namely worker resistance to machinery. Such resistance was encountered in both regions but, with one major exception, resistance did not prove an obstacle to advance in the West Riding. This was not so in the West of England where major opposition greeted all new innovations. The failure of the West of England to match the pace of change in Yorkshire in the years 1770 to 1820 was to prove crucial for that industry's ultimate ability to compete. Why this should have been so, and its implications for our understanding of the response to machinery not only in the woollen industry but in other industries and regions undergoing mechanical and structural transformation, form the themes of this discussion.

[1] R. G. Wilson, 'The supremacy of the Yorkshire cloth industry in the eighteenth century', in N. B. Harte and K. G. Ponting (eds.), *Textile History and Economic History: Essays in Honour of Miss Julia de Lacy Mann* (Manchester, 1973), pp. 225–46.
[2] J. de L. Mann, *The Cloth Industry in the West of England from 1640 to 1880* (Oxford, 1971).

I

The woollen industry experienced some of the most extensive resistance to the advent of machinery in the industrial revolution. Thus Rees' *Cyclopaedia* noted in 1819: 'The able workmen ... have made greater and more effectual opposition to the introduction of improvements in the woollen than in any other of our great manufactures.'[3] The most spectacular example of this opposition was witnessed in Yorkshire in 1812 in the Luddite disturbances when the croppers or cloth dressers attempted to stem the tide of finishing machinery, 'which both they and their employers knew perfectly well would displace them',[4] by destroying the machines and the mills which housed them. But such actions had been preceded ten years earlier by the cloth dressers in Wiltshire and Somerset,[5] and it was in the West of England where resistance to machinery proved most intractable and widespread. For example, the spinning jenny, after initial resistance, was in widespread use in Yorkshire from the later 1770s but, though first introduced into the West of England in 1776, it was not taken up in significant numbers until the early 1790s because of worker hostility. The scribbling engine spread rapidly in Yorkshire from the mid-1780s, but protracted disturbances prevented its widespread adoption in the West of England until after 1795. And the flying shuttle loom, taken up after initial opposition in Yorkshire from the early 1780s, led to disorder when introduced in the West of England in the 1790s and was still provoking riots in Frome as late as 1822.[6] Faced with this apparently deep-seated antipathy to machinery in the West of England we may be tempted to echo the words of Josiah Tucker, Dean of Gloucester, who lamented of the West Country industry in 1757:

As to Machines in the Woollen [industry], nothing very considerable hath been of late attempted; owing in a great Measure to the mistaken Notions of the infatuated Populace, who not being able to see farther than the first Link of the Chain, consider all such Inventions as taking the Bread out of their Mouths; and therefore never fail to break out into Riots and Insurrections, whenever such Things are proposed.[7]

Worker resistance to machinery receives little attention in the economic history textbooks of the industrial revolution. Historians have shown more

---

[3] A. Rees, *The Cyclopaedia* (London, 1819), vol. 38, article on woollen manufacture.
[4] E. P. Thompson, *The Making of the English Working Class* (London, 1963; Harmondsworth, 1968), p. 570. For Yorkshire Luddism see in particular Thompson, *The Making*; and M. I. Thomis, *The Luddites* (Newton Abbot, 1970).
[5] A. J. Randall, 'The shearmen and the Wiltshire Outrages of 1802: trade unionism and industrial violence', *Social History*, 7, 3 (1982), pp. 283–304.   [6] Mann, *Cloth Industry*, Chs. 5 and 6.
[7] J. Tucker, *Instructions for Travellers* (Gloucester, 1757), p. 21.

sympathy than Tucker for workers' fears of losing their bread but they have been reluctant to discern much in the way of general attitudes to machinery from such outbursts of hostility, preferring to explain them merely as symptoms of other problems. Machine breaking has in particular frequently been associated with and explained by economic depression and industrial stagnation. Thus the Hammonds noted of 1812:

It was an unfortunate time for the introduction of labour-saving machinery. There had been a bad harvest the year before; the Orders in Council had crippled the woollen industry; there were numbers of unemployed apart from those turned adrift by the introduction of new machinery. The croppers ... attributed all the evils that beset them to these new machines and determined to destroy them.[8]

Briggs described the Luddites as 'helpless victims of distress'[9] and Thomis likewise stressed the economic depression occasioned by the Orders in Council as the principal factor in the outbreak of Luddism in 1811–12.[10] Earlier resistance to the spinning jenny, scribbling engines and the flying shuttle has likewise been connected to slumps in the economy and slower rates of growth. Antipathy to these machines is said to have declined as the economy improved or growth accelerated.[11] Machine breaking thus bids fair to be seen simply as an aspect of the 'social tension chart',[12] as merely another reaction to hunger and unemployment.

Similarly the actions of the machine breakers have often been portrayed as instinctive reactions to threats of hunger, the products of desperate and backward-looking men unable to air their grievances in more constructive forms. Thus the Hammonds and more recently Thomis sought to divorce the Luddites from the wider body of workers, isolating violence as the resort of a minority unable to develop the more sophisticated responses of trade union organisation or parliamentary petitioning. Luddism, wrote Thomis of Yorkshire, 'occurred not through established trade-union machinery but in its absence'.[13] Machine breaking was therefore an indication of industrial weakness and an incapacity for organised 'orthodox trade unionism'.[14] Bythell, writing of the Lancashire power-loom riots, argued in the same vein that they were 'pointless physical violence',

---

[8] J. L. and B. Hammond, *The Skilled Labourer* (London, 1919; Harlow, 1979 edn), p. 246.
[9] A. Briggs, *The Age of Improvement* (Harlow, 1959), p. 182.
[10] Thomis, *Luddites*, Ch. 2.
[11] Mann, *Cloth Industry*, Ch. V; see also J. Stevenson, *Popular Disturbances in England 1700–1870* (Harlow, 1979), pp. 118, 152.
[12] W. W. Rostow, *The British Economy in the Nineteenth Century* (Oxford, 1948), pp. 122–5. For a criticism of this approach see E. P. Thompson, 'The moral economy of the English crowd in the eighteenth century', *Past and Present*, 50, (1971), p. 78.
[13] Hammonds, *Skilled Labourer*, Ch. 11; Thomis, *Luddites*, p. 134.
[14] E. H. Hunt, *British Labour History 1815–1914* (London, 1981), p. 196; cf. Randall, 'The shearmen and the Wiltshire Outrages'.

'a throwback to the disorganised activities of a pre-industrial age'.[15] Hobsbawm on the other hand, while recognising the existence of considerable hostility towards machinery in some areas, saw much machine breaking as part of an older tradition of 'collective bargaining by riot', a form of proto-trade union action in which machinery was attacked to bring pressure to bear on employers or to prevent other workers blacklegging. The machine was in general not attacked *per se*, and its destruction was incidental to the struggle for income.[16] This argument has found wide acceptance.[17] Thus Stevenson notes, 'even in resistance to machinery, the reaction was less hostility to machines as such but opposition to those machines which seemed most directly to threaten living standards'.[18] The Hammonds were well aware of the long history of machine breaking throughout the eighteenth century, but while they recognised that the changing character of capitalism during the industrial revolution pre-cipitated more bitter clashes over labour displacement, they nonetheless saw the machine breakers fighting merely to preserve their own incomes rather than articulating or defending an alternative economic philosophy to that of the machine economy.[19]

The variety of circumstances, the variety of response from region to region, trade to trade, and even within the same trade from place to place, has tended to dissuade historians from suggesting broader parameters to the understanding of the incidence and character of resistance to machinery. Certainly it is much easier to explain machine breaking as a spontaneous response to distress, as an understandable but ill-judged knee-jerk reaction of self-preservation rather than as a reasoned hostility to the machine economy itself. There may well be good grounds for such a cautious interpretation of machine breaking but such a view may delimit our perception of the basis of resistance to technological change. I would like to suggest three areas of approach which may contribute towards a more dynamic appreciation of hostility to the advent of machinery: the organisation and structure of work; the character of the manufacturing community; and the ideology of resistance.

[15] D. Bythell. *The Handloom Weavers* (Cambridge, 1969), pp. 180, 181.
[16] E. J. Hobsbawm. *Labouring Men* (London, 1964), Ch. 2. Hobsbawm identifies two sorts of machine breaking: collective bargaining by riot and direct hostility to the machine itself. While he notes that the latter 'was neither so indiscriminate nor so specific as has often been assumed' and that it was 'surprisingly weak', he suggests there was wide community support for such views. It is interesting that it is only the concept of collective bargaining by riot which has been widely taken up since this pioneering article first appeared in 1952.
[17] See, for example, Stevenson, *Popular Disturbances*, Chs. 6, and 7; Hunt, *British Labour History*, Ch. 6; J. F. C. Harrison, *The Common People* (Flamingo edn, 1984), Ch. 8.
[18] Stevenson, *Popular Disturbances*, p. 131.
[19] Hammonds, *Skilled Labourer* (1979 edn), introduction by J. Rule, pp. xx–xxvii.

II

A critical factor determining the response to machinery was the organisation and structure of work. Certainly there were, as various historians have indicated, considerable regional differences in workers' reactions to mechanisation. These reflected, in part, differences in the regional economic opportunities for growth and work created during the industrial revolution. Thus the more variegated economies of the Midlands and the north saw little hostility to machinery whereas the more industry-specific economies of many southern regions witnessed prolonged resistance. But in great measure these differences also reflect different organisations of work. This may most clearly be seen by examining the structure of the woollen industry of the West of England and comparing it with that in Yorkshire. Both produced the same basic product, woollen cloth. In both the basic processes were the same but their respective organisations of production were very different. In the parlance of proto-industrialisation, the West of England industry constituted a *Verlagsystem* while that in the West Riding took the form of a *Kaufsystem*.[20]

In the West of England the putting-out system reached its apogee. Here gentlemen clothiers occupied a pivotal position putting out work to large workforces, each worker a specialist with specialist skills (see Figure 7.1). Thus a gentleman clothier would employ wool sorters, pickers, scribblers, warp spinners, weft spinners, spoolers, reelers, weavers, burlers, fullers, dyers, cloth dressers, fine drawers and markers. Here there was a sub-division of labour many times more impressive than that of Adam Smith's famous pin factory. Not all these workers were employed directly by the gentleman clothier. Sorters, pickers and scribblers usually worked in the clothier's workshops but spinners and weavers were invariably outworkers working in their own homes. Some West Country clothiers owned fulling mills and dyeworks, but others would put this work out on commission to independent fullers and dyers. Some owned their own finishing shops (this

[20] The debate on proto-industrialisation continues to engage the interests of economic historians even though there is a growing recognition of the difficulties of applying the concept to the British experience. Broadly the model advanced by Mendels and developed and re-worked by others envisages two distinct and progressional modes of industrial organisation before the factory: the *Kaufsystem* characterised by artisan domestic production in by-employment with agricultural activities; and the *Verlagsystem* in which capitalist control has been extended into a putting-out system where workers, divorced from agriculture, depend entirely upon wages from industrial production. See F. F. Mendels, 'Proto-industrialisation: the first phase of the industrialisation process', *Journal of Economic History*, 32, 1 (1972), pp. 241–61; P. Kriedte, H. Medick and J. Schlumbohm. *Industrialisation before Industrialisation: Rural Industry in the Genesis of Capitalism* (English transl., Cambridge, 1982). See also S. Pollard 'Industrialisation and the European economy', *Economic History Review*, 26, 4, (1973).

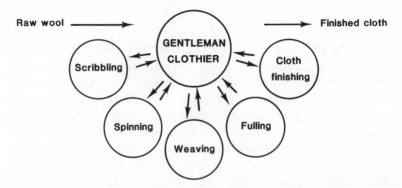

Figure 7.1   The organisational structure of the West of England woollen industry

was a growing trend towards 1800) but most employed independent master dressers who were thus generally the direct employers of the notoriously unruly cloth finishers or shearmen as they were known in the West. Nonetheless, the clothier's role as 'Paymaster', as Tucker called him, remained the same throughout. He owned the raw material at all stages and paid piece rates for all work. 'He is the Master of the whole Manufacture from first to last.'

Tucker contrasted this system of production unfavourably with that of the West Riding where 'the Woollen Manufacture is carried on by small Farmers and Freeholders'.[21] Here the industry was divided into two separate sections (see Figure 7.2). The main stages of production up to the finishing processes took place in the hands and in the workshops of master clothiers of whom there were many thousands. These master clothiers bought the raw wool and then worked it up, sorting, scribbling, carding and spinning the wool and then weaving it into cloth within an extended family unit of household, living-in and living-out journeymen. Numbers of journeymen employed in general did not exceed a handful and in consequence there was little specialisation and the product quality was generally much lower than that in the West of England. Once woven, the master clothiers had the cloth fulled by independent concerns and then sold it at the Cloth Halls to gentlemen merchants. As in the West Country several gentlemen merchants were setting up their own finishing shops towards 1800 but the majority employed master dressers to complete their cloths prior to sale.

Tucker believed that the 'domestic system' of the West Riding produced better-value products and better industrial and social relations. The West Country journeymen 'deprived of the Hopes of advancing

[21] Tucker, *Instructions*, pp. 24–5.

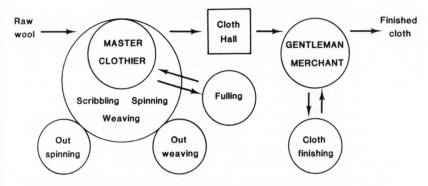

Figure 7.2   The organisational structure of the Yorkshire woollen industry

themselves ... think it no Crime to get as much Wages, and do as little for it as they possibly can, to lie and cheat, and do any other bad Thing; provided that it is only against their Master, whom they look upon as their common Enemy'. In Yorkshire, however, the journeymen, 'being so little removed from the Degree and Condition of their Masters, and so likely to set up for themselves by the Industry and Frugality of a few Years, have no Conception that they are embarked in an Interest opposite to that of their Masters'.[22] Wilson, examining the opportunities for entrepreneurial advance in both regions, concluded that Tucker's views were exaggerated. While Yorkshire master clothiers in 1794 echoed Tucker in describing the West of England system as being 'founded on a Monopoly erected and supported by great capitals', Wilson, citing Mann, correctly argues that there were many smaller clothiers in the West Country and that there were always opportunities to enter their ranks. 'Little makers' in Gloucestershire ran precarious trades 'on tick' from East India Company factors throughout the eighteenth century, while Blackwell Hall factors provided similar credit for Wiltshire clothiers.[23] Trowbridge, a major centre of the Wiltshire trade, was always famous for its preponderance of smaller and middle-sized clothiers, and the controversy over the projected repeal of the old regulatory statutes in the years 1802–6 revealed that the 'inferior' clothiers greatly outnumbered their 'respectable' counterparts.[24] However, it was the respectable clothiers who dominated the trade, both in 1700 and in

[22] Ibid.
[23] Wilson, 'The supremacy of Yorkshire', pp. 237–9; *Journal of the House of Commons*, XLIX, p. 275; J. Haynes, *A View of the Present State of the Clothing Trade in England* (1706), p. 14; S. Rudder, *A New History of Gloucestershire* (Gloucester, 1779), pp. 61–2; Mann, *Cloth Industry*, pp. 96–8, 81–3.
[24] K. H. Rogers, 'Trowbridge clothiers and their houses, 1660–1800', in Harte and Ponting (eds.), *Textile History and Economic History*, pp. 139–40; Mann, *Cloth Industry*, pp. 145–6; Randall, 'The shearmen and the Wiltshire Outrages', p. 301.

1800. Mann suggested that some 400 clothiers dominated the Gloucester-shire trade and 250 the Wiltshire trade at the start of the century. By its close there may well have been even more of a concentration of capital. The Gloucestershire clothiers' association which co-ordinated their campaign to repeal the old statutes, and which included most, but not all, of the principal firms in the county, had only seventy-eight subscribing members. Further, the costs of establishing oneself as a clothier continued to rise. In 1660 a minimum figure of £300 was suggested. By 1760 this had risen to over £500.[25] While factors might make credit available to nascent entrepreneurs, a man still needed capital of his own far in excess of that normally within the reach of a journeyman before he might expect such help. The lack of an intermediary rank of master workers further delimited opportunities. There were indeed some master spinners and more, though a declining number of, master weavers who might sub-contract work for a clothier and amass some capital and wider business knowledge, but their role was in many ways superfluous. Master dressers had better opportunities for advancement and many Trowbridge clothier families sprang from such roots.[26] However, their knowledge of the trade was confined to finishing. The wider experience needed by the clothier could prove a costly acquisition. There can be little doubt, therefore, that Tucker was broadly correct when he assumed that the West Country worker could 'never be but Journeyman'.[27]

The much clearer opportunities for social and economic mobility in Yorkshire expounded by Tucker were echoed in the Report of the Parliamentary Select Committee of 1806. The gap from journeyman to master clothier was never wide, though it too was growing. The real gap in the West Riding was that which separated master clothier from gentleman merchant. This was not as great as that between master worker and 'respectable' clothier in the West of England, but it remained substantial. However, since there was no overlap of functions and the Cloth Halls acted as an effective buffer between them, there was very little conflict until machinery aroused fears of 'Cloth Merchants becoming Cloth Makers' in the mid-1790s.[28]

The difference in the organisation of the industry in the West Country and Yorkshire therefore stemmed from the clear functional differences between gentlemen clothiers and master clothiers. The former were essentially organisers and controllers, the latter master workers. The former

[25] Mann, Cloth Industry, pp. 33–4, 146, 98.
[26] Rogers, 'Trowbridge clothiers', pp. 160–1.
[27] Tucker, Instructions, p. 25.
[28] British Parliamentary Papers, 1806. (268), III, Report of the Select Committee to Consider the State of the Woollen Manufacture; Journal of the House of Commons, XLIX, p. 275.

were large capitalists, the latter petty producers. Thus, while even the smallest 'respectable' gentlemen clothiers produced 300 or more broad-cloths per annum, the largest master clothiers rarely produced more than 150 and the majority produced many fewer. The social structures occasioned by these different organisational systems – on the one hand a society clearly divided between capital and labour, on the other a more homogeneous or graduated social hierarchy – predated the advent of machinery and were to have fundamental effects on its reception.

The sub-division of the workforce of the West of England provided that industry with highly specialist skills which enabled the production of a variety and quality of cloths which were unmatched elsewhere and gave the workers a strong sense of craft pride and solidarity. However, with the advent of mechanisation such specialisation made these workers very vulnerable to technological redundancy. An innovation in any one branch might threaten an entire trade with unemployment. This proved particularly true of preparatory and finishing machinery. From figures compiled by the West of England handloom weavers' assistant commissioner in 1838 it is posssible to conclude that the spinning jenny displaced nine in ten warp spinners, and thirteen in fourteen weft spinners in the region. The scribbling engines made nearly fifteen in every sixteen adult male scribblers redundant and the gig mill and shearing frame displaced nine in ten cloth dressers. These trades constituted major sections of the pre-industrial workforce in the West of England. Thus the mechanisation of spinning reduced the female labour required in the production of a cloth by 75 per cent. The scribblers had constituted around 10 per cent and the cloth dressers around 15 per cent of the adult male workforce.[29] They found that their carefully honed skills were rendered redundant by machinery. The impact of machinery was felt not only by those directly displaced. Since large numbers of textile workers' wives in the eighteenth century took in spinning, many family economies experienced the loss of this traditional income. Weavers felt the draught as increasing numbers of displaced women took up the loom. Craft restrictions on recruitment to different trades meant that many men in trades which were not initially affected by technological change had brothers or sons who worked in trades which were. Technological unemployment cast a chill throughout the West of England woollen-producing community.

In the West Riding of Yorkshire, however, the domestic system's

---

[29] *British Parliamentary Papers*, 1840, XXIII, Reports from the Assistant Handloom Weavers' Commissioners, Pt VIII, pp. 439–41; A. J. Randall, 'Labour and the industrial revolution in the West of England woollen industry', unpublished Ph.D. thesis (University of Birmingham, 1979), pp. 236–57.

relative lack of specialisation meant that the new technologies of the late eighteenth century did not threaten vested interests. Frequently they proved adaptable to the small workshop, as did the jenny or the smaller hand-powered scribbling engines, and energies released from preparatory hand processes could easily be re-channelled into the loom. Even when larger powered machinery was introduced into the West Riding, these could often be absorbed within the existing structure of the industry. Thus water-powered scribbling mills were frequently initiated by master fullers, who were already working on commission for the master clothiers, or by groups of master clothiers themselves in small joint-stock companies.[30] When such machinery was set up in the West of England, it was established by the gentlemen clothiers, emphasising the capitalist–labourer division and presaging the development of a factory system. Mann noted that the early mills here 'were not in most cases the imposing piles familiar to a later generation but small buildings'.[31] Nonetheless, while large mills were few, they showed a new trend towards the extension of capitalist control which alarmed the woollen workers. The extent of the fear which such mills aroused should not be underestimated. Staverton, Twerton and Uley mills were exceptional but workers many miles distant from them had heard of them, even though they had never seen them, and were frightened of their potential. The same was true of Bean Ing mill in Yorkshire.

Thus the attitude to machinery depended to a great extent on how it might or might not integrate within existing work structures. The large scribbling engines occasioned early protests in Yorkshire, but, established by the master clothiers, they strengthened the domestic system. In the West of England, however, they were not introduced until 1791 for fear of the reaction which then greeted them. Resistance in Wiltshire was fierce and was not overcome until after 1795. While rising economic improvement thereafter may have eased its introduction, it was also eased by the permanent garrison of troops stationed in the region since the riots of 1791, troops whose orders frequently stressed their duty to protect woollen mills.[32] Where work organisation was the same, however, as it was in the finishing trades in both Yorkshire and the West of England, then the reaction was the same, as the Wiltshire Outrages and the Luddite disturbances were to prove.

---

[30] W. B. Crump and G. Ghorbal, *History of the Huddersfield Woollen Industry* (Huddersfield, 1935), p. 90; R. G. Wilson, *Gentlemen Merchants: The Merchant Community in Leeds, 1700–1830* (Manchester, 1971), pp. 90–109. These small joint-stock scribbling mills often included more than six partners but, since they were organised under a trust, they did not infringe the law.

[31] Mann, *Cloth Industry*, p. 131.

[32] W. B. Crump, *The Leeds Woollen Industry* (Leeds, 1931), pp. 315–6; Mann, *Cloth Industry*, p. 135; Randall, 'Labour and the industrial revolution', pp. 315–16.

It is thus necessary to examine the way in which a machine impinged not only on a particular task but also on workplace and work practice. The same machine might liberate labour from drudgery and open up more profitable and even socially mobile prospects in one area and break down customary work relations, throw labour onto the scrapheap and widen the gap between capital and labour in another. Labour certainly did not see machinery in abstract. They recognised its direct relevance to work. But they judged its acceptability in terms of its impact upon their lives as a whole and the ways in which it might support or challenge their autonomy over their work and work custom.

III

While the workers' attitude to a new machine was determined by its impact upon work, the reaction with which it was greeted was not simply a product of its capacity to displace labour. Indeed, the reaction to a given machine varied widely. In some places it might encounter violent resistance, in others meet with passive acceptance even though its impact upon employment was identical. The reason for this variety of response therefore lay not in the machine itself but in the character of the community to which work gave rise and within which work took place. Some communities such as those engaged in the woollen manufacture in the West of England possessed both a tradition of and a capacity to sustain vigorous and forcible protest when faced with challenges to accepted norms. Others did not. Why this was the case may be better understood by an examination of the character of the community consciousness evinced in Gloucestershire and Wiltshire clothmaking parishes.

A common and crucial characteristic of the West of England woollen cloth-producing communities was their dependence upon full-time industrial production. Although both the Gloucestershire and Wiltshire textile communities existed cheek by jowl with fairly prosperous settled agrarian economies, there was very little interrelationship. The scarp slopes of the Cotswolds and the valley bottoms into which the Gloucestershire industry was concentrated were situated on the boundary of the old-enclosed pastoral Vale and the arable Wold, but the dual farming-weaving economy still to be found there in the early seventeenth century had all but disappeared by 1760. Some clothiers owned the same small plots of land held in their family for generations. Many successful clothiers bought landed estates. But few weavers owned land. The Wiltshire textile communities were if anything even more sharply divorced from agrarian production. Clothiers here were predominantly urban-dwelling and from early in the eighteenth century most weavers were rent payers with only a few owning land. Here the decline of the farmer clothier was more marked. The 'cheese' country which surrounded the woollen communities was old-enclosed and dominated by small owner-occupiers whose labour demands were usually met within their families. The surviving commons around the towns were packed with industrial workers and industrial housing to accommodate them on an extensive scale dated from the seventeenth century. There was more common land on the Gloucestershire Wold, as was the case with the Wiltshire 'Chalk' or downland. These areas' arable economies provided demand for labour in harvest time which gave woollen workers the chance of some alternative employment.[33] That apart, these workers depended for their livelihood upon loom, scribbling horse and shears, well aware that they had only their labour to sell.

The common experience of dependence upon piece-rate weekly earnings for survival was paralleled by common experience of dependence upon the market place for food supplies. Some textile workers had gardens and allotments, but few had anything like sufficient space available to produce more than a small part of their subsistence needs.[34] Bread, the staple diet of the labouring poor, had to be bought for cash in the market place, either in its finished state, as flour or as grain. This great reliance upon wheat supplies from the Wold or the Downs made the food market a potential flash-point for disorders, as steep rises in price and diminishing availability of grain in 1766 and 1795 proved in both Gloucestershire and Wiltshire. The structure of employment in the industry thus led not only to a common experience as producers but also to a common experience as consumers, thereby reinforcing the strong sense of community consciousness.

The textile workers' awareness of their proto-proletarian status was emphasised by the specialisation of their industry. A strong craft consciousness characterised all the male trades, bolstered as it was by vestigial apprenticeship controls and a powerful belief in the 'artisan' status that the 'mystery of the trade' conferred upon its practitioners. Certainly the history of the industry in the eighteenth century is littered with conflicts over wages, apprenticeship and custom. Such disputes occasionally afford tantalising glimpses of county-wide unions of all three male trades, though the bases of these larger organisations were certainly the permanent but mostly clandestine local box clubs, centred upon the sick clubs or burial societies. Each trade was zealous to protect its own economic status and

---

[33] *Victoria County History of Gloucestershire*, vol. 2 (London, 1907), pp. 164–71, 239–41: *Victoria County History of Wiltshire*, vol. 4 (Oxford, 1959), pp. 43–64; Mann, *Cloth Industry*, pp. 92, 95–6, 102, 32–3.

[34] Mann, *Cloth Industry*, p. 102.

was well aware of its own history, but craft exclusivity extended only so far. Weavers, scribblers and shearmen patronised different public houses but marriage and restrictions upon apprenticeship numbers made for close integration. This was reinforced by a common dependence upon piece rates emanating directly or indirectly from a relatively small number of merchant capitalists. It was further endorsed by the numerous clubs, societies and looser associations occasioned by common needs for sickness and death insurance, and for recreational, religious and cultural activities. This strong sense of mutuality was exhibited at times of crisis throughout the eighteenth century.[35]

While it is the West of England woollen workers' dependent relationship upon capital which strikes the economic historian, the *leitmotif* of the woollen workers' culture was their insistence upon the determination to uphold what they saw as their economic independence and independent status. 'Independence' was one of the most prized of the weavers' 'rights and privileges': the right to work in their own time, in their own home, for whomsoever they chose. In reality this independence and choice was limited by the availability of work and of employers and by the need to earn a subsistence. But the fact that work took place outside direct employer control was seen as a real sign of superior status. And the notorious worship of St Monday, so aggravating to the clothier, emphasised the weavers' autonomy and set them above those labourers whose employers regulated their every task. The scribblers and shearmen, though working in shops and not at home, held similarly strong views on their independence and were just as assiduous in their enjoyment of St Monday. While workshops had notionally fixed working hours, custom dictated that these were at very least flexible. Certainly any attempt to enforce a more rigorous regime and to rationalise work was most fiercely and generally successfully resisted.[36] Thus while the organisation of the industry and the need for income dictated the structure of work, work practice was to a very great extent dictated by custom. Attempts to pin down the components of work custom in a precise way are fruitless since custom was constantly evolving, encompassing both long-standing

---

[35] See, for example, the riots in Wiltshire and Somerset in 1726–7; the Gloucestershire weavers' strike in 1756 and the food riots in Gloucestershire and Wiltshire in 1766. J. de L. Mann, 'Clothiers and weavers in Wiltshire in the eighteenth century', in L. S. Pressnell, *Studies in the Industrial Revolution Presented to T. S. Ashton* (London, 1960), pp. 66–96; A. J. Randall, 'The industrial moral economy of the Gloucestershire weavers in the eighteenth century', in J. Rule (ed.), *British Trade Unionism 1750–1850: The Formative Years* (Harlow, 1988).

[36] The attempt to impose a standard twelve-hour day with only two, not the customary five, breaks for meals was one of the reasons behind the strike of Bradford on Avon shearmen in 1802. See Randall, 'The shearmen and the Wiltshire Outrages', p. 291; *British Parliamentary Papers*, 1802/3 (95), VII, Minutes of Evidence on the Woollen Trade Bill, pp. 336–7.

practices and recent gains or compromises. But while in some respects nebulous, custom had a firm backbone provided by the law. Thus the weavers' position was buttressed by the laws restricting the numbers of looms which might be owned by any artisan and by that which forbad clothiers from establishing loom shops. And they, like the scribblers and shearmen, well recognised the significance of the apprenticeship legislation in protecting their trades, even if no one observed any law to the letter. This common recognition of the importance of defending custom meant that attempts by the clothiers to challenge any of its aspects touched all workers and could easily provoke a widespread and collective reaction. Tucker claimed that 'as great Numbers of them work together in the same Shop, will they not have it more in their Power to vitiate and corrupt each other, to cabal and associate against their Masters?'. But though Tucker drew attention to such cabals, he was wrong in supposing they were aimed against the paymasters' 'superior Fortunes'. Woollen workers in the West in disputes invariably distinguished between the 'good honest gentlemen' who observed custom and those 'unmasterlike' masters who sought to destroy it by interfering with the workers' 'rights' and independence.[37]

Independence in work was matched by a remarkable degree of independence from external authority elsewhere. Housing, though rented, was rarely tied to employers, and local government in the woollen-producing parishes rarely seems to have been a very effective agency of social control. Furthermore, these districts were not well provided with justices of the peace. The food riots in Gloucestershire in 1766 and 1795 forcibly drew the attention of the bench there to the paucity of magistrates in or near the woollen parishes which contained between 40,000 and 60,000 inhabitants.[38] These disturbances clearly showed the means of maintaining law and order locally to be inadequate. In Wiltshire this shortage of magistrates was, to a greater extent than in Gloucestershire, made up by appointing practising full-time clothiers to the bench in the woollen towns.[39] A consequence of this was paradoxically a more violent and bitter pattern of industrial relations and a greater incidence of disorder. Where the bench could not or would not offer the possibility of impartial arbitration, the Wiltshire workers were more ready to solve their own problems by force.

Thus the organisation and character of work in the West of England produced a community consciousness that was both dynamic and defensive.

[37] Tucker, *Instructions*, p. 25. In this, the West of England woollen workers held attitudes in common with many other trades. See J. Rule, *The Experience of Labour in Eighteenth-Century Industry* (Beckenham, Kent, 1981), pp. 208–12.

[38] A. J. Randall, 'The Gloucestershire food riots of 1766', *Midland History*, 10 (1986), pp. 72–93.

[39] Mann, *Cloth Industry*, pp. 116–17.

Here we see an example of that 'rebellious traditional culture' described by Thompson, forged elsewhere by similar communities of non-agrarian independent workers, depending upon their earnings for food but divorced from the means of production.[40] 'Traditional' because, as has been shown, the woollen workers' culture put a premium upon custom and upon the maintenance of their 'rights and privileges'. But 'rebellious' because their common experiences gave them the collective basis from which to resist fiercely attempts to undermine their living conditions or way of life. It was because of this that the West of England woollen communities figured prominently in industrial disorders throughout the eighteenth century, but this tradition of protest extended beyond industrial disputes. Other protests, food riots in particular, bred a pattern of response to threats to existing notions of independence, fairness, order or custom. The response to machinery therefore fitted into an established pattern. Where such a tradition of protest was not established, however, where workers had no successful background of collective action in support of living standards, the machine met with little resistance.

This can be clearly seen in the case of the jenny in the West of England. When attempts were made in 1776 and again in the early 1780s to introduce the jenny into the main woollen towns it met with very great hostility from the woollen workers who feared the loss of an important contribution to the family economy. This hostility, however, declined in the early 1790s and the jenny was introduced in large numbers. Weavers saw the advantage of the more even yarn produced on the machine and their wives were recompensed for their loss either by taking up the jenny itself or more frequently the loom. This rapid take up of the jenny had disastrous consequences for the non-textile producing areas of Wiltshire and Somerset. In order to obtain sufficient hand-spun yarn the clothiers had been accustomed to put out spinning up to a 30 or 40 mile radius, and spinning formed an often-vital element of the family economies of large numbers of rural workers. Here the jenny caused widespread hardships.[41] Yet these non-textile areas succumbed without demur. With no tradition of organised protest and living in a more tightly controlled and dependent environment, resistance had no community platform. The main reaction in fact came from the ratepayers, faced with rocketing poor rates, who developed a deep mistrust of machinery from this time. One non-textile area, however, did react. This was the Keynsham coalfield where miners' wives supplemented

[40] E. P. Thompson, 'Eighteenth-century English society: class struggle without class?', *Social History*, 3, 2 (1978), p. 154. See also A. Charlesworth and A. J. Randall, 'Morals, markets and the English crowd in 1766', *Past and Present*, 114, (1987).

[41] Mann, *Cloth Industry*, pp. 128–9.

their menfolk's earnings by spinning. The Keynsham miners had a volatile history of protest,[42] but the distance of the coalfield from the woollen towns precluded prolonged effective resistance.

Reaction to machinery therefore depended upon the character of the community and that community's tradition of protest. In the West of England woollen districts this tradition was a rich one. Comparison of eighteenth-century industrial disturbances with protests over food marketing reveals many parallels of action.[43] Thus, just as the 'mobbers' in the food riots of 1766 insisted that all trades and workers should take their part in setting the fair price and restoring proper marketing practices,[44] so it should be emphasised that it was not merely those who were immediately threatened with displacement who took to the streets to protest against the jenny, scribbling engine, flying shuttle loom or gig mill, but a cross-section of the workforce as a whole. Just as the actions of the huckster or badger might call forth the wrath of all consumers, so the machine innovator frequently found himself the target of the community as a whole. Thus the crowd which destroyed the first spinning jennies to be set up in the region at Shepton Mallet in 1776; that which set fire to the first scribbling engine to appear in Wiltshire at Bradford on Avon in 1791; and the one which protested against that machine's first appearance in Gloucestershire at Woodchester in 1792, all included weavers, scribblers and shearmen in their ranks. Even the cloth dressers, so much more powerful in their industrial bargaining position than were the other woollen trades, received wide community support in their prolonged struggle against finishing machinery.[45]

As with the food rioters, the crowds protesting against machinery exhibited a strong sense of the legitimacy of their case and actions, and within their own limits, a degree of order and control, even under the severest provocation. There was certainly no wild orgy of destruction. For example, in May 1791 the crowd which assembled outside the house and workshop of Joseph Phelps at Bradford-on-Avon demanded that he take down his new scribbling engine and promise to refrain from using it since it would occasion much unemployment. Phelps refused, stones were thrown at his house, and he, in reply, fired upon the crowd, killing three people and mortally wounding two others. The crowd were incensed, but

---

[42] R. W. Malcolmson, '"A set of ungovernable people": the Kingswood colliers in the eighteenth century', in J. Brewer and J. Styles, *An Ungovernable People* (London, 1980), pp. 85–127; Hammonds, *Skilled Labourer*, p. 121.

[43] Randall, 'The industrial moral economy of the Gloucestershire weavers'.

[44] Randall, 'Gloucestershire food riots', p. 82.

[45] Randall, 'Labour and the industrial revolution', pp. 259–309; idem, 'The shearmen and the Wiltshire Outrages', pp. 299–300.

when Phelps, his nerve broken, then handed over the machine, their anger was assuaged. The scribbling engine was taken on to the town bridge, next to the lock-up, and, with some ceremony, condemned and set on fire.[46] The parallels between this incident and the sacking of the corn mill of a corn factor at Beckington in September 1766 are marked.[47] Likewise the way in which the crowd at Westbury in 1795, taking advantage of the temporary removal of most of the troops stationed in the town, divided themselves into separate parties to destroy the newly erected scribbling engines is very similar to the way in which the food rioters divided their forces in their attacks upon cheese factors and millers in the town in 1766.[48] And, as with the disturbances of 1766, the anti-machine rioters from 1776 to 1816 were discriminating in their actions, attacking only the property and machinery of those whom they believed were illegally or immorally trying to destroy established customary relationships. As has been noted elsewhere, it was the property rather than the persons of the innovators against which violence was directed. Phelps suffered no personal harm whatsoever (though all his windows were smashed) in spite of his 'lawful' but murderous assault on the crowd. In spite of numerous cries that innovators' lives were in mortal danger, only John Jones, the powerful arch-rival of the Wiltshire shearmen, was to be the victim of an act of attempted murder, and that did not occur until 1808.[49]

Violence was not the only method which West Country cloth workers utilised to stem the advent of machinery. As they showed at Shepton Mallet in 1776, they were prepared to negotiate a phased introduction or trial of a few machines, 'by which the surprising utility which you have asserted or the dangerous consequences which we have apprehended may evidently appear'.[50] The Gloucestershire workers were more inclined than their Wiltshire and Somerset counterparts to put their trust in the arbitration of the local gentry and magistracy, a legacy of their not-unsuccessful history of appeals to the bench in earlier disputes in the county.[51] This did not prove a fruitful choice. Sir George Paul, prison reformer and gentrified son of an old clothier family, was asked to arbitrate

---

[46] *Salisbury and Winchester Journal*, 23 May 1791; Public Record Office, W.O. 1/1048, Bradford on Avon magistrates to Sir George Yonge, 15 May 1791, Garth to Yonge, 18 May 1791; W.O. 1/1049, Lane to Yonge, 15 May 1791, Bethell to Lane, 15 May 1791.

[47] *Salisbury and Winchester Journal*, 29 Sept., 6 and 13 Oct. 1766; *Aris' Birmingham Gazette*, 22 and 29 Sept. 1766.

[48] W.O. 1/1082, Anstie to Secretary at War, 28 May 1791; *Salisbury and Winchester Journal*, 29 Sept. 1766; *Annual Register*, vol. 9 (1766), p. 138; Public Record Office, T.S. 11/1116, case against Nicholas Minty.

[49] Randall, 'The shearmen and the Wiltshire Outrages', pp. 297–8.

[50] *Bath Chronicle*, 28 Nov. 1776.

[51] Mann, *Cloth Industry*, p. 117.

in disputes over the introduction of both scribbling engines and gig mills in the early 1790s. However, he came out strongly in favour of innovation and irredeemably divided the workers. The Gloucestershire challenge to machinery thereafter generally proved much more feeble than that found in Wiltshire.[52]

The strong trade union organisation of the shearmen enabled them to mount orthodox industrial sanctions against those who introduced gig mills, and there is some evidence to suggest that Wiltshire scribblers also attempted strike action. But the strike was not a potent weapon against a machine which was anyway displacing the striker. All groups also made use of petitions and propaganda directed at a wider public, both locally and further afield. Such propaganda proved effective and demonstrated that the community basis of support extended beyond the ranks of the workers. The woollen manufacturing community encompassed small masters, struggling clothiers and shopkeepers as well as gentlemen clothiers and woollen workers, and many of these smaller capitalists shared the workers' fears of the monopolising results of the advent of machinery. They were also more susceptible to worker pressure than larger employers. Master dressers were suspected in 1802 and 1812 of covert support for machine breakers, while petitions from spinners and scribblers received support from ratepayers angered that the innovators' vision of progress might involve them in heavy costs. And these widely based fears of change were not without influence over the magistracy charged with preserving the peace. In these circumstances the innovators faced an uphill struggle. The same cannot be said of the West Riding until the later 1790s when small master clothiers began to fear the rise of a new class of merchant manufacturer who would bypass the Cloth Halls and destroy their trade.[53]

The rebellious culture of the West of England woollen workers undoubtedly had an impact on innovators. Their tradition of violence deterred all but the most determined from confrontations over machinery. Thus a Chippenham clothier wrote in 1786, 'If we in this part of the kingdom attempt to introduce machinery it must be with the risk of our lives and fortunes.' This was an opinion echoed throughout the 1790s and until well after the end of the Napoleonic War. The fear which such volatile communities of woollen workers engendered had influence beyond their immediate parishes, for they themselves did not respect such arbitrary boundaries. For example, the riots in Shepton Mallet over the introduction of the jenny in 1776 were occasioned not by the local workers who had

[52] *Gloucester Journal*, 30 April 1792, 16 and 23 June 1794; W.O. 1/1091, Paul to Secretary at War, 20 July 1795; Randall, 'The shearmen and the Wiltshire Outrages', pp. 296–7.

[53] Randall, 'The shearmen and the Wiltshire Outrages', pp. 299–300; Thompson, *The Making*, Ch. 14; D. Gregory, *Regional Transformation and Industrial Revolution: A Geography of the Yorkshire Woollen Industry* (London, 1982), Ch. 3.

been persuaded to accept a 'trial' of the machine, but by workers from the Wiltshire textile towns some 15 to 20 miles away who would not tolerate its presence.[54] In this way a riot in one place curbed potential experiments over a much wider area. We may conclude that workers' hostility to change may have greatly delayed the mechanisation of the West of England woollen industry and thereby have contributed to a slower growth rate than that in Yorkshire. Thus worker resistance may well have been responsible for depressed trade, and not the reverse as is often assumed.

IV

Since the reaction to machinery was community based, this raises the question of how far the workers' response was informed by a common view or ideology. Historians have been reluctant to accept that workers in the eighteenth century held a philosophy which was inimical to the machine. Such an alternative political economy may be discerned, it has been argued, from the 1820s but 'In the eighteenth century there was no Machinery Question.'[55] One reason for such assertions is that it was not until the 1820s that workers found access to the media, in particular through the radical press, and were able to articulate wider value systems. But there were occasions in the later eighteenth and early nineteenth centuries when workers did have such opportunities and it is possible to discern in them the elements of a political economy which was indeed hostile to the machine.

The woollen industry, particularly that in the West of England, again offers a good example, for here from 1776 onwards the innovators were engaged in a propagandist battle to win over a dubious public to the beneficent consequences of machinery. By 1802 it had become clear that the old corpus of often-archaic legislation which still technically regulated the manufacture of woollen cloth might offer the workers an opportunity to check the march of progress. Thus the innovators sought to persuade Parliament to repeal this old regulatory code, thereby presenting the workers with a national stage from which to argue their case against 'freedom' and machinery. Space precludes a detailed discussion of the points which emerged from this debate but it is important to identify the major tenets of the workers' arguments.[56]

[54] Mann, *Cloth Industry*, pp. 126, 123.
[55] M. Berg, *The Machinery Question and the Making of Political Economy. 1815–1848* (Cambridge, 1980), p. 1. See also M. Berg, *The Age of Manufactures* (London, 1985), Ch. 2, where the author makes clear that there was a growing awareness among political economists in the eighteenth century of the potential difficulties of new technologies.
[56] For a more detailed examination of this case see A. J. Randall, 'The philosophy of Luddism: the case of the West of England woollen workers c. 1790–1809', *Technology and Culture*, 27, 1, (1986).

The workers' case against machinery took two broad aspects, the social and the economic. The social arguments rested heavily on the ways in which machinery destroyed men's livelihoods, work customs and way of life.[57] The machine was guilty of theft for it rendered useless the craft skills of the artisan, skills which had been acquired through apprenticeship and which constituted a real property to the workman. Such men were driven from self-sufficiency into poverty and to the indignity of the poor rates. Alternatively, machinery forced him or his family to leave the cottage economy with its morally uplifting aspects of familial responsibility and paternal discipline to work in the morally degrading atmosphere of the factory. This close identification of the machine and the factory is worth noting. The triumph of the machine was already equated with the destruction of outwork.

It was in the economic arguments against machinery, however, that we can see most clearly the workers' justifications for their resistance to change.[58] Machines were not repudiated *per se*. Where they might 'abridge, facilitate or expedite man's labour' they were to be welcomed, but this was only true where they did not cause redundancy. Were machinery to dispense with labour, however, this would have deleterious consequences for the economy as a whole for it would reduce domestic consumption and, through the poor rates, increase domestic costs. 'A trade', the workers believed, 'is valuable to a country in proportion to the number of hands it employs.' 'Everyone knows that the more labour is employed on any article prior to sale, the more generally profitable.' Machinery by reducing labour requirements reduced the cost of producing a cloth. But this was to no advantage for 'However powerful the machinery made use of no more cloth could be produced for no more could be sold than is already sold'. Machinery would only 'lessen our home markets more than increase our foreign ones'.[59] Thus the workers held a static view of the market. If there was already demand for more cloth, then more production would have ensued. All machinery could do was to satisfy that demand in less time. And, since machine-made cloth would cost less, the overseas consumer

---

[57] See in particular R. Jackson, *The Speech of Randle Jackson to the Committee of the House of Commons Appointed to Consider the State of the Woollen Manufacture* (London, 1806); E. Wigley, *The Speech of E. Wigley on Behalf of the Woollen Weavers of Gloucestershire to the Committee of the House of Commons Appointed to Consider the State of the Woollen Manufacture* (Cheltenham, 1806); *Journal of the House of Commons*, XLIX, pp. 599–600, LXXI, p. 431; and the evidence of the woollen workers in *British Parliamentary Papers*, 1802/3 (95), VII, and 1806 (268), III.

[58] See in particular Jackson, *Speech of Randle Jackson*; *Considerations upon a Bill for Repealing the Whole Code of Laws Respecting the Woollen Manufacture* (London, 1803); *Observations on Woollen Machinery* (Leeds, 1803).

[59] *Leeds Mercury*, 5 and 12 Feb. 1803, letters from Looker: *Observations on Woollen Machinery*, p. 5; *Considerations upon a Bill*, p. 35.

would benefit at the expense of the earnings of the domestic producers whose ability to purchase other home-made products would in turn be diminished. In this way the machine would prove a long-term economic disaster.

The machine further damaged England's economic competitiveness by destroying a major national asset, the skill of her workforce. This skill justified the English artisan receiving higher wages than his continental counterpart. But the machine could, the workers believed, be worked by anyone. Thus machinery would be copied or exported and worked by foreign rivals, destroying overseas markets still further. Machinery was also accused of threatening markets in another way. It produced much worse cloth, the workers claimed, than did hand methods. Such faults might be disguised temporarily but they must inevitably show up, thus ultimately destroying the reputation of the product and the producers. In this way any short-term gains would be countered by long-term major losses.

These arguments were drawn heavily if selectively from the old mercantilist economic theories of the early eighteenth century and repudiated the new spirit of *laissez-faire*: 'this new philosophy, this emancipation from restraint ... which preceding ages have treated with the scorn it deserves', as the cloth dressers' counsel described it.[60] Such arguments suggested that only one group stood to gain from machinery, the large capitally endowed machine owners who were able to make their profits at everyone else's expense. This *motif* underlay all the arguments against machinery. The larger capitalists were intent on overthrowing all order and regulation so that by their wealth they might monopolise the trade and make a killing. The eighteenth-century hatred of monopolists was attached to the innovators. 'It is manifest that the desire for more machinery in the woollen manufactory proceeds from not public but private advantage. It is wholly a race amongst individuals.' Parliament, the workers believed, must protect them 'from falling sacrifice to the spirit of monopoly, to private cupidity in the guise of public good'.[61]

This view of machinery had much in common with the attitudes expressed by the food rioters which Thompson has described as 'the moral economy of the English crowd'.[62] Here we see the same belief that economic relations should be confined within moral imperatives, here we see the same vision of the need for regulation to maintain stability, custom and fairness for all. This was not an alternative ideology to capitalism but one in which capitalist initiative was constrained within existing structural

[60] Jackson, *Speech of Randle Jackson*, p. 43.
[61] *Observations on Woollen Machinery*, pp. 4, 22.
[62] Thompson, 'The moral economy of the English crowd'.

relations. Such a value system did not prohibit change. But change had to be evolutionary from within the existing structure of work. The machine and the factory, however, were seen as revolutionary challenges and were as such to be resisted. That there should be parallels in the attitudes of the workers to both the organisation of the food market and of work should not be surprising. For, as I have tried to suggest, it was principally the organisation of work which determined the character of the workers' community and it was principally from this community that the attitudes and reaction to machinery sprang. Any attempt to understand the hostility of groups of workers to change in the industrial revolution must take account of this.

V

By way of conclusion we may attempt briefly to relate resistance to machinery in the English woollen industry to the debate on proto-industrialisation. The *Verlagsystem* of the West of England produced reaction and resistance, both physical and ideological, to the advent of the machine whereas, with the exception of the cloth dressers, the *Kaufsystem* of the West Riding saw a much more peaceful transition. This division broadly echoes the case put forward by Thomson based on his study of the woollen industry of Languedoc. The production of high-quality woollen cloth, he notes, necessitated a *Verlagsystem* of production, a point echoed by both Wilson and Mann, but the very success of such organisations led to industrial inflexibility and to entrepreneurial decline.[63] The case of the West of England industry over the eighteenth and early nineteenth centuries seems broadly to confirm this, although it is important to note that West of England clothiers were not behind their Yorkshire rivals in their first attempts to introduce the new technologies.[64] But introduction did not necessarily mean take-up, and a crucial factor in delaying take-up was worker hostility, not just clothier inertia. Thomson also argues that a further characteristic of *Verlagsystems* was the alienation of the workforce. Opportunities for social mobility were far fewer than in a *Kaufsystem* and this tended to produce discontent and disillusionment. Indeed, he cites Tucker on the industry of the West of England to prove his point.[65] It is certainly true that opportunities for social mobility in the

---

[63] J. K. J. Thomson, 'Variations in industrial structure in pre-industrial Languedoc', in M. Berg, P. Hudson and M. Sonenscher (eds.), *Manufacture in Town and Country before the Factory* (Cambridge, 1983), pp. 83, 80–1; Wilson, 'The supremacy of Yorkshire', p. 239; Mann, *Cloth Industry*, p. 116.
[64] Mann, *Cloth Industry*, p. 123.
[65] Thomson, 'Variations in industrial structure', pp. 81–3.

West of England industry were very limited. But the 'static' nature of the industry's organisation and the advanced specialisation of the workforce also produced stable and craft-conscious communities of workers who drew self-confidence and pride from their shared proto-proletarian experience of waged but autonomous work. And from the seemingly strictly compartmentalised nature of their industry they developed a world view which assumed such fixed parameters were eternal. Just as the moral economy was a view of the legitimacy of parameters of food marketing articulated by those divorced from the production of foodstuffs, so the same sort of view of the 'rights and privileges' of the trade was developed by workers divorced from control of the means of industrial production. Thus the *Verlagsystem* of the West of England bred a workforce which may have been disillusioned with its lack of social mobility but was certainly vigilant and vigorous in defence of its own liberties and customs. We must not overemphasise the cultural or social alienation or poverty of such groups of workers. Their adaptation to the mobility delimiting but socially liberating confines of the *Verlagsystem* may with advantage be compared to that of the factory workers in the new towns of the mid-nineteenth century who were to develop another separate and self-assertive working-class culture.

Thomson further suggests that the advent of machinery may have offered greater benefits to a *Verlagsystem* than a *Kaufsystem*. The previous cost advantages of the *Kaufsystem* were eroded by machinery, while the *Verlagsystem* already possessed the requisite capital and closer worker control. The factory also eased the entrepreneurial problems of large-scale production.[66] This progression from *Kaufsystem* to *Verlagsystem* to factory has frequently been portrayed as a linear process.[67] However, just as we must not underemphasise the capacity of the *Kaufsystem* to adapt to change, nor should we overestimate the capacity of the *Verlagsystem* to transform itself into the factory system, as indeed Thomson himself shows of Carcassonne and Clermont.[68] Entrepreneurial inertia left a cloying legacy, but the workforce could prove even more reluctant to accept change than their masters for they had far more to lose. By virtue of their strong community links and their willingness to defend their position they might mount effective delays, damaging the capacity of their industry to keep pace with developing rivals and thereby ultimately losing markets and the possibility of future growth. Thus we see that the West Riding *Kaufsystem* proved highly adaptable to early mechanisation whereas the

---

[66] Ibid., p. 87.
[67] Mendels, 'Proto-industrialisation: the first phase'.
[68] Thomson, 'Variations in industrial structure', pp. 87–8. See also J. K. J. Thomson, *Clermont-de-Lodève 1633–1789: Fluctuations in the Prosperity of a Languedocian Cloth-Making Town* (Cambridge, 1982).

West of England *Verlagsystem* in comparison failed to develop as quickly in the years 1780–1816, and from 1826 was actually in irreversible decline.[69] Youthful *Verlagsystems* such as the West Riding worsted industry might have the energy to metamorphose again. Older industries, as older industries today, proved much less adaptable.

Thus, while an understanding of the organisation of an industry is crucial to any appreciation of the attitudes of its workers to machinery, it is also necessary to examine both the character and control of work and the character of the community within which work takes place. For it was from this community basis that the universal initial wariness which greeted all mechanical innovations developed in some places into the physical resistance of machine breaking, and from which an alternative political economy to the machine economy was first tentatively advanced.

[69] P. Hudson, 'From manor to mill: the West Riding in transition', in Berg, Hudson and Sonenscher (eds.), *Manufacture*, pp. 124–44; see also P. Hudson, 'Proto-industrialisation: the case of the West Riding wool textile industry in the eighteenth and early nineteenth centuries', *History Workshop Journal*, 12 (1981) pp. 34–61; Mann, *Cloth Industry*, p. 168.

PART THREE

THE DIVERSE NATURE OF THE OUTER REGIONS

Chapter 8

Two paths to economic development: Wales and the north-east of England[1]

NEIL EVANS

The industrialisation of south Wales has always been puzzling. Historians have usually reached for a colonial analogy of some kind to explain it. The Hammonds started the trend by comparing the lack of an industrial tradition and social conditions in south Wales with an African goldfield.[2] Closer observers of Welsh affairs have often agreed, and Perkin made a shrewd summary of their findings in 1969, concluding that the industrial process in south Wales had been semi-colonial.

Wales, with mineral resources and a similar but slightly more advanced society [i.e. than Ireland and the Scottish Highlands] is a still more interesting test case. There, handicapped in the early stages by lack of capital, lack of entrepreneurs and lack of a potential proletariat, industrialism had to be induced from outside. The result was a semi-colonial economy in which capital was provided in large blocks by English capitalists encouraged by favourable concessions from local mineral owners.[3]

This train of thought led a careful scholar (in a playful mood) to wonder whether Wales had truly been industrialised; its late nineteenth-century economy was concentrated (and to an increasing extent) on the primary production of commodities, notably coal. Urbanisation lagged behind the average British level, manufacturing was of little importance and most work was of a handwork, almost craft variety. Central features of nineteenth-century industrialisation were missing, and perhaps the beast itself was.[4]

Michael Hechter's book *Internal Colonialism: The Celtic Fringe in British National Development 1536–1966* (1975) took this approach to its logical

---

[1] Many people have helped with this chapter, but special thanks to Merfyn Jones, Dai Smith and Gwyn Williams for encouraging me despite my gentle disagreements with them, to John Williams for typically shrewd and helpful comments on a draft, to Pamela Kneller for typing far beyond any legitimate call of friendship, and to Liz who introduced me to the north-east.

[2] J. L. and Barbara Hammond, *The Rise of Modern Industry* (London, 1926; new edn intro. by R. M. Hartwell, 1966), p. 158.

[3] Harold Perkin, *The Origins of Modern English Society 1780–1880* (London, 1969), p. 98.

[4] L. J. Williams, 'Was Wales industrialised?', lecture at the Welsh Association, Aberystwyth, 2 Sept. 1977.

conclusion and extended it to the whole of Wales. For Hechter England had always been the core of British political and economic power and it had constantly dominated the Celtic periphery. Ireland, Scotland and Wales had essentially similar economic histories which could be reduced to this domination from the centre and a resultant cultural division of labour. This explained both the relative underdevelopment of the periphery and the persistence of its cultural distinctiveness. It had failed to be absorbed into the bland homogenisation of culture predicted by orthodox modernisation theory.

Hechter's visions were nourished by many colonial analogies, but not by much serious economic analysis. In particular the classic period of the industrial revolution was passed over in silence, with standard works receiving only passing mention. Space does not allow a dissection of his views, but his style of analysis did derive from more substantially grounded accounts and in some respects was part of a longer intellectual tradition; it did not arise simply from the influence of Gunder Frank. Most Welsh historians who have responded to Hechter have done so with antagonism. It is quite easy to spot errors of fact and interpretation and the Procrustean bed of theory is a prominent part of the book. Recent comments and analyses by Williams, Smith and Jones have broken with earlier views and stressed that the industrialisation of Wales was an integral part of British development. Indeed, so central was the role of Wales in economic development that it should be seen as part of the core, not the periphery. Hechter should be turned on his head.[5]

It is not intended to launch a frontal attack on this recent writing but merely to issue a reminder that in the necessary job of emptying the bath water a firm hold has to be kept on the baby. There is a genuine puzzle about Welsh industrialisation and generalised assimilation to the wider scheme of things does not help resolve it. The old tradition (Hammonds to Hechter) is inadequate because it simply compares Wales with an undifferentiated England, lacking in any regional variations. England is seen as one economic entity, experiencing industrialisation more or less uniformly. The newer view tends to blend Britain together, seeing Wales as part of an economically progressive core, and not enquiring into any possible variations within this sector. This is far more adequate than any crude colonial comparison, but it is in danger of ignoring the distinctiveness of Wales. This is what a sustained and realistic comparison can display.

[5] See especially, Gwyn A. Williams, 'Imperial south Wales', and 'When was Wales?', both in his *The Welsh in their History* (London, 1982); R. Merfyn Jones, 'Notes from the margin: class and society in nineteenth century Gwynedd', in David Smith (ed.), *A People and a Proletariat* (London, 1980); and David Smith in 'Tonypandy 1910: definitions of community', *Past and Present*, 87 (1980), p. 160.

Such a comparison has to be with a region of England and not with England in general. The north-east of England has an advantage in this respect. On the face of it there is a basic similarity; by the late nineteenth century south Wales and the Great Northern were the major export coalfields of Britain; both had substantial iron and steel industries. The parallel has become a commonplace, and one endorsed in recent academic discussions. Professor Coleman in his sceptical look at the idea of proto-industrialisation stressed that the development of these two areas poses a problem for the theory, that

the presence of coal and iron was of greater consequence in helping to determine the pattern of industrialization in England [sic] than was the existent distribution of so-called proto-industrialization is suggested by the industrial development of the north east and south Wales. Neither had any significant prior experience of what the theory recognizes as proto-industrialization, but both had coal and iron.[6]

Lee's recent classification of the regions of Victorian Britain points in the same direction and places Wales and the north-east in the same category – regions based on coal mining, rather than textiles, consumer services and industries or agriculture.[7] Both have also been seen as areas of under-development and backwardness; Hechter has his north-eastern analogues, as will be shown.

Approaching the old puzzle of the distinctiveness of Wales and through what is apparently its least promising angle – a comparison with a region which shared some fundamental features with it – is one means of illuminating the peculiarities of the Welsh economy. The similarities will show up best, as we shall see, in a static analysis of the late Victorian economy, but any interpretation taking a longer and more mobile view will also find important differences.

It may be helpful at the outset of this discussion to specify the regions which are being considered. The north-east of England is simply and conventionally defined as the counties of Northumberland and Durham, which were given economic unity by the presence of the Great Northern coalfield. Industrial development spread outwards from its first centres along the Tyne. By the nineteenth century it had stretched over the Tees to include portions of North Yorkshire (chiefly Middlesbrough and the Cleveland Hills) which were, in economic terms, integral to the region.[8]

Wales, by contrast, has never possessed a single, integrated, economy

[6] D. C. Coleman, 'Proto-industrialization: a concept too many', *Economic History Review*, 36, 3 (1983), p. 443.
[7] C. H. Lee, 'Regional growth and structural change in Victorian Britain', *Economic History Review*, 34, 3 (1981), pp. 446–51.
[8] Norman McCord, *North-East England: The Region's Development, 1760–1960* (London, 1979), p. 13.

and much of the response to Hechter's work has taken the form of stressing the importance of regional divisions within Wales.[9] In the pre-industrial era, however, these regions had much in common. The upland core of the Welsh massif ensured that pastoralism was the prime activity and fertile lowland areas, proto-industrial pockets, and areas of mineral working were studded into and around that core. This makes it possible to discuss those areas together. In the course of industrialisation the fortunes of the various areas diverged markedly and some consideration is given to the 'failed transitions' of mid-Wales and north-west Wales. Yet prime attention is given to the south Wales coalfield which developed as an area of heavy industry and the one most directly comparable to the experience of the north-east of England. Thus, though a variety of Welsh regions are discussed in the pre-industrial period, only one of them experienced a large-scale industrial revolution (though there was a miniaturised version in north-east Wales). Out of the diverse regions of pre-industrial Wales there was only one path to large-scale economic development and it is that which is contrasted with the north-east of England in the nineteenth century.

The economic history of the north-east has not been as fully explored as might be expected. The search for an industrial revolution based on textiles and canals largely by-passed this important pioneer area where neither was present, and the recent emphasis on proto-industrialisation offers no remedy for this situation.[10] Hughes, by contrast, once claimed that: 'Newcastle, despite its agricultural shell, is the centre of what is in all probability the oldest industrial region in the country.'[11] We need to bear in mind the qualification as well as the claim, for substantiating it would involve defining exactly what is meant by an 'industrial region'. For present purposes it is sufficient to recognise the early development of an industrial society in the area. A special correspondent employed by a south Wales newspaper to investigate social conditions in the coalfield in the 1880s made the same point (and displayed his clearly extensive knowledge of the north-east) when he referred to Welsh miners as having a prototype at Bishop Auckland.[12] The north-east was the pioneer of the coal trade, and of industrial society in Britain. The coal industry from an early stage developed a detailed division of labour and a proletariat recruited from the

---

[9] Graham Day, 'Underdeveloped Wales?', *Planet*, 45–6 (November 1978).

[10] D. J. Rowe, 'The economy of the north-east in the nineteenth century', *Northern History*, 6 (1971).

[11] E. Hughes, *North Country Life in the Eighteenth Century*, vol. 1: *The North-East, 1700–1750* (Oxford and Durham, 1952), pp. xiii–xiv. R. J. Morris recently made a similar point at the Society for the Study of Labour History Conference, London, 31 May 1980.

[12] *South Wales Daily News*, 17 Oct. 1887; he rather spoiled the point by referring to Consett as the prototype of Rhymney; ibid., 23 Sept. 1887. As will be argued later, Rhymney was the prototype of Consett.

wandering poor, criminals and civil war prisoners. Many came from Scotland and the whole workforce was given none of the status accorded to people who worked the land or to craftsmen. No guild organisation ever emerged in coal mining. The product was seen as being offensive and the people carried its taint.[13] The Newcastle area has been described as the first industrial landscape in Europe, in the sense that 'coal began to determine the physical aspect of the environment'; and in 1767 there were fifty-seven Newcomen engines in the area.[14] Defoe was impressed by a story of a wondrous underground explosion in which almost sixty people died. On the road to Newcastle he had 'a view of the inexhausted store of coals, from whence not London only, but all the south part of England is continually supplied...we [in London] are apt to wonder whence they come and that they do not bring the whole country away'.[15] Yet long-distance trade also provided the local population with problems of comprehension for 'when in this country we see the prodigious heaps, I might say mountains of coals which are dug up at every pit, and how many pits there are; we are filled with equal wonder to consider where people can live that can consume them'.[16]

Recent work by a group of radical geographers has obscured this point by portraying the history of the region as one of underdevelopment and essentially pre-capitalist forms of exploitation.[17] It makes little sense to see surplus value in the north-east as being in the hands of a 'pre-capitalist' class and one which attempted to protect its position by monopoly rather than innovation. The north-east in the early modern period was hardly a periphery. It was always in good contact with London; Newcastle was an important trading city with firm international links from at least the early sixteenth century. The term 'hostmen' used to describe its merchants was derived from their role in hosting foreign merchants. Danzig and the Netherlands were important trading partners. Durham's cathedral close maintained its contacts with the church politics of Oxford, of which it was a rather far-flung outlier. The coal industry expanded in the sixteenth century as a result of industrial growth, timber shortage and the transfer of church property in the Reformation. Between 1565 and 1625 coal shipments from the Tyne multiplied twelve times and not until the

[13] J. U. Nef, *The Rise of the British Coal Industry* (2 vols., London, 1934), vol. 1, pp. 347–9, 411–29; vol. 2, pp. 135, 67.

[14] Wolfgang Schivelbusch, *The Railway Journey: The Industrialisation of Time and Space in the Nineteenth Century* (Leamington Spa, 1986), pp. 1–2.

[15] Daniel Defoe, *A Tour Through the Whole Island of Great Britain, 1724–6* (Penguin edn, 1971), pp. 534–5.

[16] Ibid., p. 535.

[17] J. Carney, *et al.*, 'Regional underdevelopment in late capitalism: a study of the north east of England', in I. Masser (ed.), *Theory and Practice in Regional Science* (London, 1976).

eighteenth century would this rate of growth be surpassed. By 1640 it had
worked a revolution, as James phrases it, 'From Lineage Society to Civil
Society'.[18] Bands of retainers were the badge of the feudal magnates;
newcomers with fortunes derived from coal displaced them and penetrated
the Newcastle oligarchy. The Great Northern Rebellion of 1569 marked the
death throes of any group that could realistically be described as a 'pre-
capitalist' ruling class. The aristocratic rebels were already isolated and their
behaviour undermined respect for them. In 1652 a pamphleteer in the area
was denying John Donne's sense of fraternity and proclaiming that 'each
man is an island'.[19] Relations between landlords and tenants became
contractual rather than dependent. The region illustrates the dominance of
what Thompson has called an agrarian bourgeoisie:[20] 'agricultural and
industrial enterprise went hand in hand' and 'the coal industry [was] the
most prolific source of new recruitment into the gentry'. Still in the early
eighteenth century, 'Thanks to coal, there was always a greater degree of
fusion of landed and mercantile interests in these parts than elsewhere.'[21]
The confrontation of the two orders had been marked in Durham in the
sixteenth century, but by the civil war it was the possessive market society
which had won.

The persistent concern of the controllers of the north coast's coal trade
with limiting production and maintaining prices by means of monopoly
organisation could also be cited as an example of the area's primitiveness
but this would misunderstand the situation and the historical context. By
1700 this regulation of the trade owed nothing to the guild-like activities
of the Newcastle hostmen and was a means of maintaining profits during
depressions in demand. Monopoly was by then based on the economic
power of a cartel rather than the political power of a guild, and it was the
coal owners rather than the merchants who exercised this power. In the
expansionary periods combinations proved to be difficult to sustain. Yet in
the depression of the early eighteenth century the Grand Allies were able
to limit entry and keep up prices so that the producer benefited and not the
London middleman. This was not atavism but a normal means employed
by capitalist enterprises as a way of sustaining the geographical advantages
which the north-east enjoyed. A succession of such arrangements

[18] Constance Fraser, 'The early hostmen of Newcastle upon Tyne', *Archaeogia Aeliana*, fifth series, 12
(1984); Mervyn James, *Family, Lineage and Civil Society: A Study of Society, Politics and Mentality in
the Durham Region, 1500–1640* (Oxford, 1974), p. 177.
[19] James, *Family, Lineage and Civil Society, passim* and p. 189.
[20] E. P. Thompson, *The Poverty of Theory and Other Essays* (London, 1978), p. 40 (the phrase is implied
rather than used directly); Perry Anderson attacks it in 'Socialism and pseudo-empiricism', *New Left
Review*, 35 (1965).
[21] Hughes, *North Country Life*, p. xix.

dominated the trade, culminating in the Limitation of the Vend of 1770 to 1845, and only the coming of the railways proved able to destroy this. In the 1930s Nef and Sweezy well understood that the coal industry and monopoly was a crucial part of the capitalist world, though an isolated jibe of Sweezy's about the feudal proclivities of early nineteenth-century coal owners seems to have misled some development theorists.[22]

The position of the north-east was established early and it became a powerful force in the British economy. By the reign of Charles I one Tyneside pit could probably have produced the entire output of Henry VIII's reign.[23] Coal was increasingly mined in response to the phenomenal growth of London, and the gentry of the north-east flourished as a particularly market-oriented group in an increasingly commercialised society.[24] Splendid homes provide an architectural evidence of this success – Alnwick, Ravensworth, Lumley, Seaton Delaval and Gibside, the last complete with its column of British liberty, 'a splendid symbol of British Whiggery'.[25] Coal also attracted other industries to the area; salt production ran at about 1,400 to 1,500 pans per annum in the seventeenth century with 202 pans in use in 1635. Cheap coal made it competitive until the 1750s and saltmaking helped sustain the profits of the coal industry in the eighteenth century. Glass and chemical production also developed.[26]

Wales in the immediate pre-industrial period provides an instructive contrast. Newcastle's mines were 'England's Peru'; in Wales it was rawhide on hoof that Archbishop John Williams compared with the Spanish treasure fleet.[27] And the non-subsistence aspects of the regional economies of Wales were mostly marginal and ultimately externally controlled. No producer had the market dominance to create a position of strength equivalent to that of the Grand Allies. A north Wales petition of the 1640s, lobbying for

---

[22] Paul. M. Sweezy, *Monopoly and Competition in the English Coal Trade 1550–1850* (Cambridge, Mass., 1938), is the classic account whose conclusions I follow. P. Cromar's articles, 'The coal industry on Tyneside 1715–50', *Northern History*, 14, (1978); 'Spatial change and economic organisation: the Tyneside coal industry 1751–1770', *Geoforum* 10, 1 (1979); 'The coal industry on Tyneside 1771–1800: oligopoly and spatial change', *Economic Geography*, 53 (1977), are admirably clear and good at recognising capitalists. See also Hughes, *North Country Life*; Nef, *Coal Industry*.

[23] Nef, *Coal Industry*, vol. 1, p. 362.

[24] E. A. Wrigley, 'A simple model of London's importance in changing economy and society 1650–1750', *Past and Present*, 37 (1967); Roy Porter, *English Society in the Eighteenth Century* (Harmondsworth, 1982), Ch. 5; Nef, *Coal Industry*, vol. 1, part 4 Ch. 1.

[25] Hughes, *North Country Life*, p. xix; quotation from Nicholas Pevesner and Elizabeth Williamson, *The Buildings of England: County Durham* (Harmondsworth, 1983), p. 294.

[26] N. R. Elliot, 'Tyneside, a study in the development of an industrial seaport', *Tijdschrift voor Economische en Social Geographie*, 53, 11 (1962), pp. 228–9; Nef, *Coal Industry*, vol. 2; Joyce Ellis, 'The decline and fall of the Tyneside salt industry 1660–1790: a re-examination', *Economic History Review*, second series, 33 (1980), pp. 45–58.

[27] Nef, *Coal Industry*, vol. 1, p. 21; R. T. Jenkins and Helen M. Ramage, *A History of the Honourable Society of the Cymmrodorion* (London, 1951), p. 4.

safe conduct from the royal armies and for free commerce and traffic during the civil war, displays an economy of dependence:

That the sale of your petitioners' cattle and Welsh cottons being the principal and most considerable commodities of these counties, cottons being usually vented in Shrewsbury, and our cattle driven and sold in most parts of England, hath been and is the only support of your petitioners' being and livelihood, among whom there (be) many thousand families in the mountainous part of this country who sowing little or no corn at all, trust merely to the sale of their cattle, wool and Welsh cottons for the provision of bread.[28]

The most lucrative part of the trade was fattening and geography prevented Wales from sharing in this. In the eighteenth century a pair of oxen sold in Montgomeryshire for £33 fetched £60 a year later at Smithfield, after fattening.[29] Wool, the other staple trade, was firmly in the grasp of middlemen, the Shrewsbury drapers, until the late eighteenth century. Early sixteenth-century cloth production had concentrated in south Wales and had been exported via the ports of the region. The migration of the industry to mid- and north Wales in the course of the century established Shrewsbury's dominance. The drapers' role was never unchallenged, but it was only other factions in the town or other merchants who could produce any realistic opposition, and not the producers. The latter were undercapitalised, needed ready cash and were producing a poor-quality old drapery for which there was no overwhelming demand. In the late eighteenth century Thomas Pennant on one of his tours observed of the cloth trade: 'It is sent and sold in the rough to Shrewsbury; a practice very contrary to the interest of the country.'[30] Wales was not good grain-growing country, either, and its excursions into the grain trade were of dubious benefit. A lack of granaries necessitated quick sales after the harvest, when prices were low; as the next harvest approached stocks were low and would have to be replenished at the higher prices then obtaining. This meant that the farmers failed to make the maximum profit and were consequently short of the capital necessary to build granaries![31]

[28] Cited in Caroline Skeel, 'The cattle trade between Wales and England from the fifteenth to the nineteenth centuries', *Transactions of the Royal Historical Society*, fourth series, 9 (1926), p. 135.

[29] Skeel, 'Cattle trade', p. 142. For a general discussion of the role of trading relationships in dependency, see P. Cooke, 'Dependent development in United Kingdom regions with particular reference to Wales', *Progress in Planning*, 15, 1 (1980).

[30] Cited in Caroline A. J. Skeel, 'The Welsh woollen industry in the eighteenth and nineteenth centuries', *Archaeologia Cambrensis*, 79, part 1 (1924), p. 14. This section derives mainly from T. C. Mendenhall, *The Shrewsbury Drapers and the Welsh Wool Trade in the Sixteenth and Seventeenth Centuries* (Oxford, 1953); see also Caroline A. J. Skeel, 'The Welsh woollen industry in the sixteenth and seventeenth centuries', *Archaeologia Cambrensis*, 77 (1922); J. Geraint Jenkins, *The Welsh Woollen Industry* (Cardiff, 1969); idem, 'The woollen industry', in Donald Moore (ed.), *Wales in the Eighteenth Century* (Llandybie, 1976).

[31] David W. Howell, 'The economy of the landed estates of Pembrokeshire c. 1680–1830', *Welsh History Review*, 3, 1 (1967), p. 269.

Table 8.1. *Percentage of total output of*
British coal: north-east and south Wales

	1700	1750	1800
North-east	43·2	37·4	29·6
South Wales	2·7	2·7	11·3

Source: Michael W. Flinn, *The History of the British*
Coal Industry, vol 2: *1700–1830 The Industrial*
Revolution (Oxford, 1984) p. 26.

Capital accumulation in such circumstances was precarious. In the sixteenth century an anonymous clergyman saw only limited future prospects for Wales: 'for a present reformation there is no other means to be devised but to set those idle persons to work to clothing. Neither can the barren soil serve to any other trade or science, except for that of summering of cattle, or for minerals.'[32] The following centuries saw slow changes, mainly based upon minerals which were worth only a passing reference in the Tudor period. Wealden ironmasters developed the iron industry and the Mines Royal and the Mineral and Battery works went into production of metalliferous ores in the sixteenth century. Coal mining developed in the western part of the coalfield around Swansea, which dominated the industrial development. Coal shipments from Wales rose thirty times in the period 1560–1690, but the base was a very small one. There were few industries in the area to use coal and the west coast of the British Isles was an infinitely poorer market for coal than the east coast, which sustained Durham and Northumberland's growth. Nor could trading and producing monopolies develop in a coalfield with a variety of coals and scattered markets. The coal trade lacked Newcastle's singlemindedness. Wales' share of the growing production of coal in the period rose significantly only after 1750 as Table 8.1 indicates.

Iron smelting and forging became established, chiefly in the eastern part of the south Wales coalfield with Monmouthshire, perhaps the major area, benefiting from the tidal waters of the Severn and Wye, and the proximity of the Forest of Dean. Metal mining was more widespread and passed away from the chartered companies into the hands of the local gentry. Sir Carbery Pryce of Gogerddan's legal victory in 1691–2 eased the process of the transfer of mineral rights. In the next seventy years Cardiganshire's

---

[32] Cited in Skeel, 'The Welsh woollen industry' (1922), p. 233.

lead mines expanded to a mid-eighteenth century peak of production but it was a limited industry with a few multiplier effects.[33]

In southern Glamorgan the local gentry became prominent in activities which others had pioneered and contributed to the development of an infrastructure for industry. Many areas of the life of the upper classes were touched by metropolitan standards. Much of the impetus came from Bristol's merchants and Jenkins has described this zone as being a suburb of that city. Connections were certainly close, and it has been suggested that Bristol's own longer term development suffered from developing an area so far removed from its own immediate hinterland.[34] Towns in south Wales remained small and subaltern, none reaching 5,000 in population in the mid-eighteenth century. In 1801 Merthyr was the biggest Welsh town with 7,705 people. Newcastle was four times as large, a fact which helps place the extent of development in south Wales in perspective. Recent work has shown a society which changed rapidly in the eighteenth century, but not sufficiently or extensively enough to undermine the broader perspective of John's: 'With the possible exception of Scotland, no major area of Britain had less of an industrial tradition; and even when compared with Scotland, Wales lacked the stimulus provided by Glasgow and Edinburgh, two large and important commercial centres.'[35]

Industry suddenly erupted in the north-eastern rim of the coalfield in the late eighteenth century. It was not supported by agricultural innovation, by town growth or prepared for by proto-industrialisation on any great scale. Wales, with the exception of the Vale of Glamorgan, had been in the economic as well as a religious sense 'the most barren corner of the land'.[36] There was little preparation and social consensus was fragile. Two spectacular insurrections at either end of the 1830s reflected a longer period of instability. Merthyr made Trollope's curates faint at the thought of moving there: the 'black domain' to the north of Newport seemed ungovernable.[37]

---

[33] Nef, *Coal Industry*, vol. 1, pp. 52–6; William Rees, *Industry before the Industrial Revolution* (2 vols., Cardiff, 1968); R. O. Roberts, 'Industrial expansion in south Wales', in Moore (ed.), *Wales in the Eighteenth Century*, p. 17.

[34] W. Llewellin, 'Sussex ironmasters in Glamorgan', *Archaeologia Cambrensis*, third series, 34 (1863); Roberts, 'Industrial expansion in south Wales'; W. E. Minchinton, 'Bristol: the metropolis of the west in the eighteenth century', *Transactions of the Royal Historical Society*, fifth series, 4 (1954); Philip Jenkins, *The Making of a Ruling Class: The Glamorgan Gentry 1640–1790* (Cambridge, 1983), especially Ch. 3; M. J. Daunton, 'Towns and economic growth in eighteenth-century England', in Philip Abrams and E. A. Wrigley (eds.), *Towns in Societies* (Cambridge, 1978).

[35] A. H. John, 'The industrial development of south Wales, 1715–1914', in P. Leon (ed.), *L'Industrialisation en Europe au XIX siècle* (Paris, 1972), p. 514.

[36] The phrase was used by the Welsh puritan John Penry in 1587. Christopher Hill, 'Puritans and the "dark corners of the land"', in his *Change and Continuity in Seventeenth Century England* (London, 1974), p. 7.

[37] Gwyn A. Williams, *The Merthyr Rising* (London, 1978); Ivor Wilks, *South Wales and the Insurrection of 1839* (London, 1984); and especially David Jones, *The Last Rising* (Oxford, 1985), Ch. 1.

The north-east's development provides a contrast. Its early nineteenth-century growth was comparatively slow and it has been neglected in studies of the classic period of the industrial revolution. It had no canal development and has drawn the economic historian's attention chiefly to note the circumstances of the collapse of the vend.[38] It deserves more interest and provides evidence for Wrigley's contention that it was coal rather than cotton that was of central importance in the industrial revolution.[39] A bulky product posed problems of transport that textiles did not, and radical solutions like railways emerged. Already in the eighteenth century the area was criss-crossed by wagonways – indeed the expansion of the industry away from the Tyne demanded such a development. Most developments in nineteenth-century railway technology had their origins here. Deep coal mines, the product of large-scale production, posed problems which only steam engines and other fundamental changes could remedy. The technical changes in mining – primarily steam pumping and winding – have been less regarded than those in textiles, but held down the costs of a diminishing returns industry, to general economic benefit. Between 1700 and 1830 production quintupled from an already large base figure and the absolute production of almost 7 million tons in 1830 is, perhaps, the most striking fact, for it had dramatic consequences. As Leister recognises: 'Despite its antiquity the Durham sea coal industry was evidently still vigorous enough to trigger off both a mining and a transport revolution.'[40] This laid the basis for the area's later importance in engineering. Early nineteenth-century growth may have been less astonishing than in south Wales, but it was more firmly rooted in the region and its past. In the early nineteenth century changes crowded together, preparing the way for a spectacular transformation:

All these interconnected developments, the invention of the steamship and the railway, the tapping of deeper coal seams, the discovery of Cleveland iron, the building of docks on the Durham coast, the establishment of an effective Commission for improving the Tyne, and the almost simultaneous foundation of

[38] In the following discussion I draw frequently on three important general works which I will not cite again, viz.: Rowe, 'The economy of the north-east in the nineteenth century'; Norman McCord, 'Some aspects of north-east England in the nineteenth century', *Northern History*, 7 (1972); idem, *North-East England*; for the collapse of the vend, see A. J. Taylor, 'The third marquess of Londonderry and the north-east coal trade', *Durham University Journal*, 48, 1 (1955); idem, 'Combination in the mid-nineteenth century coal industry', *Transactions of the Royal Historical Society*, fifth series, 3 (1953); David Large, 'The third marquess of Londonderry and the end of the regulation, 1844–45', *Durham University Journal*, 51, 1 (1958).

[39] E. A. Wrigley, 'Raw material supply in the industrial revolution', in R. M. Hartwell (ed.), *The Causes of the Industrial Revolution* (London, 1967).

[40] Michael W. Flinn, *The History of the British Coal Industry*, vol. 2: *1700–1830 The Industrial Revolution* (Oxford, 1984), pp. 26–7 and *passim*; Ingeborg Leister, *The Sea Coal Mine and the Durham Miner* (Durham, 1975), p. 9.

Table 8.2. *Annual value of mining and manufactured products: north-east England,* c. *1863*

Coals	£6,650,471
Metallurgical products	£3,707,941
Chemical manufactures	£1,583,220
Paper	£300,000
Leather	£135,659
Glass and clay wares	£1,066,050
Iron shipbuilding	£1,643,326
Engines and machinery	£1,928,600

Source: W. G. Armstrong *et al.* (eds.), *The Industrial Resources of the Three Northern Rivers, the Tyne, Wear and Tees* (Papers read to the British Association 1863), p. iv.

Armstrong's and Palmer's set the stage for the swiftest and most remarkable period of industrial expansion in the whole history of the northern coalfield.[41]

Investment in ports and railways spread development into south Durham's concealed coalfield and the balance of coal production shifted towards the Wear and Tees.[42] In 1836, the *Newcastle Journal* was boasting: 'Newcastle is a town which is making more strides in wealth, population and importance than perhaps any other in the Empire.'[43] By the 1860s, the visiting British Association could be presented with a brave array of hard fact, as displayed in Table 8.2. Engineering and iron-shipbuilding both emerged in the early nineteenth century and became prominent along the Tyne. Shipbuilding became highly localised in two major areas and three other large single concerns, the locations determined by the availability of iron and engineering. Despite a later start the north-east was producing far more iron ships than the Clyde by 1890. Tramps and fighting ships were the local specialities, but as the *Mauretania* proved, high-class passenger ships were not outside the yards' possibilities. The availability of a local market for ships was crucial: 'Wherever possible ... the yards followed the ships'.[44]

[41] S. Middlebrook, *Newcastle upon Tyne: Its Growth and Achievement* (Newcastle, 1950), p. 195.
[42] A. G. Kenwood, 'Capital investment in docks, harbours and river improvements in north-eastern England 1825–1850', *Journal of Transport History*, new series, 1, 2 (1971). For descriptions of the industrial complexes of the period, see W. Clark Russell, *The North East Ports and Bristol Channel* (2nd edn, Newcastle, 1883).
[43] Cited in David Dougan, *The History of North East Shipbuilding* (London, 1968), p. 18.
[44] Sidney Pollard and Paul Robertson, *The British Shipbuilding Industry 1870–1914* (Cambridge, Mass., 1979), p. 56. See also Dougan, *History, passim*; Leslie Jones, *Shipbuilding in Britain, Mainly between the Wars* (Cardiff, 1957), p. 25.

Coal was a fertile basis for an economy and led to important spin-offs. These were supported by a prosperous and improving agriculture, in Northumberland in particular. The troubled history of the border left much almost virgin land available cheaply in the form of large farms. Innovators like the Culleys, brilliant pupils of Robert Bakewell, seized the chance and became a focus for the diffusion of new methods. Their correspondence, their apprentices and the movement of labourers helped spread new ideas. Heavy capital investment continued into the nineteenth century, giving the large farms their distinctive appearance – a large group of outbuildings clustered around a yard, with a tall chimney symbolising the capital input. Durham had smaller estates, smaller farms and slower development, but like the whole area it benefited from a wide and fertile coastal plain. The arable fields had been enclosed by the seventeenth century, and this laid down the framework for commercial exploitation. Large-scale growth of output followed in the eighteenth century, with productivity gains of five to sevenfold being recorded in some areas.[45] Urbanisation was extensive; in 1821 more than 60 per cent of the population lived in rural communities and none in towns of more than 50,000; in 1911 the respective figures were 25 per cent and 40 per cent. Much of the growth seemed to be locally financed and a recent study has found much continuity in the history of the great west Newcastle dynasties from the early nineteenth century onwards. It would be difficult to delineate such a regional bourgeoisie in south Wales.[46] In the late nineteenth century the economy of the north-east became more diverse. Iron-based industries grew dramatically. An area which had once been an insignificant producer of iron was by 1900 turning out a third of British pig-iron production. The key to this was the exploitation of the rich iron veins of the Cleveland Hills after 1851. The Tees, the last of the three great rivers to become an industrial highway, came into its own. The coal trade had developed there in the early nineteenth century. Large investments in ports and railways benefited the area; three docks were opened on the river in the second quarter of the

[45] D. J. Rowe, 'The Culleys, Northumberland farmers 1767–1813', *Agricultural History Review*, 19 (1971); Stuart MacDonald, 'Agricultural response to a changing market during the Napoleonic Wars', *Economic History Review*, second series, 33 (1980); idem, 'The diffusion of knowledge among Northumberland farmers 1780–1815', *Agricultural History Review*, 27 (1979); idem, 'The role of George Culley of Fenton in the development of Northumberland agriculture', *Archaeologia Aeliana*, fifth series, 3 (1975); J. W. House, *North Eastern England: Population Movements and the Landscape since the Early Nineteenth Century* (Newcastle, 1954), pp. 20–31; A. D. M. Phillips, 'Agricultural improvement on a Durham estate in the nineteenth century; the Lumley estate of the Earls of Scarborough', *Durham University Journal*, 72, 2 (1981); W. M. Hughes, 'Economic development in the eighteenth and nineteenth centuries', in John C. Dewdney (ed.), *Durham County with Teesside* (British Association, Durham, 1970), pp. 228, 231.
[46] Norman McCord and D. J. Rowe, 'Industrialization and urban growth in north east England', *International Review of Social History*, 22, part 1 (1977), pp. 30–1; Benwell Community Development Project, *The Making of a Ruling Class* (Newcastle, 1978).

century and coal shipments rose from virtually nothing in 1825 to 1·5 million tons in 1840. After 1850 Middlesbrough's astronomic growth heralded a further expansionary phase. Iron and steel dragged engineering, shipbuilding and chemicals in their wake.[47] Shipbuilding, engineering, armaments and glass production marked a new era on the Tyne. Armstrongs developed many innovations in armaments, Palmers the first successful screw-driven colliers. Consett started from a greenfield site in 1840 to become a major steel producer.[48] 'It is also a fact of great industrial and social importance that the activities of Tyneside were immensely stimulated by the competition in armaments which was the prelude to the Great War. The firm of Armstrong Whitworth is said to have employed in pre-war days as many as 20,000 persons.'[49]

In the 1920s a well-informed report could portray the economic history of Tyneside as a steady progression from one industry to another: 'quite a number of industries have risen and have decayed afterwards. Time after time it has seemed as if a term had come to the prosperity of the river; but as one industry or one market has failed, another has risen to take its place.'[50] The recent past seemed to have taken the form of a narrowing down to a dangerously small group of staples, but the long-term history provided the basis for some guarded optimism about the future. The main losses of the nineteenth century were industries like chemicals and glassmaking which failed to sustain an early promise. Taking the whole of the north-east into perspective, it is harder to see the development as a narrowing down. In the early nineteenth century one staple industry (coal) had gathered some subsidiaries around it. By the nineteenth century the minor industries had declined, but had been replaced by two further staples, ironmaking and engineering (in its many forms). And perhaps this is the place to exorcise finally the ghost of a pre-capitalist class whose dead hand is supposed to have retarded local development. There were two major changes in the predominant economic controllers. Newcastle merchants gave way to local landlords in the early modern period and landlords settled back into a rentier role from the late eighteenth century onwards as a middle class of industrialists, many of them local lawyers and colliery viewers in origin, emerged. Landlords continued to play a role in the

[47] I. Bullock, 'The origins of economic growth on Teesside, 1851–81', Northern History, 9 (1974); G. A. North, Teesside's Economic Heritage (Middlesbrough, 1975); C. A. Hempstead (ed.), Cleveland Iron and Steel: Background and Nineteenth Century History (British Steel Corporation, 1979); Kenwood, 'Capital investment'.
[48] Allan S. Wilson, 'The origin of the Consett Iron Company, 1840–1864', Durham University Journal, 65, 1 (1972).
[49] Henry A. Mess, Industrial Tyneside: A Social Survey (London, 1928).
[50] Ibid., p. 38.

partnerships which dominated the industry, and local knowledge seemed to be a vital ingredient for successful entrepreneurship. There seems to have been little import of capital.[51]

The trajectory of development in south Wales in the nineteenth century was quite different. It is largely the story of the shift from one staple (iron) to another (coal). The earlier comments on Wales emphasised its unpreparedness for industrialisation. The massive ironworks seemed to sit uneasily in the barren hills. The traveller Benjamin Malkin was struck by this in 1804 as he passed through Merthyr Tydfil, the capital of the new processes, and shock town of the Welsh industrial revolution. He was clearly influenced by Malthus, and was struck by 'the extreme disproportion between the population and the visible means of sustenance'.[52] Ironmaking came to be phenomenally successful – on one estimate something like a third of British iron production was issuing from there in the 1830s. By 1840 the Dowlais with its 5,000 employees was the largest ironworks in the world. Rails went from the rolling mills to lie on the plains and hills of Europe and North America. Before that cannon had been a major product.[53]

But it was a show in which the star was hindered by poor supporting acts. Towns and the markets they provided were notable absentees in eighteenth-century Wales and urbanisation only slowly caught up with the British norm in the following century.[54] Agriculture was the absentee that Malkin obviously had in mind and apart from a few rather isolated pockets, it remained the despair of the improvers for much of the century. Agricultural societies and reformers received little succour – largely because their 'solutions' were not as well adapted to the physical terrain as was the traditional practice of the area. Nor did Welsh farmers have the capital to experiment and small farms did not allow economies of scale to be realised. Few works of agricultural improvement were translated into Welsh, the first language of most farmers. Fortuitously the more fertile areas were contiguous with the coalfield – the Vale of Glamorgan, for example, experienced some improvement because of the demands of the industrial market. Though there were regional variations, Wales was essentially a land

[51] Ibid., Ch. 3 *passim*; Carney *et al.*, 'Regional underdevelopment'; Flinn, *Coal Industry*, pp. 267–9; M. Sill, 'Landownership and industry: the east Durham coalfield in the nineteenth century', *Northern History*, 20 (1984), pp. 145–56; R. W. Sturgess, 'The north east coalmasters: 1820–1855', in R. W. Sturgess (ed.), *Pitman, Viewers and Coal-Masters: Essays on North East Coal Mining in the Nineteenth Century* (North East Labour History Society, 1986).

[52] Cited in David Jones, *Before Rebecca* (London, 1973), p. 70.

[53] The standard work is A. H. John, *The Industrial Development of South Wales 1750–1850* (Cardiff, 1950). Michael Atkinson and Colin Baber, *The Growth and Decline of the South Wales Iron Industry, 1760–1880* (Cardiff, 1987), appeared too late for me to make use of it, as did the major collection: Colin Baber and L. J. Williams, *Modern South Wales: Essays in Economic History* (Cardiff, 1986).

[54] For a general discussion of urbanisation, see Neil Evans, 'The urbanization of Welsh society', in Trevor Herbert and Gareth E. Jones (eds.), *People and Protest: Wales 1815–1880* (Cardiff, 1988).

of large estates and small farms. Linguistic, religious and cultural differences were encrusted on the class divide and destroyed the co-partnership of landlord and tenant that was often the basis of agricultural improvement in many parts of England. There is little point in blaming landlord or tenant for this situation – it was the gulf between them that was the problem.[55]

Elsewhere in Wales industries collapsed as a national market was created in the early nineteenth century, and limited natural resources were effectively worked out. Wool, for long the staple industry, fell victim to the national market created by canals and railways: Rochdale came to sell flannel to Wales in the mid-nineteenth century. The mid-Wales industry tried to develop from undercapitalised 'proto-industrialisation' to the real thing and exhausted itself in the process. Competition was too effective and ironically in that area of Wales coal was absent as were effective links to the coalfields. Factories were built but barely opened; by the 1850s the textile industry was moribund apart from supplying local markets. In the late nineteenth century wool was re-established, on a small factory basis, in south-west Wales. But then it was entirely dependent on its proximity to the south Wales coalfield and the protected market which the taste of a largely Welsh workforce gave it.[56] Water power sustained this small-scale production in an area as lacking in coal as was north-west Wales. The West Riding had nothing to fear, and Lancashire still less.

The copper mining industry had flourished briefly in north Wales in the late eighteenth century. Large reserves of low-grade ore were cheaply worked in great open casts and gave the Anglesey solicitor Thomas Williams the economic power to dominate the world market in the 1790s. Yet within ten years both Williams and cheap ore extraction had gone. Swansea smelters looked increasingly to South America for their supplies. In copper extraction, Wales became an increasingly irrelevant backwater.[57] Industrial enterprises in mid- and north Wales generally followed the same pattern. A boom from the 1790s collapsed in the decade between 1815 and 1825 and pastoralisation was the major consequence. Marginal, small-scale production, largely based on mineral extraction and water power ran into the limits of their possibilities and declined. Unlike the industries of south

[55] Key works on agriculture are David Howell, *Land and People in Nineteenth Century Wales* (London, 1978); Richard Colyer, 'Limitations of agrarian development in nineteenth century Wales', *Bulletin of the Board of Celtic Studies*, 82, 4 (1978); Richard Colyer, *The Welsh Cattle Drovers* (Cardiff, 1976); idem, 'Early agricultural societies in south Wales', *Welsh History Review*, 12, 4 (1985); Pamela F. Michael, 'Tenant farming in Merioneth, 1850–1925', unpublished M.A. thesis (University of Wales, 1978).

[56] See Jenkins, *Welsh Woollen Industry*.

[57] J. R. Harris, *The Copper King* (Liverpool, 1964); John Rowlands, *The Copper Mountain* (Llangefni, 1966); R. O. Roberts, 'The rise of and decline of non-ferrous metal smelting in south Wales', in W. E. Minchinton (ed.) *Industrial South Wales* (London, 1969).

Wales they had often used local capital, which was sufficient for the restricted scale of production. They were not concentrated in a narrow belt as was industry in south Wales, but widely scattered across the area.[58] Geographically and in capital sources mid- and north Wales industries had a more organic connection with the area itself, growing out of local conditions. Lack of coal and exhaustion of mineral resources proved to be crippling. The two exceptions serve to prove the rule. In the north-west slate expanded rapidly between 1830 and 1880 on the basis of new markets in Britain and beyond, improved quality of production and reduced costs (largely through falling transport charges). It was a resource in plentiful supply and one which could undercut its competitors.[59] In the north-east the tiny Flintshire and Denbighshire coalfield maintained an array of industries – iron, lead smelting, bricks, etc. – but it was always constrained by the narrowness of the coal measures. In orientation it was an outlier of Merseyside and Staffordshire and took little but labour from Wales.

In the main centre in the south it was the iron industry which broke the earlier vicious circle of poverty and provided capital which could be a platform for further development, notably in the sale coal industry. Ironmasters' capital and canal building opened up the rich coal reserves of the north-east rim of the coalfield. Before the mid-nineteenth century coal was largely a subsidiary of iron in south Wales and it was with the tapping of deep steam coal seams in the Aberdare and Rhondda Valleys – in the previously underdeveloped, deep lying, central part of the coalfield – that it now came to the fore.[60] The mid-Victorian period saw a complex process of growth and decline in which the baton was passed from iron to coal. In the mid-1870s the well-informed Bishop Ollivant even wondered if growth was coming to an end. The overall expansion of the region has masked this development. Iron declined dramatically as the old beneficial leases fell in, local ore resources were exhausted and new technologies and sources of ore supplies demanded flat coastal sites rather than the inaccessible and cramped heads of the valleys. There was closure, conversion to steel manufacture, transfer of capital to coal and some new works established on the coast, notably at Cardiff and Port Talbot. No works were moved from the rim of the coalfield to the coast; the offshoot of Dowlais established at Cardiff produced ships' plates, a new trade not formerly followed. Yet in the new dispensation iron and steel in Wales remained tangential to the

[58] A. H. Dodd, *The Industrial Revolution in North Wales* (Cardiff, 1933; 3rd edn, 1971).
[59] Ibid.; the best published analysis of the slate industry is Dylan Pritchard, 'The expansionary phase in the history of the slate industry', *Transactions of the Caernarvonshire Historical Society*, 10 (1949); see also Jean Lindsay, *A History of the North Wales Slate Industry* (Newton Abbot, 1974).
[60] The classic study is J. H. Morris and L. J. Williams, *The South Wales Coal Industry 1841–1875* (Cardiff, 1958).

industry in Britain. In 1914 south Wales produced only 753,000 tons of pig iron compared with the north-east's 3,307,000 tons.[61] Only in the western part of the coalfield did any really vital growth take place in metals when the region came to dominate British (and briefly world) tinplate production.[62]

The growth of the coal industry tended to obscure all this, producing an economy which was unusually geared to the export of a primary commodity. Iron formed only a limited foundation for growth. Some iron companies went into coal production, others struggled on while their owners joined the landed gentry across the border. But there were limitations in the impact of iron on the wider economy. The firms – especially Guests and Crawshays – were huge and vertically integrated. They produced almost all their wants from raw materials to manufactured product.[63] The spin-offs in capital accumulation and the development of an entrepreneurial class were quite small. Contemporaries frequently noticed the peculiar class structure and its consequences. There were fears that truck shops inhibited the development of a middle class and tended to polarise society. The area resembled Wolverhampton in the combination of iron and coal mining and manufacture, it was noted in 1862, but entirely lacked the smaller and more varied manufacture which was so vital there. A nonconformist minister observed that the working classes of Wales were doomed to hard labour – to dangerous and exhausting trades – and lacked opportunities in the skilled metal trades.[64]

A good deal of the initial capital for the sale coal industry was derived from local sources. Two main factors accounted for this. The iron industry had generated enough pockets of wealth to provide a seed bed, and the scale of capital needed for coal was relatively modest until the second half of the nineteenth century. Early entrepreneurs included shopkeepers, a

---

[61] A. H. John and Glanmor Williams (eds.), Glamorgan County History, vol. 5: Industrial Glamorgan (Cardiff, 1980), is a convenient source for this. The comments here follow D. G. Watts, 'Changes in location in the south Wales iron and steel industry 1860–1930,' Geography, 53, 3 (1968); Ieuan Gwynedd Jones, The Valleys in the Mid-Nineteenth Century (Merthyr, 1981), pp. 7–10; B. R. Mitchell and Phyllis Deane, Abstract of British Historical Statistics (Cambridge, 1962), p. 133; for Ollivant's views, see Western Mail, 22 July 1875.

[62] W. E. Minchinton, The British Tinplate Industry (Oxford, 1957).

[63] The argument here derives from the discussion of A. H. John's paper, pp. 522–4, in Leon (ed.) L'Industrialisation; for studies in the firms see John Addis, The Crawshay Dynasty (Cardiff, 1957); J. England, 'The Dowlais ironworks 1759–1793', Morgannwg, 3 (1959); M. J. Daunton, 'The Dowlais Iron Company in the iron industry 1800–1850', Welsh History Review, 6, 1 (1972); John Davies, 'The Dowlais lease, 1748–1900', Morgannwg, 12 (1968).

[64] British Parliamentary Papers, 1852, XXI, Report on Mining Districts, 1852, 12–13, 1862, XXII, Fourth Report of the Medical Officer of the Privy Council, p. 465 (I owe this reference to Professor Ieuan Gwynedd Jones). Thomas Rees, Miscellaneous Papers on Subjects Relating to Wales (London, 1867), p. 12.

timber merchant, a bridge and railway builder, shipowners and ironmasters. Rarely did the single entrepreneur have total control of an enterprise; more typical was the partnership. Yet capital from outside the immediate region of south Wales was significant from the 1860s, and possibly it became more so as time passed and joint-stock organisation became more available. The increased capital needs of the industry as it tapped deeper seams may have contributed to this also. The bulk of new work at existing pits came from ploughed back profits and the coal industry was less dependent than most on public subscription. This was despite the fact that there was a market for shares from the 1870s and stock exchanges emerged in Cardiff (in 1892) and Swansea (in 1903). There was also a speculative fringe to the industry: investors with little serious interest who simply sought quick profits. In the final phase of expansion from the 1890s to the First World War joint-stock companies played an increasingly dominant role. Many had a limited range of major shareholders and in 1913, 43·5 per cent of employment in the coal industry was in private companies. Yet south Wales had, in the same year, 36·9 per cent of its employment in coal in public limited companies. This was the highest figure for any British coalfield and dwarfed the north-east's 6·9 per cent. It was in such companies that capital external to the region was likely to be attracted. Of shareholders in south Wales mining companies 57 per cent were external to the area. Again this was the highest figure for any British coalfield, far above the national average of 38 per cent and the north-east's 40 per cent.[65] This tends to confirm a persistent impression of capital shortage in the area; the coal owners were a large component of the limited sources for industrial capital and they appear not to have been entirely sufficient even within their own industry. This offers pointers to some of the possible reasons for the failure of industrial diversification. Coal absorbed much of what was, in all likelihood, a limited local capital supply and it also devoured the labour supply, despite the frantic pace of in-migration. It may also have tended to crowd out other development, in the simple sense of absorbing potential industrial sites with its greed for marshalling yards and the limited flat land of the valley floors and it tended to monopolise the area's transport facilities. The congestion of the railways and ports was notorious and graphically illustrated by the strike of the Cardiff seamen and dockers in the summer of 1911. Within a few days of the strike becoming general up to 100,000 miners were idle, and the threat

[65] L. J. Williams, 'The coalowners', in Smith (ed.), *A People*; Rhodri Walters, 'Capital formation in the south Wales coal industry 1840–1914', *Welsh History Review*, 10, 1 (1980); G. M. Holmes, 'The south Wales coal industry, 1850–1914', *Transactions of the Honourable Society of the Cymmrodorion*, 10 (1976); Roy Church, *The History of the British Coal Industry*, vol. 3: *The Victorian Pre-Eminence, 1830–1913* (Oxford, 1986), pp. 144–5; R. H. Walters, *The Economic and Business History of the South Wales Steam Coal Industry, 1840–1914* (New York, 1977), Ch. 3.

Table 8.3. *Percentage of British coal exports: north-east and Bristol Channel*

	1850	1880	1900
North east ports	63·6	39·5	29·7
Bristol Channel ports	13·0	39·0	41·9

Source: G. M. Holmes, 'The south Wales coal industry, 1850–1914', *Transactions of the Honourable Society of the Cymmrodorion*, 10 (1976), p. 171.

to coalfield production helped ensure a speedy settlement. This over-crowding helped doom to failure Cardiff's dreams of developing an import trade and of capturing the Midland market. All the impressive statistics which its advocates mustered could not overcome the disadvantages to importers which a massive and booming export trade presented. Pit props, grain, foodstuffs and metal ores formed a limited import trade; many vessels were paid off elsewhere and sailed to Cardiff in ballast, with only skeleton crews.[66]

In its later phases of development coal produced few spin-offs. South Wales supplied an increasing proportion of Britain's coal exports, with the consequence that much of the production was not generating any local coal-using industries. The diversity of its markets and effective competition precluded a pricing cartel though one was attempted in the 1890s. There was no equivalent of the protected market which the early north-east trade had enjoyed. The north-east had moved away from exporting, just as south Wales came to dominate British coal exports, as Table 8.3 indicates. The north-east turned away from its traditional London market and sold to local industries to an increasing extent. In 1873 evidence from a large sample of Durham collieries indicates that only 14·3 per cent of coal went to London, while 22·5 per cent was used for gasmaking, 27·2 per cent for manufacturing and 36 per cent became coke.[67] Furthermore, the mining technology and expertise for south Wales was largely imported from the north-east which

[66] M. J. Daunton, *Coal Metropolis: Cardiff 1870–1914* (Leicester, 1977); idem, 'Aristocrat and traders: the Bute docks, 1839–1914', *Journal of Transport History*, new series, 3 (1975); Robin Craig, 'The ports and shipping, 1750–1914', in John and Williams (eds.), *Industrial Glamorgan*. Graham Humphreys, *Industrial South Wales* (Newton Abbot, 1972) has some useful comments in the introductory chapter by Joe England, pp. 30–2. For Cardiff's promoters see Neil Evans, 'The Welsh Victorian city: the middle class and national and civic consciousness in Cardiff, 1850–1914', *Welsh History Review*, 12, 3 (1985). For the strike of 1911, see Neil Evans, '"A tidal wave of impatience": the Cardiff general strike of 1911', in J. Geraint Jenkins and J. Beverley Smith (eds.), *Politics and Society in Wales, 1840–1922: Essays in Honour of Ieuan Gwynedd Jones* (Cardiff, 1988).
[67] Holmes, 'Coal industry'; R. W. Sturgess, 'Factors affecting expansion of coalmining 1700–1914', in R. W. Sturgess (ed.), *The Great Age of Industry in the North East* (Durham, 1981), pp. 8–10.

had first developed deep mining and the same applied to the colliers which carried the export trade. South Wales had both the market and the basic resources for ship production. Cardiff, by the early twentieth century, registered more tramp shipping than any other port in the world and ships' plates were actually manufactured there. Investors occasionally saw a potential in shipbuilding, but in reality it was too late to effect the development of an industry already well established and having distinct regional specialisms elsewhere. A good deal of the capital for shipping came from the north-east and many of the vessels plying from Cardiff were built there – it was the obvious source of colliers. By the late nineteenth century it was difficult to break into an established structure. Pollard and Robertson confess their bafflement at the failure of shipbuilding in south Wales, for it measured well on their check list of conditions. Reluctantly they fell back on the absence of tradition as an unsatisfactory answer. If 'tradition' is the product of the trajectory of development in an area, and if we add the additional factors discussed here, perhaps their explanation can be seen as more satisfactory.[68]

The main argument of this chapter is that the lack of diversification in south Wales is the product of a particular pattern of development. Persistent local capital shortages and dependence on 'imports' of capital were the key features and ones which the iron industry failed to overcome completely because of its vertically integrated structure. Coal mining became dominant at a stage where the key innovations which it was likely to produce had already been made elsewhere. The pattern of the north-east's growth was different; its pioneer role in coal production gave it an important place in the development of engineering and shipbuilding. In 1914 it was much less dependent upon coal than south Wales was.

Something of this difference can be captured by examining the occupational distribution of the population of the two areas, as indicated in Table 8.4. South Wales' concentration on metal manufacture in 1851 is clearly displayed, and the high figure for mining (including ironstone mining and a substantial proportion of coal mining being directed at iron manufacture) is a further reflection of that fact. By 1911 south Wales was greatly concentrated on coal and while still slightly ahead of the north-east in metal manufacture cannot match it in the more sophisticated spheres of metal using – mechanical engineering and shipbuilding in particular. Such differences need to be put in perspective. On the broad view there were important similarities and both were overconcentrated in a narrowish band of activities, as the world depression of the interwar years was to reveal all

---

[68] Pollard and Robertson, *Shipbuilding*, p. 58.

NEIL EVANS

Table 8.4. *Percentage of total employed in selected occupations, 1851, 1911*

	North[a]	Northumb. & Dur.	Glam. & Mon.	Wales	G.B.
1851					
Agriculture etc.	24·9	17·0	16·9	33·6	22·0
Mining and quarrying	11·7	16·2	21·5	13·5	4·0
Metal manufacturing	4·0	5·3	12·5	6·3	3·0
Mechanical engineering	0·9	1·3	0·6	0·6	0·8
Shipbuilding and marine engineering	1·4	2·0	0·3	0·3	0·3
1911					
Agriculture etc.	7·3	4·0	3·0	10·4	7·8
Mining and quarrying	21·0	25·8	32·9	25·6	6·8
Metal manufacturing	5·6	4·6	7·0	5·9	3·2
Mechanical engineering	4·3	5·2	1·8	1·5	2·8
Shipbuilding and marine engineering	4·2	5·3	0·6	0·5	0·9

[a] North – North Riding, Westmorland, Cumberland, Northumberland, Durham.
Source: calculated from total employment tables 1851, 1911 in C. H. Lee, *British Regional Employment Statistics 1841–1971* (Cambridge, 1979).

too clearly. Yet examination of the trajectory of development has pointed to equally vital differences.

It was argued at the outset that it is not adequate to compare the development of the Welsh economy with the whole of England; yet in the end the peculiarities of Wales are highlighted by using the nearest equivalent amongst the regions of England as a control. The colonial analogy is a difficult one to maintain (though the constant dependence on external capital has been stressed here) for it suggests a straightforward concern with primary production. The Welsh economy was not always of that kind, particularly in the early nineteenth century when iron was often exported in semi-manufactured or manufactured forms. For this reason it could be argued that it is more appropriate to refer to Wales as an example of combined development – that is the combination of advanced sectors of production with quite primitive ones – 'a drawing together of the different stages of the journey, combining of separate steps, an amalgam of archaic with more contemporary forms'.[69] In the late nineteenth century Wales

[69] Leon Trotsky, *A History of the Russian Revolution* (London, 1977 edn), p. 28.

shifted back to being largely a primary exporting region – mainly as the result of this previous development.

Examination of these two regions cannot make a theory of regional economic development but it does raise some more general issues. Regional economic development has been a concern of geographers, sociologists and economists for twenty years or more. Historians have had the concern for even longer with Dodd's *The Industrial Revolution in North Wales* being a pioneer study.[70] Recent historical work on proto-industrialisation has also had a strong regional emphasis.[71] As a general theory proto-industrialisation has proved to be inadequate despite making many gains in understanding the linkage between rural outworking, family structures, agricultural change and proletarianisation. The experience of regions of heavy industry offer little consolation to the theory as the connection between domestic forms of manufacturing and iron and steel can be very tenuous. Tilly, perhaps, did as much as anyone to popularise the term, but he now recognises that there is a difficulty in the 'suggestion of a distinctive but standard stage in the creation of modern industry'.[72] The proliferation of research seems to have made him into a pluralist, stressing different regional paths to development and recognising that heavy industrial regions are a distinct category.[73]

This recognition is perhaps part of an emerging consensus in several disciplines. Massey has elaborated a general view which greatly influenced the approach of the present chapter. 'The social and economic structure of any region will be a complex result of the combination of that area's succession of roles within the series of wider national and international spatial divisions of labour.'[74] Houston and Snell's critique of proto-industrialisation starts from a different point, but arrives at a similar conclusion, though rather less emphatically: 'When discussing the causes of industrialization it would seem more helpful to consider the relations

---

[70] The book was first published in 1933 but written in the 1920s; much of its substance appeared as articles then and apparently the University of Wales Press delayed publication for some time. Dodd's inspiration was R. H. Tawney whose extra-mural classes he had attended.

[71] For example, P. Hudson, 'Proto-industrialisation: the case of the West Riding wool textile industry in the eighteenth and early nineteenth centuries', *History Workshop Journal*, 12 (1981).

[72] Charles and Richard Tilly, 'Agenda for European economic history', *Journal of Economic History*, 31 (1971). In Charles Tilly's *The Vendee* (London, 1964), an earlier encounter with the process, he described the bocage as semi-urban – the result of the uneven impact of the wider process of urbanisation on the area. For his more recent views see his 'Flows of capital and forms of industry in Europe, 1500–1900', *Theory and Society*, 12, 2 (1983), quotation from p. 129.

[73] See Tilly, 'Flows and forms'; idem, 'Did the cake of custom break?', in John M. Merriman (ed.), *Consciousness and Class Experience in Nineteenth-Century Europe* (New York, 1979).

[74] Doreen Massey, 'Regionalism: some current issues', *Capital and Class*, 6 (1978), p. 116; almost the same phrase is also used in idem, 'In what sense a regional problem?', *Regional Studies*, 13 (1979), p. 235.

between all the factors in the specific regional frameworks from which it emerged.[75] Such an approach has been attempted here; an effort at a more precise delineation of regional peculiarities through a detailed and controlled comparison. The danger of this pluralism is that it tends towards fragmentation, a distrust of generalisation and a retreat into an empiricist appreciation of distinctiveness. Tilly's evident concern to construct typologies of regional development is a valuable and necessary corrective.

Work on contemporary regional issues throws up some warnings and problems. We must avoid giving regions personalities and then blaming them for lack of growth or praising them for success. 'Regions are not actors; their inhabitants are.'[76] As Massey stresses, they are complex combinations of past and present structures but not living entities. People within *and without* the regions still make the decisions: analysis of class and power structures cannot be evaded. The definition of regions is another problem: it presents more problems in Wales than in the north-east. Both areas have clear geographical identities, but in Wales as a whole the economic identity is more open to question, though it is not for south Wales alone by the mid-nineteenth century. There were few economic links between industries in north and south Wales and they had different patterns of development. Yet labour was recruited essentially within Wales for much of the nineteenth century and perhaps Wales reached a greater level of national integration in non-economic spheres at that time than any time before or since. However, the choice of regional boundaries may influence the outcome of arguments and has to be recognised as an issue.[77] Economic boundaries may also change with time; the exploitation of iron and coal in south Wales made the coalfield into a distinctive region in the nineteenth century.

No region is an economic island and flows of capital, labour and resources between them are important issues to be considered. Othick has argued that compared with nations, regions are, in both economic and political terms, 'open'. Some areas clearly had surplus capital to export –

---

[75] R. Houston and K. D. M. Snell, 'Proto-industrialization? Cottage industry, social change and industrial revolution', *Historical Journal*, 27 (1984), p. 490.

[76] Peter Alexis Gourevitch, 'The re-emergence of peripheral nationalisms: some comparative speculations on the spatial distribution of political leadership and economic growth', *Comparative Studies in Society and History*, 21, 3 (1979), p. 304.

[77] Massey, 'Regionalism'; idem, 'In what sense a regional problem?'; Brinley Thomas, 'Wales and the Atlantic economy', in Brinley Thomas (ed.), *The Welsh Economy* (Cardiff, 1962); Neil Evans and Jon Parry, 'Gogs, Cardis and Hwntws: region, nations and state in Wales, 1840–1940', revised version of a paper presented to the eighth Lipman seminar on Ireland, Belfast, 5–7 September 1986 (available on request). Recently Dudley Baines and Brinley Thomas have debated the nature of migration patterns in Wales; see Baines *Migration in a Mature Economy: Emigration and Internal Migration in England and Wales, 1861–1900* (Cambridge, 1985); and Thomas, 'A cauldron of rebirth: population and the Welsh language in the nineteenth century', *Welsh History Review*, 13 (1986–7).

Merseyside is one clear example – while others (Wales has been stressed here) were importers.[78] Trends within the wider capitalist economy will influence regional fortunes in a powerful way. Again Othick usefully stresses that links to the outside world are not unmitigated blessings for some regions in the course of industrialisation, but become simply channels for inter-regional imports and the destruction of local enterprise. The mid-Wales woollen industry's fate in the mid-nineteenth century is a classic example of this. Such 'backwash' effects are concentrated in periods of slower growth. 'Spread' effects – the beneficial aspects of inter-regional influence – will concentrate in eras of rapid expansion: the south Wales iron industry between 1780 and 1815 and coal in the 1850s and 1860s would be good examples of this.

We need to develop a sense of the interaction of economic factors at a regional level. The theory of proto-industrialisation has achieved this only partially: the dove-tailing of industrial and agricultural production is one of the themes. Yet another emphasis in some of the writing is on industry as a compensation for poor agricultural endowment.[79] It would also be useful to understand how agricultural prosperity may have contributed to industrial growth; north-eastern landlords poured their profits into coal mines. As far as Scotland is concerned Harvie has argued that: 'Industrialization ... had its roots in the land' and Cobbett seemed to be observing the same phenomenon on Lowland farms when he described them as 'factories for making corn and meat, chiefly by means of horses and machinery'.[80] In Germany, joint-stock companies were a means of mobilising agrarian capital for industry, and as Hobsbawm observes in pre-industrial societies the very size of the agricultural sector gives it a central role in development.[81] Some landlords in south Wales invested in industry in the eighteenth century and Jenkins has recently emphasised their role. What he cannot show (and he does not try to) is that this dramatically modifies our traditional picture of the sources of capital for the new, coke-based iron industry; that late eighteenth-century capital was mainly imported and was distinct from this earlier eighteenth-century development.[82] General economic growth in the north-east benefited from a

---

[78] John Othick, 'The economic history of Ulster: a perspective', in Liam Kennedy and Philip Ollerenshaw (eds.), *An Economic History of Ulster, 1820–1940* (Manchester, 1985); A. G. Kenwood, 'Fixed capital formation on Merseyside 1800–1913', *Economic History Review*, second series, 31, 2 (1978).   [79] E. L. Jones, 'The agricultural origins of industry', *Past and Present*, 40 (1968).

[80] Flinn, *Coal Industry*; Christopher Harvie, *Scotland and Nationalism: Scottish Society and Politics 1707–1977* (London, 1977), pp. 77, 80.

[81] Hans-Ulrich Wehler, *The German Empire 1871–1914* (Leamington Spa, 1985), p. 12; E. J. Hobsbawm, 'Scottish reformers of the eighteenth century and capitalist agriculture', in E. J. Hobsbawm *et al.* (eds.), *Peasants in History: Essays in Honour of Daniel Thorner* (Calcutta, 1980) p. 3.

[82] Jenkins, *The Making*.

rather more prosperous agriculture, and a more complex and varied pattern of towns than in Wales. In Wales, by the nineteenth century, it was industry that was subsidising agricultural rents – at least on some of the great estates with vast industrial incomes.[83]

An emphasis on the whole picture within a region fits easily with a greater stress upon geography and natural resources than has recently been fashionable. Hobsbawm has tended to reduce the significance of coal supplies as a cause of the industrial revolution, though he does see the early development of the industry as one of the factors which differentiated Britain from Europe[84] Nef emphasised particular reasons why coal emerged as a key industry early in Britain and while his stress on a general crisis in fuel supply would no longer gain assent, many of these factors remain important.[85] Wrigley, Flinn and Thomas have all recently stressed the contribution of coal to the industrial revolution and Nef's old suggestion that coal resources had an impact on the fortunes of what would now be called 'proto-industrial' enterprises is worthy of further investigation.[86] It is one (perhaps rather obvious) answer to the question of which sense of outworking prospered in the long run and which did not. Cameron makes the presence or absence of coal one of his key variables in his analysis of the patterns of European industrialisation.[87]

Geography does not, of course, determine history; it is the actions (intentional and unintentional) of people which do that. Some emphasis has been given here to the kinds of trading relationships which exist between regions and the way in which these can influence capital accumulation. Monopoly was a form of organisation which kept reproducing itself in the north-east and it gave the region several centuries of protected profits. Hausman has recently questioned the size (but not the existence) of these monopoly profits. His conclusion that they added only slightly to the price of a chaldron of coal in the period 1700–1845, and had less impact on prices than did taxes on coal, is more important for London than it is for the north-east. Obviously this slight price advantage would be a higher proportion of profits than it was of price. Thus, even if his complex calculations gain assent, they do not destroy the argument presented here, and entry to the coal trade was probably easier to prevent in the early eighteenth century

[83] John Davies, *Cardiff and the Marquesses of Bute* (Cardiff, 1981), Ch. 4.
[84] E. J. Hobsbawm, *Industry and Empire* (London, 1968), pp. 22, 31.
[85] Nef, *Coal Industry*. For an unreconstructed statement of his views, see his 'An early energy crisis and its consequences', *Scientific American*, 237, 5 (1977).
[86] Flinn, *Coal Industry*, Ch. 13; Wrigley, 'Raw material supply'; Brinley Thomas, 'Towards an energy interpretation of the industrial revolution', *Atlantic Economic Journal*, 8, 1 (1980).
[87] Rondo Cameron, 'A new view of European industrialization', *Economic History Review*, second series, 38, 1 (1985).

than it was later.[88] Sweezy's and Cromar's view that excess profits stimulated entry and ultimately excess capacity which would have depressed the rate of return in the long run seems to be more significant.[89] In south Wales the coal trade because of its diversity of markets and coals never lent itself to such organisation, though the larger firms in the iron industry had been enabled by their resources to rise above the pressures of competitive pricing during depressions.

It is a frequent response to historical problems to argue for going back to the regions and their distinctiveness. There have been many gains from such approaches, but there also needs to be synthesis if they are to contribute to broader arguments. Wider views also help to locate the region. Comparison is one of the best – and ultimately perhaps the only – method of establishing the specific characteristics of an area. This inevitably leads into more general and theoretical issues and could help establish the basis for theories which are grounded in, and can be tested by, empirical research. We will need to take care of regional distinctiveness, but cannot afford to assume that the overall patterns of national and international development will thus take care of themselves.

[88] William J. Hausman, 'A model of the London coal trade in the eighteenth century', *Quarterly Journal of Economics*, 94, 1 (1980), pp. 1–2, 11; idem, 'Cheap coals or limitation of the vend? The London coal trade, 1770–1845', *Journal of Economic History*, 44, 2 (1984), pp. 321–2, 327; idem, 'Market power in the London coal trade: the limitation of the vend 1770–1845', *Explorations in Economic History*, 21 (1984), pp. 398–9.

[89] See n. 22.

Chapter 9

Proto-industrialisation in Scotland

IAN D. WHYTE

The origins of the industrial revolution in England have long been debated but Scotland is often treated as only marginally important in the industrialisation of Britain. Scotland's economic development in early modern times remains in many ways a puzzle. An impoverished country with essentially medieval trading patterns and an underdeveloped economy at the end of the seventeenth century, Scotland rapidly caught up with her southern neighbour in the eighteenth century.[1] Scotland's industrialisation has the appearance of an 'economic miracle' compared with progress south of the border. Traditionally, Scotland's success has been attributed mainly to external influences, particularly the Union of 1707 giving access to expanding English domestic and colonial markets.[2] To explain everything in terms of the Union is, however, inadequate, as Devine has suggested.[3] Much of Scotland's eighteenth-century development was shaped by indigenous influences but the nature of these has been insufficiently explored.

Scotland's case is not only intrinsically interesting but comparison with England and other European countries offers the possibility of new insights into the causes and mechanisms of industrialisation more generally. Although proto-industrialisation theory has been applied to Ireland,[4] there has been little theoretical work on the development of pre-factory industry in Scotland. Given the recent interest in proto-industrialisation within western Europe and the lack of research on the origins of Scottish industrial development this chapter attempts to analyse some of the distinctive characteristics of Scottish industry in the seventeenth and eighteenth

---

[1] The character of the Scottish economy at the end of the seventeenth century is described in T. C. Smout, *Scottish Trade on the Eve of the Union, 1660–1707* (Edinburgh, Oliver and Boyd, 1963). Scotland's industrialisation in the eighteenth and nineteenth centuries has recently been surveyed by R. H. Campbell, *The Rise and Fall of Scottish Industry 1707–1939* (Edinburgh, John Donald, 1980).
[2] Campbell, *Rise and Fall*; T. M. Devine, 'The Union of 1707 and Scottish development', *Scottish Economic and Social History*, 5 (1985), pp. 23–40.   [3] Devine, 'The Union of 1707'.
[4] E. L. Almquist, 'Pre-famine Ireland and the theory of European proto-industrialization: the evidence of the 1841 census', *Journal of Economic History*, 39 (1979), pp. 699–718; B. Collins, 'Proto-industrialization and pre-famine emigration', *Social History*, 7, 2 (1982), pp. 127–46.

centuries in the hope of generating some new questions about Scottish social and economic development and their place within the British industrial revolution. The theoretical yardstick of this analysis is found in hypotheses raised by the proto-industrialisation literature. As industrialisation in Scotland was preceded by widespread rural manufacturing, particularly of textiles for distant as well as local markets, the proto-industrialisation model offers a useful framework within which to explore the country's rapid economic progress in the eighteenth century. The theoretical approaches associated with the concept of proto-industrialisation are useful in highlighting many important questions such as those concerning the links between regional specialisation in industry and agriculture, the relationships between agrarian structures, landownership and household production, and the importance of gender divisions in both agricultural and industrial labour.

THE REGIONAL DISTRIBUTION OF RURAL TEXTILE PRODUCTION IN EARLY-MODERN SCOTLAND

A good deal of effort has been given to defining the environmental, economic and social criteria which characterised regions where large-scale rural industry developed in the past, though it must be appreciated that such criteria relate to idealised situations which are not likely to exist in all or even most proto-industrial regions.[5] Proto-industrialisation is thought to have developed mainly in upland areas among peasant smallholders practising a pastoral economy. Such people developed industrial activities to supplement inadequate incomes from marginal farming. Typical proto-industrial regions were characterised by dispersed settlement where controls generated by open-field systems, nucleated villages and tightly organised manors or estates were weak or absent. The lack of marked seasonal peaks of labour in pastoral farming strengthened the commitment to industrial production as did the individuality generated by geographical isolation. The large reserves of wasteland in such areas could be encroached on piecemeal by squatters producing a pattern of small holdings which in turn encouraged the taking up of by-occupations in industry. There are problems in trying to apply this model situation too rigidly, as Coleman has pointed out.[6] The idea only begins to fit England if the definition of

---

[5] F. F. Mendels, 'Proto-industrialisation: the first phase of the industrialisation process', *Journal of Economic History*, 32, 1 (1972), pp. 241–61; P. Kriedte, H. Medick and J. Schlumbohm, *Industrialisation before Industrialisation: Rural Industry in the Genesis of Capitalism* (English transl., Cambridge, Cambridge University Press, 1982).

[6] D. C. Coleman, 'Proto-industrialization: a concept too many', *Economic History Review*, 36, 3 (1983), pp. 435–48.

'upland' is broadened to include lowland wood-pasture areas. Most early advocates of proto-industrialisation agreed that areas of commercial cereal production with extensive open-field systems and strong landlord controls were less favourable to the development of large-scale rural industry. In such areas neither the pattern of landholding structures nor the marked seasonal demand for labour encouraged proto-industrialisation as opposed to subsidiary by-employments, as Snell has indicated.[7] Gullickson's work on the Pays de Caux has, however, suggested that the link between proto-industrialisation and unfertile areas of subsistence farming has been overstressed in the past and that other influences such as landlessness and lack of employment in agriculture for women could generate proto-industrialisation in areas of large-scale cereal production.[8]

How did the distribution of rural textile production in Scotland during the seventeenth and eighteenth centuries compare with the model? To some extent this depends on the scale at which the problem is approached. At a European level Scotland was a peripheral, marginal, largely upland country with a mainly pastoral economy. Scotland's settlement pattern was one of dispersed farmsteads, cottages and hamlet clusters with few nucleated villages. With such a broad perspective the development of rural industry anywhere in Scotland could be reconciled with the model.

But proto-industrialisation is a regional concept and must stand or fall by its ability to explain developments at this scale. If one examines Scotland more closely, discrepancies begin to appear. To appreciate this it is necessary to make some regional division of Scottish agriculture in the early modern period. The definition of 'farming regions' in early modern England, and the industrial activities associated with them, has reached a high level of refinement.[9] The same cannot be said for Scotland. The concept of farming regions may not even be strictly applicable. There are indications that there were less marked regional variations within Scotland in settlement patterns, farm structures, field systems and types of husbandry as well as social structures and inheritance patterns than there were in contemporary England or France.[10] Contrast between the Gaelic Highlands and the anglicised Lowlands were important at a macro-scale, as were

[7] K. D. M. Snell, *Annals of the Labouring Poor: Social Change and Agrarian England 1600–1900* (Cambridge, Cambridge University Press, 1985), especially Chs. 1 and 4.

[8] G. L. Gullickson, 'Agriculture and cottage industry: redefining the causes of proto-industrialization', *Journal of Economic History*, 43, 4 (1983), pp. 831–50.

[9] J. Thirsk (ed.), *Agrarian History of England and Wales*, vol. 4: *1500–1640* (Cambridge, Cambridge University Press, 1967), pp. 1–112; idem, J. Thirsk (ed.), *Agrarian History of England and Wales*, vol. 5, part 1: *1640–1750 Regional Farming Systems* (Cambridge, Cambridge University Press, 1985).

[10] I. D. Whyte, *Agriculture and Society in Seventeenth-Century Scotland* (Edinburgh, John Donald, 1979), pp. 19–22.

differences between neighbouring estates at a local level. Marked regional variations at an intermediate scale are harder to identify.

Within Lowland Scotland there was nothing comparable to the contrast between champion and wood-pasture which occurred in lowland England.[11] However, much of the eastern Lowlands from the Moray Firth to the Berwickshire Merse, and some parts of the western Lowlands such as the lower Clyde Valley and central Ayrshire, were oriented towards cereal production. Many of these areas were substantial exporters of grain in the later seventeenth century. Other parts of the Lowlands, even northern areas like Caithness and Orkney, also produced enough grain to be periodic exporters. On the other hand the Southern Uplands were pastorally oriented with an emphasis on sheep rearing in the eastern Borders and cattle raising in the south-west. Even in the Southern Uplands arable farming was important in the broader dales and all livestock farms except the most high-lying produced some grain for subsistence purposes until well into the eighteenth century. The Highlands too had an economy based on pastoral farming with a subsistence arable element.[12]

Within this broad framework where did rural industry occur? On the basis of the traditional proto-industrialisation model one would look to the Southern Uplands and the Highlands for concentrations of industrial activity analagous to the Pennines or Alpine areas. Unfortunately, whilst the physical environment of these areas might have favoured such developments, the social and cultural milieu did not. The Borders had a sheep-rearing tradition whose origins lay in medieval monastic farming.[13] However, while a certain amount of woollen cloth was exported from the region, the limited scale of activity in the seventeenth and early eighteenth centuries does not indicate large-scale production for distant markets.[14] It was only later in the eighteenth century, with a reorganisation of farm structures linked to the development of more commercial livestock farming, that labour was released to allow the development of commercial woollen production.[15] The Highlands were even less attractive for industrial

[11] J. Thirsk, 'Industries in the countryside', in F. J. Fisher (ed.), *Essays in the Economic and Social History of Tudor and Stuart England* (Cambridge, Cambridge University Press, 1961), pp. 70–88.

[12] The basis of this regional division is discussed in Whyte, *Agriculture*, pp. 19–22. The regional diversity of agriculture in early modern Scotland is also considered in R. A. Dodgshon, *Land and Society in Early Scotland* (Oxford, Clarendon Press, 1981), pp. 157–73.

[13] T. B. Franklin, *A History of Scottish Farming* (London, Nelson, 1952); J. A. Symon, *Scottish Farming, Past and Present* (Edinburgh, Oliver and Boyd, 1959).

[14] Smout, *Scottish Trade*, pp. 232–6.

[15] R. A. Dodgshon, 'Agricultural change and its social consequences in the Southern Uplands of Scotland', in T. M. Devine and D. Dickson (eds.), *Ireland and Scotland 1600–1850: Parallels and Contrast in Economic and Social Development* (Edinburgh, John Donald, 1983), pp. 55–6.

development, being isolated culturally and linguistically from the rest of Scotland.[16] Much of the area was remote from urban centres and, even after the pacification following the 1745 rebellion, remained unattractive to merchant capital. As will be discussed below, parts of the southern and eastern Highlands did become linked with Lowland textile production through the commercial spinning of linen yarn, but the remaining textile processes, particularly weaving, failed to gain a foothold there.

Map 9.1 shows the distribution of concentrations of textile production in Scotland during the late seventeenth and early eighteenth centuries. Woollen and linen cloth were significant exports in the sixteenth century but little is known of the distribution or scale of production outside the burghs at this time.[17] By the start of the eighteenth century, although woollens and linen were being produced throughout Scotland, commercial production was markedly concentrated. Evidence for the stamping of linen after 1727 shows that the industry was located principally in five counties: Forfarshire, Lowland Perthshire and Fife in the east, Lanarkshire and Renfrewshire in the west.[18] The map emphasises the importance of the larger burghs as centres for financing, organising and marketing rural textiles. The counties which specialised in linen production contained, or were adjacent to, the five largest towns as well as many second-rank burghs.

The woollen industry was less buoyant than linen manufacture in the later seventeenth century and suffered from English competition after the Union.[19] There were concentrations of activity in Aberdeenshire, including the knitting of hosiery as well as the weaving of coarse plaiding, and in the Borders. Elsewhere, as with linen manufacture, production was closely tied to the towns and their immediate hinterlands.

This concentration partly reflects the strength of the monopolies of the major Scottish burghs even in the seventeenth century. In contrast to England, where the medieval structure of monopolies and restrictive guild practices was rapidly disappearing, Scotland's larger medieval towns retained considerable control over the country's trade and manufacturing. The ancient urban foundations, known as royal burghs, held their charters direct from the crown. They were mainly medieval foundations and included all the larger towns. Their collective interests were united and

---

[16] A. Youngson, *After the Forty Five* (Edinburgh, Edinburgh University Press, 1973); M. Gray, *The Highland Economy 1750–1850* (Edinburgh, Oliver and Boyd, 1957).

[17] S. G. E. Lythe, *The Economy of Scotland in its European Setting 1550–1625* (Edinburgh, Oliver and Boyd, 1960), pp. 38–40.

[18] A. J. Durie, *The Scottish Linen Industry in the Eighteenth Century* (Edinburgh, John Donald, 1979), p. 24.

[19] Smout, *Scottish Trade*, pp. 253–6; Campbell, *Rise and Fall*, pp. 6–20.

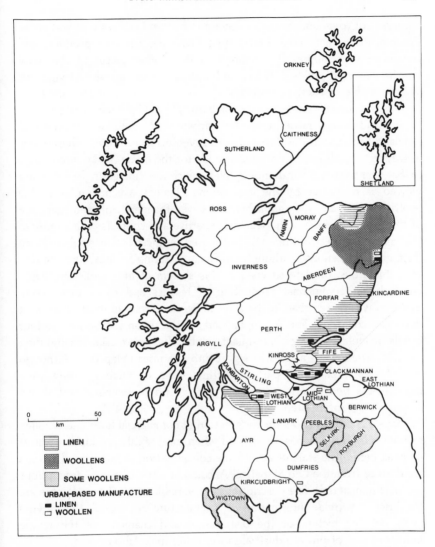

Map 9.1   The distribution of large-scale rural textile industries in Scotland in the late seventeenth and early eighteenth centuries

promoted by the Convention of Royal Burghs, an organisation which had considerable influence with the central government until after the Restoration. The royal burghs contributed substantially to crown revenues through taxation and in turn were allowed to retain their extensive privileges. These included a monopoly on foreign trade within defined hinterlands or 'liberties' which covered the entire country. In theory only burgesses of royal burghs were allowed to buy and sell within these areas. Trading, other than direct barter type exchanges between producer and consumer, was supposedly confined to the market places of the royal burghs. The craft guilds of the royal burghs were still active and vigorous and were able to exert considerable control over rural manufacturing.[20]

A new type of centre, burghs of barony, holding their charters from larger landowners rather than the crown, had multiplied throughout Lowland Scotland in the sixteenth and seventeenth centuries. These were, however, only allowed to produce goods for the home market until 1672. In that year the royal burgh monopolies, which were increasingly becoming viewed as restrictive by the landowning element which dominated the Scottish Parliament, were abolished. However, the merchants and craftsmen of the royal burghs had the wealth, expertise and contacts which ensured that manufacturing continued to be focused on these towns until well into the eighteenth century. Although rural manufacturing for local consumption was ubiquitous, the late survival of this system of monopolies probably ensured that commercial production of textiles and many other commodities was more urban in character in Scotland than in most other west European countries. This is emphasised by the urban location of various textile 'manufactories' for high-quality cloth which were established during the late seventeenth and early eighteenth centuries (Map 9.1). Although landed capital played a part in setting some of them up they were nevertheless tied to urban locations where entrepreneurship and skilled labour were concentrated.

Maps 9.2 and 9.3 show the distribution of commercial linen and woollen manufacture in the 1790s, the period when rural textile production was at its peak before the start of large-scale concentration in factories. The data are derived from the Old Statistical Account, a series of parish descriptions by local ministers.[21] The descriptions are variable in quality and some are too brief to provide information on manufacture but overall they give a fairly detailed picture of the distribution and character of the textile industries and of proto-industrialisation using male labour.

Map 9.2 shows that the weaving of linen was still concentrated in the same areas as a century earlier. The parishes shown are those for which linen is recorded as being produced in some quantity for distant markets. A notable feature is the spread of the spinning of linen yarn to remote districts like Highland Perthshire, the Moray Firth, Ross and even Orkney. The small-scale subsistence character of agriculture in many of these Highland and northern areas may have left women freer to take up

[20] T. C. Smout, A History of the Scottish People, 1560–1830, (London, Collins, 1972), pp. 146–65.
[21] Sir John Sinclair, Statistical Account of Scotland (21 vols. Edinburgh, Creech, 1791).

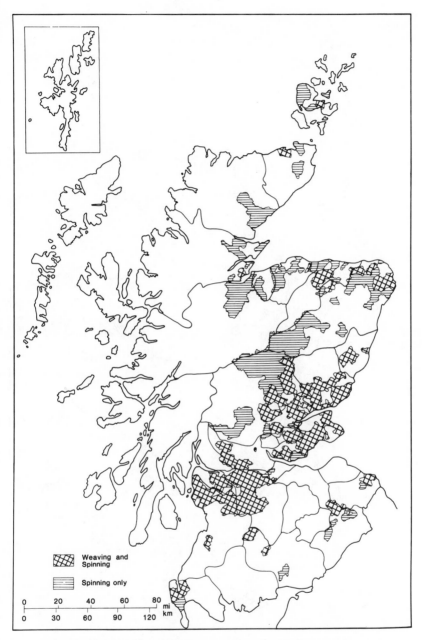

Map 9.2   Distribution of commercial linen production in the 1790s
Source: Based on information derived from Sinclair, *Statistical Account*

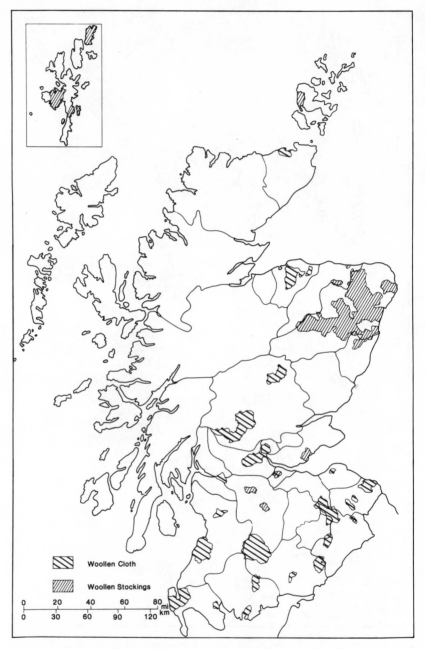

Map 9.3   Distribution of commercial woollen manufacture in the 1790s
Source: Based on information derived from Sinclair, *Statistical Account*

commercial yarn spinning once urban manufacturers had started to penetrate the region. In these parishes there was no significant commercial weaving of linen but a high proportion of the women produced yarn for sale. Sometimes they grew their own flax but mostly they obtained their raw materials from urban manufacturers, often at a considerable distance, or from their local agents. The manufacture of woollen cloth was much less important than linen by the end of the eighteenth century and had a scattered distribution with concentrations in south Ayrshire, the eastern Borders between Galashiels and Hawick, and at the foot of the Ochils. Allied to this was the distribution of stocking knitting. In southern Scotland this was mainly urban based but in the north there were major concentrations in two rural areas. Aberdeenshire and Orkney and Shetland.

If we focus on linen, Scotland's premier manufacture for much of the eighteenth century, its production was mainly located in arable rather than pastoral areas. In Perthshire commercial production did not begin to penetrate the upland districts until the middle of the century and even this was confined to spinning.[22] Here we have an apparent paradox. In the proto-industrialisation model such areas appear unsuitable for the development of rural industry. Moreover, while the settlement pattern throughout Scotland was predominantly dispersed, arable farming was nevertheless tied to an open-field system, infield–outfield, which required co-operation between neighbours at a township level.[23] Such communal controls, supposedly unfavourable to the development of large-scale rural industry, were more significant in the arable Lowlands than in upland pastoral districts. The manorial courts which regulated activities within English open-field systems had their counterparts in Scottish baron courts.[24] In Scotland landowners had a high degree of control over the rural population compared with England, while the kirk sessions controlled population mobility through the issue of testimonials.[25] Such controls are likely to have been more effective in Lowland areas where estates and parishes were smaller and the rural population was more closely supervised by landlords, estate administrators and kirk session elders.

One possible reason why hill areas like the Southern Uplands did not have large concentrations of industrial activity like parts of the Pennines was the way in which much upland rough pasture was held. In England hill pastures were grazed in common by surrounding communities but the land was generally in single ownership. This encouraged the small-scale intake

[22] Durie, *Scottish Linen Industry*, pp. 35–9.
[23] Dodgshon, *Land and Society*, pp. 141–73.
[24] Whyte, *Agriculture*, pp. 41–51.
[25] R. A. Houston, 'Geographical mobility in Scotland 1652–1811: the evidence of testimonials', *Journal of Historical Geography*, 11, (1985), pp. 379–94.

of land by squatters who could eventually be brought before the manorial court and charged rents for their new tenements.[26] In Scotland, however, much hill pasture was held as commonty. Commonties were owned jointly by two or more proprietors. Unauthorised squatting on such land was an infringement of the shared property rights of the various landowners. These rights could remain effective only if the land was preserved as stinted pasture. Taking in a portion of commonty and converting it to arable was generally opposed in the interests of all the landowners concerned. Despite their potential for colonisation commonties were effectively tied up as rough pasture and could not be converted to arable without a division by general agreement.[27] Such agreements were made only occasionally during the seventeenth century.[28] In 1695 the Scottish Parliament passed an act simplifying divisions where unanimous agreement could not be reached, but it was only later in the eighteenth century, when the economic advantages were more manifest, that many divisions were undertaken.

The bringing into cultivation of new land by establishing smallholdings at the fringes of the existing improved area was more characteristic of areas like Aberdeenshire in the period of improvement from the later eighteenth century.[29] But where this was done it was generally to create a reservoir of part-time labour for the large farms rather than to encourage rural industry. In addition, population pressure, encouraging the small-scale intake of marginal land, was lacking in Scotland in the century before the 1750s. Periodic subsistence crises in the Lowlands until the late 1690s and in the Highlands into the eighteenth century, combined with high levels of emigration, prevented a build-up of population which might have encouraged such land to be taken into cultivation.[30]

One part of Scotland had the classic preconditions for the development of large-scale textile production during the later eighteenth century: the northern and western Highlands. Here a rapid build-up of population, partly a result of lower age of first marriage than in the rest of Scotland,[31] progressive sub-division of already smallholdings, and the adoption of the potato occurred under conditions of bare subsistence.[32] The small sizes of the holdings – whether on the old joint farms or in the new crofting townships – forced people to take up activities outside agriculture to make

[26] G. H. Tupling, *The Economic History of Rossendale* (Manchester, Chetham Society, 1927).
[27] I. H. Adams, 'Division of commonty in Scotland', unpublished Ph.D. thesis (University of Edinburgh, 1967).
[28] Whyte, *Agriculture*, pp. 213–14.
[29] M. Gray, 'North East agriculture and the labour force 1750–1875', in A. A. MacLaren (ed.), *Social Class in Scotland* (Edinburgh, John Donald, 1976), pp. 86–110.
[30] M. Flinn (ed.), *Scottish Population History* (Cambridge, Cambridge University Press, 1977).
[31] Ibid., p. 274.   [32] Ibid., pp. 31–7.

even a precarious living. Yet large-scale textile manufacture did not develop. The options which were tried included kelp burning, fishing and seasonal migration to the Lowlands, but few Highland landowners seem to have seriously considered textiles. Attempts to establish centres for weaving at places like Lochbroom, Lochcarron and Glenmoriston were unsuccessful.[33] Only at the end of the nineteenth century did weaving of Harris tweed develop, mainly in the Outer Hebrides, as a cottage industry in combination with crofting agriculture. The north-west Highlands and Islands have many parallels with Ireland, where large-scale linen manufacture was established successfully under not dissimilar circumstances. In the Highlands, however, textiles failed to provide a solution to the area's problems partly because of lack of skill among the workforce and the sheer distance from urban markets and urban capital. Even in the southern and eastern Highlands, where attempts to develop textile industries were made, success was limited. Here, too, lack of skill in weaving was blamed. At a time when quality control was becoming increasingly important, even for coarser linen, it seems to have been impossible to provide adequate instruction and supervision to weavers in Highland areas. In addition, the remoteness of the north-west Highlands from urban markets, and its far-flung, fragmented geography would have been major disincentives to the development of proto-industrialisation.[34] This restricted weaving to Lowland areas within easy reach of the towns.

It is clear then that in the seventeenth and eighteenth centuries rural textile manufacture in Scotland did not correspond closely to the distribution of upland, or even lowland, pastoral areas. Some of the reasons for this have already been mentioned in passing but the phenomenon is more fully explained if we examine the structure of Scottish rural society. As an introduction to this theme it is useful to consider to what extent Scotland's demographic experience at this period fits the model.

POPULATION PATTERNS AND RURAL INDUSTRY

Proto-industrialisation stresses the demographic impact of the development of large-scale rural industry.[35] As a result of the rise of industry as an alternative source of employment to agriculture the inhabitants of areas of rural manufacture became increasingly divorced from agriculture and the

[33] Durie, *Scottish Linen Industry*, pp. 89–90.
[34] F. F. Mendels, 'Seasons and regions in agriculture and industry during the process of industrialisation', in S. Pollard (ed.), *Region und industrialisierung* (Göttingen, Vandenhoek und Ruprecht, 1980), p. 183.
[35] The demographic aspects of proto-industrialisation are discussed in L. A. Clarkson, *Proto-Industrialization: The First Phase of Industrialization?* (London, Macmillan, 1985), pp. 39–50.

controls which the limitations of environmental resources and agricultural technology placed on population levels. It became unnecessary to postpone marriage and the setting up of an independent household until land or capital had been inherited or built up, as income from industrial work allowed financial independence at an earlier age. This, it is argued, encouraged a fall in the age of first marriage and larger average completed family sizes producing substantial increases in population compared with areas which concentrated on agriculture. In-migration to areas where it was possible to clear land from the waste and combine small-scale agriculture with domestic industry has sometimes been accorded a limited role by exponents of proto-industrialisation[36] although some earlier studies have considered that in-migration was a significant factor in causing population growth in such areas.[37]

How well do regional demographic trends in Scotland during the seventeenth and eighteenth centuries fit this model? Some of the ministers who contributed to the Old Statistical Account suggested that the growth of the textile industries, especially linen manufacture, did have demographic and social effects similar to the ones postulated in the model. The high wages which could be obtained from weaving and spinning allowed young people to become independent and marry earlier than in purely agricultural communities, largely because they were able to by-pass the period of farm or domestic service which a high proportion of young people in agricultural areas underwent. The income from spinning, knitting and especially the embroidering of muslins discouraged young girls from going into service, allowing them either to remain at home and contribute to the family's income or to set up house on their own. Lower age at first marriage was specifically linked with larger families and an increase of population in some parishes.[38] For instance, the minister of the parish of Kettle in Fife wrote that 'the looms find employment for women and children; and hence, a family being advantageous, the men marry early; and hence one of the principal causes of the increased population'.[39] It should be stressed that until more detailed local studies of communities are undertaken there are no clear indications of how age at first marriage and completed family size varied between rural communities with or without industry. Moreover, the evidence for high levels of population mobility in Scotland in the late eighteenth century[40] suggests that in-migration is likely to have been as

[36] Kriedte, Medick and Schlumbohm, *Industrialisation before Industrialisation*, make very little reference to migration as a factor influencing population growth in proto-industrial areas.

[37] Thirsk, 'Industries in the countryside', pp. 76–7.

[38] Sinclair, *Statistical Account*, vol. 1, p. 378.

[39] Ibid., vol. 1, p. 378, vol. 2, p. 200, vol. 4, p. 474, vol. 6, p. 515, vol. 9, p. 476.

[40] Ibid., *passim*.

important as increased fertility in causing population growth in the linen manufacturing areas; but this still remains to be demonstrated.

Some indications of the extent to which rural textile manufacture encouraged population growth can be gained by comparing population figures from the Old Statistical Account of the 1790s with those from a census conducted by parish clergy in 1755.[41] In Perthshire, Forfarshire and Kincardineshire only 64 per cent of linen-weaving parishes increased their populations between 1755 and the 1790s. The average rate of growth over the period was 5 per cent. In Fife too 64 per cent of textile manufacturing parishes had increased their population at an average rate of 8 per cent. In Ayrshire, Lanarkshire and Renfrewshire the figures were 72 per cent and 27 per cent respectively. The experience of parishes which had only commercial spinning or knitting without any significant weaving was very different. Of the purely spinning parishes north of the Tay 65 per cent were in decline (at an average rate of 5 per cent). Of the stocking-knitting parishes of Aberdeenshire, 81 per cent had experienced a fall in population at an average rate of 8 per cent.

It is impossible, however, with the current state of knowledge to isolate the impact of textile manufacture on population from a variety of other influences which were encouraging growth in parts of the rural Lowlands. The population of Scotland increased by 23 per cent between 1755 and the 1790s but large areas of the Southern Uplands lost population absolutely as did many Lowland parishes in eastern and north-eastern Scotland. The other main area of absolute decline was the southern and eastern Highlands. The parishes with the highest growth rates were mainly urban and suburban, the populations sometimes doubling or trebling, but some rural parishes in the main textile-producing areas experienced increases in population well above the national average. On the other hand, some weaving parishes were clearly losing population relatively and even absolutely to nearby towns, while net growth also occurred in some rural areas without the benefit of large-scale textile manufacture: the Lowland parishes of Dumfries-shire and Galloway for example. At a local level activities such as the factory spinning of cotton, bleachfields, coal mining and fishing could encourage population growth independent of textile weaving. Again, detailed local studies are required to explain the high degree of variation in patterns of population change at this time.

Did proto-industrialisation in Scotland bring poverty and misery to the manufacturing population? All the evidence indicates that by the later eighteenth century the demand for textiles was sufficiently great to give a

---

[41] The census is published in G. Kyd (ed.), *Scottish Population Statistics* (Edinburgh, Scottish History Society, 1952). Its reliability is discussed in Flinn, *Scottish Population History*, pp. 58–64.

substantial proportion of weavers a higher level of income than other artisans or even many middling farmers.[42] Murray has, however, cautioned against the uncritical acceptance of a late eighteenth-century 'golden age' before the days of power-loom weaving.[43] There were marked differences in income depending on the type and quality of the cloth woven, while periodic trading slumps could cause much hardship.[44] Female textile workers in otherwise agricultural areas, whether spinners or knitters, seem to have been particularly vulnerable in the later eighteenth century. As their incomes became more vital to the economies of their families they were open to exploitation as well as to the effects of changes in the demand for their products. Following the bad harvest of 1782 the Aberdeenshire stocking knitters were forced to redouble their efforts in order to maintain family incomes as a slump in demand for stockings resulted in a fall in prices.[45] Competition from frame knitting and from overseas producers was also helping to drive down prices, forcing many of them to change to spinning linen yarn.[46] During the seventeenth century, as well as trade slumps caused by foreign wars interfering with overseas markets, subsistence crises also cut home demand for industrial products. The effects of such fluctuations on rural industrial workers have yet to be studied.

The Old Statistical Account paints a generally rosy picture of the lifestyles of weavers in the late eighteenth century but some ministers also stressed the negative side: the generally poorer health of men and women who worked mainly indoors in conditions which were sometimes damp, poorly ventilated and badly lit.[47] We must remember the authors' prejudices though. The picture drawn by some of the ministers of the virtues of agricultural life is too arcadian to ring true while their descriptions of the ill-health, vice and moral degradation which, for them, was an inevitable accompaniment of high wages in the textile industries is also likely to be overdrawn.

In some respects, then, Scotland's demographic patterns fit the proto-industrialisation model. In others they do not. Are there any aspects of Scotland's rural social and economic structures which might help to explain the apparent anomalies as well as highlighting the underlying causes of the very specific geographical distribution of textile manufacture described earlier in this chapter?

[42] Durie, *Scottish Linen Industry*, pp. 80, 100.

[43] N. Murray, *The Scottish Handloom Weavers 1790–1850* (Edinburgh, John Donald, 1978), p. 41.

[44] Ibid.

[45] Sinclair, *Statistical Account*, vol. 7, p. 270.

[46] Ibid., vol. 2, p. 539, vol. 9, p. 469, vol. 13, p. 85.

[47] Ibid., vol. 5, p. 20, vol. 7, p. 113, vol. 9, p. 388, vol. 14, p. 460, vol. 16, p. 96.

RURAL INDUSTRY AND RURAL SOCIAL STRUCTURE

In the traditional proto-industrialisation model the stereotype rural industrial worker is a peasant farmer living under marginal conditions in an upland pastoral area, working a holding too small to provide adequate support for himself and his family. He engaged in rural industry using his own labour and that of his family to supplement his household's income. How true was this for Scotland? To answer this question we need to know more about how textile production fitted into the agricultural economy of particular regions and how landholding and gender division of labour on the land influenced the possibilities of rural manufacturing, especially with the increasing commercialisation of agriculture and the expansion of textile production during the course of the eighteenth century.

If we start by considering the late seventeenth and early eighteenth centuries, the indications are that the spinning of woollen and linen yarn was done throughout the country by a high proportion of adult and young women in the tenant class and below. In the 1780s it was estimated that some 80 per cent of the female population of Scotland did some spinning.[48] This proportion had probably not changed materially from earlier decades. Spinning would have been done by the wives of tenant farmers, by their daughters and living-in female farm servants, by the wives of cottars, as well as by widows and unmarried women. Spinning for non-local consumption was more concentrated in its distribution, however, being centred in the main weaving areas (Map 9.1). Weaving had a more limited base both in the numbers employed and the social groups from which weavers were drawn. Within the rural Lowlands it is probable that tenant farmers with larger holdings were employed more or less full time in agriculture. Most of the weavers were cottars, men who sub-let small shares of arable land with attached grazing rights from the tenant farmers and in return provided them with labour to help cultivate their holdings. The blanket term 'cottar' hides many gradations and regional distinctions. In some districts, such as the Lothians, married cottars were employed as ploughmen by the tenants, receiving land, grazing and even a small fee in return.[49] Details of the employment of such men sometimes specify that the cottar's wife was to spin as part of the contract but not that the man was to weave. These ploughmen were probably too fully occupied in agriculture to have had much time to spare for weaving. Other cottars supplied labour on a less regular basis, in some cases principally during the main peaks of the agricultural year. Such men had more scope for engaging

[48] Durie, *Scottish Linen Industry*, p. 159.
[49] Smout, *History*, pp. 135–6.

in weaving. This is sometimes suggested in the poll tax records of the 1690s by the dual designation 'cottar and weaver'.[50]

Proto-industrialisation emphasises the tendency for holdings to be small in potential rural industrial regions and for them to be further reduced once large-scale industry had become established through partible inheritance. Most of the land in Scotland was held by substantial landowners. Owner-occupiers, peasant proprietors, formed a limited group in most areas. These 'bonnet lairds' were more common in parts of the western Lowlands but even there they did not dominate rural society and their numbers diminished from the seventeenth century to the eighteenth as they were engrossed by the larger estates.[51] Partible inheritance of land by small owner-occupiers can be eliminated as a significant influence behind the rise of rural industry in Scotland. It is more appropriate to consider temporal and geographical variations in the sizes of holdings occupied by tenants, the main group which worked the land. A rise in the rural population might, in theory, have led to the sub-division of tenanted holdings beyond subsistence level, encouraging people to turn to textile production. There is, however, no evidence for this during the seventeenth and early eighteenth centuries. As a result of the epidemics of the 1640s, famine in the 1690s and substantial emigration throughout the seventeenth century, population levels at the time of Webster's census in 1755 were probably not much above those of the mid-seventeenth century.[52] After 1600 the trend was indeed towards the gradual amalgamation of holdings in many areas rather than their sub-division, partly due to landlord policy and possibly also to modest capital accumulation by some sections of the tenantry.[53]

As regards geographical variations in holding sizes, Dogshon has shown that farms and holdings were comparatively small in the north-east where many tenants probably worked less than 20–30 acres of land. Holding sizes tended to increase southwards through Forfarshire, Fife and the Lothians to Berwickshire. South of the Forth it was not uncommon for some tenants to have holdings of 300 acres or more. Holdings were also relatively small in the western Lowlands, probably comparable in size with the north-east.[54]

---

[50] The poll lists for Aberdeenshire and Renfrewshire have been published: J. Stuart (ed.), *List of Pollable Persons within the Shire of Aberdeen, 1696* (2 vols., Aberdeen, Spalding Club, 1844); D. Semple (ed.), *Renfrewshire Poll Tax Returns* (Paisley, 1864).

[51] L. Timperley, 'The pattern of landholding in eighteenth-century Scotland', in M. L. Parry and T. R. Slater (eds.), *The Making of the Scottish Countryside* (London, Croom Helm, 1980), pp. 137–54.

[52] Flinn, *Scottish Population History*, pp. 181–4.

[53] Whyte, *Agriculture*, pp. 141–52; I. D. Whyte and K. A. Whyte, 'Debt and credit, prosperity and poverty in a seventeenth-century Scottish rural community', in R. Mitchison and P. Roebuck (eds.), *Economy and Society in Scotland and Ireland, 1500–1939* (Edinburgh, John Donald, 1988).

[54] Dodgshon, *Land and Society*, pp. 214–17.

While Aberdeenshire and Renfrewshire may have had a preponderance of smaller holdings, Forfarshire and Fife, which were also important centres of rural textile manufacture, did not. Many tenants were probably working holdings which were too small to give them anything other than a bare subsistence due to high levels of rent and low crop yields. This did not necessarily mean that they had enough free time to engage in industrial activity on a commercial scale to supplement their incomes though. On many estates a good deal of the tenants' free time was taken up performing labour and carriage services for the proprietor.[55]

The lack of correspondence between smallholdings and concentrations of rural industry introduces the possibility that the relationship between the two may have been the reverse of the one usually postulated. The classic argument is that rural industry usually developed where holdings were small and liable to further sub-division, and that they were located away from areas of large-scale grain production. In Scotland rural textile production was concentrated in areas which were oriented towards cereal production and in which holdings were not particularly small. The apparent paradox is resolved if one considers Scottish farm structures as a two-tier system. The cottars rather than the tenants were the group which had access to land but without enough to make a full living from agriculture. Proto-industrialisation usually envisages rural industrial workers as acquiring smallholdings through sub-division due to partible inheritance, or squatting on the waste. Neither of these factors was important in Scotland. The group which occupied small plots of arable land was not located in remote upland areas but was fully integrated into the Lowland farming economy. The parallels between cottars in Lowland Scotland and the land-poor smallholders and labourers of the eighteenth-century Pays de Caux studied by Gullickson are striking.[56] Upland areas lacked rural industry not only because of restrictions on squatter settlement. Farms in some upland areas like west Aberdeenshire were multiple-tenant ones with few cottars. In other districts, as in the eastern Borders, they were large single-tenant sheep runs where the continuation of a subsistence arable element alongside commercial livestock rearing absorbed much of the labour which might otherwise have been directed into textile production.

In lowland arable areas the demand for labour on the land was characterised by seasonal peaks and periods of underemployment. Where holdings were relatively large a good deal of the farm work was done by people who were not members of the tenants' families. Some of this labour was provided by living-in farm servants but such people had to be

[55] Whyte, *Agriculture*, pp. 35–6.
[56] Gullickson, 'Agriculture and cottage industry'.

maintained throughout the year by the tenant. They would not have been engaged unless they could have been kept in full-time employment. Cottars provided the extra labour for ploughing, sowing, harrowing, carting, peat cutting and harvesting. In the slack periods between, as well as working their own holdings, they could supplement their incomes by engaging in weaving or other craft activities. This may explain how weaving came to be centred in areas like Forfarshire and Fife which were also major grain producers. Studies of rural industry in early modern Eruope have produced other examples of areas which concentrated on arable farming yet had textile industries geared to distant markets: Armagh for instance.[57] In Scotland it was evidently the related patterns of agriculture and rural social structure which produced this link.

A gradual trend towards the reduction of tenant numbers per farm has been identified in many areas during the later seventeenth and early eighteenth centuries.[58] This was achieved by gradually consolidating the fractions of multiple-holding farms until they were converted to single tenancy. This increased holding sizes, decreased tenant numbers and raised the demand for non-tenant labour as society became more polarised. However, as long as a system of cottar labour remained, streamlining farm structures in this way tended to increase the smallholding element in the rural population which had to depend in part on rural industry. Agriculture and rural textile production in Lowland areas would only have become separated when the cottar system was replaced by one where landless labourers were employed full time for money wages instead of receiving smallholdings, with migrant labour brought in from outside to cope with seasonal peaks of demand such as the harvest. The cottar system only began to decline in this way during the later eighteenth century.

How did textile manufacture in Scotland integrate with agriculture? There was little problem with spinning which was done almost entirely by women and could be fitted into the slack periods of virtually any household or farm economy. Although women provided an important part of the rural labour force during harvest time they did not normally work in the fields at other seasons until the spread of root crops towards the end of the eighteenth century increased the demand for weeding. As a result, to a greater degree than men, women were liable to seasonal underemployment in the traditional Lowland farming system and thus had the time, and the incentive through lack of alternative employments, to try to increase their families' incomes by spinning, as was the case in the similar economy of the

[57] Clarkson, *Proto-Industrialization*, pp. 35–6.
[58] Whyte, *Agriculture*, pp. 35–6.

Pays de Caux.[59] A notable feature of the second half of the eighteenth century is the spread of commercial spinning outside the main weaving areas into adjacent Lowland agricultural parishes and to more distant Highland and northern districts (Map 9.2). This spread is likely to have been in part a result of demand for yarn outstripping the capacity of spinners in the main weaving areas. Moreover, in such areas there were competing sources of employment for women; the embroidering of muslins was enticing many women away from the spinning wheel in the 1790s as it paid better.[60] So did work in the bleachfields and the new cotton mills. Manufacturers were forced to look further afield for their yarn. In areas like Highland Perthshire and Aberdeenshire spinning quickly became a mainstay of the economy, providing much of the cash needed to pay the rent.[61] Following the bad harvest of 1782 yarn spinning kept many poor families in such areas alive.

Stocking weaving in Aberdeenshire was another example of a rural industry centred in a Lowland region with a predominantly female labour force. Aberdeenshire had been a major producer of woollen plaiding as well as knitted stockings in the later seventeenth century but by the end of the eighteenth century the area made little cloth for commercial sale. Over much of the county, however, a high proportion of the women, as well as many boys and old men, knitted stockings. In the early eighteenth century the industry had been based on local wool supplies. Agricultural changes with the adoption of new rotations greatly reduced the sizes of the flocks in Lowland parishes.[62] This allowed Aberdeen merchants to extend their influence over the industry by turning to imported English wool and controlling its supply. As with the spinning of linen yarn, stocking knitting had become crucial as a source of cash to pay the rents of poorer smallholders. The stockings were exported to London and Holland but the area faced competition from knitters in Jersey, Guernsey and Germany which, along with the spread of frame knitting, was driving prices and wages down.[63] Although spinning linen yarn was potentially more profitable and was, in some parishes, taking over from stocking knitting, there was considerable resistance to the changeover. The minister of the parish of Keith-Hall recorded that a woman could knit 'and do some little things about her house at the same time. Or she can work at her stocking while feeding her cows.'[64] Knitting was considered less physically

---

[59] Gullickson, 'Agriculture and cottage industry'.
[60] Sinclair, *Statistical Account*, vol. 7, p. 381, vol. 9, p. 370.
[61] Ibid., vol. 2, p. 469, vol. 16, p. 341.   [62] Ibid., vol. 2, p. 539.
[63] Ibid.   [64] Ibid., vol. 9, p. 469.

demanding, less sedentary and more healthy than spinning. In Orkney and Shetland stocking knitting was also geared to overseas markets. Shetland provides an interesting example of a domestic rural industry which survived with little change from the eighteenth to the twentieth centuries.

The literature on proto-industrialisation has relatively little to say concerning industries where the work was performed entirely by women though the importance of the gender division of labour in the local economy of areas in which commercial manufacture takes root is beginning to be appreciated.[65] Such industries could fit into a variety of economies: mixed farming in Aberdeenshire, livestock rearing in Highland Perthshire and a crofting–fishing economy in Shetland. It is interesting to speculate why these areas did not develop weaving as well. Sheer distance from the manufacturing centres and a lack of inherent skills in the population may have been the case in the Highlands and the far north. The prosperity of fishing in Shetland may have prevented the development of weaving while the adoption of improved systems of farming in Aberdeenshire may have had the same effect. These areas of purely female employment were fairly transient phenomena representing the apotheosis of the putting-out system before factory-based manufacturing began to concentrate employment. In terms of the model they are rather special cases of de-industrialisation.

Traditional domestic weaving also integrated well with agriculture. Under this sytem weavers were dependent on local families handing over their yarn for making up. Demand was often seasonal, being slack in summer when additional labour was needed in agriculture and picking up again after harvest when there was more money available and less need for labour on the land.[66] The seasonality of this demand allowed rural weavers to provide a reserve of farm labour. As the commercial side of the industry grew, rising demand not only led to an expansion of the labour force but also to a growing time commitment on the part of established weavers. Durie has suggested that in the early part of the eighteenth century it was probably difficult for weavers tied to purely local markets to obtain more than six months' work in any year[67] By the end of the century, however, a weaver working for distant markets could operate virtually full time, the steadiness of the demand from international markets reducing the seasonal element in his working year.[68]

Such weavers must have become increasingly distanced from their agricultural background. The demand for greater efficiency in the use of

---

[65] Gullickson, 'Agriculture and cottage industry'.
[66] Sinclair, *Statistical Account*, vol. 10, p. 244.
[67] Durie, *Scottish Linen Industry*, pp. 43–4.
[68] Ibid.

agricultural labour also encouraged a split between the full-time agricultural and industrial worker. By the end of the eighteenth century the involvement of many weavers in agriculture must have been confined to harvest work. Changes in farm organisation, particularly in the later eighteenth century, encouraged the removal of cottars whose shares of land reduced the size and efficiency of farms. They were replaced by wage-earning landless labourers supplemented in some areas such as the north-east by crofters settled on newly reclaimed land who provided occasional day labour for the larger farms. Most arable areas began to make considerable use of migrant female labour to help with the harvest. As there was a shortage of such labour in the Lowlands and a high proportion of women in the southern Highlands were working at home spinning, this labour was drawn from the more distant northern and western Highlands beyond the reach of the textile industries.[69] Increasing commercialisation of agriculture squeezed the cottar-weavers off the land at precisely the time that increasing demand from the industrial sector allowed them to move into textile manufacturing full time and earn good wages.

Where did the weavers go when they were phased out as cottars? Some stayed on the land as labourers, their former holdings absorbed into the reorganised farms. Others carved out plots of land from the waste and continued to combine agriculture with industry. Many migrated to the towns where the decline of guild restrictions was making it easier for incoming weavers to set up. Some moved only a short distance to the new planned estate villages which landowners were establishing throughout Scotland. One of the objects of such villages was to absorb labour which was being released from the land by the reorganisation of agriculture.[70] Lockhart has shown that they recruited from very local hinterlands. Some of their original inhabitants were tenants or their sons who had been forced to leave the land due to farm restructuring. Others were cottar-weavers moving into textile manufacture on a more full-time basis. Weaving was an important element in many planned villages and the principal activity in some.[71] In such villages smallholdings were usually available and agriculture remained an important element.

Proto-industrialisation usually considers external demand as the main influence in encouraging specialisation in rural industry in areas of increasingly smallholdings. In Scotland, however, the development of

---

[69] Ibid. p. 158.

[70] T. M. Devine, 'Highland migration to Lowland Scotland 1760–1860', *Scottish Historical Review*, 62 (1983), pp. 137–49.

[71] D. G. Lockhart, 'Sources for studies of migration to estate villages in North East Scotland 1750–1850', *Local Historian*, 14 (1980), pp. 35–43.

commercial agriculture may have played a positive role in creating a more specialised industrial workforce by encouraging cottars to move into full time textile manufacture. At the same time independent weavers became increasingly drawn into putting-out systems controlled by urban manufacturers. There is little evidence of highly organised putting-out systems in Scotland during the seventeenth and early eighteenth centuries. The ones which are known were usually closely focused on the suburbs and immediate hinterlands of the major burghs. Most cloth was either produced for local use or by independent weavers for sale in local fairs or nearby towns. Urban clothiers would travel round these fairs buying the cloth from individual weavers. Putting-out systems developed greatly in scale and importance during the eighteenth century. Although there were still a few customary weavers producing cloth for purely local consumption, in the early nineteenth century putting-out systems had long since dominated production.[72] The details of this development require further study. By the 1790s independent weaving was more characteristic of the woollen industry. This was probably because woollen manufacture, being more concerned with the home market than linen production, remained more traditional and loosely organised to a later date.[73] Where independent weavers survived in the linen industry it was often in the more peripheral parts of the main manufacturing areas. Growth of demand for linen beyond the capacity of Scottish flax production, and an increasing reliance upon imported raw materials, probably allowed merchants to extend their hold over the producers faster than in the woollen trade where home-produced wool remained important.

CONCLUSION

In this chapter it has only been possible to outline a few aspects of a complex topic, the nature of the early phases of industrialisation in Scotland. Many aspects of Scotland's economy and society combined to produce the distinctive patterns of proto-industrial production in the seventeenth and eighteenth centuries. The strong trading monopolies which the ancient royal burghs retained until the later seventeenth century enabled them to exert powerful control over industrial production in their rural hinterlands. In some respects this promoted rural industry as Scottish burghs functioned more as trading and finishing centres than as foci of industry. On the other hand, as entrepreneurship was overwhelmingly located in the burghs this is likely to have encouraged textile production

[72] D. G. Lockhart, 'The planned villages', in Parry and Slater, *The Making*, pp. 249–70.
[73] Durie, *Scottish Linen Industry*, pp. 43–4.

to concentrate in lowland areas around the major towns rather than in more remote upland areas.[74] The growing importance of temporary migration to the Lowland harvest from the more distant parts of the Highlands during the later eighteenth century also worked against the development of commercial cottage industry in this area. One of the most important influences which determined the distribution and character of rural industrial production was the agrarian structure of Lowland Scotland. In particular, the dependence until the later eighteenth century on a class of smallholding cottars, who formed the majority of rural families in most areas, created a social group with only limited access to land and every incentive to try to diversify their activities into industrial work to increase their incomes. It is clear that the proto-industrialisation model is not completely effective in explaining the distribution and character of rural textile industries in seventeenth- and eighteenth-century Scotland. This resulted from particular combinations of cultural, social and economic structures and the nature of some of these have been considered. On the other hand, the application of the model does focus attention on a range of questions which have been neglected or side-stepped by historians of Scotland's industrial and social development. This emphasises the need for more detailed analyses of rural social structure in Scotland and the role of industry in relation to it. It is hoped that this chapter has been able to demonstrate the advantages of fitting such analyses into a more rigorous theoretical framework which facilitates comparison with rural industry in other countries and regions.

---

[74] Sinclair, *Statistical Account, passim*; M. Lynch, 'Continuity and change in urban society 1500–1800', in R. A. Houston and I. D. Whyte (eds.), *Scottish Society 1500–1800* (Cambridge, Cambridge University Press, 1989).

Chapter 10

The environment and dynamic of pre-factory industry in Northern Ireland

LESLIE A. CLARKSON

I

Irish history is apt to be obscured by a cloud of semantics so, at the outset, Northern Ireland is defined as the historic nine-county province of Ulster: Antrim, Armagh, Cavan, Donegal, Down, Fermanagh, Londonderry, Monaghan and Tyrone. This is neither geographically nor economically a homogeneous region but the outcome of an amalgam of Gaelic-Irish and Anglo-Irish lordships and subjected to substantial English and Scottish settlement from the late sixteenth century. Since 1922 six of the nine counties have formed a smaller political unit – also called, confusingly, Ulster or Northern Ireland – and as with the larger area this too lacks an economic unity.

By virtue of physical geography and climate there exist many variations in landscape and settlement patterns in Ulster. These range from extensive areas of lowland in the valleys of the Lagan, Bann and Foyle, the Lough Neagh basin, Counties Fermanagh and Cavan, and the eastern lowlands of Antrim and north Down to the mountain masses of the Sperrins and Mournes, the rocky uplands of north-west Donegal and north Antrim and the chain of drumlins stretching from south Donegal to the Ards peninsula. Rainfall and temperature made Ulster natural pasture country but local needs and, in the later eighteenth and early nineteenth centuries, the demands of distant markets, created an extensive mosaic of small tillage farms producing mainly potatoes and oats, the former for subsistence and the latter for sale.

Is there then any sort of unity that justifies treating the nine-county Ulster as a single region in the pre-factory age, a period defined for present purposes as roughly 1700–1850? Three unifying themes can be identified. The first is the growth of population, not, admittedly, unique to Ulster, which changed the land–labour ratio and made imperative the laying of an alternative economic base to agriculture. The creation of such a base, in the form of a commercialised linen industry, provides the second theme. This industry was demonstrably 'pre-factory', striking its roots in the small farms and cottages of the Ulster countryside. The development was largely an Ulster phenomenon. Thirdly, Ulster became unmeshed in the fabric of international trade. The process had commenced in the early seventeenth century as English and Scottish settlers produced cattle and cattle products for markets in Britain and beyond, but from the late seventeenth century linen yarn and cloth became the dominant items of trade. Commercial ties were stronger in 'inner Ulster' (Antrim, Down, Armagh and Londonderry) than in 'outer Ulster' (Donegal, Tyrone, Fermanagh, Cavan and Monaghan). Even so, by the end of our period Ulster was 'the most monetised of the Irish provinces'.[1]

Linen was not the only pre-factory industry in Ulster. As settlers filled the plantation towns they generated a demand for essential consumer goods and gave rise to a scatter of manufacturing craftsmen: leatherworkers, woodworkers, building craftsmen, clothing workers, butchers, bakers, maltsters, brewers, and so on. As Hunter has pointed out, 'such a range of occupations is likely to represent the common core of pursuits in most of the small inland towns'.[2] The survival of a local census from the cathedral town of Armagh in the south of the province taken in 1770, shows how this urban manufacturing pattern remained intact, even in a part of Ulster much affected by the growth of the linen industry. Over a quarter of the occupied population in the town was engaged in manufacturing, the most important crafts being leatherworking, clothing, woodworking and building. In addition, since no hard and fast line can be drawn between manufacturing and trading, a considerable proportion of the workforce involved in the dealing sector of the economy were also intimately engaged in such activities.[3]

As late as 1841 vestiges of this pre-industrial pattern survived throughout Ulster. In that year the occupied population totalled 1·1 million, of whom 478,000 worked in agriculture and 496,000 in manufacturing. Of the latter, 381,000 were employed in the now mechanising textile industry, but there were 133,000 workers (12 per cent) in manufacturing occupations outside textiles.[4]

The history of the non-textile activities in the later nineteenth century is instructive. Industries such as shipbuilding and engineering expanded in

[1] Liam Kennedy, 'The rural economy, 1820–1914', in Liam Kennedy and Philip Ollerenshaw (eds.), *An Economic History of Ulster, 1820–1940* (Manchester, Manchester University Press, 1985), p. 34.

[2] R. J. Hunter, 'Ulster plantation towns, 1609–1641', in David Harkness and Mary O'Dowd, *The Town in Ireland* (Belfast, Appletree Press, 1981), p. 71.

[3] L. A. Clarkson, 'An anatomy of an Irish town: the economy of Armagh', *Irish Economic and Social History*, 5 (1978), pp. 34, 44–5.

[4] *Census of Ireland for the Year 1841*, British Parliamentary Papers, 1843, XXIV, p. 364.

the Belfast region, evolving not from traditional handicrafts but as creations of a new generation of entrepreneurs whose arrival in Belfast was largely fortuitous; that is to say, the earlier crafts were not the pre-factory precursors of the industrial base of late nineteenth-century Ulster. On the contrary, many of the old consumer crafts declined in the face of competition from other parts of the United Kingdom; for such occupations the experience of the late nineteenth century was de-industrialisation.[5]

The focus of this chapter is on the great success story of the eighteenth century: the linen industry accommodated in the farmhouses and cottages of rural Ulster which dominated much of the Ulster economy from the end of the seventeenth century until the emergence of factory flax spinning in the 1830s and 1840s.

II

The growth of the industry throughout Ireland is most clearly indicated by the export statistics.[6] From an annual level of between 1 and 2 million yards of cloth in the second decade of the eighteenth century, exports grew to 10–12 million yards by the early 1750s and to 25 million yards in 1771. During the 1770s and early 1780s trade was disrupted by the American wars, but there was a rapid recovery from 1784 to 1796 when exports totalled almost 47 million yards. Thereafter wartime disturbances and competition from cotton created a long period of stagnating and sometimes depressed markets (see Figure 10.1). Yarn exports followed a different path: varying between 10,000 and 15,000 cwts in the early 1730s, rising to over 30,000 cwts by the early 1770s, then fluctuating around a stable trend before falling away from the 1790s (see Figure 10.2).

Production for the home market can only be guessed at. Gill, the early historian of the industry, assumed a per capita consumption of cloth of 5·5 yards per annum. On this basis home demand was 12·1 million yards in 1725, 24·2 million yards in 1791 and 37·4 million yards in 1821.[7] Thus the proportion of total output exported increased from well under half in the 1720s to roughly two-thirds in the 1790s. Gill's estimate of home demand in 1821 is probably too high since it takes no account of the switch from

---

[5] Philip Ollerenshaw, 'Industry, 1820–1914', in Kennedy and Ollerenshaw (eds.), *Economic History*, pp. 86–96.

[6] Conrad Gill, *The Rise of the Irish Linen Industry* (Oxford, Clarendon Press, 1925), pp. 341–3.

[7] Ibid., pp. 160–1. The population figures used for these estimates are those printed in L. A. Clarkson, 'Irish population revisited, 1687–1821', in J. M. Goldstrom and L. A. Clarkson (eds.), *Irish Population, Economy and Society: Essays in Honour of the Late K. H. Connell* (Oxford, Clarendon Press, 1981), p. 26.

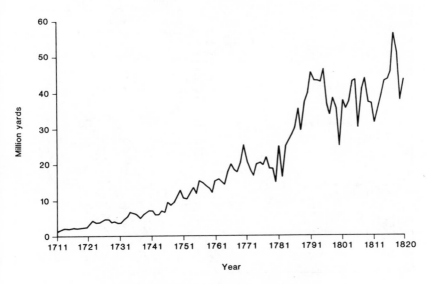

Figure 10.1 Linen cloth exports, 1711–1820
Source: Gill, *Irish Linen Industry*, pp. 341–3.

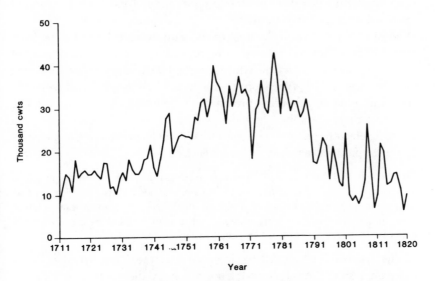

Figure 10.2 Linen yarn exports, 1711–1820
Source: Gill, *Irish Linen Industry*, pp. 341–3.

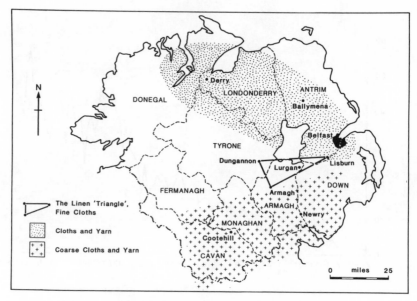

Map 10.1   Ulster and the principal linen regions, *c.* 1780s

linen to cotton. Most likely the proportion of total output exported remained at around two-thirds.

Most of the cloth and the bulk of the yarn made in Ireland came from Ulster. In the 1770s and 1780s over 80 per cent of all production originated in the province, despite the efforts of the Linen Board to promote the industry elsewhere.[8] When production was at its height, yarn spinning spread into the neighbouring provinces of Connaught and Leinster, but it was from these areas that the industry first retreated in the early decades of the nineteenth century.[9] The concentration of linen manufacture in Ulster had been pronounced even in the earliest days.

The Scotch and Irish in that province [reported Richard Lawrence in 1682] addicting themselves to spinning of linen yarn, attained to vast quantities of that commodity, which they transported to their great profit, the conveniency of which drew thither multitudes of linen weavers, that my opinion is, there is not a greater quantity of linen produced in like circuit in Europe.[10]

The heartland of the Ulster industry was the 'linen triangle' lying between Lisburn, Armagh and Dungannon in the south-centre of the

---

[8] Gill, *Irish Linen Industry*, p. 161.
[9] Brenda Collins, 'Proto-industrialisation and pre-famine emigration', *Social History*, 7, 2 (1982), pp. 127–46.
[10] Quoted in W. H. Crawford, 'The origins of the linen industry in North Armagh and the Lagan Valley', *Ulster Folklife*, 17 (1971), p. 43.

province. Writing of County Armagh in 1795 Robert Stephenson reported that 'the linen manufacture has made amazing strides...within the last 50 years'. The finest linens – lawns, cambrics, diapers, damasks – were made around Lurgan, while weavers to the west of Armagh city specialised in good-quality yard-wide linens. Along the river Callen, running west and south-west of Armagh city, thirty-six bleach yards were at work in 1771 and another fifteen elsewhere in the county.[11]

Unlike many European regions of rural industry the land of much of the linen triangle was fertile and capable of supporting commercial agriculture. Yet, as Arthur Young exclaimed in a famous passage:

> you there behold a whole province peopled by weavers; it is they who cultivate, or rather beggar the soil, as well as work the looms; agriculture is there in ruins; it is cut up by the root; extirpated; annihilated; the whole region is a disgrace to the kingdom; all the crops you see are contemptible; are nothing but filth and weeds. No other part of Ireland can exhibit the soil in such a state of poverty and desolation. A farming traveller, who goes through that country with attention, will be shocked at seeing wretchedness in the shape of a few beggarly oats on a variety of most fertile soils, which, were they in Norfolk, would soon rival the best lands in that county.[12]

These strictures are remarkably similar to those that Young directed at agriculture in the Pays de Caux in Normandy some years later, another area of generally good agricultural land where the peasantry nevertheless clung to domestic industry (in this case cotton manufacture) despite the spread of cereal farming. The desire of smallholders and labourers for a supplementary source of income, and the need to find employment for their wives and daughters that was not readily available in arable farming except at harvest time, encouraged the development of cottage industry. We do not know whether similar mechanisms were at work in south Ulster. Yarn spinning was universally regarded as a female activity but we know too little about the structure of agriculture in the linen triangle to say whether it generated insufficient employment for women. Certainly there were substantial farmers in the region who specialised in food production; it was their activities, contrasted with those of the farmer-weavers, that so enraged Arthur Young.[13]

---

[11] 'Robert Stevenson's View of County Armagh, 1795' (Public Record Office of Northern Ireland, D 562/1270).

[12] Arthur Young, *A Tour in Ireland...Made in the Years 1776, 1777, and 1778...* (2 vols., London, 1780), vol. 2, p. 119.

[13] Arthur Young's comments on the Pays de Caux are quoted by G. L. Gullickson, 'Agriculture and cottage industry: redefining the causes of proto-industrialization', *Journal of Economic History*, 43, 4 (1983), p. 838; see also pp. 840–3. For Ulster, see W. H. Crawford. 'Economy and society in south Ulster in the eighteenth century', *Clogher Record* (1975), pp. 241–8.

South of the linen triangle, extending westwards into Monaghan and Cavan and eastwards into south County Down, was an area specialising in the production of coarse cloths and also in yarn. Much of the latter was sold to weavers in other parts of Ulster, but some went to manufacturers in Drogheda town in County Meath, one of the few centres of linen production outside Ulster.[14] To the north of the linen triangle, spinning and weaving were scattered throughout the countryside of north Down, west Antrim, County Londonderry and into Donegal.[15]

The relative importance of the main regions can be gained from the statistics of sales taking place in the urban cloth markets. In 1784 roughly 46 per cent of cloth (by value) was sold in towns serving the linen triangle, including Belfast. The most important markets in order were Lurgan, Lisburn, Armagh, Dungannon and Belfast. Over 20 per cent of sales took place in south Ulster towns, with Cootehill in County Cavan and Newry on the Down–Armagh border being the most important. The remaining sales were handled by the northern towns including Ballymena in mid-Antrim and Derry City which served the west County Londonderry and east Donegal regions.[16]

The linen markets were visited weekly by weavers from the surrounding countryside with their unbleached cloths which they sold for ready cash to linen drapers or bleachers. Sales took place in inns and doorways although towards the end of the eighteenth century market halls were constructed in many towns. Most towns concentrated on trade but there was some urban linen production, notably in Lisburn where John and William Coulson established a damask 'factory' in 1764 capable of producing cloth able 'to vie with anything of the kind in Europe'.[17] The cost, size and complexity of the looms, and the high degree of skill involved, made centralised production of damask economically advantageous, offsetting the benefits of cheap labour that the countryside offered. The Coulsons also employed weavers making cheaper cloths in their own houses close to the factory. Lisburn also developed as a cotton manufacturing town in the late eighteenth century and by 1821 one third of all households were engaged in some form of unmechanised textile production.[18]

More typical, though, was Armagh, a town at the centre of the linen

[14] John Fitzgerald, 'The organisation of the Drogheda economy, 1780–1820', unpublished M.A. thesis (University College, Dublin, 1972), pp. 132, 144–5.
[15] For a general account see T. W. Freeman, *Pre-Famine Ireland: A Study in Historical Geography* (Manchester, Manchester University Press, 1957), pp. 269–307.
[16] Gill, *Irish Linen Industry*, pp. 336–8.
[17] John Dubourdieu, *A Statistical Survey of the County of Antrim* (Dublin, 1812), pp. 391–3.
[18] L. A. Clarkson and Brenda Collins, 'Proto-industrialization: Lisburn 1820–21', in Pierre Deyon and F. F. Mendels, *La Protoindustrialisation: théorie et réalité* (Budapest, 8th International Congress of Economic History, Section A2, 1982), pp. 5–8.

triangle, but the home of very few weavers.[19] Stuart, the historian of Armagh, noted in 1819 that

it is not at all necessary to the advancement of that trade, that either the spinners or the weavers should be collected into overgrown cities, or congregated into crowded and unwholesome factories. Those branches of the linen business, which are their peculiar concern, can be perfectly well managed in their respective cabins. The linen weavers of Ulster, unlike the mere manufacturers of Great Britain, are free agents, whose employments are diversified and rational. They are sometimes engaged in the labours of the loom, and sometimes in the cultivation of their farms, and in this voluntary alternation of business, they find health and recreation ... It cannot, therefore, be a matter of wonder, that in the county of Armagh, the towns are of small extent, and that every hill and vale should abound with rural habitations.[20]

Stuart's rosy opinion of rural manufacture contrasted with those of Arthur Young who believed in the 1770s that manufacturing should be confined to towns to the benefit of countryside and town alike, and Sir Charles Coote who in 1804 condemned farmer-weavers as an 'illiterate and uncivilized peasantry'.[21]

Stuart identified a second important feature of the Ulster linen industry. Not only were most weavers country dwellers, they were also 'free agents' in the sense that they were independent producers combining agriculture with linen manufacture. Their links with the outside world were through the drapers and bleachers who thronged the markets, not through large-scale capitalist employers. At the time Stuart was writing a good deal of textile manufacturing in Great Britain had indeed retreated into overgrown cities and operatives had become wage-workers in unwholesome factories. The process was occurring even in Ulster.[22] Nevertheless, the 'free agent' continued to be the typical worker in the linen industry into the nineteenth century.

III

How is the emergence of a commercialised, rural-based linen industry in Ulster to be explained? We need to consider four interlocking reasons: entrepreneurial skills, markets, technical improvements and labour costs.

The origins of the linen industry lay within Ulster itself which in the late sixteenth and early seventeenth centuries was already producing con-

---

[19] Clarkson, 'The economy of Armagh', p. 36.
[20] James Stuart, *Historical Memoirs of the City of Armagh* ... (Newry, 1819), p. 467.
[21] Young, *Tour in Ireland*, vol. 1, p. 120; Sir Charles Coote, *Statistical Survey of the County of Armagh* (Dublin, 1804), p. 263.
[22] Gill, *Irish Linen Industry*, pp. 144–7.

siderable quantities of yarn for export, as well as coarse cloth for local consumption.[23] The crucial turning point was the 'commercialization of peasant techniques'[24] – in the later seventeenth century by enterprising producers and landlords who spotted the opportunities for selling Irish linens in England at the expense of Scottish and European cloths.

Two groups were particularly responsible for the transformation of a local industry into an international undertaking. The first were immigrant weavers, many from the north of England, who arrived in Ulster following the Cromwellian resettlement in the 1650s.[25] Especially prominent were Quakers who settled in towns such as Lurgan and Lisburn. The first Quaker meeting house in Ireland was built in Lurgan in 1654 and Quaker families such as Hoope, Edmondson, Webb, Robson, Wright, Pierson, Bradshaw, Turner, and others, formed a tight-knit body possessing manufacturing and market skills, capital and – above all – entrepreneurial talent. A similar, although less cohesive, network existed within the Church of Ireland community, including Arthur Brownlow the landlord of Lurgan.[26] Altogether less important were the Huguenots whose role was exaggerated by Louis Crommelin, the leading member of the group.[27] Huguenots settled in Lisburn in 1698 because the industry was already well established in south Ulster. Their main contribution was to publicise the industry to the English and Irish Parliaments, which were well disposed to assist it, and to stimulate the weaving of fine linens.[28]

Landlords were the other major stimulus to the development of the linen industry. From the late sixteenth century much of the land in Ulster passed from native Irish to English and Scottish ownership. The uprising of 1641 disrupted the process but settlers returned in large numbers from the 1650s. Landlords were faced with the problem of finding satisfactory tenants for their estates. They therefore offered extraordinarily beneficial terms: in towns and villages renewable three-life leases (in effect perpetuity leases); in the countryside three-life leases and leases for long periods of years. Furthermore, landlords turned a blind eye to the sale of the unexpired portions of leases by tenants and to the use of leases as a pledge or mortgage to borrow money. Thus tenants were possessed of a valuable

[23] Ibid, pp. 6–7.
[24] D. C. Coleman, 'An innovation and its diffusion: the "New Draperies"', *Economic History Review*, second series, 22 (1969), p. 421.
[25] Crawford, 'Origins of the linen industry', pp. 46–7.
[26] F. X. McCorry, 'The history of Lurgan, 1610–1963', unpublished Ph.D. thesis (Queen's University, Belfast, 1986), pp. 22–3, 28–9, 40, 47–9.
[27] *British Parliamentary Papers*, 1840, XXIII, Reports from the Assistant Handloom Weavers' Commissioners, Pt III, p. 616; Gill, *Irish Linen Industry* pp. 16–20.
[28] Crawford, 'Origins of the linen industry', pp. 47–8.

asset which they could use to raise capital to sink into the textile industry – or indeed into any other activity – if they so desired.[29]

Landlord involvement in the linen industry was even more direct than the granting of beneficial leases. It was, of course, primarily the responsibility of the tenant to discover a profitable use for his farm but it was in the landlord's interest to give a helping hand. In the early days the rearing of livestock for the English and Scottish market was the readiest way of exploiting underpeopled estates but the Cattle Acts of 1663, 1667 and 1681 killed the export trade in live animals. Many northern graziers, unlike their counterparts in the south of Ireland, were ill-placed to switch to the burgeoning export trade in provisions to southern Europe and the West Indies. Instead, landlords in the north encouraged weavers to settle on their estates by setting up markets where yarn and cloth could be bought and sold.[30] The best known example is that of Arthur Brownlow, landlord of Lurgan and grandson of its founder, who in the later seventeenth century personally purchased cloths at a loss until the business could be conducted on a profitable footing.[31]

Immigrants and landlords were the catalysts that set the industry moving; its continuing success depended on more enduring circumstances. The most obvious need was an assured market. By an act of the English Parliament in 1696 Irish hemp, flax, yarn and all kinds of linen were permitted into the English market duty free; and from 1705 coarse brown and white linens were also permitted into colonial markets. Further encouragement to colonial trade came in 1743 when a system of export bounties, introduced in England, was extended to Irish linen. As a result a proportion of Irish cloths consigned initially to English ports was re-exported to the American colonies.[32] Bounties may explain the surge in exports in the later 1740s;[33] and disturbances in the American markets in the late 1770s and early 1780s were at least partly responsible for the disruption to Irish exports in those years.

Valuable as these concessions were they were not sufficient to ensure success since Irish linens still had to compete with English, Scottish and continental cloths. For much of the eighteenth century English linen production exceeded the combined imports from Ireland and Scotland.

---

[29] W. H. Crawford, 'Landlord–tenant relations in Ulster, 1609–1820', *Irish Economic and Social History*, 2 (1975), pp. 8–10.

[30] Ibid., p. 9; idem, 'Economy and society', pp. 245–6.

[31] McCorry, 'History of Lurgan', pp. 23–4.

[32] A. E. Murray, *A History of the Commercial and Financial Relations between England and Ireland from the Period of the Restoration* (1903; reprinted by Books for Libraries Press, New York, 1970), pp. 119–20.

[33] For a dissenting voice see Gill, *Irish Linen Industry*, p. 71.

Sales of Scottish linen south of the border were considerable. And, duties notwithstanding, there continued to be some import of linens from the Continent, especially Germany.[34] Irish linen thus had to compete in the market on the basis of quality and price.

It was the initiative of Ulster manufacturers that raised quality to standards acceptable in the English market. In 1696 a County Armagh landlord reported that 'I have as good diaper [a cloth woven in geometric patterns], made by some of my tenants nigh Armagh, as can come to a table, and all other cloth fit for household uses.' Diaper weaving had probably been introduced by English weavers who, in turn, had learned it from the Dutch. For example, in the early eighteenth century a Quaker weaver from Armagh, James Bradshaw, visited Holland to learn weaving techniques and – if family tradition is to be believed – narrowly escaped with his life from this excursion into industrial espionage.[35] The Linen Board, established in 1711, also engaged in multifarious projects to raise standards in the growing and preparation of flax, and in spinning, weaving, finishing and marketing. Eventually, though, the Board became 'a positive hindrance' because of its increasingly conservative attitude towards technical innovation.[36]

More fundamental were technical advances occurring in the several finishing processes designed to turn brown linen into an attractive bleached white cloth. There were four important developments: the switch from home-produced kelp (burnt seaweed) and weed ashes to imported barilla and potashes as bleaching agents; the move away from bran and buttermilk sours – used to neutralise the bleaches – to vitriol (i.e. sulphuric acid); the introduction of water-powered washing and beetling machinery; and careful quality control. Some of these skills were learned from the Dutch although they were refined within Ulster; all were important in enhancing the quality of Irish cloth while at the same time increasing the volume of output to match rising demand.[37] And all made finishing the most capital-intensive branch of the industry.

In all stages of production up to bleaching, however, labour not capital was the most important input. The cost of labour was a major determinant of the final cost of cloths, and cheap labour was an important explanation

[34] N. B. Harte, 'The rise of protection and the English linen trade', in N. B. Harte and K. G. Ponting (eds.), *Textile History and Economic History: Essays in Honour of Miss Julia de Lacy Mann* (Manchester, Manchester University Press, 1973), pp. 85, 93, 107.

[35] Stuart, *Historical Memoirs*, pp. 422–3.

[36] H. D. Gribbon, 'The Irish Linen Board 1711–1828', in L. M. Cullen and T. C. Smout (eds.), *Comparative Aspects of Scottish and Irish Economic and Social History 1600–1900* (Edinburgh, John Donald, 1977), p. 82.

[37] The most comprehensive discussion is in Aileen L'Amie, 'Chemicals in the eighteenth century Irish linen industry', unpublished M.S.Sc. thesis (Queen's University, Belfast, 1984), *passim*.

for the success of the Ulster linen industry. It was particularly important for the middling qualities of linen that comprised the bulk of the exports. The evidence is ambiguous, but the Irish product seems to have been cheaper, quality for quality, than its continental, Scottish, and English counterpart.[38]

Labour costs are crucial in explaining not only the success of Irish linens in England but also the particular location of the industry in the Ulster countryside. It was not the case that the whole of Ireland had an advantage over England or Scotland in respect of labour charges, but there was a distinct advantage in the linen regions of Ulster. We have to look to the nineteenth century for firm evidence. Witnesses before the Commission on Handloom Weavers in 1840 stated that weavers' earnings in Ireland were lower than those of weavers in other parts of the United Kingdom, although R. M. Muggeridge, one of the commissioners, observed that 'cheap labour is dear labour'.[39] Low wages were all too often offset by low productivity. However, this was at a time when the labour market was overstocked and the bulk of textile earnings were in the form of wages.[40] In the eighteenth century the majority of linen workers had been self-employed family workers. Their incomes were in the form of profits or, in the case of wives, children and apprentices, a share in the family subsistence. It is very difficult to calculate earnings in these circumstances. Arthur Young believed that spinners' and weavers' earnings were 'from double to near treble those of husbandry labour throughout the kingdom [of Ireland], and yet complaints about poverty are infinitely more common among these people than in those parts of the kingdom that have no share of the manufacture'.[41] He drew a distinction between skilled and unskilled labour, arguing that skilled labour cost the same in Ireland as in England. On the other hand, 'husbandry labour [in Ireland] is very *low priced*, but by no means *cheap*', because of the low productivity of Irish labour. This is the identical point to that made by Muggeridge seventy years later. Young observed, though, that in the north of Ireland productivity was high.[42] Comparisons between Ireland and Scotland point in the same direction: little difference in the price of skilled labour, but unskilled labour cheaper in Ireland than unskilled labour in Scotland.[43]

This low cost of 'husbandry labour' was important at two stages of linen production. The first was in flax growing and preparation. Flax was a

[38] L. M. Cullen, *Anglo-Irish Trade 1660–1800* (Manchester, Manchester University Press, 1968), pp. 66–8. [39] Handloom Weavers Commissioners' Report, pp. 598, 726.
[40] Ibid., pp. 594, 595, 596, 600. [41] Young, *Tour in Ireland* vol. 2, p. 114.
[42] Ibid., pp. 105, 157.
[43] L. M. Cullen, 'Incomes, social classes and economic growth in Ireland and Scotland, 1600–1900', in T. M. Devine and David Dickson (eds.), *Ireland and Scotland 1600–1850: Parallels and Contrasts in Economic and Social Development* (Edinburgh, John Donald, 1983), p. 250.

profitable crop on the small farms of the north of Ireland where it was rotated with potatoes. However, the land needed careful spading, ploughing and manuring, and the crop required constant weeding. It was harvested by being pulled out by the roots and then dried before being retted and hackled to separate the fibres from the stalk. Young calculated that in County Armagh labour accounted for 60 per cent of the cost of producing an acre of flax; the other costs he attributed to rent and seed.[44]

The other processes in which labour costs were important were spinning and weaving. Excluding the highest quality cloths such as damasks, capital expenditure on wheels, looms and related equipment was relatively low and fixed costs were kept low by the use of the domestic system. The earnings of spinners and weavers dominated the cost structure of the initial stages of linen manufacture. Unit labour costs were further kept down by the extensive use of part-time labour, particularly the labour of women and girls as spinners and in the various decorative processes. The finishing stages of washing, beetling and bleaching were another matter. Capital costs were dominant because of the expense of the equipment and the duration of the bleaching process. Labour was expensive because of the use of skilled man-power, but labour costs formed a small fraction of total finishing costs.[45]

Contemporaries explained low labour costs in Ulster by the cheapness of provisions stressing, in addition, the importance of small-scale – and slovenly – farming in providing weavers and their families with oats, potatoes and milk. For example, in County Antrim in 1812 'inferior' weavers were said to earn only 2s or 3s a week as employees of master weavers, but their small garden plots supplied them with sufficient potatoes to live on.[46] Economists offer a more subtle approach, explaining a low price of labour in terms of opportunity costs. We noted earlier that, following the embargo on live cattle exports to England and Scotland, labour (and capital) in Ulster moved into the linen trade. In other parts of Ireland factors of production shifted into dairying, the provisions trade and into sheep and wool production. For reasons of climate and geography these openings were not profitable in Ulster. Linen manufacture thus absorbed labour that had few alternative uses.

Even so we must distinguish between various parts of the province. There was, for instance, little weaving in Fermanagh in west Ulster where the main economic activities were dairying and the rearing of beef cattle for

[44] Young, Tour in Ireland, vol. 1, p. 106, vol. 2, p. 113; Coote, Statistical Survey, pp. 197–8; L'Amie, 'Irish linen industry', pp. 18–29.
[45] Gill, Irish Linen Industry, pp. 46–51, 323.
[46] Handloom Weavers Commissioners' Report, p. 622

sale to the linen counties. In Monaghan, in the south-west, and, Donegal in the north-west, weaving did not seriously challenge corn and cattle until the 1740s when harvest failure and cattle disease eroded traditional sources of income.[47] In 1729 Arthur Dobbs, a County Antrim landowner, identified the counties in Ulster concentrating on weaving as Antrim, Armagh, Down, Londonderry and Tyrone. There was also extensive spinning in these areas but the yarn was used within the household by the farmer-weavers; the family operated as an integrated unit. On the other hand Cavan, Donegal and Monaghan were engaged principally in spinning, the yarn being sold to the weavers in other counties.[48]

The distinction between the yarn, and the cloth and yarn, counties implies that the former had more female labour than male surplus to the requirements of agriculture than the latter. At all events the distinction between the two groups of counties did not change fundamentally during the eighteenth and early nineteenth centuries; indeed, it increased. As linen production expanded, spinners in marginal areas in west Ulster were pulled in to supply yarn to weavers in the east. These same marginal regions were the first to give up linen as the industry contracted, although as late as 1821, 31 per cent of Ulster's textile workforce was still located in the three counties of Cavan, Donegal and Monaghan; two decades later the figure had dropped to 13 per cent.[49]

IV

Underlying explanations of industrial location in terms of labour costs is the fact that the supply of labour was increasing in eighteenth-century Ulster as a result of population growth. Between 1660 and 1760 the population of Ulster grew from roughly a quarter of a million to roughly one million; by 1821 it had doubled again to two million.[50] Province-wide statistics fail to do justice to the intensity of population growth in the linen regions. In 1841 Ulster as a whole had the highest population density of the four provinces, and Armagh was the most densely settled county in Ireland. In the principal weaving counties more than 40 per cent of farms were 5 acres or less in size; these were the pocket handkerchiefs on which farmer-

---

[47] Crawford, 'Economy and society', pp. 245–8.
[48] E. R. R. Green, *The Lagan Valley 1800–1850: A Local History of the Industrial Revolution* (Manchester, Manchester University Press, 1949), p. 62.
[49] Kennedy, 'Rural economy', p. 12.
[50] William Macafee and Valerie Morgan, 'Population in Ulster, 1660–1760', in Peter Roebuck (ed.), *Plantation to Plantation: Essays in Ulster History in Honour of J. F. McCracken* (Belfast, Blackstaff Press, 1981), pp. 47, 52; Stuart Daultry, David Dickson, and Cormac O Grada, 'Eighteenth-century Irish population: new perspectives from old sources', *Journal of Economic History*, 41 (1981), pp. 624–5.

weavers eked out a living.[51] That shrewd observer, James Stuart, commented in 1819 that the 'diffusion of the populace over the whole face of the county [Armagh] is neither the result of any settled plan, nor of mere accident. It has its origin in the nature of the linen manufacture, so essential to the prosperity of the province.'[52]

At the general level there seems to be a clear association between population growth and the linen industry, each stimulating the other. Yet the nature of the link has not been worked out in detail. According to the model of proto-industrialisation rural industry stimulates population growth by providing the economic support for marriage and by encouraging young marriages; both lead to high fertility. The only study specifically addressing these issues in Ireland is that of Almquist which uses evidence taken from the census of 1841. He showed that spinning and weaving, high nuptiality and high population density did indeed go together: 'most of the hypotheses proposed by Mendels and others [i.e. the theory of proto-industrialisation] are confirmed for Ireland in 1841'.[53]

Almquist's work relates to a time when the textile industry was in decline and when rural industry was no longer a powerful force working on population. Even in the linen counties it had never been the only stimulus to growth; an abundance of land capable of yielding potatoes in profusion also encouraged high rates of increase.[54] Mokyr, indeed, has argued that the presence of cottage industry in the three counties of Mayo, Sligo and Leitrim (all in the province of Connaught, not Ulster) made only a marginal difference to the speed at which population increased in the immediate pre-famine years.[55] Finally, high nuptiality and low age at first marriage seems to have been commonplace throughout Ireland from the seventeenth century.[56] If the evidence existed it might reveal that rural industry was only one among a number of stimuli to population growth in Ulster. It might also clarify whether the demographic consequences of the domestic system – employing the 'free agents' described by Stuart – were different from those of the putting-out system in which spinners and weavers worked as employees.

Another thread of the proto-industrialisation hypothesis is that rural industry created 'immiseration'. Contemporaries generally agreed that

[51] Freeman, Pre-Famine Ireland, pp. 270–1.   [52] Stuart, Historical Memoirs, p. 467.
[53] E. L. Almquist, 'Pre-famine Ireland and the theory of European proto-industrialization: the evidence of the 1841 census', Journal of Economic History, 39 (1979), p. 709.
[54] Ibid., pp. 710, 712, 717.
[55] Joel Mokyr, Why Ireland Starved: A Quantitative and Analytical History of the Irish Economy, 1800–1850 (London, Allen and Unwim, 1983), p. 294.
[56] Joel Mokyr and Cormac O Grada, 'New developments in Irish population history, 1700–1850', Economic History Review, second series, 37 (1984), pp. 478–9.

farmer-weavers and their families in the north of Ireland lived more comfortably than agricultural labourers. Arthur Young grudgingly admitted that linen manufacturers 'live better than the labourers', although he did not approve of the fact that weavers' wives 'drank tea for breakfast'. He also asserted that weavers were imprudent in their spending and irregular in their working habits.[57] Sir Charles Coote was scarcely less grudging in 1804, describing 'a general gloomy poverty' prevailing among the peasantry of County Armagh. Nevertheless, he was forced to 'confess that the extraordinary comforts, so eminently enjoyed by the people of this county, was a matter of astonishment to me, who had been well acquainted with the relative situation of those classes in other counties of this province'. He concluded that the prosperity of the Armagh population over their neighbours arose from two causes:

one of which is, that more money can be earned by the manufacture of fine, than of coarse linen; Armagh being more engaged in fine webs than the counties of Ulster which lie west of it. But the other is the primary and chief cause; the people are more industrious and sober, and their earnings are seldom spent in the dram shop.[58]

Other writers were more enthusiastic about the benefits of industry. According to Edward Wakefield in 1812 the linen industry permitted the weaver to supply 'work to everyone under his roof, [and] he is enabled by their earnings to consume oatmeal instead of potatoes and to allow his wife and daughters to wear cotton or linen gowns'.[59] As for Stuart writing in 1819, we have already seen that he was enthusiastic about the benefits of the linen industry to the Armagh countryside. As late as 1840, when the Ulster industry was in decline, the Commission on Handloom Weavers found that linen earnings compared favourably with other manufacturing occupations and were superior to the incomes of agricultural labourers.[60]

The superior standards of living enjoyed by linen workers possibly owed something to their status as free agents which permitted them to work at their wheels and looms as they pleased, subject, of course, to the demands of the markets. Their smallholdings provided them with a cushion of subsistence, and landlords, for their part, were happy enough with an army of smallholders on their land for it provided a buoyant rent roll. Indeed, it was in the linen counties of Ulster that landlords first began to squeeze middlemen off their estates in order to enjoy the rising rents that their undertenants could afford to pay. Conversely, it was the income gained

[57] Young, *Tour in Ireland*, vol. 1, p. 103, vol. 2, p. 114.
[58] Coote, *Statistical Survey*, pp. 263–4.
[59] Edward Wakefield, *An Account of Ireland, Statistical and Political*, vol. 2 (Dublin, 1812), p. 740.
[60] Handloom Weavers Commissioners' Report, pp. 594, 621–2.

from linen that enabled small undertenants to pay the higher rents exacted by middlemen and desired by landlords.[61]

V

A major theme within proto-industrialisation is that of 'proletarianisation': the metamorphosis of 'free agents' into wage-workers as the market for their products expanded. Many linen workers in Ulster ceased to be independent producers in the second quarter of the nineteenth century. Even in the eighteenth century farmer-weavers without sons of an appropriate age had employed apprentices and journeymen to help work the looms and some of these journeymen never graduated to the rank of master.[62] Large-scale employers of wage-labour also existed in the high-quality branches of the industry such as damask and diaper. Furthermore, finishing had been capital intensive from the 1720s; bleachers consequently had employed wage-labour from an early stage. Some bleachers also employed weavers to ensure an adequate supply of cloths.[63]

The decisive stimulus to the growth of wage-labour was the mechanisation of flax spinning. Machinery developed in England at the end of the eighteenth century made little impact in Ireland because the yarn it produced was too coarse for general use. However a wet-spinning process, permitting the spinning of fine yarn, was invented in England in 1825 and was introduced by James and William Murland in Castlewellan, County Down, in 1826, and into Belfast by Thomas and Andrew Mulholland in 1829. Wet-spinning spread quickly through the Irish industry.[64] Weaving remained a manual process until the 1860s, but with the advent of mill-spun yarn, 'manufacturers with large capital and extensive connections now give out webs to weavers ready to be put on the loom, and pay by the yard for the weaving of the piece'.[65] Wet-spinning thus heralded the arrival of the factory system. It also marked the contraction of the rural textile industry throughout much of Ulster and its concentration in the industrial city of Belfast and a few other locations in east Ulster.

The path into de-industrialisation for all but Belfast and its hinterland was not straightforward. For sixty years cotton manufacture made substantial progress in east Ulster and at any time up to about 1820 it appeared that a factory-based cotton industry might grow successfully out

[61] David Dickson, 'Middlemen', in Thomas Bartlett and D. W. Hayton (eds.), *Penal Era and Golden Age: Essays in Irish History, 1690–1800* (Belfast, Ulster Historical Foundation, 1979), pp. 179–80.
[62] Collins, 'Proto-industrialization', pp. 132–3.
[63] Gill, *Irish Linen Industry*, pp. 144–5, 154–5.
[64] Ibid., pp. 264–72, 316–19; Ollerenshaw, 'Industry', pp. 69–70.
[65] Handloom Weavers Commissioners' Report, p. 597.

of the pre-factory linen industry. Cotton manufacture had developed in Ireland from the mid-eighteenth century, initially around Dublin and Cork, but it eventually became concentrated in east Ulster. The first cotton was made in Belfast in the early 1780s using the labour of pauper children; the first water-powered factory, equipped with English carding and spinning machinery, was built near Belfast in 1784. The first steam-powered factory was erected at Lisburn, 10 miles from Belfast, in 1790 and a second one, also in Lisburn, three years later. Thereafter there was an erratic growth of investment and employment in cotton spinning, reaching a peak of twenty-one cotton mills and 3,600 employees in 1826.[66]

The cotton industry in Ulster was the creation of local and English entrepreneurs already connected with the textile trades. In the present state of knowledge it is impossible to say how the capital was raised to finance machinery purchased from England and Scotland and to pay for the purpose-built factories. The Linen Board made a few grants for steam engines but it seems probable that the bulk of the capital came from existing producers in the linen industry diversifying or switching into cotton production.[67] In the late 1820s, significantly, the best known of the new wet-flax spinners were the Mulhollands who had previously been cotton manufacturers but who moved out of cotton after their premises had been destroyed by fire. Capital evidently switched readily from one textile fibre to another.

As capital was mobile so too was labour. Just as the first steam-powered factories were getting into production, muslin weaving was introduced into Belfast and spread quickly throughout the hinterlands of Belfast and Lisburn. Muslin weaving was organised mainly by Scottish agents who imported fine-quality yarn from the west of Scotland. It attracted labour from flax weaving initially by the high wages it offered. It also recruited women who had at one time made a living from spinning flax, possibly because they commanded lower wages than males. The phase of high earnings did not last. In the 1820s and 1830s the hand-loom cotton industry survived only by cutting wages. As a low-wage occupation, however, offering supplementary earnings to agriculture it remained important throughout the period, allegedly employing as many as 100,000

---

[66] Gill, *Irish Linen Industry*, pp. 227–34; Green, *Lagan Valley*, pp. 95–9; Frank Geary, 'The rise and fall of the Belfast cotton industry: some problems', *Irish Economic and Social History*, 8 (1981), pp. 31–8; David Dickson, 'Aspects of the rise and decline of the Irish cotton industry', in Cullen and Smout (eds.), *Comparative Aspects*, pp. 100–11.

[67] Gill, *Irish Linen Industry* pp. 232–3. Impressionistic evidence suggests that the pattern of investment in the Ulster cotton industry was similar to that in the English textile industry at the same time. For a recent discussion see Pat Hudson, *The Genesis of Industrial Capital: A Study of the West Riding Wool Textile Industry, c. 1750–1850* (Cambridge, Cambridge University Press, 1986), pp. 14–24.

women at its peak in 1857. Production fell rapidly during the 1860s as fashions changed and the demand for muslin declined.[68]

The eventual failure of the Irish cotton industry has long been debated by Irish historians. In its formative years it had enjoyed a degree of protection and in 1792 new tariffs imposed on English imported muslins and printed calicoes were effectively prohibitive. Following the Act of Union the duties on muslin and calico were lowered and eventually abolished between 1808 and 1813; duties on yarn were removed in 1824. Nationalistically minded historians early this century argued that the removal of protection exposed the Irish industry to destructive competition from other parts of the United Kingdom, but the chronology of contraction does not support the case. The existence of duties in the first place possibly assisted the growth of the infant industry, but its decline from the 1820s was part of a wider process of concentration affecting the industry throughout the United Kingdom as a whole. The decisive switch from cotton spinning to linen after 1828 was a simple matter of opportunity costs. Once the machinery for spinning fine counts of linen yarn was available it was more profitable to use capital and labour to make linen, leaving cotton to the more favoured producers on the United Kingdom mainland.[69]

From the 1830s, therefore, the future of the Ulster textile industry lay with flax spinning factories concentrated in the east of the province. Flax weaving was still a cottage industry at this time, but it clustered ever closer to the factories that now provided the bulk of the yarn. With the mechanisation of linen weaving during the Cotton Famine the hand-loom weavers of the province received the final mortal blow. Simultaneously muslin weaving decayed. Pre-factory industry was at an end. In its place was left insubstantial farming throughout most of the region and some survivals of the old handicraft regime in the form of embroidery, knitting and shirtmaking. There also remained one great factory town – Belfast – the last creation of the industrial revolution in the British Isles.

[68] Green, *Lagan Valley*, pp. 103–8; Ollerenshaw, 'Industry', pp. 68–9.
[69] Dickson, 'Cotton industry', pp. 104–9; Geary, 'The rise and fall of the Belfast cotton industry', pp. 47–8.

INDEX

Aberdeenshire, rural industries in, 237, 241, 245, 247–8
age of marriage, 12; in Lancashire, 49, 55, 57; in Scotland, 240; in Ulster, 266; in the Weald, 159
agricultural implements, manufacture of, 109
agriculture, 7, 43; in Cumbria, 135, 139, 140, 141, 143, 154; in Lancashire, 50–1; in the north-east, 206, 213; and proto-industrialisation, 24–5, 27; and Scottish rural industries, 229–31, 234, 237–8, 239–40, 243–50; in Ulster, 252, 253, 257, 264–5, 265–6, 267; in Wales, 215–16, 222; in the Weald, 160, 170–2; in the West Midlands, 107, 121, 123, 124; and the West Riding woollen industry, 76–7; and woollen manufacture, 55, 72–3; see also cattle farming; smallholdings
Almquist, E. L., 266
American colonies, trade with, in the West Midlands, 115
Anderson, B. L., 86
apprenticeships: in the West of England, 186, 188; in the West Midlands, 120, 129
Armagh, 256, 257, 258–9, 262, 264, 267; farmer-weavers in, 265–6
Ashburnham, William, 170
Ashton, T. S., 86
Atlas of Industrialising Britain, 17, 18
attorneys: in Lancashire, 61; in the West Riding, 71, 79, 81, 82–3, 86, 98

banks and banking, 17, 29; in Manchester, 61; in the West Midlands, 127; in the West Riding, 71, 79, 81, 83–4, 93, 98, 99
Belfast, 258, 269, 270
Berg, M., 26, 27
Birmingham, 19, 105, 110, 111, 117, 119–21, 127, 129, 131
birth rates, in Lancashire, 55, 56–7, 61
Black Country, 124, 127, 129
Blackburn, 42, 46, 66
blade mills, 108

blast furnaces: in the Weald, 164; in the West Midlands, 123, 124–5
bleaching, linen, 262, 264
bloomeries, in Cumbria, 141–2
bobbin manufacture, in Cumbria, 134, 135, 152
Bolton, 45, 46, 62, 65, 67
Bradford, 19, 71, 97
Bradshaw, James, 262
Briggs, A., 177
Browne, John, 166, 170
Browne, Thomas, 163
Brownlow, Arthur, 260, 261
Bungar, Isaac, 168–9
burghs, royal, in Scotland, 232–4
Burnley, 42, 52, 66
Bury, 53, 54, 58
Bythell, D., 177–8

calico industry, 63; in Cumbria, 134, 146, 151–2
Calverley, 73, 74–8, 80–1, 82, 84
Cameron, Rondo, 226
canals, 2, 15, 17, 66, 70
capital and capitalists, 37–8; in Cumbria, 148–9, 151, 155; industrial, markets for, 16–17; in Lancashire, 57–8, 61–2, 63; in the north-east, 206–7; and proto-industrialisation, 24, 27; in Ulster, 260, 269; in Wales, 209, 218–19; in the Weald, 159, 160, 172–3, 174; in the West Midlands, 109–10, 121, 127–8; and the West Riding woollen industry, 69–99
carding: in Cumbria, 139; mills, in the West Riding, 90, 95; in the Weald, 160
Cardoso, F., 162, 163
Carlisle, 134, 135, 136, 137, 139, 145, 146, 151–2, 153, 154
Carus–Wilson, E. M., 136
Catholic households, in Lancashire, 60
cattle farming: in Cumbria, 149; in Lancashire, 55; in Ulster, 253, 264–5; in Wales, 208; in the Weald, 159, 171
charcoal production: in Cumbria, 149–50; in the West Midlands, 117–18

271

woollen manufacture (cont.)
152, 153; in Lancashire, 45, 46, 51–9; in
Scotland, 231, 232, 233, 234, 236, 237, 250;
in Wales, 208; in Yorkshire, 22, 31, 45, 63,
69–99
worsted manufacture: in Lancashire, 56, 63; in
the West Riding, 63, 72, 73, 74, 81–2, 85,
87, 89, 92, 97
Wrightson, K., 12
Wrigley, E. A., 11, 13, 26, 49, 211, 226

yarn, linen: exports of, 254, 255; in Scotland,
234, 237, 242, 243, 247; spinning, 242, 243,
247, 256, 257; in Ulster, 256, 257

yeomen: in Cumbria, 132, 138, 140–1, 142,
148–9; in the West Midlands, 106, 107, 114,
121; in the West Riding, 77–8
Yorkshire woollen industry, 22, 29, 31, 45, 63,
69–99; and hand-knitting, 145; and
technological change, 175, 176, 179, 180–1,
182–3, 184, 192
Young, Arthur, 49, 145, 257, 259, 263, 264,
267

Zeitlin, J., 32–3, 35